Communities

Libraries and Information Services

Items should be returned on or before the last date shown below.

Any item **not required** by another reader may be renewed at any library, by phone, or on-line at www.calderdale.gov.uk.

To renew, please give your library membership number.

DATE DUE FOR RETURN

0 9 MAR 2019

1 5 APR 2019

D1609994

SEDUCTION AND DESIRE
The Psychoanalytic Theory
of Sexuality since Freud

Ilka Quindeau

Translated into English by John Bendix

KARNAC

First published in 2013 by
Karnac Books Ltd
118 Finchley Road
London NW3 5HT

British Library Cataloguing in Publication Data

A C.I.P. for this book is available from the British Library

ISBN-13: 978-1-78049-089-2

Typeset by V Publishing Solutions Pvt Ltd., Chennai, India

Printed in Great Britain

www.karnacbooks.com

CONTENTS

INTRODUCTION

Drive, desire and seduction: approaches to a new formulation of the psychoanalytic theory of sexuality

The myth of sexuality is obsolete. Today, in contrast to Freud's time, talk about sexual wishes and fantasies has become highly trivialized, not least through talk shows and "reality TV." What was once considered "perverse" has long since lost that label: rubber, latex and leather seem to have come out of the closet and moved into many bedrooms. It has become a matter of course today for young women to take advantage of artificial insemination rather than—as used to be the case—becoming pregnant through sexual intercourse.

These three facets illuminate the profound changes in the sexual realm that we encounter not just in everyday life but in therapeutic practice as well. It is not only disorders of sexual function in the narrower sense that has changed; rather, an entire spectrum of the most varied phenomena can be observed. A century after Freud's groundbreaking *Three Essays on the Theory of Sexuality* (1905d), psychoanalytic thinking faces a great challenge, and a situation altered in manifold ways. It calls for a reconsideration of sexuality, pleasure, and desire, and a rethinking of our ideas about men and women, the relations among them, and their relationship to one another. The *Three Essays*, the central text of psychoanalysis with regard to sexuality, needs to be fundamentally revised.

This detraditionalization and pluralization of sexual lifestyles has been observable since the late 1960s. It encompasses sexual orientations and preferences, new forms of relationships and families, and notions of what is male and female, masculine and feminine. The student, women's, and gay and lesbian movements set fundamental changes in motion that are commonly labelled as a "sexual revolution," though that term mythologizes it. Institutions like church or state, which set norms in the sexual realm in the past, have become largely irrelevant. Traditional sexual morality has yielded to a negotiated morality (Schmidt, 2004), which presupposes partners more or less equally strong and neither emotionally nor economically dependent on one another. This new morality presupposes sensitivity to the wishes and limits of the other, and demands high reflective abilities which cannot be assumed to be self-evident. A negotiated morality goes hand-in-hand with considerable changes in sexuality between men and women, and is reflected not least in changes to court decisions in cases of sexual assault. One can put it more pointedly: A democratization of sexual relationships is underway.

Changes in sexual morality are also reflected in a shift in the meaning of the institution of marriage. On the one hand, it is losing its monopoly on defining and legitimating relationships and families. On the other hand, it remains a pivotal societal institution. Faith in marriage apparently remains undiminished, as indicated both by high remarriage rates and by same-sex civil partnerships, which are legitimated by analogy to the marriage model.

Alongside matrimony, Giddens (1993) sees a new relationship form emerging, one he calls the "pure" relationship: A love relationship hardly serves reproductive or maintenance functions anymore, and it no longer needs the institution of marriage to legitimate it either. Instead, it is entered into for its own sake. While this form of relationship is more evident among same-sex pairs, heterosexual pairs are increasingly drifting in this direction as well. A relationship is maintained only as long as both partners feel comfortable; permanent instability is one of its characteristics. Permanence for its own sake would contradict the perceptions of the ideal, and as Reimut Reiche (2004a) deftly characterizes it, "serial monogamy"—a term used already in the 1950s by U.S.

anthropologists—is practiced instead. In such relationships, sexual activity primarily serves to establish intimacy and to express desires for closeness, security and affection.

The drawback of this intimacy-giving aspect of sexuality can be seen in the displacement of private and public spheres, which is accompanied by a high degree of commercialization. The omnipresence of the sexual in the everyday—whether in advertising, on television, in the movies or on the internet—leads to a permanent arousal that simultaneously deadens individuals. The consequences this has for sexual experience, or for wishes and fantasies, can scarcely be foreseen in detail.

Still, it is within established partnerships that the vast majority of sexual activities continue to take place. This surprising finding, in stark contrast to the media image of the omnipresence of the sexual, is the result of an empirical study on sexual relationships in Germany. In it, there were remarkable continuities between different age groups. Cohorts of thirty, forty-five and sixty year-olds of both sexes were interviewed over a thirty-year period, in Hamburg and Leipzig, and the results showed that around ninety-five per cent of all sexual intercourse took place in established relationships, a finding independent of sex, age, and place of residence. Only about one per cent occurred in external relationships and only five per cent among those who were single, though they constituted about twenty-five per cent of the respondents (see Schmidt, 2004, 2005). These results make actual sexual behaviour look far more prosaic than garish media productions would have one believe.

The decisive change during the last years is probably the oft-proclaimed, general decline in the importance of sexuality. Thus, the large symbolic importance attributed to sexuality in the context of the sexual revolution that was part of the student movement in the 1960s is clearly being reduced again today. Sexuality is no longer seen as a boon or promise of happiness through which entire societies can be liberated. By now, it appears to have become less burdened, more self-evident, and more relaxed. A coexisting tendency now, however, is to mystify the new forms of sexuality in a negative manner, following the positive mystification of sexuality as a means for liberation, rapture or ecstasy, and to associate these new forms with a deprivation of liberty, or with violence, abuse, illness and gender hierarchy.

The German sexologist Volkmar Sigusch (2001) describes the transformation of sexuality over the past decades as composed of three distinct processes: dissociation of the sexual domain, dispersion of the sexual fragments, and diversification in the forms of relationships. These transformations have introduced fundamental changes in sexual life that are of direct importance to every individual, both in terms of sexual practice and in terms of wishes and fantasies.

Dissociation of the sexual

The key dissociation separated the sexual sphere from that of reproduction. This process, which took place over decades, led in the late 1960s to the emergence of the idea of a putatively "clean" and pure sexuality with the reproductive functions no longer superimposed on it. This separation, helped by numerous technological innovations, continues into the present. Thus, the process of reproduction, including early embryo development, has been increasingly transferred outside the female body. Cloning techniques for the first time have made even reproduction without sex possible, hence also separating the reproductive from the sexual sphere.

It is only an apparent paradox that this separation was accompanied by a further dissociation: the formulation during the 1970s of an "autonomous" female—and hence also male—sexuality. At the time, sexuality was given a gender, though it certainly had always had one, due to its implicitly androcentric orientation. Now, however, the assumption was that sexuality was separated by gender, and a distinction was then made between female and male sexuality. From that point on, the sexual was seen in terms of gender difference, and the hierarchical processes and conflicts associated with it. This dissociation into "male" and "female" sexuality is paradoxical because it was established just when sex, with respect to reproduction, was losing its importance. It thereby takes on the function of cementing a culture of two sexes, and thereby underscoring its function in supporting the social order.

The dissociations of the sexual find further expression in an older but still valid sexological distinction that remains the basis of the current discourse on gender. John Money, in his research on intersex development, distinguished at the time between sex, gender role and gender identity (Money, Hampson & Hampson, 1955), dimensions of the sexual that to that point had been assumed to coincide. While social expectations of behaviour today hardly seem bound to an individual's biological sex anymore, and this dissociation as a result has become part of everyday understanding, the separation of biological sex and gender identity often seems far less self-evident. Law and medicine, however, seem to be ahead of common understanding here. Thus, it is now legally possible for a person assigned as male at birth who has become a transwomen to marry a former woman who has become a man. In the specialized terminology used, this is a marriage between a male-to-female (MtF or M2F) transgender person and a female-to-male (FtM or F2M) trans-gender. In the current International Classification of Diseases (ICD-10) published by the World Health Organization, trans-sexuality is listed as a "gender identity disorder" that calls for treatment. The dissociations thereby become fixed and receive societal acknowledgement. What is interesting about all these phenomena is that the difference between the sexes is both losing importance and being solidified at the same time. Nowhere is the significance of biological sex more evident than in trans-sexuality—which simultaneously makes it clear that anatomy is not destiny but can be changed through medical operations.

While transsexuals affirm cultural bisexuality with their bodily and mental suffering, it is seriously questioned by other groups such as the intersexuals. These are people of unclear sex, with both male and female biological features, an ambiguity that led them to be called "hermaph-rodites" in earlier ages. They seem to elude definitive assignment to one sex. Current practice is to forcibly assign a sex in infancy, reinforced by operations that need to be repeated multiple times in the course of development. Those so affected now claim this is a violation of human rights and an assault on the body. These phenomena also make clear that it is not just "gender" but also "sex" that is culturally constructed. This is the main argument in the contemporary gender discourse, par-ticularly as put forward by Judith Butler (1993a, 1997). Her deconstruc-tionist and politically subversive effort has been to try to abolish the culture of two sexes, making her a target of criticism from all possible directions (see, for example, Nussbaum, 1999 and Reiche, 2004b). Nevertheless, we have this debate to thank for the important impetus it has given to the psychoanalytic discussion of male and female, mascu-line and feminine.

A further dissociation lies in the separation of the sphere of sexual experience from the realm of bodily reaction. A good example is the development of Viagra®, which for the first time makes the sex act on the part of men possible (almost) without sexual arousal. If erectile dys-function, especially when it occurred only under certain circumstances, used to serve as an important indicator of underlying mental conflicts, today it is usually biochemically outsmarted. Aside from in the medical realm, this dissociation of the sexual from the physical today takes place on a large scale through the media, whether in the form of telephone sex, e-sex, or cybersex. These offers, whose current range is immense and whose impact is immeasurable, provide fundamentally new possibilities for sexual arousal and encounters, the consequences of which are increasingly evident in therapeutic practice.

Last, one can observe a final dissociation in the separation of the realm of the libido from the realm of *destrudo*, the urge to destroy, the separation of a loving, tender aspect of sexuality from its aggressive, destructive side. This separation found prominent expression in the discourse on abuse and violence during the 1980s and 1990s. On the one hand, it served to sensitize the public to sexual violence, in particular that directed against children, and its serious consequences. On the other hand, it often equated male sexuality with violent or oppressive sexuality. Meanwhile, women too have become perpetrators. That robs them of an exclusive claim to the role of victim. At the same time, it generally and newly restores an aura of indecency to sexuality, one that seemed to have been shed in the "sexual revolution" of the 1960s.

Sexual dispersions

"Sexual dispersion" is the term Sigusch (2001) uses to characterize the fragmentation and dissociation of elements, social segments, and lifestyles. That process goes hand in hand with the cultural dissociation of previously unitary "sexuality" and with an all-encompassing commercialization of its individual spheres. Commercial interests carve apart previously interrelated actions in order to offer, and correspondingly market, the smallest possible units. German newspaper and internet ads hence offer ZK (French kisses)—more expensive now, in the era of AIDS—or GB ("facials") or BW (nipple eroticism), always in abbreviations that are not easy to decipher or that presuppose a certain degree of familiarity. This dispersion process is also reflected in the disclosure of all sorts of intimacies in radio and television talk shows. The functions of such displays are certainly manifold, and could betray a compulsion to confess, to which Foucault (1977b) argues sex has been subject for centuries. They could simply be an effort to drive the feeling of shame out of a mass audience, an impulse Freud regarded as the powerful counterpart to the "impulse to watch". Not least as a result of these manifestations the boundary between normal and abnormal, and between public and private, has shifted enormously. During the "sexual revolution" of the 1960s, sexuality was presented in the mass media for the first time, in the form of nudity, partner relationships, and methods of contraception. Today, the media presents things far beyond what was previously thought "normal", and increasingly stages the unusual, which, in Freud's sense of "partial drives" or "perversions", shows off smaller and smaller elements of what used to be a unitary "sexuality". An example would be television shows depicting cages used by sadomasochists or repair workshops for dildos. What this means at the level of the psyche remains to be seen. We seldom see this dispersion of the sexual in psychoanalysis now, but in terms of socialization, its effects can hardly be overestimated. What seems to be especially significant for analytic practice, on the one hand, is the constant media staging of confessions and declarations, which pushes back the boundaries of intimacy. It makes the intimacy of treatment, and its inherent compulsion to confess, appear in a different light. On the other hand, from an analytic perspective one can also regard these dispersions, like the dissociations and diversifications, as the current manifestation of a defence against "the activity of the sexual drives", the pressing, uncontrollable element of desiring.

Diversifications of the sexual

In speaking of changes to the institution of the family, Sigusch (2001) uses "diversification" or "deregulation" to characterize the trends towards contraction and devaluation of that institution as well as the multiplication of traditional relationship and lifestyle forms. They enable the aforementioned "dispersions" and "dissociations" to occur, but are also triggered by, or coincide with, them. What is decisive for these diversifications is a market-like demand for greater flexibility in all areas of life, including in the sexual realm. Rigid social roles and psychological identities, as well as stable life-plans, are scarcely compatible with this general increase in flexibility. Instead, what is demanded is a "modular self that functions like a tool-box whose parts can be taken out as needed, augmented and linked to one another" (2001, p. 32, translated for this edition). This increased flexibility is also evident in sexual orientation, for example, which often no longer remains the same throughout life, or by which individuals no longer wish to be defined (Düring, 1994; Schmidt, 2004). Thus, after having a family, a woman may opt for a lesbian relationship, or a man who has lived as a homosexual may indulge his wish to have children and marry a woman. In an earlier era, this might have been taken as evidence that these individuals had repressed their "genuine" sexual orientation, but now it is seen as a sign of increasing liberation. Since previous boundaries are becoming increasingly permeable, and identities ever more fragile or even fluid, the conventional rigid division into homosexual, heterosexual, and bisexual is losing its significance, too. All forms of sexuality are put up for discussion and differentiated, and even heterosexuality is no longer taken for granted either culturally or theoretically—which Freud already perceptively mentioned in a footnote (1905d, pp. 30–31). Still more important, given the circumstances of the three aforementioned transformations, the forms of sexuality no longer constitute an identity. If homosexuality and heterosexuality are no longer mutually exclusive but instead inclusive, then bisexuality, understood psychologically, takes on a new meaning. Mainstream psychoanalytic theory by now sees it basically as infantile megalomania or as averted homosexuality, but I consider it a very promising concept whose theoretical significance and potential is still far from being exhausted.

Challenges for psychoanalytic theory and practice

Studies of cultural changes in sexuality reveal basic alterations that deeply shake all psychoanalytic concepts of sexuality and gender, of sexual wishes and fantasies, and of what is regarded as diseased and regarded as normal in this area. With the exception of theories of the female in the realm of the sexual, psychoanalytic theorizing even today essentially remains guided by Freud's *Three Essays*. Yet it needs to take account of these changes and give them a conceptual grounding. Freud's pioneering work on sexuality, which decisively influenced the twentieth century, contains a number of significant insights that, despite all the criticism levelled against them, have lost none of their relevance. Three central and innovative aspects of this theory that remain significant are worth briefly noting: 1) the expanded notion of sexuality that is not only confined to genitality; 2) a non-normative concept that allows for a fluid boundary between the normal and the perverse, and between what is healthy and what is diseased; and 3) the assumption of an autonomous infantile sexuality.

For many decades, in occasional studies covering diverse areas, Freudian notions of sexuality have been repeatedly taken up and expanded upon. Still, the questions raised have been highly fragmented and devoid of inner coherence. As a result, an integration of the individual aspects into a cohesive theoretical framework is still lacking. That would make the interior links between the concepts clearer, or to put it more trenchantly, would provide an overall, seamless concept of the varied facets of sexuality. Thus, the development of the male and masculine cannot be understood without the development of the female and feminine, for example. The concept of the genesis of sexuality has an effect on the understanding of infantile sexuality or of perversions— or on the perception of maleness and femaleness, and so forth. Such systematization has clinical utility as well, for sexual practices, wishes and fantasies are not only the object of every analysis or therapy; rather, as before, the sexual continues to constitute the core of the unconscious.

The present study is organized in three long Chapters. The first addresses the genesis and emergence of sexuality. The second puts the question of sexual dimorphism at its heart and examines male and female sexuality. Chapter Three examines sexual orientation with respect to heterosexuality, homosexuality and perversions.

With respect to the genesis of sexuality, which I discuss in Chapter One, Freud was initially ambivalent. In his later work, he increasingly took the view that it arose endogenously, and believed that human sexuality followed an innate biological program. His views create a number of problems. An innate program implies a biological function, which in the case of sexuality would consist of reproduction. But without a doubt, human sexuality encompasses far more than procreation: Reproduction seems clearly subservient to psychological factors, and technological innovations have increasingly separated reproduction from sexuality itself. Assuming that human sexuality is a genetic endowment also implies that sexual forms—heterosexuality, homosexuality, even perversions—would be determined prenatally. Sexual orientation thus would not be acquired and would tend not to be flexible, but rather fixed throughout life.

In the place of a biological plan in which human sexuality is the result of maturation processes, I suggest substituting a sexuality whose foundation lies in an interpersonal relationship. For this, I turn to the early Freudian writings on seduction theory and its further elaboration by Jean Laplanche. I want to emphasize the influence of the Other on the genesis of sexuality, not in the sense of sexual assaults or sexual violence, as Freud postulated in his theory of seduction, but as a universal structure. As a rule, the early parent-child relationship is such a locus of universal, unconscious seduction and elementary gratification. Desire is inscribed in the infant's body.

I close Chapter One with a discussion of infantile sexuality. For more than a century, childhood sexuality has been described again and again by empirical sexologists, but in more recent writings on infancy, it seems to have again become controversial whether one can really ascribe sexuality to children (see the overview in Dornes, 2005). In this context, the publications by analysts of the first and second generations, now almost forgotten, remain meaningful. They provide vivid examples of infantile forms of pleasure and gratification, and of oral, anal, and urethral eroticism, which continue into adulthood, and under certain circumstances even provide the basis for so-called "perversions".

In Chapter Two, I turn to the question of male and female sexuality, and start with the difficulties in determining both. While biological sex and psychosocial sexual identity have until now been regarded as one and the same, it is not least the transsexuals who have questioned this apparently "natural" connection. Not just *Geschlecht* identity but biological sex as well can be interpreted as culturally manufactured and assembled. Freud himself had already remarked on "constitutional bisexuality" and regarded "maleness" and "femaleness" as conventions, but his explicit theory of sex and gender was clearly phallocentric, and one in which the female had to appear as the inferior, second sex. Even in Freud's lifetime, this construction of the female and femininity was attacked from many quarters and rejected. In the meantime, the notion of an independent, genuinely female and an independent, genuinely male sexuality has established itself in psychoanalytic discourse. This clear separation does not entirely convince me, however. My question is whether male and female sexuality, as in other areas of behaviour and experience, are more similar than they are different. Speaking sociologically, the question is whether variation within the sex or gender is larger than variation between the sexes or genders. If so, then a rigid categorization of a male and a female sexuality is not valid. Instead, one would need to conceive of a general human sexuality in which men and women were less different from one another than among themselves. What significance then would be ascribed to body dimorphism, generativity, fantasies, or identification would need to be examined in each case.

From a therapeutic perspective, I also want to call into question the binary coding of sex and gender assignment. Even if it has long since become impossible in our society to state what a "real man" or a "real woman" is, patients still frequently suffer under the burden of imagined standards they do not think they meet. That could be a successful business woman who has no children, and at high risk to her health subjects herself to the ministrations of reproductive technology. Or it could be a man who believes he can stabilize his virility only with the help of Viagra®. These behavioural patterns have meanwhile become possible through technical innovations, but those affected by them often pay a high psychological price. Psychological theories increase this degree of suffering if they contribute to these idealized notions by using rigid notions of male and female.

Freud indicated a way to overcome this division into two sexes and genders with his notion of bisexuality. The difference between the sexes/genders is not thereby superseded, it merely loses its apparent clarity and its all-encompassing nature, one that essentializes existing differences into the basis for personality. Maleness and femaleness can, by contrast, exist in a complementary manner inside a person, and be thought of as elements that mutually reinforce rather than mutually exclude one another. Particularly in the realm of the sexual, one finds both phallic as well as receptive traits which go beyond the anatomical attributes of the primary sex organs, but are not difficult to translate into the most diverse practices. To limit female sexuality to the receptive and male sexuality to the phallic is something I find quite problematic, however, even though this is repeatedly implicit in some efforts to conceptualize an autonomous female or male sexuality. Numerous studies of the development of sexual identity have resolved a key misinterpretation in Freud's exposition: While Freud did not perceive an autonomous female development before puberty and regarded the girl as a "little man", these studies describe an independent path the girl takes from birth onwards.

Most likely due to this devaluation, and to the consequent, unavoidable efforts at demarcation, such studies tend to engage in a latent idealization of femaleness. In a manner that is too one-sided, they emphasize what an asset it is for a girl to become aware of her femaleness. On the one hand, this ignores the renunciation that accompanies adopting an unambiguous sexual identity—the renunciation of identifications with the other sex/gender. From this perspective, I describe the development of a gender or sexual identity as a melancholy process: unlike sorrow, it cannot name the loss. This loss, of course, applies to both genders. On the other hand, the acquisition of a gender or sex identity is regarded in some psychoanalytic theories as a quasi-indisputable developmental element resulting from the Oedipus complex, and in consequence is addressed too little as a psychological process which has to be worked through.

In Chapter Three, I address the question of "object-choice" (in Freudian terms) by seeing the three forms of sexuality—homosexuality, heterosexuality, perversion—as different but psychologically equivalent variants of object-choice. In the psychoanalytic discourse, there has been widespread consensus until now that sexual orientation is fixed in childhood or at the latest during adolescence. Research findings, however, cast increasing doubt on that view (Düring, 1994; Schmidt, 2004). The extent to which these observations can be brought into accord with psychoanalytic conceptualizations remains to be established. As with the development of a gender identity, this "setting of the course" (in Morgenthaler's sense) with respect to sexual identity is also linked to losses that call for working through the sorrow or melancholy. The "object-choice", the formation of sexual identity, should therefore also be understood as a "developmental task".

The psychological equivalence of homosexuality and heterosexuality is today unquestioned. The development towards heterosexuality, as Freud already noted, also is not self-evident but is a psychological task. But the evaluation of the so called "perversions" as psychologically equivalent is far less clear. The transformations in the sexual realm already described (Sigusch, 2001) mean that much once regarded as pathological is now seen as within the bounds of the "normal" and has lost the aura of shamefulness or wickedness adhering to the "aberrant". Psychoanalytic conceptualizations such as those offered by Fritz Morgenthaler or Joyce McDougall have become correspondingly more influential, though Janine Chasseguet-Smirgel, for example, suggests a diametrically opposed view. The implications of the various standpoints need to be examined in detail to establish their utility for contemporary psychoanalytic theory and practice. In this context, the implication of re-designating "perversions" as "paraphilia" in the

World Health Organization's ICD manual also needs to be examined. On the one hand, the "perversions" thereby lose their central sexual content, while on the other hand they also lose their stigmatization. The cultural changes in sexuality are most evident in this transformation of "perversions". So the conceptualization of sexuality also raises one of the greatest challenges for current psychoanalytic thinking. What is called for is a Lacanian "return to Freud", a renewed attention to Freud's original texts to think beyond or to take them further.

CHAPTER ONE

Seduction, desire, and sexuality

Seduction: the emergence of sexuality

Freud's seduction theory—an underappreciated idea

The theory of seduction holds a curious place in psychoanalytic theory, for like no other concept, it is essentially understood in terms of its rejection. Freud himself, in fact, never spoke of a theory—that label was first given by historians of psychoanalysis—but rather of a "grave error" that he tried hard to rectify throughout his life (1925d, p. 33). As originally formulated, it was meant as a way to get to the bottom of the riddle of hysteria. In the meantime, it—or rather, its repudiation— has come to be invoked for the most varied topics and problems. In the eyes of critics, it was only through this retraction that Freud discovered infantile sexuality, recognized the significance of unconscious fantasies, or even made the emergence of psychoanalysis possible. In the eyes of advocates, Freud's rapid rejection instead marked the beginning of the end of psychoanalysis, with some even suggesting that dishonest personal motives lay behind this change in paradigm (Masson, 1985; Krüll, 1986; Quindeau, 2004a). I will leave these controversies, which I regard as not very fruitful, to one side and instead turn to more constructive perspectives based on Freud's early writings that can extend

1

psychoanalytic theory. In the seduction theory, I see the first efforts to formulate a theory of sexuality: It suggests theses both for the aetiology of neuroses and for the emergence of human sexuality.

What is at issue in this theory? Unlike the medical theories common at the time, Freud did not trace hysteria back either to hereditary or to somatic, "degenerative" factors. Instead, he suggested a model of trauma in which the psychological processing of an event as memory—and not the event itself—plays the decisive etiological role. This insight was pointedly expressed in the celebrated quip, "the hysteric suffers mainly from reminiscences" (1950a, p. 286). In so doing, this theory moves beyond the traditional medical theory of trauma, which contrasts the (objective) event with the (subjective) experience, describing a dialectic, interwoven relationship between "inner" and "outer", and between "subject" and "object".

Freud's considerations regarding seduction theory originated in his preoccupation with mental illnesses such as hysteria and obsession, which he called defensive neuro-psychoses. The neurotic symptoms originated in the effort to ward off intolerable and embarrassing thoughts and feelings that could be traced back, in his view, to sexual experiences during early childhood or during pre-pubescence. His female patients who suffered from hysteria had talked about them during treatment, and included sexual or erotic relationships ranging from seduction to violent sexual assault carried out by adult carers, relatives, teachers of both sexes, or even by somewhat older children. Freud saw these experiences as a major factor in the genesis of neuroses, though he wondered how frequent such events could really have been. There could not possibly have been so many perverse adults, and he was surprised that they appeared so regularly in the life histories of his hysterical female patients.

Plagued by doubts about this regularity, Freud took a step with far-reaching consequences to free himself of his "overestimation of reality and underestimation of fantasy" (1896c, p. 440). He subsequently came to interpret such reports from female patients less as descriptions of real sexual experiences and more as expressions of unconscious fantasies. Taking this step set off a controversy that has continued with greater or lesser vehemence ever since. Hardly worthy of discussion here is the frequent, but thereby no less absurd, accusation that Freud, and psychoanalysis itself, downplayed or even denied the reality of the sexual abuse of children.

Nonetheless, it is worth pursuing his paradigm shift to further develop psychoanalytic theory. As valuable as Freud's insight into the significance of unconscious fantasies is, his "underestimation of reality" remains problematic, as does the sharp separation of fantasy from reality. The constitutive importance of "seduction" in socialization, as well as the interplay of fantasy and reality in determining the psychological development of every human being, would only be worked out much later in Jean Laplanche's "general seduction theory". Through his work, the concept of seduction has led to an enrichment of psychoanalytic theory, because it immensely extends our understanding of psychological development and how psychological structures are formed. He describes the seduction situation not as a contingent experience of abuse, but instead as a regular and universal aspect of the relationship between child and adult (Laplanche, 1988).

Nachträglichkeit—the central mode in the formation of sexuality

Freud's most important theoretical accomplishment in conjunction with the seduction theory is the concept of *Nachträglichkeit*. With it, he departed from the conventional linear notion of time in which the future emerges from the present, and the present emerges from the past. The succession of past, present, and future seems inviolable to our everyday consciousness. The concept of *Nachträglichkeit*, however, allows the past to emerge from the present. In the course of life, earlier experiences and events, or rather, the traces they leave, are lent new meaning or reinterpreted in accordance with the actual present at the time, or with a particular stage of development. I wish to describe the key psychological functions with the help of this concept of *Nachträglichkeit*, for it lies at the heart of all psychological development and takes on particular meaning in the emergence of the sexual. In fact, human sexuality is constituted in the mode of *Nachträglichkeit*.

What exactly does this mean? It can be described more fully by using one of Freud's early case histories (1950a). As an adult, Emma suffered from not being able to go into shops alone. During her treatment, she remembered having gone shopping as a twelve year-old, and there having encountered two shop-assistants who were laughing. Frightened, she ran away. She connected this laughter with her dress; in addition, one of them had been sexually attractive to her (Scene I). This scene, which initially appears incomprehensible especially in its affect of fright, was augmented by a second memory. "On two occasions when she was a child of eight she had gone into a small shop to buy some sweets, and the shopkeeper had grabbed at her genitals through her clothes (Scene II). In spite of the first experience she had gone there a second time; after the second time she stayed away. She now reproached herself for having gone there the second time, as though she had wanted in that way to provoke the assault" (ibid., p. 354).

In this example, one sees several scenes from her personal history combined together in a constellation to form a memory with a traumatizing effect. It is only in light of the second scene that the first scene makes sense. In analysis, the patient surmised a possible association between the two by suggesting that the shop-assistants' laughter unconsciously evoked the grinning shopkeeper—and thus the memory of the sexual assault. Owing to the maturation brought on by puberty, this unconscious memory had triggered a sexual reaction, though the repression barrier made this reaction inaccessible to the conscious mind and it was instead transformed into a reaction of panic. Key to Freud's argument is the *nachträgliche* sexual arousal, meaning the retrospective attribution. With it, memory receives an affect the earlier experience did not have. The change brought about by puberty allows for a different understanding of what was remembered. The common objection is that the ground was pulled out from under this explanation by Freud's "discovery" of infantile sexuality soon thereafter, however, putting his notion of *Nachträglichkeit* in doubt. Nevertheless, he made later use of it in the Wolf Man case (1918b, p. 45).

The judgment that *Nachträglichkeit* is an antiquated idea tied to superseded suppositions is often found in the English-speaking world, which may be due to its problematic, if not faulty, translation as "deferred action" in James Strachey's Standard Edition of Freud's works (Laplanche and Pontalis, 1973). Seeing it as action that is delayed or shifted in time would reduce *Nachträglichkeit* to a behavioural level. That would associate it with Freud's early model of trauma, which saw it as physiologically-based, and that model is, with good reason, today regarded as dated.

An interpretation of *Nachträglichkeit* based on this faulty translation runs more or less as follows. Because stimulus satiation at a very early point in the development of an individual can make a still-immature ego unable to act, action is deferred until it becomes possible, meaning when the ego is more mature. In this reading, patient Emma's panic would then be seen as an affect of fright, a deferred response to the shopkeeper's assault, as she was not capable (owing to stimulus satiation) of responding to the assault at the time. This, however, sees trauma as an external event, which is an antiquated view not least because libido development and the ascription of meaning by the subject play no role.

As an alternative to this problematic reading, I advocate broadening the potential scope of *Nachträglichkeit* so that it refers less to actions themselves than to attributions of meaning in the sense of inscriptions. To do so, Freund's own restricted views need to be transcended. In the context of his meta-psychological considerations used to explain hysteria, *Nachträglichkeit* was initially intended to describe arousal processes with the language of neurophysiology. That was meant to explain why the memory itself, rather than the event, was traumatic in the sense of stimulus satiation. Freud regarded the ascription of meaning, or in other words, the sense that patients themselves made of certain experiences at various times in their lives, as less important.

Let us return to Emma's case to explore the problematic aspects of the Freudian line of argument. Of key importance is the neural triggering of sexual arousal that first becomes possible after puberty (called sexual release: see his notions of attachment and release in the Project for a Scientific Psychology, first formulated in 1895, in Freud, 1950a). But in the wake of the *Three Essays on the Theory of Sexuality* (Freud, 1905d), where he postulated a theory of two phases of human sexual development as well as the notion of infantile sexuality, this argument can no longer be supported. I believe it far more likely that the childhood scene with the shopkeeper was already accompanied by feelings (though possibly ambivalent ones) of lust or desire. Speaking in favour of that are later feelings of guilt and Emma's thought she might have wanted to provoke the assault by returning a second time. In light of the later development of Freud's theory, I see the traumatic scene as follows. Apart from the laughter, which she regarded as the key link between the two scenes, such linkage also can be created through sexual arousal. This is given a different interpretation in Scene II—in accordance with the child's developmental stage—than during or after puberty. The conjoining of the two scenes in the remembering process lends Scene I a sexual dimension as well, and ties in with the significance not understood at the time, one which afterwards frightens the girl and is expressed in feelings of guilt and self-reproach. The feelings of lust or desire one can assume in Scene II, which probably seemed unproblematic to Emma as a child, become offensive and unbearable for Emma in light of her post-puberty genital sexuality. One can add to this that in her memory, Emma does not see herself as a girl subjected to the assault of an adult. Instead, what was passively experienced is later transformed into what was actively induced, which weakens her feelings of helplessness and vulnerability but at the same time increases her feelings of guilt.

With an increased horizon of understanding, earlier experiences can—*nachträglich*—be given different meaning. Even in my revised reading of the Freudian concept of *Nachträglichkeit*, this remains bound to the underlying bodily processes. However, I no longer see these as pure quantities of arousal but instead as memory traces in the form of neurological pathways. As I will explain in greater detail, these memory traces are differently efficacious at various stages in psychosexual development, in particular when subject to drives and their fates, conceived of as contrasting pairs.

In my reading, the concept of *Nachträglichkeit* would therefore need to be understood as follows. In addition to cognitive development, it is primarily psychosexual development or, in adulthood, dominant, unconscious, psychosexual conflict constellations that lend previous experiences, at various points in time, altered if not new meanings. These conflict constellations incorporate psychological conflicts that are currently relevant, and that result from various incompatible internal psychological players and processes. Unlike in constructivist models, for example, what is of particular importance in these processes of constructing meaning is that they are not about the retrospective ascription of meaning to earlier experiences.

The past is not wilfully constructed, but instead the unconscious, conflict-laden dimension of earlier experiences continually forces new inscriptions. *Nachträglichkeit* thus designates a complex temporal movement that operates not only from the present into the past, but also from the past into the present. In so doing, the ordinary linear concept of time from past to present, which sees the present as emerging causally from the past, is nullified. I call this complex temporal movement a constellation, meaning a mental conjoining of experiences and events from highly diverse periods in an individual's life course, in order to make clear that a linear, temporal ordering does not underlie the psychological processes. Instead, it is the psychological processes themselves that create such an order (in detail, Quindeau, 2004a).

If we again return to Emma's case, Freud argues from a purely economic, or energetic, concept of trauma. Despite the problems associated with this concept, with its help, he was able to transcend the rigid juxtaposition of "interior" and "exterior" and turn trauma into a relational term. Trauma consists in a surge of arousal that supersedes the ability of the particular individual to deal with it in his or her psychic structure. In Emma's case, the trauma consisted in the fact that the memory of the scene with the shopkeeper released such a high degree of sexual arousal that it could not adequately be dissipated and as a result was transformed into fright and flight. I emphasize yet again that the trauma does not lie in the assault of the shopkeeper, that is, not in the event itself, but in the interaction of the two scenes in memory. The trauma is to be sought in the recollection, for that is what triggers the increasing arousal and flight.

These considerations shed light from yet another perspective on the conceptualization of the sexual. In this case study, sexual arousal is evoked through memory and not only through, say, visual perception or tactile stimulation. Even if one can add to the Freudian view, as I have suggested, the fact that Emma was already sexually aroused in the scene with the shopkeeper, the high degree of arousal that ultimately led to flight developed only years later in the scene with the shop assistants, and thus out of linking current perception with memory. In my view, it is one of the key characteristics of human sexuality, in contrast to other living creatures, to be (largely) independent of specific sensory stimuli.

In this interpretation of trauma, designating the constellation and interaction of "interior" and "exterior" as well as (at least) two points in time, one can recognize the genuine achievement of the Freudian theory of seduction. True, Freud often, even emphatically, rejected this theory at various times in his subsequent work, but one can be suspicious of this revocation. It seems rather, as if he never entirely gave up on it. After all, with this retraction, he departs from a direction in the development of his theory that Laplanche (1999a) calls his Copernican, decentralized thinking. Laplanche divided Freudian thought into Ptolemaic, recentring and Copernican, decentring modes; poles between which Freud constantly oscillated. The Copernican revolution is "still more radical, in that it suggests that man, even as subject of knowledge, is not the central reference-point of what he knows. No more than they orbit around him do the stars recognize the primacy of man's knowledge" (1999a, p. 57). This insight into the decentring of the subject finds its expression in the concept of a dynamic unconscious, which, as is well-known, Freud with irony called the third narcissistic blow to mankind after Copernicus and Darwin (Freud, 1916–17).

This dynamic unconscious differs from the descriptive unconscious, as used in other scientific disciplines such as neurobiology. The difference has less to do with the idea that behaviour and experience are essentially steered by it, and to a much smaller degree by conscious intent, and more to do with the assumption that the unconscious is an area of human experience that cannot be described positively, by detailing its contents, or by contrasting it with the conscious mind. As an area fundamentally at some remove from experience (Waldenfels, 2002), or as a concept for something that is lacking (Gondek, 1990) which tries to understand the paradox of the unconscious—there is something beyond experience that nevertheless is known—the unconscious puts the self-understanding of the modern subject as autonomous permanently in question. The theory of seduction, which emphasizes the primacy of the Other, also points in the same direction.

This primacy of the Other is clearer in Laplanche's reading than in Freud's version. One can develop a structural model of the development of the psyche based on Laplanche's general theory of seduction (Quindeau, 2004a). If one understands seduction as a basic structure of socialization, then this opens the possibility of understanding human sexuality as finding its origins in the Other.

The universality of seduction—desideratus ergo sum

If, with Laplanche, I interpret the theory of seduction structurally, it means I see the seduction situation not as a violent sexual assault but rather as part of the development of the psychic structure within a social context. Seduction provides the basic pattern for the early relationship of a child to an adult, male or female. The general psychological structure of the child develops from it, as does sexual desire more specifically. In consequence, I see the origin of human sexuality essentially in a social situation. Biological assumptions, according to which the genetic equipping of a human also provides organs for reproduction, are certainly compatible with this thesis. Yet such theories, which understand sexuality essentially as constitutionally given, do not explain the decisive characteristic of human sexuality: the independence of sexual arousal from sensory perception. That points to the significance of conscious and unconscious sexual fantasies, which I regard not as genetically based but rather as the result of introjection and identification processes that occur in social interactions. The term seduction, in addition to emphasizing the primacy of the Other in the development of the subject, also brings out the fundamentally sexual character of this relationship, which is shaped by enigmatic sexual messages sent from the adults to the child.

Laplanche (1988) differentiates among three levels of seduction: primal seduction, precocious seduction, and paedophile seduction. The most important in his theory is primal seduction, and he barely addresses the other forms. While the last refers to contingent, more or less violent, sexual experiences of a child with an adult, precocious seduction is of more general significance because it accompanies the ordinary and unavoidable acts of infant care. By contrast, the term primal seduction does not refer to behaviour but instead describes the universal structure of the relationship of a child to an adult. This relationship is marked by a fundamental asymmetry. Here a child, whose psychic structure is just beginning to develop, encounters an adult who already has a developed psychic apparatus. Laplanche's theory emphasizes this basic and momentous difference between child and adult and asks what its consequences are for human development.

This way of thinking is irritating at first, because it reverses the usual view of the parent-child relationship: A child's development is customarily seen from the perspective of the child as the subject of this development. The paradigm of modern developmental psychology is to regard individuals "as producers of their development" (Lerner & Busch-Rossnagel, 1981). The parent-child relationship is essentially conceived of as an interaction, however, as a relationship between what are, in principle, equal partners who influence each other. In this view, in contrast to Laplanche's perspective, the emphasis is on likeness and not on difference. This paradigm shift in how the child is viewed began to enter developmental psychology about thirty years ago and today influences everyday understanding as well. "For a long time, it was taken for granted that the behaviour of the parents was taken as precondition and the behaviour of the children as consequence. More recently, one finds the opposite view (the child as the cause of the behaviour of the parents) more frequently expressed, or one finds an analysis of the interaction of a parent-child system" (Oerter & Montada, 1982, p. 22; translation for this edition). Up to this point, the behaviour of the parents was regarded as condition and the behaviour of the child regarded as consequence, but since then one finds a reversal: now the child is the causes the behaviour of the parents (Oerter & Montada, 1982).

Developmental psychology has continued to follow this line up to the present (see Oerter & Montada, 1995), in particular in research on infants using terms such as the "competent infant" (Dornes, 1993; Stern, 1985, 2004). Only a few decades ago, infants were regarded as more or less passive beings, who in the first months did little other than sleep and eat, and who correspondingly needed, other than emotional attention, little beyond basic care.

But today, from the first moment of life, children are considered active, curious, communicative, and competent. They want to discover the world, and they prompt adults to behave according to their wishes and needs. Though all these behaviours can certainly be observed in infants, this list, with few changes, can almost be taken as a job description for senior managers. The ideals of modern society are projected into the images of early childhood. Self-determination and autonomy are apparently constitutive, at the moment, for human self-image and thus influence, at least in broad contours, our ideas of the infant.

Laplanche contrasts that view with an approach based on difference theory, and emphasizes the asymmetry in the relationship of child and adult. He focuses on the structure of the relationship and not on the interactive, reciprocal behaviour of those involved in it, a position which is opposed to that held in today's developmental psychology. He does not see the child as the "producer of his own development" in the current sense of the modern autonomous subject. Instead, he sees the child as structurally subordinate to the Other (as a "subject" in the literal Latin sense of *sub-iectum*). Human development therefore does not start with the ego but is conceived of as stemming from the Other, the unfamiliar, the unavailable. This point of view—the primacy of the Other—corresponds with the central preoccupation of psychoanalysis, which sees experiences and feelings as determined, at their core, by the unconscious; thus by what is inaccessible and unavailable to the ego.

Laplanche regards primal seduction as a basic, anthropological situation: From the moment of birth, the child is confronted with the world of the adults. "However, the adult world is not an objective world which the child has to discover and learn about in the same way that it learns to walk or to manipulate objects. It is characterized by the existence of messages (linguistic or semiological messages, meaning pre-linguistic or paralinguistic) which ask the child questions it cannot yet understand. The child has to make sense of them and give an answer." (Laplanche, 1989, p. 124). The infant's encounter with the adult world consists, in particular, in being confronted with "enigmatic messages". These messages are "enigmatic", for one thing, because they can be only very inadequately processed or translated owing to the infant's still underdeveloped capacities to respond somatically, cognitively, or affectively. At the same time, they are not completely available to the adult, either: they do not consist only of conscious elements but are laced with unconscious aspirations as well. The messages therefore become enigmatic signifiers for both parties, forcing the infant to make efforts at translation. A claim emanates from these messages to which the child cannot not respond.

I regard the notion of claim and response, as formulated for example in Bernhard Waldenfels's (2011) phenomenological philosophy, as more adequate for describing the seduction scene than calling it a message. Inherent in the term "message" is the idea that there is something to communicate or transmit, something that could be precisely identified and named. But in a "enigmatic message" we are dealing, rather, with something that is obscure even to the person sending that message. The German term *Anspruch*, "claim," also has the corresponding dual meaning, appropriate in the seduction context, of both appealing to someone and making a demand: Whenever I address someone, I unavoidably also assert claims to which the other person must react (Waldenfels, 2011).

Through these "enigmatic messages", the infant is confronted with the desires of an adult, and with unconscious sexual fantasies that are unavoidably mobilized by this intimate relationship. This last point is worth re-emphasizing. It is unconscious fantasies that are being evoked in the relationship to the infant, and they act as enigmatic messages. These fantasies are also inaccessible to the parents—a crucial, basic point, because under no circumstances is this about real sexual acts. In the relationship to the child, the unconscious desire of the adults is perceived as a claim that forces the child to respond. That claim is thereby transformed and introjected into the child and is physically inscribed in the child. The unconscious sexual fantasies of the adults become part of the mental and physical structure of the child through the processes of introjection and identification. I will describe various aspects of this more fully in the ensuing chapters.

Laplanche regards this seduction scene, this confrontation of the child with the unconscious, the desires, and the sexuality of adults, as a traumatic incursion into the child's world. The enigmatic signifiers are implanted in the child and create an internal foreign object not amenable to any kind of metabolic processing (Laplanche, 1999a). These considerations have by now shown themselves to be extremely constructive for psychoanalytic theory—they serve, for example, to conceptualize the genesis of psychic structures, the unconscious, and sexuality, or to untangle processes such as repression, introjection and transference (see Bayer & Quindeau, 2004).

However, Laplanche's line of argument also raises a number of problematic and still unresolved points. For example, it gives the impression that the adult world stands in opposition to a "child's world". Instead, I would like to emphasize that this child's world is only being constituted through this process: one cannot speak of an "incursion" as that would presuppose something that already exists. Rather, the notion of a "child's world" independent of adults serves the cliché of the asexual, "innocent" child. This kind of paradisiacal state before the fall from grace can be found, for example, in Ferenczi (1933), whom Laplanche justly critiques because the child is dependent initially for its existence on "external assistance" and without an adult, would not survive.

But there are other reasons for my questioning whether it makes sense to describe the infant's confrontation with adult desires as a "traumatic incursion". The question can be put more sharply: Is this encounter necessarily a confrontation? I am well aware that in putting it this way, I question a broad consensus in psychoanalytic theory. Though they give it different shadings, analysts from the most diverse backgrounds, be they Freudians, (neo-) Kleinians or Lacanians, are unanimous in arguing that there is a traumatic confrontation between the world of the adult and the world of the child. I would like to encourage questioning of what is taken as self-evident, because the notion of a traumatic encounter of child and adult has a number of problems and inherent contradictions. To resolve them, I suggest a fundamental shift of emphasis in psychoanalytic theory with respect to the genesis of the subject, of the unconscious, and of sexuality: a shift from the trauma of the (emerging) subject to the desire of the Other.

As a fundamental objection, I first want to emphasize that both traumatic incursion and confrontation presuppose the (ego) structure—so that something can even be attacked or overcome in the first place.

The genesis of that structure should first be explained, however. If the (sexual) unconscious is ascribed a basic, central importance in the psychic apparatus, it seems problematic to assume that prior to its genesis, a different psychic structure exists. Laplanche (1988) discusses a similar question with respect to suppression, which he distinguishes from primal repression to avoid turning the *explanans* into the *explanandum*. But as far as I can see, he is not referring here to the problem of trauma.

Laplanche's main argument, which speaks for the traumatic character of this relationship, is the inadequate somatic, emotional, and cognitive equipment an infant has for processing the enigmatic messages. Of particular importance here is the sexual immaturity of the child, as human sexual development takes place in two widely separated phases. It is only *nachträglich*, after sexual maturity sets in, that the (former) child can access the meaning of adult sexuality. As in Emma's case, it is at this point, beyond puberty, that the universal trauma of the general seduction situation takes place. However accurate the assumption of inadequate means for processing may appear, the assumption that this occurs in a traumatic manner seems inconclusive to me, for another reason as well. Current psychoanalytic theory regards trauma as composed of a triad of intrusion, denial, and arousal (see Fischer & Riedesser, 1998).

These three dimensions would need to be recognizable in order to speak of trauma in a clinical sense. But is the infant really overwhelmed by the "enigmatic messages"? Does the level of physiological arousal evoked by the presence of adults rise to such a degree that it can barely be curbed? Since this is not likely as a rule to be the case, I find it not very appropriate to ascribe a traumatic character to the relationship between adult and child. In my critique, I am concerned with the theoretical ascription of a fundamentally traumatic quality to the parent-child relationship, but certainly do not deny that there are overwhelming experiences for an infant. Yet as a rule, these do not occur in the context of interactions but are caused instead by the absence of a (caring or protective) Other.

But I would also like to point to a further significant aspect in this context that could speak for retaining the notion of trauma: the idea that the enigmatic message is transported into the psyche of the child "like a foreign object" and forms the unconscious there. To designate this realm of the Other, foreign, and inaccessible, the term trauma seems to be extremely appropriate again after all, as it also describes an alien object that must be sealed inside the psychic structure and contained so that mental functioning is possible.

Yet one could ask at this point whether it is actually sensible to assume that the enigmatic message is only encapsulated and remains in this form in the child's psyche. The image of the sealed-off foreign object evokes possibly inapplicable notions, for it is, after all, the very confrontation with this message that activates productive psychological processes such as the construction and differentiation of the psychic structure. What strikes me as more appropriate, therefore, is the idea that in the process of confrontation, this message changes. Though it ultimately remains a foreign object, albeit a continually changing one, it is partially processed and integrated. In terms of metaphor, I would like to augment the image of the foreign object with the image of the trace the "enigmatic message" leaves or inscribes in the body and in the developing mental structure, a trace that leads to further reinscriptions.

Proceeding from Laplanche's argument, I take a different path and emphasize not the traumatization of the (emerging) subject but instead the desire of the Other. I conceive of the relationship between the child and the adult as a place where the psychic structure of the child, the unconscious mind, and infantile sexuality emerge in a non-endogenous and not necessarily traumatic manner. It is not the trauma of the subject but rather the sexual desire of the Other that is of central, constitutive, significance in my approach. The desire of the adult is directed at the infant, as a claim or demand that is being made. The infant responds to this demand by generating his or her own infantile sexual desire. The constitutive process of sexuality, and beyond this, of the entire psychic structure, could be taken as a pointed modification of the famous Cartesian *cogito ergo sum*, and formulated as *desideratus ergo sum*: I am desired, therefore I am.

This formulation takes account of the fundamental heteronomy of human existence. The passive form *desideratus* points to the prior structures associated with the individual, structures to which the subject is subjected, and at the same time to the dependence on the Other in the course of his or her development. Sexual desire thereby is neither an endogenous process, meaning something already inherently present in humans, nor is the individual either the subject or the creator of his or her desires. Rather, I take every instance of desiring as a response to being desired. If one formulates the origin of desire as under the primacy of the Other, one is making not only an assertion about the situation in early childhood. Every desire, even in adulthood, is a response to these internalized scenes from early childhood, of being desired by mother, father, or other guardians. The desire of the Other constitutes the subject's psychic structure and desire. This, in my reading and put succinctly, is the essence of the Freudian theory of seduction.

Desire as inscription in the body

"Desire" instead of "drive": reformulating drive theory

The concept of drives is at the heart of Freudian psychoanalysis. With justification, Wolfgang Mertens (1998) regards it as a constitutive element of the entire theory. At the same time, in the last few years it has increasingly been seen as obsolete and superseded. This loss of significance, however, carries grave consequences both for psychoanalytic theory and for therapeutic practice (see Quindeau, 2005). Freud developed his drive concept in coming to terms with the problem of human sexuality. Over the years, this idea was expanded into a theory of drives and frequently revised. But these revisions continued to lead further and further away from the sexual. To more closely define the sexual, I return to Freud's original drive concept and amass arguments that speak for maintaining the concept and modifying it. However, the designation "drive" cannot be salvaged but must be replaced—though I do so reluctantly, because it unavoidably entails a shift, and thus also a loss, in meaning.

Freud (1905d) used the term "drive" (*Trieb*) for the first time in the *Three Essays on the Theory of Sexuality*. The term was not his own creation but was commonly used at the time in medicine by the then leading sexuality researchers (see, among others, Krafft-Ebing, 1877; Moll, 1897; Ellis, 1898). I suspect that many of the misunderstandings concerning the theory of drives are the result of this long history of the term. Freud took a prevalent term and filled it with different content, but was not able to prevail and, particularly in his later works, often reverted to the use of the conventional meaning, one heavily influenced by German idealism. The term drive served to describe the motives and determinants of human behaviour. In drives (impulses), Kant had seen a natural propensity:

> The predisposition to animality in mankind ... is threefold: first,
> for self-preservation; second, for the propagation of the species,

through the sexual impulse, and for the care of offspring so begotten; and third, for community with other men, i.e., the social impulse. (1934, p. 22)

Unlike Hegel, who discerned in drives a quest for reason (*Vernunft*), Schopenhauer and Nietzsche in particular expanded on the notion of drives as the dark side of human nature. At the end of the nineteenth century, Albert Moll, a pioneer in the study of human sexuality, a field based in medical science, published his studies on the "sex drive", a subject into which little serious research had been done (Sigusch, 2005b). Moll opposed the then-prevalent assumption of a reproductive drive and argued instead for a sex drive that was composed of a "detumescence drive"—which he described as an organic urge to empty a secretion—and a "contrection drive" which led to a convergence of body and spirit (Moll, 1897, p. 94). Even if Freud did not make explicit reference to Moll, he apparently was deeply impressed by his works (Sulloway, 1979). In many respects, however, and particularly regarding the concept of drives, Freud went much further.

Yet the connotation of drives as a dark, inherent part of human nature has remained right up to the present and apparently cannot be exorcized from the term. At least in everyday understanding, and worse, even in German criminal law, the sex drive, which in its cruder form is usually ascribed to men, is regarded as a biological force that is difficult to keep under control and that determines behaviour. For Freud, though, at least in his early works, drives were neither inherent forces nor predispositions. In his later works, Freud clearly assigns drives to human nature, but his earlier conceptualizations can be read in terms of socialization theory as well: The drive, or the "destiny" of drives (*Triebschicksal*), first originates, rather, in the interaction of adult and child, and is not to be understood as innate and dependent on maturation.

But this subtle view, to which even Foucault (2005)—who otherwise does not much esteem psychoanalysis—gives credit to for addressing the entwined unit of desire and interdiction, apparently did not resonate among Freud's audience. Paradoxically, Freud is criticized for a drive concept he never advocated. Thus, for example, he is supposed to have proposed a "sex drive" in a functional, hydraulic sense—a kind of "boiler model" for letting off steam—which might fit Moll's "detumescence drive" but completely misses the mark with respect to Freud's conception of drives. However, the series of misunderstandings in the reception history of the psychoanalytic concept of drives seems to take no end, and not just in the English-speaking world—as reconfirmed by a wide variety of contributions in a recently published collection of articles about the *Three Essays* (Dannecker & Katzenbach, 2005).

But to return to the *Three Essays* themselves, even on the first page, and with deliberate rhetorical intent, Freud discusses the assumption of a biological "sexual instinct". This is part of our everyday understanding, Freud says, and immediately begins to rebut the "errors, inaccuracies and hasty conclusions" (1905d, p. 135) existing in public opinion. While the energetic dimension of the drive concept was already prefigured in Freud's early distinction between external and internal stimuli (Freud, 1950a), here he differentiates the source, object, and goal of the drive. Unlike instincts, which describe hereditarily fixed behaviour that is necessary in a biological sense for the preservation of the species, drives have neither a fixed object nor a predetermined goal. The sources of the drive can also be quite varied, at least in Freud's first formulations, where he distinguishes between direct and indirect sources, direct stimulation of the erogenous zones through various stimuli as well as general "muscular activity," "affective processes", or "intellectual work" (Laplanche & Pontalis, 1973, p. 424).

It is only in the later revisions of the theory that Freud tries to give drives an exclusively somatic basis by locating their source in the organs of the body (Freud, 1915c). Yet Freud does not decide the question of whether it is a somatic force or mental energy that underlies drives. Likely with deliberate intent, he retains the ambiguity of the drive in all his writings, seeing it as lying in a liminal area between the mental and the physical. In his late works he finally reaches the well-known assessment, "The theory of the instincts is so to say our mythology. Instincts are mythical entities, magnificent in their indefiniteness" (1933a, p. 95). Yet as much as one may agree with Freud in his appreciation of the indeterminate and indefinable, making a mythology the core of a science is not without problems. That does not imply an immediate rejection of drive theory as unusable; instead, it calls for renewed reflection to fathom and pursue the unrealized potential still contained in this theory.

I see such potential for the drive concept in Freud's early writings, because it is not yet weighted down by the ballast of mystifying speculations about Eros and Thanatos, nor is it as yet understood as, at its core, a biological predisposition.

But neither can one simply reverse the shift in the meaning Freud gives to the idea of drives in his works. To preserve what, as before, remains a meaningful concept in a modified form, I suggest replacing the term "drive" with less encumbered terms. One among them is the term "wish" (*Wunsch*), which Freud elaborated on in *The Interpretation of Dreams* in conjunction with his analysis of hallucinatory wish-fulfilment. Comparable to the drive, the wish is regarded as "the motor of any mental activity" (1900a). Yet despite obvious similarities between the two notions, I do not see the term "wish" as really suitable either, as it relies too much on mental processes and ignores the somatic dimension. As an alternative, the term "desire" suggests itself instead. In Freud's work, it had no place, though it is the key concept in Lacan's psychoanalytic theory. It is of course difficult to disregard Lacan's usage of the word, and it makes my venture a tricky one, but nonetheless I want to revisit the term "desire" without making (explicit) reference to Lacan, in order to continue the discussion of Freud's original concept of drives. If the result is congruence with Lacan, this is more coincidental than intended.

To triangulate on the term desire, I first want to turn to the most important aspects of the Freudian drive theory: Desire lies, as a liminal concept, between the somatic and the mental. It is rooted in the body and is at the same time a mental representation. With "desire" we also gain a concept that, in contrast to the concept of drive, is not associated with the problematic dimension of heredity and the biologically innate. With this, it becomes possible to understand the emergence of desire in a manner explicitly connected to socialization, and place it in a social, "inter-subjective" space.

I intentionally use the term "inter-subjective" guardedly, as many quite diverse phenomena are understood by this term nowadays in the psychoanalytic discourse. By "inter-subjective," I do not mean to designate interactions between *subjects* but instead, following the more recent phenomenological discourse (as in Waldenfels, 2002), designate the *interstice*, the intervening space between the "subject" and the Other. Here, "subject" no long means the subject as autonomously agent, in the sense of the "cogito" as used in the Enlightenment and German Idealist traditions, but rather as the one subjugated to the Other, and which makes the emergence of the subject possible in the first place. The primacy of the Other encompasses language and culture as well as social structures and functions, and extends to specific persons. The Other I understand in this context as existing prior to the subject.

It is not just the term "drive" that is problematic. The drive concept's increasing loss of significance might be related to various later distinctions Freud undertook with respect to the theory of drives. In the *Three Essays*, Freud spoke only of a single drive—the sexual drive—but in his later works, he diversified drives, distinguishing between the sexual drive and the ego or ego-preservation drive in *Instincts and their Vicissitudes* (1915c), and finally contrasting the libido with the death drive in *Beyond the Pleasure Principle*, his last essay on the theory of drives (1920g). The last concept, in particular, probably the most speculative and controversial, in which Freud both borrows from mythology and anchors drives in biology, arguably sealed the fate of Freudian drive theory. With these distinctions, the prominent position he had given the sexual drive was lost, and it became re-conceived as one drive among others; thus, he himself contributed to reducing the significance of the sexual. Freud's successors have added other drives arbitrarily, with Adler (1924) adding self-assertion and Bowlby (1951) adding attachment, while Balint (1933) replaced libido with primary love. This process has continued in the notions formulated by psychologists of the self, right up to the newer theories of infancy in which, for example, the drive concept merges into non-specific motivation(al) systems (as in Lichtenberg, 1989).

While psychoanalytic theory has largely accepted this diversification of drives, there are hardly any theories that build on the primacy of the sexual, as formulated originally in the *Three Essays*. The only exception is Laplanche's (1999b) general theory of seduction, noted above, which regards the death drive as a sexual drive as well, and thereby reasserts a monism in the drive theory that emphasizes the central significance of the sexual.

Yet should one continue to give sexuality such a central place in psychoanalytic thinking? I certainly do not intend to perpetuate the pan-sexualism of the nineteenth century and assume that every set of symptoms is of sexual origin. Instead, I inquire about the importance and relative significance of the sexual in a theory of humankind in general.

The drive theory is of paramount importance for psychoanalysis for three reasons: 1. as a science of the unconscious, 2. as anthropology, and 3. as a theory of socialization (Quindeau, 2005). It is indispensable in psychoanalytic thinking, for without it, it is difficult to make sense of the contradictory, conflict-laden, and non-identical dimension presented by the psychic life of civilized man.

Sexual desire is paradigmatic for the unconscious, for the Other, for that which is foreign to the ego. By conceptualizing an unconscious that goes beyond the descriptive unconscious to encompass what is not (yet) conscious, Freud ascribes the central motive force in humans, that is, everything that is key in determining a person's behaviour and experience. Yet this is something that eludes the (self-)consciousness and the (self-)determination of the modern subject.

With his drive theory, Freud brought a fundamental matter into relief: in desire lie the roots of conflict and yet desire is largely inaccessible to conscious awareness. The lines of conflict run between the conscious and the unconscious, but also inside the unconscious and between individual subjects. Conflict is thereby unavoidably inscribed in the psychic structure, and is not a disorder or deviation, as some theories in psychology or psychotherapy argue.

How significant the idea of conflict is for constructing psychoanalytic theory can also be seen in developmental psychology concepts, such as that of psycho-sexual development (a topic I will return to in greater detail below). In the course of psychosexual development, a child acquires (or searches for) various modes of gratification and these are organized as polar contrasts between the active and the passive. These wishes are tied to basic body processes and experiences and are associated with various zones or areas of the body. Thus there are the gratification modes of orality (with the contrast pair "ingesting, devouring" and "being eaten or devoured"), of anality (with the contrast pair "holding on" and "releasing") and of genitality/phallicity (with the contrast pair "penetrating" and "receiving"). Emotional conflicts arise from the polarity of these gratification modes. For one, simultaneous achievement of active and passive wishes is contradictory: One cannot both hold on and release at the same time, or both enter and receive. For another, the wishes are often at odds with one another, as when there a simultaneous (oral) wish for merging and an (anal) wish for demarcation or individuation. These conflicts are represented doubly. On the one hand, they are located within internal psychological processes, and on the other, they manifest themselves in object- relations. As a rule, such conflicts are mastered through psychological defence mechanisms, as a functioning defence enables a broad spectrum of gratification modes. Only during a crisis, as in the case of mental illness, does this spectrum become more limited, with desire being distorted into a symptom. These distortions of desire are what psychoanalytic therapy tries to treat in order to make the full variety of gratification modes available again. Thus, at the end of an analysis the goal is less a pleasant identity construct than a heightened tolerance for ambiguity, as well as the insight that the contradictions of desire can never be resolved.

In the *Three Essays on the Theory of Sexuality*, Freud turned against the prevailing understanding of human sexuality as basically instinctual behaviour or biological programming. At the same time, he described the essential features of anthropology: desire, the striving for pleasure and gratification, as the main driving force of human action. That force applies not just to sexual activity in the narrower sense but lies the base of all human activity.

By no means is this driving force, which Freud called the sex drive or libido, to be understood as organic and endogenous or as a biological predisposition. Instead, it develops over the course of an individual's life. Freud was far more indecisive on this point, though, for on the one hand, he regarded the drive as liminal and lying between the mental and the physical, and neither unequivocally the one or the other. On the other hand, throughout his life he clung to the hope of someday finding and demonstrating the organic foundation of drives. I will not pursue at this point the possible reasons for this continued back-and-forth between psychology and biology—one finds it, incidentally, in other places in his works (see Quindeau, 2004a)—but instead want to emphasize Freud's hesitation. The history of reception shows that Freud's successors were far more decisive, increasingly regarding drives as an endogenous, biological predisposition. My argument takes a different direction, as I regard drives as something acquired during the course of life, something that finds expression in somatic processes or structures. Drives, in my view, do not belong to the biological endowment of humans, they are not predispositions that develop into behavioural or experiential patterns during the course of maturation. Rather, drives constitute themselves and arise in the relationship between the child and an adult.

Wish and need

The effort to better understand the sexual while maintaining the indeterminate, in an oscillating process, is not confined to the term "drive". Other facets of the sexual can be discussed by using the idea of the wish, as Freud sketched out in *The Interpretation of Dreams* (1900a), in connection with the infant's primary experience of gratification. Freud derived his concept of hallucinatory wish-fulfilment from these experiences, and wish-fulfilment is regarded as the most important function of dream-work. Beyond that, it is also of significance for other forms of psychic work as well as quite fundamental in the construction and differentiation of psychic structure. For the infant, the experience of gratification—as exemplified by nursing or feeding—comes about through the actions of another person. Formulated in Freud's terms, the gratification that results from removing the tension of unpleasure requires an object that cancels the inner stimulus.

> An essential component of this experience of satisfaction is a particular perception (that of nourishment, in our example) the mnemic image of which remains associated thenceforward with the memory trace of the excitation produced by the need. As a result of the link that has thus been established, next time this need arises a psychical impulse will at once emerge which will seek to re-cathect the mnemic image of the perception and to re-evoke the perception itself, that is to say, to re-establish the situation of the original satisfaction. An impulse of this kind is what we call a wish; the reappearance of the perception is the fulfilment of the wish ... (1900a, pp. 565–66)

The notion of the wish has central importance in Freudian thought, for it is the main feature of human sexuality. "As opposed to love, desire is directly dependent on a specific somatic foundation; in contrast to need, it subordinates satisfaction to conditions in the fantasy world which strictly determine object-choice and the orientation of activity" (Laplanche and Pontalis, 1973, p. 421 et seq).

The wish concept does not designate an intentional process or one that is consciously accessible; instead, Freud uses it to describe the working method of the unconscious. The wish, and in particular wish-fulfilment, are the key characteristics of the psychic work of the unconscious. What should be emphasized in the aforementioned attempt at definition is the demarcation of wish from need. While need makes reference to vital physiological requirements such as nourishment, sleep, warmth and so forth, wishing is a psychological category, a movement in the mind that leaves traces in memory and that wants to re-establish the perception of gratification. Unlike in everyday understanding, there is no sexual *need* under this definition, as human sexuality is not based on an absolute demand that must be met for survival. Rather, it is a wish whose aim is gratification, but such gratification cannot be achieved fully or for all eternity.

The term wish alone does not adequately encompass human sexuality, however, as it only insufficiently accommodates the somatic dimension. This, by contrast, is contained more fully in the concept of "need", which is why it makes sense to connect the wish idea with certain elements of the idea of need. Differentiating wish from need leads to differing respective forms of fulfilment. The need, the releasing of an inner tension, requires a particular, "specific action", as well as an object in order to achieve gratification.

One can readily see this in the need for nourishment. Hunger makes itself noticed as a tension and a displeasure that can be allayed by taking in nourishment: the food itself functions as object while eating functions as a "specific action". A wish, by contrast, cannot be fulfilled in such a material, specific manner. Its "fulfilment" consists much more in psychic activity—the re-cathexis of memory traces with the goal of creating a "perceptual identity", that is, a repetition of the particular perception tied to the gratification of the need. "The structure of *Wunsch* has taught us that a wish or a desire is not a tension that can be discharged; desire, as Freud himself describes it, reveals a constitution that is insatiable" (Ricoeur, 1970, p. 322). For Paul Ricoeur, the wish is a liminal term lying between the organic and the psychological, which points to the affinity of this concept with Freud's later notions of the drive. While the wish, in this early version of *The Interpretation of Dreams*, appears as a largely solipsistic event freed from the inter-subjective matrix of its genesis, its inter-subjective character is much more clearly evident in the drive concept. With respect to the conceptualization of sexuality, what is of importance is the inter-subjective context of origin—in the form of the seduction scene between child and adult—as well as the at least partial or temporary gratification, that, similar to the need to reduce tension—for example, in an orgasm—can be achieved. The term wish makes evident that this is not a purely physiological activity but instead rests on psychological processes. It shows on the one hand why sexual desire is fundamentally insatiable, or can be gratified only partially and temporarily, and continually renews itself. On the other hand, this underscores the constitutive meaning of fantasy in sexual experience, which aims at a repetition of the perception of gratification, and to that end, not only cathects memory images but also changes and reshapes them.

The wish goes back to a memory. It consists of the cathexis of an image, in memory, of a situation of gratification, and the striving for renewed gratification that is bound to it. In that regard, the wish can be regarded as the motor of every psychic activity. With the concept of hallucinatory wish-fulfilment in the *Interpretation of Dreams*, though, Freud focuses exclusively on mental processes and ignores the bodily dimension. On this point, it would therefore be necessary to add a link between the two formulations, one that derives not just the concept of wish-fulfilment but also the genesis of sexual arousal and of the erogenous zones from the primary gratification experience of the infant.

Trace and reinscription

In his theory of sexuality, Freud transcended the mind-body problem and in addition—though this was certainly not his intent—provided a starting point for formulating an exogenous, socially-based constitution of sexuality. Here, I cannot fully play the intellectual game of radically deconstructing what appears to us to be so natural and immediate—the level of the body and the somatic—but can only indicate the direction of a further discussion of Freud's texts.

As in the past, it is common to ascribe a constitutive significance for sexuality to bodily processes. They provide the basis on which psychological activities such as fantasies are added, and thus lend human sexuality a specific cast. In his early theory of sexuality, Freud tended to replace this primacy of the body with the primacy of the psychological. However, this change in perspective was not entirely successful, and for that reason Freud repeatedly fell back into the traditional view, as in his repeated—unsuccessful—attempts throughout his life to search for the origin of sexuality in endogenous, somatic processes, in preference to completely rejecting the original thought.

However, with the concept of erogenous zones, he paved the way for a different perspective, and described how the body of a newborn becomes a sexual body, one that can be sexually aroused. From this, I derive the thesis that sexuality, the striving for pleasure and gratification, is inscribed in the body through a social process, namely in the encounter an infant has with an adult.

To regard desire as inscription is certainly an unconventional way of reading the Freudian text. With this thesis, I draw on Freud's early conceptualizations in which he was preoccupied with the connection between memory and the origin of psychic structure. In a December 6, 1896 letter to Wilhelm Fliess, he laid out his completely new insights about how memory worked. It did not simply depict perceptions but rather recorded them in various systems of signification. In doing so, the psychic structure was both constituted as well as continually altered:

> As you know, I am working on the assumption that our psychic mechanism has come into being by a process of stratification: the material present in the form of memory traces being subjected from time to time to a *rearrangement* in accordance with fresh circumstances—to a *reinscription*. Thus what is essentially new about my theory is the thesis that memory is present not once but several times over, that it is laid down in various kinds of indications. (Masson, 1985, p. 207)

He had ambitious plans at the time he was developing this reinscription model, and was convinced that "if I could give a complete account of the psychological characteristics of perception and of the three registrations, I should have described a new psychology" (ibid., p. 208), but he apparently never pursued the idea.

Alfred Lorenzer's theory of socialization contains a notion of forms of interaction that I see as an elaboration of the Freudian idea of multiple coding, though Lorenzer does not make reference to it. Lorenzer distinguishes between different levels of interaction forms that are formed, in the course of ontogenesis, out of interaction practices, and that can be understood as reinscriptions, or as particular forms of interaction that are emotionally symbolic and linguistically symbolic (Lorenzer, 1977). These forms are the traces that remain of a variety of actual interactions that took place between a child and his or her reference person, and they form a structure underlying later behaviour and experience, in the sense of a pattern of expectation and orientation. With respect to the question discussed here, it is the earliest structures or forms of interaction, ontogenetically, that are of particular interest, and these are laid down at the sensory, motor, organismic, and pre-verbal level.

As an example, one can examine the way a child is taken into the arms of his or her mother. This gesture creates a kinaesthetic memory trace that as much shapes the active behaviour of the child as it fixes a passive expectation for the future. This is underscored by many clinical observations that mothers usually have a self-evident sense of how to carry their child. Evidently, memory traces of their own childhood experiences are expressed here, reflecting the way they themselves were carried. Impressive evidence of these kinaesthetic memories also can be found in the well-known case history of "Monika" provided by René Spitz (1959).

The countless repetitions of this interaction are then reflected in an interaction structure or a "specific form of interaction". This registration, in a pre-verbal, sensory-motor, organismic period, is an inscription in the body that takes place without a reflective consciousness. Going beyond Lorenzer, I want to propose the thesis that the inscription or of sensory-motor interactions not only structures a kind of body memory but beyond that, reinscription structures this body itself and its perceptual abilities.

Erogenous zones

I want to use the erogenous zones to illustrate this formation of the sexual body based on memories. With the term "erogenous zone", Freud designated a "skin or mucous membrane in which stimuli of a certain sort evoke a feeling of pleasure possessing a particular quality" (1905d, p. 183). This pleasurable feeling does not primarily adhere to that area of the body; hence it does not originate in the genetic equipping of the body and is then triggered in some manner. Rather, it first arises through the actions of another person.

Take breast-feeding as an example. By suckling at the mother's breast, the lips and mouth of the child becomes an erogenous zone. The experience of gratification shapes the infantile sexual body, supplying it with a specific ability to be aroused. "The satisfaction of the erotogenic zone is associated, in the first instance, with the satisfaction of the need for nourishment" (ibid., pp. 181–82). This "attachment" is a key characteristic of infantile sexuality and predestines certain areas of the body to be erogenous zones. At the same time, sexual activity frees itself from these zones and "precisely as in the case of sucking, any other part of the body can acquire the same susceptibility to stimulation as is possessed by the genitals and can become an erotogenic zone" (ibid., p. 184).

The erogenous zones are thereby formed through the sexual activity, by the experience of pleasure and gratification whose starting-point is in the care activities of the adults. This is true, of course, not only of breast-feeding but of all body contact between an adult and a child, from changing diapers and bathing to playing and cuddling. In the first months of a child's life, interactions are basically body-oriented. From these experiences, a body memory develops that particularly focuses on those areas especially sensitive to pleasure. This view is supported by the observation that though certain areas of the body are erogenous in all humans, individuals also have highly individualized erogenous zones, areas of the body that evoke feelings of pleasure in some people but not in others. It is just this idiosyncrasy that surely cannot be adequately explained if one argues for a biological equipping—as in the sense that for certain people, sensitive nerve endings are bundled at certain points on the body. It is far more plausible to argue that interaction experiences are the reason for the differences. Every new-born has specific individual experiences in bodily interaction with his or her parents, and therefore develops specific erogenous zones.

Thus, erogenous zones are memory traces of early gratification experiences that are inscribed on the body. Sexual arousal is based not on the particular physiological condition of individual zones of the body but instead on unconscious memories. These memories may be activated by stimulating the erogenous zones, but this is not necessarily needed. In my view, the fundamental independence of sexual arousal from sensory perception is specific to human sexuality, for such arousal also can certainly be triggered by fantasies and memories. That makes sexual arousal a highly complex, multi-layered mental process that cannot be activated mechanically or technically through particular stimuli. Rather, it results from an interaction between fantasies and memory that can be intensified through tactile and kinaesthetic as well as visual and auditory perceptions.

Memory and fantasy

Freud conceptualized a connection between memory and fantasy in his early writings:

> The aim seems to be to reach the earliest (sexual) scenes. … For fantasies are psychic façades produced in order to bar access to these memories. Fantasies simultaneously serve the tendency toward refining the memories, toward sublimating them. They

are manufactured by means of things that are heard, and utilized
subsequently, and thus combine things experienced and heard,
past events (from the history of parents and ancestors), and things
that have been seen by oneself. They are related to things heard, as
dreams are related to things seen. In dreams, to be sure, we hear
nothing, but we see. (Masson, 1985, p. 240)

Fantasy is based on perceptions, such as auditory impressions that are
later processed and embellished. Fantasies are therefore—in this early
view of Freud's—ways of processing memory traces. In Freud's later
writings, this origin of fantasy in life history is increasingly rejected in
favour of a universal, phylogenetic origin. Yet with respect to sexual
desire, it is particularly interesting. Whilst Freud regards the "primal
scene"—the sexual act between parents that is the origin of one's
own existence—basically as the origin of hysterical illness, I see it in
addition, against the backdrop of the general seduction scene between
adults and child, as a means for processing this seduction. The primal
scene thereby is a universal expression of the creation of sexual fantasy,
a prototype out of which extremely different variations develop in
the course of life. Unlike those versions that see the primal scene as
a universal structure or phylogenetic inheritance, fantasy in my view
is based on actual perceptions that are nonetheless organized within a
socially predetermined scheme: the triad of father, mother and child.
In this primal scene, perceptions with the most diverse origins have an
influence. A specific perception of parental intercourse is thereby neither necessary nor in a particular manner conducive to the construction
of this scene. On the other hand, the specific experiences with parents
and other reference persons have great importance. This is particularly
true for the seduction scenes in Laplanche's reading of the general
seduction situation. These unconscious dimensions of the parent-child
interaction are processed in and with the primal scene. This scene thus
becomes an organizer in structuring the "enigmatic" messages, bundling them together like a prism, and subsequently, *nachträglich*, lending them a form.

These constructs of the primal scene change in the course of child
development, and in adulthood. In an ideal-typical manner, and like
memories, they are subject to a permanent process of reinscription,
nachträglich. Thereby they are accommodated to the specific cognitive
and affective stage relevant at the time. They also correspond to the

needs, and, in particular, change in response to the unconscious conflict constellations of that particular moment.

> We must not suppose that the products of this imaginative activity (…) are stereotyped or unalterable. On the contrary, they fit themselves in to the subject's shifting impressions of life, change with every change in his situation, and receive from every fresh active impression what might be called a "date-mark". The relation of a fantasy to time is in general very important. We may say that it hovers, as it were, between three times—the three moments of time which our ideation involves. Mental work is linked to some current impression, some provoking occasion in the present which has been able to arouse one of the subject's major wishes. From there it harks back to a memory of an earlier experience (usually an infantile one) in which this wish was fulfilled; and it now creates a situation relating to the future which represents a fulfilment of the wish. What it thus creates is a day-dream or fantasy, which carries about it traces of its origin from the occasion which provoked it and from the memory. Thus past, present and future are strung together, as it were, on the thread of the wish that runs through them. (1908e, p. 147)

Though Freud wrote this in the context of artistic fantasy, I would like to apply his remarks to the realm of sexual fantasy. By this, I do not mean just fantasies with an explicitly sexual content. Far more decisive is their function. "Sexual fantasies" are therefore those that lead to sexual arousal and not just the fantasy but also the arousal can remain unconscious. What is particularly interesting is the tension between a permanent transformation and reshaping of the fantasies in the course of a life, on the one hand, and the immutability of the unconscious infantile wishes on the other. As I will detail, the gratification modes of the various phases of psychosexual development are reflected in sexual fantasies.

I assume that in the course of child development, the corresponding phase-specific dominant modes—orality, anality, phallicity—also dominate fantasy life. While I regard these modes, which Freud called partial drives, as subsequent (*nachträgliche*) inscriptions and reinscriptions of the infantile gratification experiences I also see puberty as the decisive juncture for these reinscriptions. It is here that these experiences are newly structured, under the primacy of the genital, and reinscribed into an adult sexuality. The partial drives thereby come to take on new meaning, *nachträglich*.

The concept of *Nachträglichkeit* is, in my view, the main point of the Freudian theory of sexuality. Astonishingly for a concept given great prominence in other early works, it is not mentioned in the *Three Essays* at all. Therefore, I want to inscribe this aspect into the Freudian theory of sexuality—as it were, as a *nachträgliche* reinscription of this theory. As described above, experiences, impressions, and memory traces are, at a later point in time, reworked as a result of new experiences or because of a new stage of development. With this reworking, the earlier experiences simultaneously gain new meaning and new psychic effectiveness. What is decisive is the dissolution of a linear concept of time: earlier experiences are just as significant for later ones as later experiences are for earlier ones. If one looks at sexuality in this manner, not as something that inheres in the body "by nature" and that merely unfolds in the course of maturation, but instead as the bodily inscription of pleasurable experiences, then it is precisely such a constellational understanding of time that is useful for understanding human sexuality. For in every sexual activity, numerous experiences, gained at the most differing times, come together and are processed as a new reinscription.

Infantile sexuality

The concept of infantile sexuality is likely the most significant accomplishment of the Freudian theory of sexuality. Among psychoanalysts, the concept remains an undisputed element of the theory, yet its actual meaning seems increasingly unclear. How does infantile sexuality manifest itself? Can a sexual character be ascribed to infantile behavioural manifestations at all, or is it not rather a matter of (retrospective) projection by adults? There are many empirical psychoanalytic studies on these questions, the best-known of which are the classic investigations by Spitz (1962), Spitz and Wolf (1949), and Kleeman (1966).

Yet such questions can hardly be answered empirically. There is no need to enter into a discussion of the details of empirical research and debate whether the individual research designs are appropriate. As soon as meaning or inner, non-observable concepts such as fantasies come into play; research needs actors capable of speech who can provide information. That is precisely what infants or small children cannot (yet) do. The memories of adults or of older children, who often are called upon to act as substitutes in such research, do not seem very reliable and are often informed more by current discourse than by what actually occurred earlier. What remains is a comparison of the different arguments with respect to what it means—both for thinking about human beings in general and for understanding sexuality specifically—to ascribe sexual experience and behaviour to new-borns.

An extended understanding of sexuality was a central concern for Freud. It was neither to be confined to adulthood nor reduced to genitality, but was meant to encompass a broad spectrum of possibilities for pleasure and gratification. That is, sexuality possessed a "polymorphously perverse" character and began with the infant's very first manifestations of life, hence with suckling. The designation "polymorphously perverse" may sound pejorative, but Freud did not use the term "perverse" with a normative intent. Rather, it was meant as a more general way for describing forms of sexuality that did not serve the goal of reproduction, thus including not only infantile sexuality but also the so-called perversions. The many different forms in which infantile sexuality was expressed were described as "polymorphous". In Freud's understanding, infantile sexuality was quite clearly separated from adult sexuality. Moreover, it was also thought of as auto-erotic.

Before turning to the problems with the Freudian line of argument, I first want to look at what can be gained from it. Accepting the existence of infantile sexuality means it lies along a continuum with adult sexuality. That reveals, for one thing, a perspective suggesting a continuum of sexual experience and behaviour, and for another, the diversity of this continuum. Sexuality is not confined to a biological, reproductive function but expresses itself in various psychically equivalent forms. This applies both to heterosexual and homosexual object-choice and to the so-called perversions. This concept of sexuality, which was originally broadly conceived and neither conventionally judgmental nor hierarchically ordered, is found in particular in the first of the *Three Essays*. However, Freud himself kept retracting and changing it so that it more closely approximated the prevailing "common understanding". Yet the original formulation offers a number of advantages, and it is for that reason that I want to return to and expand on it.

What strikes me as of special significance is that this model avoids creating a normative hierarchy of sexual experience and behaviour. The possibility of conceptualizing psychologically equivalent forms of sexuality calls for a concept of sexuality that does not begin only in adulthood, meaning with the sexual maturation accompanying puberty. The primacy of genitality at that point perforce carries with it a primacy of reproductive function that subsumes other forms. In terms of psychological equivalence, however, the question of pathologizing sexual behaviour and experience can also be put differently. Thus, as is generally the case in the psychoanalytic understanding of illness, a specific behaviour is not to be regarded as pathological. Rather, the function that behaviour performs is the key to determining whether an illness is present or not. Accordingly, the boundary-line between so-called normal and deviant or pathological behaviour can be determined only in the individual case and not in general terms.

The concept of infantile sexuality can be, paradigmatically, divided into two large groups or positions: homological and heterological (Schmidt, 2005). In research on sexuality, the former is associated with the work of Albert Moll, who in the early twentieth century wrote a comprehensive work on the sexual life of the infant (Moll, 1912). He emphasized the structural similarity of infantile and adult sexuality, and was primarily interested in the quantitative differences. He regarded infantile sexuality as a precursor to the later sexuality of adults. This view was shared by Havelock Ellis, one of Moll's contemporaries, as well as by later researchers like Alfred Kinsey. One still finds this view today among researchers who engage in empirical studies, including John Bancroft. What is investigated includes both sexual behaviours (such as masturbation or sexual activity with others) and sexual responses (such as orgasm, arousal and erection) as well as psychosexual aspects (such as fantasies) or socio-sexual phenomena (such as being in love). In methods used are observation, and survey of carers or retrospective interviews. There is consensus among sexologists that nearly all the sexual expressions found among adults can also be observed among small children, from sexual curiosity to arousal to orgasm, with all the characteristics, including the "lost gaze", rapid breathing, and muscle spasms.

These behavioural expressions differ in their frequency from those of adults, and are both far less common and far less goal-oriented. Thus, about sixty per cent of younger adults today remember pre-pubescent sex play with others, and about forty per cent, pre-pubescent masturbation (Schmidt, 2005). Compared with Kinsey's surveys, the frequency has increased, and there is a marked convergence in accounts from both women and men (Bancroft, 2003). Similar trends are also evident among children, reflecting the changes in sexual behaviour among adults and youths: liberalization and "gender equalization" (Schmidt, 2004). However, what remains open is whether behaviour has genuinely changed, or whether this is not simply remembrances in accord with current discourses. For in the course of liberalization, such memories currently, unlike earlier, are not only wholly unproblematic but probably even socially desired. In addition, research shows only minimal differences in homosexual and heterosexual activity in childhood and, in addition, a steady rise in sexual activity as puberty approaches. In light of such findings, the psychoanalytic assumption of a latency period cannot be empirically confirmed (Schmidt, 2005).

As informative as such a quantifying perspective is, the meaning of the findings is often not sufficiently considered. Even if similar sexual behaviours are observable in children and in adults, they can hardly be expected to carry the same meaning. The shift in meaning during the life span, the role played by (changing) fantasies, and the overall influence of personality development on sexual experience and behaviour are given too little attention by advocates of the homological position. In this research, sexuality is only one variable, and it is kept largely separate from other areas of experience and behaviour. One can therefore agree with Gunter Schmidt (2005) when, in referring to the contribution the homological position makes to arguments about sexual socialization, he describes it as insufficiently complex.

By contrast, meaning is emphasized in the heterological position, the most prominent example of which is the Freudian conception. What is crucial in this position is the clear differentiation between infantile and adult sexuality. However, some authors regard this distinction as so rigid that in the end it is unclear whether an infant's behavioural expressions are about sexuality at all. Unlike those who promote the homological position, Freud wrote that "we much reject as being too narrow-minded" (1916–17, p. 320) the reduction of the sexual to the genital and to the reproductive function. However, that leaves one with the difficult task of making plausible why the pleasurable activities children engage in, which at first glance do not appear sexual, should in fact be called "sexual."

In his *Introductory Lectures on Psycho-Analysis*, Freud discussed the difficulty of precisely determining the sexual, finally suggesting one completely abstain from efforts to define it. Instead, he described "deviant", "perverse" sexual activities and showed their connection with so-called "normal" sexuality. Freud arrived at infantile sexuality through the perversions in assuming that "all these inclinations to perversion had their roots in childhood" (1916–17, p. 311). He had arrived at this view through careful observation: Perverse sexuality was "nothing else than a magnified infantile sexuality split up into its separate impulses" (ibid., p. 311). Correspondingly, he then called infantile sexuality "polymorphously perverse." To make his meaning clear, I must add that the term "perverse" is not meant in its pejorative, colloquial sense; instead, it encompasses all forms of sexuality that do not aim at the genital and potentially reproductive union of man and woman. Unlike many researchers engaged in empirical research, Freud admitted that these observations of infants essentially rested on interpretations— in this case, on interpretations that emerged from the retracing of symptoms during the process of analysis. This procedure, as is well known, is extremely vulnerable to attack. Yet the positivist claim, raised repeatedly in the empirical research on infants, that the observation is theory-free or theory-independent also cannot be sustained. It leads back again to the point that the question whether infantile sexuality exists cannot be empirically answered. One can only examine whether it is a theoretically meaningful construct. I have already noted above in what manner it would make sense. The concept of infantile sexuality makes it possible to give explanations for how adult sexuality emerges or develops that go beyond arguing it results from the sudden onset of endogenous maturation processes. In this manner, one can avoid reducing sexuality to the reproductive function, which is unavoidable if one argues from maturation processes. This, in turn, enables non-normative, non-judgmental conceptualizations of sexual activities that are psychologically equivalent. This applies as much to heterosexuality and homosexuality as to the "perversions". All these forms can be diagnosed as illnesses, but are not to be regarded from the outset as pathological.

What is today uncontested with respect to homosexuality—at least there is a broad consensus today that this is not an illness—does not yet seem to be the case for the "perversions". On the one hand, the spread of what are called neo-sexualities (McDougall, 1995; Sigusch, 2005a) gives the impression that sexual forms once regarded as "perverse" have now become mainstream. On the other hand, renaming what were earlier called "perversions" as "paraphilia" or disorders of sexual preference in the World Health Organization's International Classification of Diseases makes evident that sexual practices such as fetishism, voyeurism or sadomasochism are—albeit only beyond a certain extent—per se regarded as pathological. In the psychoanalytic understanding of illness, pathology only begins when such activities serve a specific (defensive) function in mental functioning. This classification once again provides evidence that a non-normative definition of sexuality still does not exist in clinical practice. Yet the concept of infantile sexuality can contribute to formulating such a definition.

Sándor Ferenczi, in a widely regarded essay on the "Confusion of Tongues between Adults and the Child" (1933), drew a particularly clear distinction between infantile and adult sexuality. Ferenczi, even more than Freud, can thereby be regarded as a decided representative of a heterologous position. In his essay, Ferenczi revisited the Freudian theory of seduction and emphasized how important the "exogenous moment" was for sexual development in infancy. After revising his theory of seduction, Freud increasingly gave dispositional and constitutional factors the key role in the aetiology of neuroses, so Ferenczi drew attention yet again to the sexual offences often perpetrated on children, and the devastating effects these have on mental functioning. He distinguished between the infant's language of tenderness and the adult's language of passion, describing the psychodynamics of a "relationship of abuse" as follows: Unlike in a loving relationship between a child and his or her carers, whose interaction could certainly take on erotic aspects, yet remains at the level of tenderness, sexual abuse is characterized by a crossing of this boundary. The child then is mistakenly taken to be a sexually mature person. That child does not react, as one might expect, with refusal or disgust but is instead absolutely paralysed by enormous anxiety and fear. This fear forces the child to submit to the will of the assailant, whose desires need to be guessed and followed. In other words, the child must identify with the aggressor.

Though the introjection of the aggressor, the aggressor disappears as external reality and becomes internalized in the psyche. Thus the earlier level of tenderness can be maintained. The introjection of the aggressor includes his or her feelings of guilt, so the child feels not only threatened by the assault but guilty as well: "The misused child changes into a mechanical, obedient automaton ... his sexual life remains undeveloped or assumes perverted forms" (1933, p. 163). This identification with the aggressor, into which a weak, underdeveloped ego is forced, has often been confirmed in research on trauma. Thus the ego tries to defend itself from further regression or fragmentation.

More controversial is Ferenczi's distinction between tenderness and passion (see the critique, for example, in Laplanche, 1988). With Freud, Ferenczi quite rightly pointed out that object love is preceded by an identification stage, which he called a stage of passive object love or tenderness. However, the question is what the child identifies with. The sexual desire of the adult includes both tenderness and passion. Both are so amalgamated, however, that it is difficult to imagine that a child can separate them and then only identify with the tenderness. Ferenczi himself, in an appendix to his essay, admitted that he had only meant to differentiate descriptively between tenderness and passion, which "leaves open the problem of the real nature of the difference" (1933, p. 166). He saw the decisive difference in the feeling of guilt, which in adult eroticism subjects the love-object to ambivalent emotions, while such ambivalence is lacking in the tenderness of the child. Still, even this differentiation can be assumed only among very small children, because the guilt feelings appear with the constitution, in about the third year of life, of a conscience. By contrast, ambivalence is already present in orality, in what is called oral sadism, which I will discuss in greater detail below. The next criterion Ferenczi employs to differentiate infantile from adult sexuality is also questionable. Infantile eroticism remains at the "pre-pleasure level" and only knows gratification in the sense of "satiation", but not the "feelings of annihilation" of orgasm (ibid., p. 167). Ferenczi did not expand on these feelings, but likely meant the feeling of the dissolution of ego boundaries. Even if it cannot be empirically determined how the child experiences an orgasm, one can assume such feelings are not wholly alien to the child. On the contrary: I assume that "feelings of annihilation" during adult orgasm are relics from experiences in very early childhood.

Variants of infantile sexuality

Oral eroticism

The first sexual activities of an infant are sucking, or to use Freud's term, *ludeln* (a repetitive, rhythmic suckling, sometimes on inappropriate objects), and ingesting objects. The sexual shows itself in a manner similar to other vital functions, in this case the need to take in nourishment. Initially, it accompanies the intake of nourishment, but then it becomes separate and independent. The sexual wish consists in the cathexis of a memory trace, as Freud described in connection with primary gratification in *The Interpretation of Dreams*. While hunger can be stilled through nourishment, *ludeln* is insatiable, and though it can be satisfied for a time, it keeps re-emerging anew. This fundamental insatiability distinguishes pleasure—and thus the sexual—from need. The experience of pleasure and gratification equips the infant body with the ability to be aroused, and erogenous zones form, initially in the area around the mouth and lips.

In suckling at the mother's breast, Freud sees the genesis of sexual development and "the unmatched prototype of every later sexual satisfaction" (1916–17, p. 314). The breast is the first object of the sex drive, which is transformed and substituted in numerous ways during the life span. A first substitution and transformation is the activity of sucking. It enables the infant to become independent of the mother's breast by replacing it with a part of its own body (the tongue, the thumb). The pleasure gained thereby becomes independent of the consent of the outside world.

With this independence, a key characteristic of infantile sexuality is named: auto-eroticism. Infantile sexuality seeks and finds its objects on its own body. But as convincing as it is to regard sucking at the mother's breast as an infant's first sexual activity, Freud's subsequent argument is implausible.

In my view, it over-emphasizes the child's striving for autonomy and auto-eroticism, relegating the constitutive function of the mother or the nursing scene to the background. If one starts with the primacy of the Other, the breast—in the manner stated, conceivable only as biological equipment—does not seem to be the first object of the sexual drive. Rather, it is the other way round: It is the "breast", representing the overall nursing or feeding scene, which first evokes the sex drive and sexual desire. Auto-eroticism in that sense is a secondary manifestation, a response to being desired and to the loss involved with being desired, owing to the repeated necessity of being parted from the "breast". Pleasure is generated as a memory of the experience of gratification. Put more pointedly, gratification precedes pleasure. Freud himself had argued this in discussing the primary gratification experience in *The Interpretation of Dreams* (1900a), but had apparently forgotten his reasoning only a few years later. The child's striving is directed at (re-)

establishing the perceived identification with the original gratification, yet that can never be achieved. In that sense, pleasure or desire is insatiable and at the same time cannot be stilled. This search starts at the beginning of life and continues until death. In terms of structure and function, infantile sexuality thus does not differ from adult sexuality, though it takes on other forms and is therefore also associated with other functions.

One can of course question whether this striving for pleasure and gratification can properly be called "sexual". There are those (see, for example, Dornes, 2005) that contest it and cite empirical studies, though without suggesting an alternate term. But regardless of that, to refer to empirical studies is extremely questionable: Like other psychological constructs, "infantile sexuality" is highly dependent on interpretation and must be deduced from the specific behaviour than can be observed. That problem bedevils other, comparable constructs—intelligence, attachment behaviour, sexuality—as well. There are no facts that can be empirically proven beyond a doubt. There are only assumptions that make more or less sense. As noted above, the assumption that an infantile sexuality exists has a number of advantages with regard to theory formation, but conversely, I do not see what advantages there would be in a theory of human beings that does not regard a child as a sexual being. Such a rationale has thus far not been produced.

But, to follow Freud as well as return to the psychosexual development of orality, in addition to sucking, an important part of oral eroticism is the ingesting of objects. In its early form, it has cannibalistic elements, which you still find in expressions such as liking someone so much you "could eat them up". This is explainable by noting that in this phase of a child's development, individuals are not perceived as objects but rather as providers of food or as nourishment themselves. By ingesting, you become one with the object. Oral introjection is conducive to primary identification at the same time. The notion of eating objects, or of being eaten by them, determines how the union with the object is unconsciously represented (Fenichel, 1946, pp. 63–66). That is also shown impressively by the Catholic ritual of communion, which is supported by the conviction that by ingesting the host, which has been transubstantiated into the body of Christ, the believer will become more similar to the incorporated object.

Iris Därmann (2004) has discussed this mixture of person and gift in a quite different context and in a very subtle manner. Using Marcel Mauss's theory of the gift, she reconstructs Laplanche's general theory of seduction to argue that nourishment stands for the gift. The nursing or feeding situation makes the mixing of person and gift clear. With the gift, a person gives of himself or herself, and that gift is taken in by the recipient, the infant. Thus, the infant is literally "possessed" by the other person. With this theory, Därmann puts the idea of inter-subjectivity on an alimentary-oral-cannibalistic basis. In this view, the carer makes a gift of her or his own sexual life—a gift to which that carer has no access—and thereby endows the infant with sexuality. Därmann shakes up biological certainties by arguing this way, not only for sexuality but also for the notion of self-preservation. In the end, it reveals itself to be the preservation of the self through the other.

Beyond the modalities of pleasure, one can also name specifically oral fears and anxieties. They correspond to the goals of oral eroticism. However, their pleasurable character is hidden and appears rather as fears, the most frequently observed of which among children, according to Fenichel, is the fear of being eaten. One can see in this the desire to be incorporated by a larger object and in that way gain security and/or omnipotence (1946, pp. 63–64). The goal of oral incorporation often takes on sadistic overtones, which as Melanie Klein (1962) suggests, may have constitutional causes, or which, according to Fenichel, may be the result of frustrations. Without wishing to pursue this controversy in detail, I want to note that the oral incorporation of an object does in fact destroy it, giving oral erotic goals an ambivalent character. However, it does not seem sensible to speak of destruction until the child has developed a notion of objects. Only then—once an infant can perceive an object separate from itself—can one assume destructive, sadistic features. This distinction goes back to Abraham (1925) who differentiated between a pre-ambivalent stage in the oral phase, where no object is yet present and the infant only wants to suckle pleasurably, and an ambivalent stage when, in addition to the object, the first teeth and thereby the goal of biting appear. Fenichel, on the other hand, correctly points out that this connection between the development of the object and the emergence of oral-sadistic impulses is not only manifested by biting, as oral-sadistic elements also occur in sucking fantasies, such as in vampirism. On the other hand, the analysis of sadistic perversions indicates that their symptoms ultimately go back to the oral goal of biting (1946, p. 65).

I want to emphasize that these early forms of oral sadism are not about aggression. The child does not bite out of aggressiveness, perhaps because it is angry or frustrated, but instead out of pleasure. As a mode of pleasure, biting is a variant of sucking. This distinction between oral sadism and aggression stands in contrast to everyday understanding. It is not a matter of inflicting pain that could be pleasurable; pain is rather a side-effect that results from searching for pleasure. This may also cast a different light on certain "perversions", in particular sado-masochistic practices generally associated with aggression and pain and less with pleasure modalities in the early phase of life.

The example of biting also shows that desire and prohibition are interwoven. An infant who bites during breastfeeding leads the mother to turn away and interrupt the pleasurable game. Pleasure is not thereby dissipated; rather, the state of tension and arousal is maintained. Through the delay, hence, the prohibition intensifies the pleasure.

Oral eroticism remains in force, in various forms that are more or less altered, to the end of life. Decisive for these feelings of pleasure is the stimulation of the mouth or mucous membranes, as in kissing, in eating and drinking, or also while smoking. On the other hand, the incorporation of objects is also sensual, as is true for swallowing and for breathing.

Anal eroticism

Freud, as was typical for his time, conceived of psychosexual develop-ment as taking place in phases or stages, with the anal and phallic-genital phases following the oral phase. But the notion of stages is misleading, as the pleasure and gratification modalities of the individual phases do not succeed one another but continue simultaneously throughout life, albeit with changing significance and intensity. I therefore regard it as more useful to abandon the Freudian notion of stages and to speak more precisely of orality, anality, phallicity or genitality as different expressions of human sexuality that emerge at particular points in life and remain in force.

According to Freud, infantile sexuality continues to develop along the lines of elementary organic needs, as in the case of sucking or *ludeln* (1916–17). What was clearest in the case of feeding is repeated in part in excretion. Erogenous zones also form through the voiding of the bladder and intestines, so feelings of pleasure accompany elimination processes as well as become independent of them. In early psychoana-lytic theory, these feelings of pleasure were investigated and described with considerable specificity. Now, perhaps incorrectly, these categories play hardly any role in psychoanalytic practice (on anal eroticism, see, among others, Ferenczi, 1914; Jones, 1919; Abraham, 1923). Thus, Abraham differentiated between pleasure at actual excretion and enjoyment of the products of that process, in which pleasure at both the sight and the smell play a role. These feelings of pleasure can be most clearly observed among children, and undergo multiple metamorphoses over time. In his article "Character and Anal Erotism" (1908b), Freud documented the interweaving of bodily and mental processes in these transformations. Upbringing contributes its part to limiting the pleasure taken in infantile coprophilia and in the excretion process. By and large, this pleasure is repressed in adulthood and can only be found in rudimentary forms, or it becomes visible again only under particular conditions, as in the form of "perversions."

Unlike oral gratification, which to a large extent remains unchanged even in adult sexuality, anal pleasures are far more affected by repression and transformation processes. The fate of anal eroticism thus far more often became the object of psychoanalytic investigation than did oral eroticism (Abraham, 1925). Characteristic of anal eroticism, and less subject to later transformations, according to Abraham, is the pleasure taken in the tension, which is far more pronounced than in oral eroticism. This tension arises because the child realizes it is not just the process of excretion itself that is pleasurable, but so is holding it back, as that leads to more intense stimulation of the intestinal mucous membranes. Retention thereby intensifies the feelings of pleasure at defecation. This intensification through retention is not only found in excretion processes but exists in every form of postponing or delaying feelings of pleasure.

According to Freud (1905d), the intestinal contents have considerable significance for the infant. They are first dealt with as a part of its own body, and are the first "present" that, by relinquishing them, the child makes. The child shows that they are compliant with adults, and by refusing to comply, can show their resistance. Fenichel (1946) points out that faeces are first part of one's own body and then become an external object, serving as a model for all that can be changed and thereby lost. They thus stand on the one hand for "possession", that is, for external things that simultaneously have an ego quality. On the other hand, they also stand for "loss" of a part of one's own body or one's own person and thereby are "the model of anything that may become lost" (p. 67). This second sense underscores the melancholy aspect of excretion, and reflects the difficulty of parting with certain things. According to Fenichel, for the infant, control of its sphincter is connected with a feeling of social power that is reflected in the most diverse scenarios between parents and child in the course of toilet training, which offers ample scope for "sensual and hostile gratifications" (1946, p. 67).

Regardless of whether this toilet training is conducted in a permissive or a disciplined manner, in light of the above mentioned feelings of pleasure at excretion and at holding back, it is evident that this is not just a question of power and control but also a variant of love play. Once again the adults perforce take on the role of the child's seducers. Remarkable in this example is that at their core, the feelings of pleasure here are not the result of actually touching the other person. The "love play" consists less in the parents touching the child than in verbal or gesticular interactions around the "potty". Excretion or retention processes are embedded in the parent-child relation and are—in whatever manner—commented upon. Even if parents do not intend it, the pleasurable feelings of the child are thereby addressed and supported, praised or even reprimanded.

Of particular significance here is prohibiting the child from taking pleasure in his or her excretion process or products, though today this is mostly implicit. As Lou Andreas-Salomé (1916) established, this prohibition is decisive for the entire development of the child. The child is first confronted with an environment that is antagonistic toward the "stirring of its drives", and he or she must dissociate its own being from that hostile, foreign world. Then he or she is forced to the first repression of his or her pleasure. After that, the "anal" stands for all that is to be rejected, for all that is undesirable, and it undergoes various transformations intended to make it unrecognizable, or comes to light again as a "perversion" that serves to override the repression. At least, to judge by the innumerable sources of advice, ranging from glossy magazines to television programs, one can see a vestige of what were once modalities for pleasure in the high significance many people bestow on bowel movements.

In the context of anal eroticism as well, frustrations create specific, characteristic anxieties. In this case, it is the notion that one might, say, be robbed of what one has inside. This fear often appears as "revenge" for anal-sadistic tendencies, with the idea that what "one wished to perpetrate anally on others will now happen to oneself" (Fenichel, 1946, p. 68). The anal-sadistic variants are largely analogous or similar to those found in oral sadism. While there is an aspect of social power or control as in orality, it is far less pronounced, owing to a lack of physiological possibilities to exert comparable control over the respective bodily functions. Like the oral striving, the striving for anal pleasure is ambivalent with respect to the object. In its archaic manner, anal pleasure can be as much expression of love and tenderness as of antagonism and contempt. The latter is encouraged particularly by the prohibition on anality. Karl Abraham divided anality into an earlier phase shaped by "a sadistic aim in excretory pleasure without consideration of the object, and a later period characterized by a prevalent retention pleasure" (ibid., p. 68) in which the object remains intact. The concern about the welfare of the Other, the basis of all love, is constituted in this later phase and reveals itself first in the willingness to sacrifice the faeces for the sake of the love object.

Urethral eroticism

Urethral eroticism plays a particular role in conjunction with the pleasures at excretion, one that, and rightly so, was understood in the early days of psychoanalysis as an independent form of sexual expression. This differentiation has been lost over time, and what remains, if anything, is anal eroticism—hardly as an expression of "normal" pleasure but instead ostracized as a "perversion". That is unfortunate, as it is precisely such voiding processes that often play a significant role in clinical practice—by which I mean an urge to urinate, that cannot be delayed, sometimes manifested by patients during analysis sessions. For understanding transference, the aspect of pleasure and gratification it entails seems to me of great significance, and not just what is commonly focused on in this context, namely resistance, defensiveness, or (castration) anxieties. In a distorted form, urethral eroticism can also be expressed in (what are usually chronic) illnesses of the urinary tract.

The primary goal of urethral eroticism lies in the pleasure gained by urination. As with the anal, I see a urethral pleasure at retention as well as conflicts that arise from such retention. Urethral eroticism is also closely connected with infantile genital eroticism. In urinating, the child inevitably becomes aware of the difference between the sexes, from which the castration complex takes its power. Earlier analysts, in a manner today seen as problematic, began from the premise that girls felt castrated and inferior in this situation, and boys feared suffering the same fate. In the meantime, the topic of castration has been extended to apply to both sexes in the sense of a threat to the inviolability of the body. Envy, in addition, is not directed only at the penis but as much to the ability to give birth. With respect to sex differences, the task of development, conflict-ridden, is to force both girls and boys to give up the illusion of their bisexuality, hence of omnipotence, and confront the limits of their respective sex. I will revisit this topic in subsequent chapters. In any case, the bisexual illusion continues to be effective in the unconscious. It is manifested in urethral eroticism, for example, by the fact that the pleasure taken in urination can have phallic significance for both sexes.

Following Fenichel, urination becomes the equivalent of active penetration, and can incorporate sadistic admixtures such as fantasies of damage or destruction. A further dimension of meaning, found among both boys and girls, is contained in the notion of letting flow as a form of passive self-abandonment and the relinquishing of control. Thus, small children often urinate intentionally in their pants or in their beds, just for the pleasure of it. Among older children, by contrast, bed-wetting no longer occurs with intent but is better understood as the unconscious equivalent of masturbation. The active goals of phallic urethral-erotic pleasure among boys, in their subsequent development, in essence merge with genitality. But the passive goals can readily come into conflict with genitality; that is why these goals sometimes merge with sadistic fantasies, as in serious cases of premature ejaculation. The idea of letting flow is often, particularly among girls, displaced from urine to tears (1946, p. 69). Urethral erotic difficulties manifest themselves among girls usually in conflicts related to penis envy.

According to Fenichel, the pleasure at retention is less pronounced in urethral eroticism than in anal eroticism, and among boys is often completely absent. Urethral erotic conflicts are therefore less characterized by the opposition between "eliminating" and "retaining" and far more by the contradiction between the wish to enjoy pleasure and arousal (through urination) on the one hand, and on the other hand, the narcissistic gratification or pride resulting from a successful control of the bladder. Fenichel (ibid., p. 69) describes the close connection between urethral eroticism and a sense of shame. He regards shame as a resistance to urethral-erotic temptations, comparable to the oral or anal anxieties of being eaten or of being robbed of one's innards. Ambition, often regarded as the product of urethral-erotic conflicts, is the fight against such shame.

The eroticism of skin and sight

In addition to the oral, anal, and genital zones of the body, skin is a further, significant erogenous zone. Depending on the subjective experiences of the individual, it can be stimulated to different degrees at various sites. This excitability is formed, as in the case of the other erogenous zones, in the interaction of infant with adults, as during bodily hygiene or play. From the stimulation of the skin, a specific pleasure at being touched emerges, one which has both active and passive components. The mode of caressing and being caressed surely ranks among the most basic forms of experiencing pleasure and gratification. The goal of this desire to be touched can be, as with oral eroticism, a form of incorporation. In Lewin's view, such "introjection through the skin" plays as important a role in magical thinking, in the most diverse cultures, as it does in unconscious sexual fantasies and in forms that are manifested as "perversions" (Lewin, 1930). In more recent psychoanalytic thinking, the skin is seen less in terms of its pleasure-giving properties than in its communicative and ego-forming aspects—or in conjunction with limitations brought about through illness, as in neurodermatitis (see Anzieu, 1986; Pines, 1994).

Through this de-sexualization, which can be observed in numerous other realms, I see a serious limitation in psychoanalytic thinking: The constitutive meaning of the energetic moment in the dynamic (sexual) unconscious can no longer be made intelligible. Absent the notion that unconscious desire becomes effective and forces actions and experiences, influencing them in a fundamental way, psychoanalysis becomes one psychology among others.

In the interaction of an infant with his or her parents, additional feelings of pleasure are created, for example in the kinaesthetic realm. It is not just being touched: being rocked or cradled also can lead to arousal in the infant. Among children, and even among some adults, one can still observe vestiges of this in an enthusiasm for being on swings or riding on carousels. An increase in basic anxieties is also connected with the sexualisation of the sense of balance or space. Thus, Alice Balint (1933) starts from the premise that the infantile fear of losing his or her balance could be the basic pattern on which all further fears are modelled.

Beyond the kinaesthetic, there are also erogenous effects proceeding from other modalities of the senses—hearing, smelling, tasting—that are of significance both in infant and in adult sexuality. While taste has a close connection with oral eroticism, smell is more connected with anal eroticism (see Abraham, 1923). The sexually arousing function of the voice and of experiences with smell and taste is well known from everyday clinical practice and to a high degree has been commercialized and used to increase sales. Despite its evident significance, hardly any psychoanalytic investigations exist that address the erogenous relevance of these sense modalities.

Sexual pleasure in looking and being looked at is analogous to pleasure in being touched. While the erotic goal of such gazing lies initially in regarding the sexual object or—as Freud notes—in gazing at the genitals or watching the process of excretion, the excitability of the eye as a sexualized sensory organ increasingly separates itself and becomes independent. "Sexualized seeing" means that seeing is not only about perceiving but also about searching for sexual pleasure and gratification. In the most obvious case, this consists in looking at what is arousing. Less obvious though no less significant is that watching itself is arousing. Voyeuristic curiosity can therefore be satisfied in de-sexualized contexts, for example through reading or in the cinema. (There is a broad psychoanalytic literature by now on such curiosity, or scopophilia, in the cinema, much of which is Lacanian; see Mulvey, 1989)

Following Fenichel, the sexualisation of sensory impressions has all the characteristics necessary for perception: the activity of the organs of perception, the motility needed for perception, and the "incorporation" of what has been perceived, with the consequent change to the ego. The ego accommodates itself to what is perceived. Scopophilia, visual pleasure, thereby functions according to the symbolic equivalence of watching = devouring (Fenichel, 1937), which one can also note in the locution "to devour something with one's eyes".

Incorporation is found in all erogenous zones, and Fenichel distinguishes between oral, anal, epidermal, respiratory, and even ocular introjections. Incorporation is not the only goal, though; there is also the phallic significance of the eye, the moment of penetration into the Other. In all these processes, the eye plays a dual role, both active-penetrating and passive-receptive. Fundamental to all developmental processes is introjection as a form of identification: The infant watches something to imitate it, to become similar to that which is seen. Later, this identification is phantasmal; one wants to observe something in order to empathize with it. The pleasure of a voyeur who observes couples largely comes from identifying with the partner of the opposite sex (Fenichel, 1937). Pleasure in watching is closely associated with sadistic impulses, also orally tinged: One wants to watch something so as to destroy it, or to reassure oneself that the attempt at destruction failed. The very process of looking at something can be a (weakened) symbolic form of destruction. Thus, in fairy-tales and myths, the power of the gaze to enchant or bewitch or paralyse those being looked at recurs again and again.

According to Fenichel, the wish to look is one of the chief components of sexual curiosity among children, and one that has an arousing character. "Knowing about sexuality", or wanting to, could then substitute for actually observing sexuality itself (Lewin, 1939). The "knowing about" can be displaced onto other topics, and thereby unleash a flood of ceaseless questions that drives adults at times to distraction. This curiosity is stimulated or blocked on the one hand by actually observing sexual activity among adults, and on the other hand by the birth of a sibling. As a particularly characteristic anxiety, one corresponding to the shame accompanying urethral eroticism, is the shyness connected with the pleasure at observing (Fenichel, 1946, p. 72).

Exhibitionism is a complement to scopophilia. The two mostly occur together, which Freud (1915c) attributed to both having a common sexual goal, namely to observe oneself. For this reason, exhibitionism is more narcissistic than any other partial drive. The pleasure gained from it is associated with a (temporary) increase in the sense of self, achieved by having the Other—in reality or in anticipation—observing the subject. Exhibitionism in early childhood aims in both sexes to display the genitals and other erogenous zones. In the course of later development, this becomes largely fixated on the genitals among men, though it is displaced onto the entire body among women (1946, p. 72, p. 316).

However, the notion of "displacing" female exhibitionism away from the genitals and onto the entire body is evidence, in my view, of the problematic view of women as "castrated" and deficient beings.

Correspondingly, Fenichel also noted that it is only in men, under special circumstances, that the close relationship to the castration complex can also lead to the formation of an exhibitionist perversion. Among women, by contrast, one does not observe such a perversion. As I will show in the following Chapters in greater detail, exhibition-ism among women is by no means "displaced". It is far more the case that the entire female body can function as a sexual organ (see Pines, 1994). In fact, there are numerous, widely distributed and by no means pathological phenomena that allow exhibitionism among women to be expressed, whether in clothing and the fitness studio or in apply-ing make-up or tattoos. It is just that these phenomena are rarely discussed in such terms. In addition, various authors provide clinical case histories of female patients who show exhibitionist behaviour (see Welldon, 1988).

Genital eroticism

Sexual arousal becomes concentrated on the genitals towards the end of the development of infantile sexuality, and they become the leading erogenous zone. Freud therefore speaks of the phallic or the infantile-genital phase of psychosexual development, and that phase prefigures the final form sexuality takes among adults (Freud, 1923e). The simi-larity is largely that an object-choice, as is characteristic for puberty, is made during this phase: All sexual strivings focus on a single person, through whom the goals are to be realized. The other characteristic of adult sexuality—the subordination of the partial drives under the pri-macy of the genital—begins to manifest itself. Freud regarded the emer-gence of the primacy of the genital, in the service of reproduction, as the last phase of sexual organization.

At this point, I agree with the critique of the Freudian theory of sexu-ality that is frequently raised. The central significance of reproduction, which Freud introduces here, is not plausible. Adding this biological aspect unavoidably creates a hierarchy of the various sexual forms, and it is one that prescribes norms and by and large supports a particu-lar social order. Arguing for the primacy of reproduction means that "polymorphously perverse" sexuality, the diversification of modalities for pleasure and gratification as found in infantile sexuality, is to remain confined to childhood. If it nevertheless persists into adulthood, it is regarded as potentially pathological, "perverse" or immature.

According to Roiphe and Galenson (1981), genital activity begins between the fifteenth and eighteenth months and is accompanied by erotic thoughts and feelings associated with the mother. The authors trace this association back to the use of soft toys and blankets that function as transitional objects and hence stand for the mother. In addition, the connection with the mother results from the unavoidable sexual stimulation in the course of infant care.

According to Freud, the most important characteristic of infantile genital organization, and one that simultaneously distinguishes it from that of the adult and that is relevant to both sexes, is the idea that only one genital apparatus, the male, is important. More precisely, genital primacy is a primacy of the phallus. Despite all the justified critique of his assumption, and it is one often dismissed out of hand, it is nevertheless worthwhile to more closely examine this single-sex focus with respect to its importance for the theoretical edifice of psychoanalysis.

Freud uses the contrast of "phallic" and "castrated" to form a basis for discussing the castration complex. His intent is to describe the developmental task of how to deal with the difference between the sexes, and the anxieties and fears typically associated with it. This task, of course, is one both sexes face, even if Freud only addressed male development.

As I will discuss below in Chapter Two, the perception of a difference between the sexes, and psychologically working through what this means, is a major challenge for the child. The child must come to terms with their bisexual fantasies of omnipotence and the unquestioned assumption that they can be both sexes. They must integrate that loss and the fact that they are limited to being only one sex. That is the main task of infantile genital organization. Fear of castration is regarded as characteristic for this phase, much like the oral fear of being eaten, and it is also the highpoint of all fears related to damage the body can suffer. The intensity of the castration anxiety corresponds to the special valuation of the genital (Fenichel, 1946). The typical conflicts in conjunction with phallicity consist in penis envy among girls and in a corresponding envy of the vagina or of the ability to give birth among boys. These conflicts also emerge from the need to abandon the bisexual fantasies of omnipotence.

Such considerations make evident that the phallic phase need not stand as the paradigm for male development. In my view, still more basic than embracing one's own sex or acquiring a gender identity is the perception of the child that it has a sex at all. In this phase, sex becomes relevant as an (additional) category for distinguishing between people, and yet also stands for desire: The child becomes the subject of its desire, and becomes aware of its desire. That is seen particularly in the Oedipal constellation. In the phallic phase, the child (actively) adopts what it has thus far (passively) experienced. With the adoption of phallicity, it reverses the constellation of the general seduction situation. The seduced child becomes the seducing child. Unlike in the previous phases, it becomes conscious of its ability to seduce others.

I therefore suggest shifting the emphasis of the phallic phase to the acquiring of desire. Thus the alternative suggested by Freud of either having a phallus or being castrated can be recast as the ability both sexes have to feel pleasure and to experience themselves as the subject(s) of desire.

Yet a problem remains in the Freudian construct of phallic monism, which equates "phallus" with male genitalia and thereby insinuates a valuation that separates the sexes. In the alternative Freud poses—either having a phallus/penis or being castrated—female development is unavoidably characterized as having a fundamental lack. Critique of this conceptualization of femaleness began already during Freud's lifetime, as from Karen Horney, and has continued ever since.

Among girls, phallic sexuality is generally associated with arousal of the clitoris. But there are also studies that speak of an early vaginal sexuality (Eissler, 1939; Lorand, 1939). Karen Horney (1933, Chapter Two.), in her vigorous controversy with Freud and Jones about female sexuality, even saw, in the heightened erogeneity of the clitoris, an overcompensation for denying the role of the vagina. Whatever their relative significance is judged to be, one should at least note that the infantile genital sexuality of girls is characterized by two major erogenous zones: the clitoris and the vagina. Following Fenichel (1946, p. 83), male genitals, in accordance with their bisexual nature, also have two such centres: the penis and the seminal colliculus (or verumontanum), a point in the prostatic urethra. In particular, men with marked passive anal or urethral desires mention this—or often, incorrectly, the nearby perineum or root of the penis—as the location of the most intense sexual sensations.

Genital erogeneity is just as elemental as oral or anal erogeneity. The erogenous zones do not shift but remain present and co-exist. Nevertheless, a concentration on genital arousal develops in the course of maturation, while other areas of the body lose erogeneity and their cathexis is yielded, in part, to the genitals. Only in the case of fixations do these shifts fail to occur, and pre-genital excitability remains at full strength, though according to Freud this can lead to limitations on genital sexuality. Just as with other forms of pleasure, genital eroticism starts at the beginning of life; genital masturbation can be observed already in infants. The urinary organs and the genitalia are largely identical, so the first efforts at genital activity are closely connected with the urethral-erotic. Infantile genitality is primarily expressed in masturbation, seldom in interactions with others, and it is rare to observe acts bearing similarity to adult intercourse. While masturbation among infants is generally confined to simple stimulation of the genitals, during the phallic phase it becomes associated for the first time with fantasies relating to objects (ibid., p. 75).

René Spitz (1962) describes early childhood masturbation as an indicator of healthy development in the small child. In his investigation of development during the first three years of life, he found a connection between the quality of the mother-child relationship and the occurrence of infantile auto-erotic activity. He observed genital play significantly more frequently among children who had a good relationship with their mothers. Beyond this, such play was regarded as an indicator of the developmental stage of the child. Spitz even regarded the lack of genital play as evidence of a developmental disorder. Abandoning masturbation at elementary school age, and not because it was denounced, could also point to a disruption in psychosexual development. Clower (1980) concludes that children's urge to touch their own genitals means they want to re-evoke the pleasant feelings they had while being cared for by their mother or father.

Other authors, such as Marina Gambaroff (1977, 1984) or Maria Torok (1994), regard infantile masturbation as a form of separation behaviour by which a child loosens its bonds to its mother. Masturbation serves the childish wish for autonomy: Since I can do it myself, the child says, I have overcome those who decided, at will, to provide or keep pleasure from me. Infantile sexuality is understood as an emancipatory act, one even more important for girls than for boys, who, owing to their "different" bodies, are more able to dissociate themselves from their mothers. How important masturbation is for separation is also confirmed by empirical findings indicating girls or women masturbate less frequently than boys or men of the same age (Schmidt, Klusmann & Zeitschel, 1992). This indicates how much more difficult it is for daughters to dissociate themselves from their mothers, and how much the emergence of their own sexual autonomy is thereby hindered.

Freud understood masturbation primarily as an auto-erotic activity, adding the relationship to an object only later. He called auto-eroticism the most important characteristic of infantile sexuality, though noting this was a secondary development by which the child made itself independent of the mother's breast. While Freud focused in his theory on the increasing independence of the child—the child separates from the mother by selecting itself as an object—Ernst Simmel (1948) specifies this process in greater detail with respect to its significance in the relational involvement of adult and child. He described infantile masturbation as a social act, and as the processing of loss:

> In the stage of developing its object relations, masturbation may be regarded as the infant's first social activity. For through this activity the child withdraws from the disappointing object which rejects its love and stimulates aggressive destructive reactions. In its own body, the child finds a substitutive gratification for the narcissistic trauma, replacing the object by its own genital as an object, and finding in itself a way of discharging object-directed erotic and aggressive tendencies. It has thus renounced direct instinctual gratification from the real objects, but keeps an ideational relationship with them in masturbatory fantasies. (1948, p. 15)

From this sketch, as brief as it is plausible, of the psychodynamics of infantile masturbation, one can conclude that the Freudian thesis regarding autoeroticism in infantile sexuality is not particularly apposite. As numerous investigations have shown, satisfying object relations are in fact a pre-condition for masturbation (Spitz, 1961). The child, in striving for pleasure, is not independent of the mother or of adults in general, but rather remains oriented to them, even when—or especially when—it turns away. The maintenance of the relationship, as Simmel argues, occurs as phantasm, as in masturbation fantasies. The fantasy thus proves to be a form of working through "reality", in this case a way of coming to terms with a loss or a separation.

In addition, I regard masturbation as a form of remembering, one that preserves a gratification that cannot be attained again. Even if masturbation repeatedly reanimates the loss, at the same time it permits the separation to be overcome. This does not take place only phantasmally—that is, on the path fantasy provides, as Simmel describes it—but also is oriented to action and to the body. The question is whether masturbation recapitulates what an infant has experienced as parental attention and caregiving. He or she would thereby actively enact what had been passively experienced. On the other hand, it would not be a pure repetition but always a remaking or re-forming as well, a type of reinscription. Thus, it is not only the parents and the elementary organic needs that structure the sexually excitable body of the child but the child himself or herself who does so as well, through masturbatory activity.

In Freudian notions of psychosexual development, phallic sexuality in my view acquires an odd dual role that results from Freud's one-sided focus on male development. Like oral, anal, and urethral sexuality, phallic sexuality is a partial drive and hence a form through which infantile sexuality is expressed in both sexes. On the other hand, in the Oedipus complex, and as part of the phallic phase, it derives from the identification of the boy with his father. That means that phallicity for Freud was also characteristic of adult male sexuality, which is, in addition, completely in accordance with how it is commonly understood. Yet this means subsuming genital sexuality under one of those partial drives that—at least in the Freudian view—are supposed to be subordinated to it.

For that reason, I would like to suggest seeing phallicity as a form of infantile sexuality that exists among both boys and girls, and to dissociate adult male sexuality from it. The latter, in my view, consists far more in integrating the bisexual aspects of the "male" phallic and the "female" receptive forms. Applied to the male body, that means, in Fenichel's sense, an integration of the two genital centres, the penis and the seminal colliculus, and thus an integration of inner and outer male genitality (I discuss this at greater length below). This integration occurs analogously in female sexuality, in which the "male" and the "female" parts can be assigned to the various areas of the female genitalia, to the "male"-clitoral and a "female"-vaginal modalities of lust, pleasure and gratification. This assignment follows traditional psychoanalysis with respect to differentiation between a clitoral sexuality that is regarded as "male" and a "vaginal" sexuality that is regarded as "female". However, such a differentiation may simply create more confusion when it comes to understanding the fundamentally bisexual character of sexuality in both men and women—one thinks here of the fruitless debate over "vaginal" vs. "clitoral" orgasm. In contrast to the Freudian view, I regard the integration of "male" and "female" parts not as a change or shift in the key erogenous zones but much more as a linkage leading to a comprehensive unity. Male sexual development calls for just such an integration, though it is one often hidden by the primacy of the phallic, and is anatomically not as evident as in the female body (see also Chapter Two).

Oedipal desire

The highpoint and culmination of the phallic phase in infantile genital organization is the Oedipus complex. It plays an essential role in structuring personality more generally and structuring sexuality in particular. Despite its core importance, Freud never systematically elaborated it (see Laplanche & Pontalis, 1973). At the synchronic and structural level, its function is directed at recognizing the limitations of one's own sex. At the diachronic level, it is directed at recognizing the difference between the generations. Key in this context is establishing the incest taboo. With respect to the development of sexuality, one should emphasize the simultaneity of both homosexual and heterosexual object-choice.

Freud formulated the Oedipus complex at about the same time as, in the context of his self-analysis; he abandoned the seduction theory (see letters 139, 141, and 142 to Fliess in Masson, 1985, pp. 285–86, 290–293):

> A single idea of general value dawned on me. I have found, in my own case too, [the phenomenon of] being in love with my mother and jealous of my father, and I now consider it a universal event in early childhood. … If this is so, we can understand the gripping power of *Oedipus Rex*, in spite of all the objections that reason raises against the presupposition of fate. … Everyone in the audience was once a budding Oedipus in fantasy and each recoils in horror from the dream fulfilment here transplanted into reality, with the full quantity of repression which separates his infantile state from his present one. (ibid., p. 272)

Freud (1923b) distinguished between "positive" and "negative" forms of the Oedipus complex, which—depending on the basic bisexuality of the child—together formed the "complete" Oedipus complex. The positive form is drawn from the Oedipus myth and describes the love felt for the parent of the opposite sex and the simultaneous rivalry with and death wished upon the parent of the same sex. In the negative form, the love is felt for the parent of the same sex, while the rivalry is directed at the parent of the opposite sex:

> A boy has not merely an ambivalent attitude towards his father and an affectionate object-choice towards his mother, but at the same time he also behaves like a girl and displays an affectionate feminine attitude to his father and a corresponding jealousy and hostility towards his mother. (ibid., p. 33)

The ambivalence that results from bisexuality characterizes the object-relations to both parents. Out of these four efforts comes identification with the father and with the mother in the resolution of the complex. The identification with the father fixes the mother object in the positive complex (in the case of the boy) and simultaneously replaces the father object in the negative complex. The identification with the mother proceeds in a similar fashion. This mechanism of replacing an object-relation through identification and introjection of the earlier object can be first found in Freud's study of Leonardo da Vinci, in which he describes homosexual development: The boy replaces his love for his mother by identifying with her (Freud, 1910c). In *The Ego and the Id* (1923b), finally, Freud sketches the emergence of the super-ego out of these identifications, which then take the place of Oedipal object-relations.

Freud sees the denouement of the Oedipal situation in identifying with the father or mother, as dependent in both sexes on the relative strength of their sexual predispositions, which he sees as biologically determined. Their expression is manifested in the differing strength of the identifications:

> The broad general outcome of the sexual phase dominated by the Oedipus complex may, therefore, be taken to be the forming of a precipitate in the ego, consisting of these two identifications in some way united with each other. This modification of the ego retains its special position; it confronts the other contents of the ego as an ego ideal or super-ego. (1923b, p. 34)

It remains unclear why Freud regards sexual orientation as biologically predisposed, for he describes it in the same breath as the result of identification, hence as the result of social interaction. What is important to emphasize is that the super-ego takes the place of the abandoned love relationship; in this manner it is preserved as an introjection in the psychic structure. This melancholy mode of sexual development will be addressed again in Chapter Two.

Following Freud, the super-ego thereby establishes the choice of love-object:

> In order to complete our picture of infantile sexual life, we must also suppose that the choice of an object (…) has already frequently or habitually been effected during the years of childhood: that is to say, the whole of the sexual currents have become directed towards a single person in relation to whom they seek to achieve their aims. (1905d, p. 199)

Following the Oedipal play with homosexual and heterosexual components, the definite fixing of the love-object occurs in two stages, in the Oedipal phase and during puberty, whereby the first presages the second. In his essay on *The Infantile Genital Organization of the Libido* (1923e), Freud assumes that a "complete object selection" took place already in childhood.

The Oedipus complex provides the child—corresponding to the bisexual predisposition—with two possibilities for gratification, one active and the other passive:

> He could put himself in his father's place in a masculine fashion and have intercourse with his mother as his father did, in which case he would soon have felt the latter as a hindrance; or he might want to take the place of his mother and be loved by his father, in which case his mother would become superfluous. (1924d, p. 176)

The dual aspect of the Oedipus complex, with its active and passive variants, corresponds to the active and passive sexual goals of both sexes. In the sexual life of the child at this time, masturbation, together with the Oedipal complex, has an important role: "masturbation is only a genital discharge of the sexual excitation belonging to the complex, and throughout his later years will owe its importance to that relationship". (ibid., p. 176)

In Freud's view, the Oedipal complex ends in different ways for girls and for boys. While it "shatters in the threat of castration" among boys, it only "slowly leaves" girls, because the girl's desire to receive a child as a gift from her father is not fulfilled (ibid.). The libidinous strivings that belong to the complex are repressed, de-sexualized, and sublimated, transformed into tender emotions. In the process, the repressed Oedipal wishes are preserved in the unconscious. Or so Freud asserts for the development of girls. Among boys, ideally, the complex is completely destroyed and nullified. This notion brought critique from many quarters, and I discuss them in greater detail in Chapter Two.

Puberty and adolescence: the transition to adult sexuality

In the *Three Essays on the Theory of Sexuality*, Freud (1905d) argues that human sexual development, unlike that of other life-forms, is a diphasic process that can be traced to delayed sexual maturity. After a period of latency, the developments of pleasure and gratification modalities, introduced during the Oedipal phase, are taken up again. The Freudian notion of latency, according to which the abating of the Oedipus complex is accompanied by an almost complete de-sexualisation of the relationship to the parents, has meanwhile come under doubt. Nonetheless, in the psychoanalytic literature, there is widespread consensus that during this time, a clear weakening of Oedipal desire takes place, and that until adolescence, no new sexual goals, that is, forms of gratification, are developed (see Blos, 1967). Beyond that, the development of the ego experiences further differentiation and stabilization which allow for increasing control over the demands made by drives. Sexual activity in this phase has the role of a temporary counterbalance of tension. Blos notes that a key criterion for latency is the shift in cathexis from external to internal object: cathexis is replaced by identifications.

With puberty, changes start taking place that convert infantile sexual life into its final, adult form. In the *Three Essays*, Freud describes the following processes: "The sexual instinct has hitherto been predominantly auto-erotic; it now finds a sexual object" (1905d, p. 207). Now "the erotogenic zones become subordinated to the primacy of the genital zone", and the partial drives are bundled together under this primacy to focus on a new sexual goal. The new sexual goal assigns different functions to the two sexes, and among women, there is even a kind of "involution" in sexual development. Among men, "the new sexual aim … consists in the discharge of the sexual products", and the prior sexual goal—achieving pleasure—becomes tied to the final act of the sexual process: "The sexual instinct is now subordinated to the reproductive function; it becomes, so to say, altruistic" (ibid., p. 207).

With the primacy of the genital, according to Freud, comes a differentiation of various kinds of pleasure, in particular initial or preliminary pleasure (*Vorlust*) and terminal or end pleasure (*Endlust*). In this context, the erogenous zones of the body serve the new function by bringing about anticipatory lust, and through this preparation, help make possible the greater gratification that results from discharging the sexual products. This differentiation leads to creation of a hierarchy of different forms of sexual activity. Compared with coitus, there (or these) are "inferior" pleasures that can add little to the increase in pleasure.

With this conceptualization of the primacy of the genital in the service of reproduction, Freud gives us a highly conventional reading of adult sexuality, which is clearly demarcated from the variety and aimlessness l found in infantile sexuality. Conceptually, during the course of adolescence the dominance of heterosexuality is reasserted, and a polarization and hierarchy of the sexes is established. Thus, Freud asserts that "it is not until puberty that the sharp distinction is established between the masculine and feminine characters. From that time on, this contrast has a more decisive influence than any other upon the shaping of human life" (ibid., p. 219). An example of the reversion to conventional views that Freud signals in his theory is his depiction of female sexual development as "involution". With this, he means a "fresh wave of *repression*, in which it is precisely clitoridal sexuality that is affected. What is thus overtaken by repression is a piece of masculine sexuality" (ibid., p. 220). In the adult woman, by contrast, the clitoris only has "the task, namely, of transmitting the excitation to the adjacent female sexual parts, just as—to use a simile—pine shavings can be kindled in order to set a log of harder wood on fire" (ibid., p. 221). Thus, the woman also switches her leading "erotogenic zone" during puberty, while the man retains his from childhood.

In the further course of the *Three Essays*, however, some aspects are augmented or relativized in a manner that again runs counter to the tendency to give a conventional account of sexuality. Thus, in passing, the new sexual goal of the man is described as "penetration into a cavity in the body which excites his genital zone" (ibid., p. 222), a formulation that limits the primacy of heterosexual coitus. In addition, the aforementioned "predominantly auto-erotic" sexual instinct in infancy is downplayed by the observation that the sexual instinct only becomes autoerotic after the loss of the mother's breast, and that "the finding of an object is in fact a refinding of it" (ibid., p. 222).

Since, according to Freud, it is natural to return to the sexual objects of early childhood after puberty, "time has been gained in which the child can erect, among other restraints on sexuality, the barrier against incest and can thus take up into himself the moral precepts which expressly exclude from his object-choice, as being blood-relations, the persons whom he has loved in his childhood" (ibid., p. 225). This incest taboo is, according to Freud, at its heart a social demand. In psychoanalytic treatment, by contrast, one can recognize "how intensely the individual struggles with the temptation to incest during his period of growth and how frequently the barrier is transgressed in phantasies and even in reality" (1905, p. 225). While incest in parent-child relations is today discussed as a punishable offense, the transgressing of the incest barrier among siblings is even today a topic that is largely taboo. Though sexual relations between siblings including coitus are repeatedly reported during analysis, and generally, though not exclusively, occur during adolescence, there are barely any publications about this problem.

The choice of object takes place during puberty, and it is initially at the level of fantasies, that is, imaginings not meant to be carried out. These are connected to infantile exploration of the genitals, which was abandoned already in childhood, and are held either wholly, or in part, unconsciously. Freud regarded them as very important because they created a place where the repressed components of the libido could be satisfied. Among them one frequently finds the "primal fantasies", universal, often stereotyped, fantasies that are largely independent of the experience of the individual. They are about overhearing the parents having intercourse, or being seduced at an early age by a loved person, or the threat of castration, or being in the mother's womb. In these fantasies, the infantile tendencies re-emerge with increased intensity due to changes occurring to the body, and as a rule in the positive Oedipal constellation. In overcoming and rejecting the incestuous fantasies, and in the detaching from parental authority that accompanies it, Freud saw one of the most significant, but also most painful, psychic achievements of puberty, "which is so important for the progress of civilization, between the new generation and the old" (ibid., p. 227). Insufficient separation from the parents and retention of the incestuous object-choice were, by contrast, the cause of numerous psychological symptoms and illnesses. Yet even without an incestuous fixation, this early choice of object remains viable. While the first serious infatuation of a boy is often directed at an older woman, and that of a girl at an older man; the later choice of object is "freely related" to these models. Unconscious "memory images" from earliest childhood play a particular role here, and in Chapter Three, I will return to this question of object-choice, in conjunction with modern psychoanalytic conceptualizations.

While Freud and many other early analysts usually spoke of puberty, "adolescence" has largely replaced that term by now, as a more comprehensive designation with respect both to biology and to psychosocial aspects. In earlier psychoanalytic theory, this phase of life was apparently largely ignored, with Anna Freud (1980) calling it the "stepchild" of psychoanalytic theory and therapy. It does not even warrant an entry in what has become the near-canonical *Vocabulary of Psychoanalysis* (Laplanche and Pontalis, 1973). However, psychoanalytic interest in adolescence has grown since the 1950s, as witnessed by work conducted by Peter Blos (1941, 1967), Moses and M. Eglé Laufer (1984), and Louise Kaplan (1984). It is precisely this phase of life that is of great significance for psychosexual development and the development of gender identity.

In psychoanalysis, the first to address adolescence was Helene Deutsch, who dealt specifically with the development of female adolescence in the context of her *Psychology of Women* (1944), a work that closely adhered to the controversial Freudian conceptualizations of the female. Even so, with the exception of a normative emphasis on sex polarity and the primacy of heterosexuality, she was able to create a quite differentiated, sensitive picture of female adolescence. It paved the way for many later theories, and for that reason I wish to present her approach a little more fully, though not uncritically. I focus particularly on her conceptualization of bisexuality with respect to the development of a gender identity and object-choice—as it were, as the new staging of the Oedipal event—as well as the integration of the bodily, especially the genital, developments into the psyche.

Helene Deutsch understood adolescence as a revolution in the psyche that was at heart a "clash of two worlds" (1944, p. 115). It is manifested in all that happens during these years: progressive and regressive forces collide. With the notion of a new staging and new structuring, the author contradicts the thesis often put forward in psychoanalytic theory of "psychic determinism" of early childhood, after which adolescence is only at heart a repetition of infantile conflicts. Kurt Eissler (1958) returned to this notion in characterizing adolescence as a "second chance." What, according to Deutsch, can be progressive or facilitating in certain areas can at the same time work in a regressive or inhibitory manner in others. Thus, for example, increased narcissism can be beneficial with respect to ego development but can hamper the development of object-relations. One and the same psychic form of expression serves countervailing tendencies, so the identification of the girl with her mother, for example, can mean that she accepts her femininity, but can also embody all the Oedipal difficulties and be more of a hindrance in accepting that femininity. Adolescents are torn between the opposed wishes to "be grown up" or to "remain a child". Helene Deutsch devotes particular attention to the pre-puberty phase and its onset, and comes to the important insight that the psychological manifestations occurring then are not confined to adolescence: "In varying degrees we all carry our infantilism, our prepuberty, and our puberty with us right into old age" (1944, p. 4).

In both sexes, according to Deutsch, the libidinous tendencies directed at the mother, as the first love-object, are reanimated in prepuberty. Central to this is the conflict between separating from the mother while simultaneously loving her. Even if the shift in object is never fully successful, disengaging from the mother is decisive for the autonomy and independence of the girl. That disengagement is underscored by a shift in the homoerotic love for the mother towards intense friendships with other girls, as well as a fondness for older women that can even take on tones of rapturous infatuation. Adolescence thus not only has the goal of working through the Oedipus complex and overcoming it, but also of transforming the primary bond to the mother into a more mature form.

While the prepuberty period is characterized by homosexual love-relations—to the mother as well as to girlfriends—this relationship structure shifts to a bisexual triangle that includes a male love-object. Fundamentally, however, this phase of early adolescence is governed by a "general sexual disquiet, usually without the presence of a real heterosexual impulse" (ibid., p. 37). Among girls during this phase, the bisexual orientation is less repressed than it is among boys. Girls are often proud of their "manliness" and process it in manifold day-dreams and fantasies, while boys are more ashamed of and denying their "femaleness".

Deutsch links the bisexual love-desires with the development of gender identity in an insightful manner. If a girl, owing to external or internal inhibitions, is not able to express her love-wishes in both directions, whether through direct relationships or through sublimation, there is a danger that the "bisexual tendencies may remain locked up in her psyche without an object. Her problem in this dangerous case is not "Do I love men or women?" or "How will I manage these two emotional tendencies?" but "Am I a man or a woman?" (ibid., p. 86). In this manner, the question of object-choice changes into a question of gender affiliation. This indecisiveness, according to Deutsch, is often the object of typical fantasies among young girls in which they take on both the male and the female roles, and thereby stage what has been lost: membership in the other sex.

The processes of prepuberty and early adolescence are basically continued during "actual" adolescence, according to Deutsch. At the centre stands liberation from the dependencies of childhood: "the old emotional ties must be cast off, and new ones created" (ibid., p. 91). The casting-off of emotional ties is accompanied by an increase in narcissism, because the earlier object cathexis is retracted into the ego temporarily. This makes adolescents not just very sensitive and intolerant of criticism but also much more vulnerable during this phase of life. In the further course of adolescence, new object relations develop from these narcissistic cathexes, and in them, currents of tenderness and sexuality flow together (ibid., p. 115). Helene Deutsch calls sexual currents those which at heart serve biological reproductive needs, and thereby argues for a clear separation of the sexuality of the child from that of the adult. Unavoidably accompanying this is the primacy of heterosexuality and a normative hierarchy of the various forms of sexuality.

The differing physicality of men and women also leads, in Deutsch, to diverging psychological developments. She justifies stereotyped sex roles in this manner:

> The path to be followed by the boy is traced in advance by the functional readiness of his organ; his progressive goal is clearly and unequivocally before him, and the only difficulties he has to solve

are the dissolution of old object ties, the discovery of new ones, and
the mastering of passive tendencies. (ibid., p. 117)

With this, she proposes an extremely limited image of maleness that
one-sidedly emphasizes phallicity and wards off passivity and receptivity. Similarly, female sexuality is curiously disembodied. While the
erotic fantasies of the boy are accompanied by direct arousal of his genitals, eroticism among girls, in the view of the author, remains separated
longer from bodily reactions: "the vaginal sensations cannot be compared with the pressure of the male organ" (ibid., p. 119). She summarizes her view of sex differences as: "The organic contrast between the
extroverted activity of the boy's sexual apparatus and the veiled, less
consciously perceived, and less urgent activity of the girl's is reproduced
in the life of the psyche" (ibid., p. 130). The most important sex-specific
difference she sees is a greater degree of willingness to identify, to fantasize, to be more subjective, and to use intuition, which she regards as
stemming from the fundamental passiveness inherent in women.

Such formulations betray how time-bound Helene Deutsch's theory
is (see also the critical comments in Chapter Two). What is interesting,
though, is the persistence of such ideas in everyday awareness even
today. In Chapter Three, I will discuss in greater detail what Deutsch
regards as the key issue of adolescence: the development of homosexuality and heterosexuality.

Peter Blos (1967) divides the process of adolescence into five phases:
pre-, early, actual, late and post-adolescence, devoting particular attention to its pre-Oedipal and pre-genital aspects. However, the conceptual distinction he draws between puberty, as a term for the bodily
manifestations of sexual maturation, and adolescence, as a term for the
corresponding psychological accommodations, isolates somatic from
psychic processes in a problematic manner, based as it is on a unidirec-
tional assumption that bodily sexual maturation influences the psyche.
This view obscures the possibility that it may be the other way around
or that the influences may be mutual. Blos describes the goal of adolescent development, as the answer to the assault of the drives on the ego
during puberty, as achieving a "stable ego and drive organization".

He summarizes the processes of change during adolescence as
follows: "The urgent necessity to cope with the novel condition of
puberty evokes all the modes of excitation, tension, gratification, and

defence that ever played a role in previous years—that is, during the psychosexual development of infancy and early childhood" (1967, p. 11). The emotional needs and conflicts must be recapitulated before new solutions can be found that have qualitatively differing goals for the drives and ego-interests. Alongside this, the pre-genital phases of sexual organization continue to exert influence and try to gain the upper hand. They stand opposed to the maturation process: "The gradual advancement during adolescence toward the genital position and heterosexual orientation is only the continuation of a development which temporarily came to a standstill at the decline of the oedipal phase" (ibid., p. 12). Here, too, one revisits the problem of a normative model of development: The manifold aspects of human sexuality become lost in the process.

According to Blos, the heightened "instinctual pressure" in pre-adolescence or pre-puberty leads to indiscriminate cathexis of all possible libidinal modes of gratification from early childhood. Every experience can have a sexually stimulating effect, and it is not necessarily an erotic stimulus that calls forth genital arousal. The first ejaculations that occur in a waking state are more often the result of a random affect than of erotic stimulation. As an example, Blos cites body-oriented competitions such as wrestling where spontaneous ejaculations occur: "This state of affairs in the boy entering pubescence testifies to the function of the genital as a nonspecific discharge organ of tension: this is characteristic of childhood up to adolescence proper, when the organ gradually acquires exclusive sensitivity to heterosexual stimuli" (ibid., p. 58).

Such formulations influence the image of male sexuality and, with respect to psychoanalytic theory-formation, can only astonish. This view ignores key psychoanalytic concepts such as the unconscious, for one thing, in the form of sexually simulating yet unconscious fantasies, making it clear that sexual arousal is by no means as indiscriminate and non-unspecific as might appear, and for another, in the form of (unconscious) bisexuality with respect to gender identity as well as to sexual orientation, which preserves, life-long, the receptiveness of the male genitals to homosexual and heterosexual stimulation.

Similar objections to this theory are relevant for its conceptualization of maleness and femaleness, as Blos largely adopts Freud's controversial model of femaleness. Blos, too, assumes a sex-specific development in adolescence that plays out differently for boys and for girls. In Chapter

Two, I will discuss these differing paths again, in the context of the formation, among both men and women, of an adult gender identity and sexuality.

From Freud and Deutsch to Blos, Eissler, and Laufer and Laufer, there is consensus in the psychoanalytic discourse that separation from the primary love objects—along with the revitalizing and overcoming of the Oedipal conflict—is the key task of "actual" adolescence. Adolescence thereby is an opportunity to compensate for adverse influences during early childhood and modify them. Otto Fenichel (1946, p. 113) already pointed out that experiences "in puberty may solve conflicts or shift conflicts into a final direction". Kurt Eissler (1958) took this further, clinically, seeing in adolescence a "second (and in most cases, last) chance." Adolescence grants, so to speak, a respite and allows the acquired psychological conflict structures and their processing patters to become more fluid. Adolescents can now encounter the re-activated Oedipal conflicts in a different manner, and turn to love objects outside the family. The goal is to overcome the narcissistic and bisexual ambitions, to enable heterosexuality and object-love to prevail, and to satisfy the search for love objects outside the family. This description of goals makes clear that during adolescence, all youths are subjected to a remarkable degree to social notions of order, and the "polymorphously perverse" infantile sexuality becomes socially regimented. This "submission", however, is rewarded by a hitherto unattained pleasure: the orgasm of genital sexuality. The primacy of genitality, under which all partial drives are subsumed, is in that sense an ambivalent achievement. On the one hand, it limits the variety of possibilities for pleasure and gratification, now downgraded to "anticipatory pleasures", but on the other hand this is compensated for by a distinct gain in pleasure through orgasmic experiences. Sexuality, too, is now placed in an interpersonal context: Sexual activity and experience is based on manifested reciprocity. Infantile sexuality, on the other hand, was by and large, or at its core, auto-erotic because of the incest taboo. The only exceptions to this were sibling relations or erotic play with peers, though largely confined to the preschool years.

A concept of adolescence less oriented to societal notions of order can be found in the work of Lillian Rotter, another early analyst who argued the young were always rebellious and disruptive, and keen on overturning the existing order (1989, p. 191). She provides interesting insights into the question of masturbation during adolescence, which she understands not just as an aspect of separation but also as an effort at self-healing (ibid., p. 198). Masturbation not only serves to heighten pleasure, but also has a soothing function, as true for menstrual cramps as for psychological tension. In this manner, disquiet and sorrow can be discharged or dissipated. The content of adolescent masturbation fantasies is, as before, childlike but takes on a narcissistic tinge pervaded with pride, and at its core is derived from Oedipal wishes.

Lillian Rotter points out that during puberty, the young must engage in grief work, mourning their first love-objects, as well as their lost childhood. Only then can there be separation, replacement, and the achievement of maturity (ibid., p. 187). The changes occurring in puberty brings also confront parents with great psychological challenges—how children experience puberty often depends on how their parents experienced, and assess, their own lives and especially their own puberty (ibid., p. 190). During their children's puberty, parents experience a second puberty. Ulrike Schmauch (2004) takes this thought further and sees a mutual sexual socialization of adolescents and their parents. Important to the analysis of adolescence is that it be understood within a relational structure, most particularly with respect to sexual experience. Whether sexuality is experienced with fear and a sense of guilt, or with delight and enjoyment, and whether new means of pleasure ensue, depends very heavily on the relationship between parents and adolescents, and indeed in both directions: Parents and adolescents mutually influence one another here.

Vera King (1992) has addressed the potential for conflict that exists in the psychic acquisition of female genitality during adolescence, particularly against a backdrop of the cultural devaluation of femininity. During puberty, the girl's sexual wishes and fantasies are connected for the first time with the possibility of pregnancy. Helene Deutsch (1944) and Judith Kestenberg (1968) point out that with the onset of menstruation inner genitality takes on a new significance and needs to be integrated. Identification with the mother plays an important role here. This process is made more difficult by a cultural definition of femaleness that is based on an antagonism between motherhood and sexual passion (Poluda-Korte, 1986). The young woman is then faced with the dilemma that the physical changes brought on by puberty, such as menstruation, breast growth, and pleasurable vaginal sensations, form the body-ego anew. These are connected with sexual fantasies and wishes, yet on the other hand the cultural image of motherhood seems incompatible with sexuality. For that reason, the positive cathexis of female genitality, and often of the entire female body, is highly conflicted. Additionally, the culturally isolated and devalued realm of motherhood, highly threatening images have been created of an all-powerful mother and of a father "castrated" and robbed of power by the mother. Hence it is much harder for girls to acknowledge their mother's desire and to "mirror" it in their own arousal, meaning to identify with their mother and yet be her rival. In bodily terms, for a daughter to be like her mother is both arousing and fear-inducing at the same time. In the desire(s) of the mother, the daughter sees her own desire(s) reflected and vice versa. This recognition implies both a homoerotic-narcissistic component in the mother-daughter relationship and the perception of desire and passion between the parents (King, 1992).

This notion of a reciprocally influenced formation of desire(s) on the part of mother and daughter seems to me extremely productive. In it, however, I see less the character of a "mirroring" than of a mutual reshaping and new staging. One can also ask what role the father might play as the man in the adolescent restaging of female desire.

Finally, I would like to return to the question raised at the outset about the difference between infantile and adult sexuality, in other words, the contrast between the homological and the heterological position. The notion that adult sexuality differs from infantile sexuality, the heterologous position, is supported by the Freudian notion of a diphasic human sexual development occurring at two different points in life: in early childhood and during puberty. This proposal leads to the dual difficulty noted above. On the one hand, it is debatable whether one is even dealing with sexuality at all in infant behaviours, and on the other hand, whether one wants to abandon what the concept of infantile sexuality engendered: a non-endogenous, non-hierarchical, "polymorphously perverse" multiplied sexuality.

As a result, my question is whether infantile and adult sexuality are really as fundamentally different as the Freudian notion of a diphasic process, and its associated primacy of genitality, makes them appear. Perhaps the assumption of a fundamental difference owes more to efforts to make psychoanalytic theory more conventional, which Freud did engage in at various points in his work. If one takes Freud's reversion to conventional notions as a failure in psychoanalytic theory-formation as Peter Passett (2005) suggests then other perspectives open. Passett denies the primacy of the genital, and sees instead precisely the infantile, polymorphously perverse as the central characteristic of human sexuality. The question, unlike in Fenichel, is then not why infantile sexuality can be called "sexual" (Früh, 2005). Rather, it is the "infantile"—meaning the "polymorphously perverse"—that is seen as the specifically human element of sexuality. Here no linear, quasi-natural development from infantile to mature, adult sexuality is assumed. Instead, a subjective history of sexuality is shaped by the subject (Passett, 2005). Also untenable, following this view, is the thesis of a diphasic sexual development, a thesis that, astonishingly, is barely questioned in psychoanalytic discourse. However, it is worth considering how sensible the conceptualization of such a break as the diphasic model proposes might be, as it calls for starting over again. For one thing, bodily maturation, which in the traditional view requires such a restarting of the developmental process, is not a one-time, datable event, but rather a multi-year process occurring on many levels. For another, it is also quite problematic to divorce the physical, bodily development from its psychological and social dimensions. Instead, one needs to see the three dimensions as a complex, interrelated set of conditions.

The perspective of the general theory of seduction, described in detail initially, which serves as the foundation for my own notions, provides an alternative to the diphasic theory. Adolescence is not so much a new start as a specific constellation, a junction-point in the course of development where various reinscriptions at various levels come together. The "enigmatic messages" are newly interpreted, in light of the body's development and of genital developments in particular, and worked through to come to new answers. Using the metaphor of a continuous reinscription, I want to suggest a more distinct connection between the various pleasure and gratification modes, including their conflicts, than the thesis of a diphasic process allows. At the same time, seeing adolescence as a juncture where various reinscriptions are concentrated emphasizes the special character of a specific phase of life and development. Finally, the concept of reinscription permits socialization experiences to be understood as inscriptions in and on the body. Bodily changes during adolescence are understood thereby not only as endogenous and caused by maturation but also as dependent on psychological and social factors. This perspective, which brings into focus the influence of interactive experiences on the body and the structure of the body, has thus far been largely ignored in psychoanalytic discourse. I see it as an important direction for future research.

A brief digression on adult sexuality

There is a not infrequent complaint about psychoanalytic notions of human sexuality that they end with adolescence and give little separate attention to the love life of adults. The discussion of psychosexual development here, too, ends with adolescence. That should not be understood as a deficit that shows gaping holes in research, but is instead based on the specific logic underlying psychoanalytic theory about human development. As is well known, psychoanalysis is interested less in phenomena that deal with the manifold expressions of human (love-) life than in the structures and functions underlying them. In that sense, the chronicity of the course of human life plays a relatively subordinate role in theory-building. As noted initially in this chapter, it is the "constellations" that are of interest, the conjunction of various scenes from different points in a life-history at least as compared with linear time.

But there are other reasons for psychoanalytic accounts of psychosexual development to end with adolescence. The underlying modalities of pleasure and gratification, and the unconscious conflicts associated with them, become fixed in the psychic structures by that point. They remain there for life, not in an "original" form but rather by being permanently reinscribed in the course of life and development. In the best case, the ways of consciously and unconsciously handling pleasures modes and their conflicts—the so-called defence formations—are expanded in the subsequent course of life. In the worst case, they become limited, as with mental illnesses. In certain situations of life, the conflicts may again become virulent and call for special psychic work. I have already described such situations as junction-points, junctures where the most differing reinscriptions, at different levels, come together. I regard adolescence as such a point in the course of psychosexual development. Menopause is a similar juncture, but so are life-events such as pregnancy, parenthood in its various stages, and experiences of loss in its diverse manifestations (death, illnesses, separations).

Such a conceptualization of development is not so chronologically oriented with respect to the life course. In this model, a temporal perspective is only necessary to indicate the particular point in time when individual pleasure and gratification modes, including their conflicts, emerge in the psychic structure or develop psychic effect. That is the case for establishing orality, anality, phallicity and oedipality, basically, up to the period of latency. Adolescence, by contrast, is not without further ado to be subsumed into this scheme. In the developmental logic of classic psychoanalysis puberty/adolescence is regarded as a repetition of the infantile psychosexual phases, though with the innovation of establishment of genital primacy.

It is thus understandable that Freud described psychosexual development only up to that point in life. Even without agreeing with these Freudian assumptions, though, I regard it as sensible to see adolescence as a separate unit of sexual development—one similar to the infantile modes of pleasure and gratification. I would like to emphasize again that, in contrast to academic developmental psychology or everyday understanding, psychoanalysis does not see relevance in adolescence as a specific, chronological, stage of life. Even though genitality, in the Freudian sense of a primacy that subordinates the other pleasure and gratification modes, is not established in adolescence, the unique feature of adolescence is in a fundamental alteration of genitality. This results from the acquisition of a sexually mature body and, through orgasm if nothing else, generates a pleasure differing from that of infantile genitality. This step in development is ideal-typically located in adolescence, though this does not mean it is completed during this phase.

In the love-life of adults, the "polymorphously perverse, infantile" modalities of pleasure and gratification—orality, anality and phallicity—are just as present as is genital desire. The one is inseparable from the other, since the individual modes stand in a complex, reciprocal relationship to one another. In addition, there is the potential reproductive function which also helps determine what is sexually experienced. I return to the topic of the acquisition of the sexually mature body as a key task of adolescence in Chapter Two, and address it from a gender-specific perspective. There I also discuss other junctures in sexual development, for example, menopause.

The modes for pleasure and gratification are reinscribed in a multitude of ways in the course of a life, depending on subjective experiences and life conditions. Differing sexual goals and sexual objects can take on significance at differing times. This variability and changeability applies in principle to sexual orientation or sexual preferences, too—an object-choice that may be heterosexual, homosexual, or "perverse", a topic I return to in greater detail in Chapter Three. Limitations on the spectrum of pleasure and gratification modes as well as on their flexibility appear as "pathological" or as "disorders" of sexual life, though

I only mention them in passing in this book, and will address them in a separate publication.

From the psychoanalytic perspective, the significance of early childhood sexual socialization for the later love-life of adults is obvious. This is not the view in other disciplines. Thus, Gunter Schmidt (2005) assumes every love relationship means a "new opportunity". Psychoanalysts as a rule regard the scope of "new chances" as more limited. Early childhood experiences with the various pleasure and gratification modes create the framework in which adult sexuality develops, in the sense of reshaping and reinscription. That does not allow for new chances every day, but at least it provides sufficient scope for some change.

CHAPTER TWO

Masculine—feminine

Freud's views on masculinity and femininity

Freud's remarks on masculinity and femininity are arguably the most controversial in all of his works. The phallic monism of his theory, and the exclusive focus on the male in his discussion of sexual development, has been deservedly rejected. For in his view, the female is not an independent sex but is distinguished by a fundamental deficit: A woman is a woman because she lacks a penis. In his early theorizing, Freud was not much interested in conceptualizing gender-specific development. For him, the differentiation between man and woman basically does not begin until puberty. In addition, as cultural differentiation into two genders is not easy to discern in the sphere of the psyche, he also rarely uses the sociological terms "men" and "women", preferring to employ "masculinity" (*Männlichkeit*) and "femininity" (*Weiblichkeit*) instead.

Freud's most differentiated treatment of these terms can be found in a footnote, added in 1915, to the *Three Essays on the Theory of Sexuality*. These terms do not describe characteristics one could assign, respectively, to men or women. Instead, they are currents found in every individual, in different proportions. While it is well known that Freud did not use these terms consistently in his works, and continually reverted to conventional gender stereotypes, it is worth examining this key differentiation:

> It is essential to understand clearly that the concepts of "masculine" and "feminine", whose meaning seems so unambiguous to ordinary people, are among the most confused that occur in science. It is possible to distinguish at least *three* uses. "Masculine" and "feminine" are used sometimes in the sense of *activity* and *passivity*, sometimes in a *biological*, and sometimes, again, in a *sociological* sense. The first of these three meanings is the essential one and the most serviceable in psycho-analysis. When, for instance, libido was described (...) as being "masculine", the word was being used in this sense, for an instinct is always active even when it has a passive aim in view.
>
> The second, or biological, meaning of "masculine" and "feminine" is the one whose applicability can be determined most easily. Here "masculine" and "feminine" are characterized by the presence of spermatozoa or ova respectively and by the functions proceeding from them. (...) The third, or sociological, meaning receives its connotation from the observation of actually existing masculine and feminine individuals. Such observation shows that in human beings pure masculinity or femininity is not to be found either in a psychological or a biological sense. Every individual on the contrary displays a mixture of the character-traits belonging to his own and to the opposite sex; and he shows a combination of activity and passivity. (1905d, pp. 219– ; emphases in the original)

Freud uses the term *Geschlechtscharakter* here, by which he means the connection between biological and psychological levels, so to render this as "character traits" in English is rather misleading.

Freud takes this mixture of masculine and feminine currents in the individual into account in his concept of bisexuality, and I will discuss this further in Chapter Three. The striking differentiation in the concept of *Geschlecht* is noteworthy here. The conventional clarity in how sex/gender is understood is overturned, but rather than being sustained, the differentiation is submerged beneath the prevailing gender ideology, which Freud also reproduces in his conceptualizations. Formulations such as this give us a potential starting point for further psychoanalytic thinking about sex and gender. This opens up a way of thinking that adopts Freud's scepticism toward the apparently unambiguous differentiation into "masculine" and "feminine", carries it further, and rather than assigning this distinction to specific individuals, interprets it as "positions". The core of such a gender concept lies in bisexuality and the resulting multiplicity of gender identifications, and psychic as well as somatic dispositions.

This concept, additionally, is linked to newer developments in gender discourse conducted in the social sciences and cultural studies, a discourse from which psychoanalytic theory has profited for many years. Since difference theory—which emphasizes the differences between women and men—is now being challenged, for example in post-structuralist gender theory, it is probably time to reconsider how helpful such a conceptualization of sex-differentiated development actually is for psychoanalysis. To answer this in substantiated manner, I will present a number of exemplary psychoanalytic concepts of masculinity and femininity in chronological order, and discuss the different lines of argument in this discourse. In my historical reconstruction of the development of theory, it is of some significance that in the "classic", monistic conceptions, one largely finds theories of female development. Male development, by contrast, is not an independent focus of research, and is instead addressed—if at all—only to more clearly articulate and demarcate femininity. This is all the more remarkable because feminist-oriented psychoanalytic concepts of femininity have been part of mainstream psychoanalytic theory for at least twenty years—often contrary to the field's own self-understanding. Might this mean the earlier, monistic view secretly lives on, but, in contrast to Freud, as a way to explain female rather than male development?

Since the 1970s, at the latest, the question of masculinity and femininity has largely been addressed in terms of identity in the psychoanalytic discourse. Psychosexual development has faded into the background. Identity is "not acquired at a particular stage of development but is instead a process. The formation of identity leads to a progressive individualization and to an increasingly complex organization of the self. Development does not end, as was assumed in earlier psychoanalytic ideas of development, in a stable character formation. Rather, the development of identity is a lifelong dialectical process" (Bohleber, 1997, p. 112, translation for this edition). If one applies this reasoning to the development of gender identity and emphasizes psychic (identity) work, one can conclude that gender identity in both men and women is formed in a lifelong dialectical process that moves between the poles of masculinity and femininity. Gender identity is thus not a "stable character formation" but is instead continually reinscribed throughout life. The ascription of gender identity, which occurs at birth, if not before, should not be understood as a finished (completed) package delivered to an individual, and that must be appropriated. Instead, a more appropriate psychoanalytic understanding of gender identity is the metaphor of a shell or container in which the most varied conscious and unconscious aspects of masculinity and femininity are stored. These come in individual mixtures and proportions, and they have differing somatic, psychic and social dimensions. Thus, in our culture, which constructs gender as a dichotomous system, there are only two kinds of containers or shells; they can hold the same or similar things. The metaphor also makes evident that, with respect to gender identity, we are not dealing with something uniform or monolithic. Rather, this identity is made up of many individual masculine and feminine aspects, some of which are in contradiction or irreconcilable. With this metaphor, I advocate a view of gender identity different from that of Robert Stoller, whose notion of gender identity has more or less explicitly stood at the core of psychoanalytic discourse for nearly forty years. I invert Stoller's perspective, which starts from a core, as an inner structure, and focuses on the layers around this core. Instead, I start from the visible exterior surface and turn my gaze onto the various aspects lying beneath it. While the shell fulfils a central function in the social order, and its binary coding is presented as indispensable to modern societies, in the psychoanalytic context I regard the container's contents and variety as much more interesting. I therefore want to argue, in conjunction with the aforementioned Freudian differentiation, that gender diversification should take the place of cultural dichotomy in psychoanalytic thinking. The advantage in so doing lies in turning away from the more or less rigid sex/gender norms that play a significant role particularly in the North American discourse, "where popular worries concerning the feminization of American males had found expression since the 1930s in psychological tests defining personality norms for men and women, that is, distinctive sex roles that were deemed essential for mental health" (Friedman, 1986, p. 89f). These established models have in the meantime penetrated deeply into everyday understanding and are of great significance for the self-concept of each individual. The conflict-laden aspect, the often unconscious fear of not adequately conforming to these norms and not being a "real" man or a "real" woman, emerges in many analyses. Given the great cultural significance ascribed to gender and its comprehensive claim as a feature of the social order, this mental struggle prejudices nearly all areas of life, from how one deals with one's own body and with sexuality, to how one arranges one's life, starts a family, or chooses a career. In that sense, addressing the conceptualization of masculinity and femininity also has high practical relevance for psychoanalysis, especially if gender norms are not to be unwittingly perpetuated.

Freud's first systematic account of male and female sexual development can be found in the *Three Essays on the Theory of Sexuality* (1905d). Adult sexuality develops differently in the two sexes:

> "Now, however, a new sexual aim appears, and all the component instincts combine to attain it, while the erotogenic zones become subordinated to the primacy of the genital zone. Since the new sexual aim assigns very different functions to the two sexes, their sexual development now diverges greatly. That of males is the more straightforward and the more understandable, while that of females actually enters upon a kind of involution". (ibid., p. 207)

While the new sexual goal of the man is to discharge the sexual products, linked to attaining the highest pleasure in the act of sex, Freud provides no information about the sexual goal of the woman. The differentiation of man and woman has its origin in puberty, and afterwards a "sharp distinction is established between the masculine and feminine characters" (ibid., p. 219). In his later writings, Freud relocated the onset of sex-specific development to the phallic phase (see "The Development of the Sexual Function" in Freud 1940a), probably less for reasons inherent in his theories than as a result of external influences. This revision was undertaken in connection with a long-standing and massive controversy during the 1920s and 1930s, which I will describe in detail below. But even beforehand, though in a rather offhand manner, he notes that male and female predispositions can already be seen in fledgling form during childhood. Thus, sexual inhibitions (such as disgust, shame, and pity) develop earlier in girls. Their tendency to engage in sexual repression seems greater and their partial drives frequently appear in passive forms. However, there is congruence between the sexes with respect to auto-erotic and masturbatory manipulation of the erogenous zones. Based on this congruence, the difference between the sexes prior to puberty is nullified, and Freud is of the view that "the sexuality of little girls is of a wholly masculine character" (1905d, p. 219). This masculine bent in little girl's results from the male character of the clitoris, seen as homologous to the penis. Only the clitoris and not the vagina, according to Freud, is decisive for infantile masturbation. With puberty, upon "becoming a woman", clitoral sexuality—as part of male sexuality—becomes repressed. In the genital sexual act, the role of the clitoris is now far more to pass arousal on to the neighbouring female genital areas, "just as—to use a simile—pine shavings can be kindled in order to set a log of harder wood on fire" (ibid., p. 221). This shift in the leading erogenous zone, together with the repression of infantile masculinity during puberty, creates a particular disposition both in sexual dysfunction as well as in the development of neuroses such as hysteria.

In his lecture on "Femininity" (1933a), Freud again addresses the pairing of the terms *Männlichkeit—Weiblichkeit*, this time in the sense of active—passive. He disavows the notion of a sex-specific libido:

> "There is only one libido, which serves both the masculine and the feminine sexual functions. To it itself we cannot assign any sex; if, following the conventional equation of activity and masculinity, we are inclined to describe it as masculine; we must not forget that it also covers trends with a passive aim. Nevertheless, the juxtaposition "feminine libido" is without any justification". (Freud, 1933a, p. 131)

As sensible as this theory of curtailment is from an architectonic standpoint, it appeared quite offensive in subsequent reception with respect to the drive concept. The statement is frequently misinterpreted to mean that Freud denied that women had any desire. The question of whether an independent, "genuine" female desire exists has pervaded psychoanalytic discourse up to the present.

Freud (1914c) regards penis envy as a fundamental element of female sexuality, one that originates in the discovery of the anatomical difference between the sexes. Viewing the male genitalia, the little girl feels deprived and wishes to have a penis. As part of the castration complex, which is characterized by the assumption, shared by boys and girls, that there is only one sex, namely the male, the lack of a penis is assumed to have resulted from a castration the girl has already experienced. In the brief essay "On Transformations of Instinct, as Exemplified in Anal Erotism", Freud (1917c) describes the most significant transformations of penis envy as, first, the desire to have children, following the symbolic equivalence penis—child, and, second, the desire, independent of this equivalence, for a man as an "appendage to the penis" (ibid., p. 129).

Controversies concerning freud's ideas about femininity

As is well known, massive objections were made to these ideas about femininity. The first alternative models were formulated by Karen Horney, who conducted a vigorous controversy about the psychology of women with Freud and Jones during the 1920s and 1930s. It is worth taking a close look at this debate, since the arguments and counter-arguments made at the time were repeated in nearly identical terms a good thirty years later during the second women's movement (see the articles collected in Chasseguet-Smirgel, 1970). The clear differences between the positions taken in the earlier debate provide numerous interesting insights into the psychodynamics of female sexuality. The debate can be followed in four essays by Karen Horney: "On the Genesis of the Castration Complex in Women" (1924), "The Flight from Womanhood" (1926), "Observations on a Specific Difference in the Dread Felt by Men and by Women Respectively for the Opposite Sex" (1932), and "The Denial of the Vagina" (1933). It is also reflected in three essays by Jones: "The Early Development of Female Sexuality" (1927), "The Phallic Phase" (1933), and "Early Female Sexuality" (1935), and in three essays by Freud: "The Dissolution of the Oedipus Complex" (1924d), "Some Psychical Consequences of the Anatomical Distinction between the Sexes" (1925j), and "Female Sexuality" (1931b). In addition, there is an essay by Melanie Klein, "Early Stages of the Oedipus Conflict" (1928), in which she participates indirectly in the controversy. I only briefly address the ideas of Helene Deutsch and Marie Bonaparte regarding female masochism, as it is an issue that, despite all the criticism levelled at it, has become deeply ensconced in the everyday understanding of femininity. As contrast, I also address the quite original approach proposed by Lillian Rotter, which focuses on female powers of seduction and fantasy.

These essays already contain the most important lines of argument for a psychoanalytic understanding of female psychosexual development. The psychodynamic dimension presented in them is of particular importance. In contemporary theory formation this dimension is regrettably too rarely considered, though it is the bedrock of psychoanalytic thinking. In these contributions by early analysts, the focus is on the (re-) construction of the "destiny of drives", that is, on the course of development of libidinous, sexual cathexes both of one's own body and person as well as of other persons and objects. Such processes can also be seen as reinscriptions. The central juncture in the reinscription of maleness and femaleness is represented by the castration complex, which involves the perception and psychic processing of the difference between the sexes. The primary point of controversy in this earlier debate was the psychic incorporation of the female genitalia, and whether the vagina has significance in early childhood (and if so, what significance), or whether it is only the clitoris that initially fulfils a pleasure-giving function. By contrast, the incorporation of the male genitalia was not mentioned at all in this debate, and at the time was apparently taken for granted. In this context, the envy of the other sex—of the penis, or of the vagina and the ability to give birth—and its various psychic functions, along with the unconscious fantasies that emerge in early childhood and accompany sexual experience throughout life, play important roles. The dimensions of pleasure and gratification have become increasingly neglected in the ensuing psychoanalytic discourse on gender, though they are of central importance with respect to the development of sexuality. In the earlier debate, however, the connection between envy and its functions on the one hand, and infantile pleasure and gratification modes on the other, is presented in some detail in particular by Karen Horney. Another important focus of this debate is the question of the development of female sexual orientation and of gender identity. The theory of a "primary" and innate femaleness is contrasted to the Freudian assumption of a constitutional bisexuality, from which an attempt is subsequently made to conceptualize an independent, "genuinely" female, mode of desire.

This stimulating controversy, which lasted more than a decade, began with Horney's talk at the Berlin congress about the female castration complex (1924). Interestingly, it is not mentioned at all in Ernest Jones's biography of Freud (Jones, 1953–57), though as one of the main actors, Jones, in his essay on the phallic phase (1933), tries to clarify and present a thorough account of the different positions taken.

The main point of departure for Karen Horney's critique was Freud's notion of penis envy, along with its (supposed) central importance for the structuring of female sexuality. Horney (1924) disputes Freud's assumption that a girl's penis envy is, as it were, a natural reaction to her "constitutional inferiority", and develops a psychodynamic explanatory model to make this phenomenon understandable in a different way. In the process, she distinguishes between different forms of penis envy: an early, primary form, as well as a secondary form associated with the Oedipus complex. She sees the most visible expression of primary penis envy in the girl's wish to urinate like a man. That wish has three parts: first, there are exhibitionist and voyeuristic desires, in which the boy, because of the visibility of his genitals, is at an advantage. His sexual curiosity can be legitimately gratified, so to speak, every time he urinates. Second, a urethral-erotic omnipotence fantasy is connected with it, one which arises out of the narcissistic overvaluation of the processes of elimination. And third, suppressed masturbation wishes play a role. In the fantasy of the little girl, the anatomical necessity of the boy to hold his genitals while urinating is the equivalent of permission to masturbate, whereas she herself is usually forbidden to touch her own genitals. It is from this feeling of disadvantage that a denial of her own femininity can develop later, supported by the idea that men enjoy far greater freedom in their sexual lives.

According to Horney, the degree of penis envy resulting from scopophila is particularly significant, because the visibility of the boy's genitals provides him with significant information about his organ, while such information is hidden from the girl: "Just as woman, because her genital organs are hidden, is ever the great riddle for man, so man is an object of lively jealousy for woman precisely on account of the ready visibility of his organ" (1924, p. 53). The result of these considerations is that the girl does not feel primarily inferior, but at most feels disadvantaged in her possibility of gratifying certain partial drives that are especially important during the pre-genital phase. Horney goes a step further in her assessment and regards this not as a subjective feeling of the girl but as an actual disadvantage. Her argument is that only when one awakens to the reality of this disadvantage can one understand penis envy and acknowledge its significance as a "near-necessary phenomenon in the life of the female child".

In the Freudian view, the girl has two ways to overcome the penis envy complex in a manner "advantageous to her". The autoerotic-narcissistic wish to have a penis can, through identification with the mother, lead either to the female yearning for a male (meaning the father) or to the maternal yearning for a child (from the father). Here, it is revealing that both wishes—which often appear to be "natural"—issue from a narcissistic motive, in the sense of "wanting to possess". Identification with the mother produces further characteristic phantasms that Horney summarizes as "female primal fantasies" in the form of rape fantasies. According to Horney, such fantasies, at first regarded by female patients as real incidents, express the total possession of the mother by the father, which the daughter witnesses in an identificatory process. Such love fantasies are contrasted with a rejection in reality that in some cases is experienced as so painful that the daughter feels betrayed or abandoned. In some cases, she even develops doubts about her purchase on reality, and this doubt can spread to all other areas of her life. Such a grave disappointment can lead to giving up the desire for a child along with relinquishing the father; those wishes are replaced by regressive anal ideas and the old desire for a penis. Through this psychodynamic process, Horney makes it clear that penis envy is not the primary trigger for the emergence of neurosis but has other functions, including giving expression to the envy of a child which the mother, rather than the daughter, has received from the father.

Karen Horney expands on these differing psychic functions of penis envy. Thus, she specifies the particular circumstances of the female Oedipus complex that induce a secondary penis envy, and, under certain conditions, a neurotic "castration complex" or "masculinity complex" among women. Basing her conclusions on numerous case studies, Horney sees this secondary penis envy as a defence mechanism that consists in identifying with the father in order to sever the Oedipal tie. The little girl—both disappointed and threatened—relinquishes the Oedipal wishes she directs against her father and instead identifies with him. Horney views this identification as a regression that impedes the development of femininity. Under certain circumstances, such a regressive identification will become solidified over time into a "neurotic masculinity complex". The term "masculinity complex" is misleading, inasmuch as for the female patients concerned, the point is not to be a man but instead to "play the father's part" (Horney, 1924, p. 61). Horney cites a case of a little girl who was disappointed that her mother, rather than the girl herself, had had a child with the father, and who warded off this disappointment by identifying with the father, though this reinforced her (primary) penis envy at the same time.

Horney's arguments make very clear how culturally dominant and effective the binary coding of gender is. Identification with the opposite sex is regarded as regression, or in general as a defence against intolerable wishes, a defence that can solidify in a neurotic manner into pathology. Yet from the perspective of diversifying gender roles and the possibilities for identification, as discussed at the outset of this Chapter, such cross-sex or cross-gender identification takes on a different meaning. It does not necessarily need to be relinquished or appraised as neurotic, but can instead be seen as a "normal" or inevitable phase of development. In these identifications, one can also see the girl's sorrow at her father's rejection, because in sorrow, the lost love object is ordinarily internalized through introjection or identification.

Unlike Freud, Karen Horney did not believe the Oedipus complex of the girl begins with the perception of being "castrated" or that anger at her inadequate equipment drives the girl away from her mother and towards her father. In Horney's view, the Oedipal turn towards the father instead develops from an innate femaleness that passes through different maturation stages. This conviction, one Horney shared with Jones (1935), later brought her much criticism from feminist psychoanalysts like Chodorow (1978) or Mitchell (1974), who denied such "biologism".

Karen Horney saw two "cores" in the female castration complex. One core is the process of identifying with the father and repressing the love for the father that preceded this identification. Thus, she reversed the Freudian argument. It is not penis envy, but rather disappointed love for the father that leads to identifying with him. Only through identification is primary penis envy revived. This psychodynamic is also the basis for the development of female homosexuality, in Horney's view: "To play the father's part always amounts also to desiring the mother in some sense" (Horney, 1924, p. 61). However, she assigns same sex desire to homosexual development, and does not regard it as part of every female's development, though given her line of argument, that certain is conceivable.

The father's rejection is connected to massive guilt feelings on the part of the girl, due to her incestuous fantasies. Incest and castration fantasies thus are connected in another manner. The second "core" of the female castration complex, according to Horney, is the girl's basic fantasy "of having suffered castration through the love-relation with the father" (ibid., p. 63), so to speak, as a punishment for incest. This female fantasy is highly significant. These desired fantasies of castration, simultaneously accompanied by feelings of fear and guilt, are warded off by the opposite illusion, namely of having a penis. In clinical terms, these castration fantasies are revealed on the one hand through antagonistic attitudes towards men, in part in the sense of devaluation and in part in the sense of wanting to castrate or cripple (ibid.,). On the other hand, they often take the form of a fear of "not being built right" in the genital area, a feeling of "soreness" or of other genital sensations experienced as unpleasant or abnormal. In the latter cases, these symptoms can be ascribed the function of confirming the castration as having already taken place. Therefore, they serve to alleviate the feelings of guilt as well as the fear of an impending castration. As an expression of unconscious memory, these symptoms both preserve the suppressed love and also bear witness, in some manner, to the reality of this love relationship—which might make the tenacity with which many female patients cling to it more understandable.

Karen Horney saw the point of departure for the development of homosexuality as well as for the castration complex, in both sexes, in the identification with the parent of the opposite sex: The man's fear of castration corresponds to the woman's desire for a penis. The analogy between fear and desire, however, is not symmetrical in both sexes. Nevertheless, hidden behind the man's castration *fear* is a castration *desire*, but one much more strongly repressed than the woman's desire for a penis. For one, this is because it touches on very deep fears of being punished and can be made a reality only by inflicting the most massive bodily harm, and for another, likely because it stands diametrically opposed to the social hierarchy of the sexes.

Karen Horney was the first author who drew attention to these various issues so fundamental to female development. But for Freud, by contrast, these considerations were unacceptable. One can only speculate what the reasons were: he may have categorically rejected Horney's assertion that an independent, libidinous, female sexuality exists. For in his view, femininity arises secondarily from phallic monism. The girl develops her Oedipal wishes vis-à-vis her father precisely because of the fantasy that she has been castrated. Freud regarded castration fantasies as the cause of Oedipal desires, while Horney saw them as the consequence.

Freud initially responded to Karen Horney's propositions with two essays: "Dissolution of the Oedipus Complex" (1924d) and "Some Psychical Consequences of the Anatomical Distinction between the Sexes" (1925j). In the first, there is a significant shift in Freud's theorizing; for the first time, he states that there are differences in the Oedipal development of boys and girls. Until that point, and most recently in *The Ego and the Id* (1923b), he assumed a largely analogous development of the two sexes. It is also interesting that for the first time, Freud makes a clear statement about the origin of the Oedipus complex here, as "a phenomenon which is determined and laid down by heredity and which is bound to pass away according to programme" (1924d, p. 174). In the boy it passes away, as described above, through the threat of castration. In the girl, by contrast, the material is "far more obscure and full of gaps" (ibid., p. 177). Even though a phallic organization, a castration complex, a super-ego, and so forth are ascribed to the girl as well, Freud emphasizes that the "feminist demand for equal rights for the sexes does not take us far, for the morphological distinction is bound to find expression in differences of psychical development: 'Anatomy is Destiny'" (ibid., p. 178).

With this, Freud quite fundamentally dissents from Karen Horney's line of argument. In his view, the girl perceives that she has been short-changed and explains this lack or deficit by assuming that she also had a penis at one time but lost it through castration. In girls and boys "the essential difference thus comes about that the girl accepts castration as an accomplished fact, whereas the boy fears the possibility of its occur-rence" (1924d, p. 178). As compensation for the loss, the girl develops a wish to have a child: "She (the girl) slips—along the line of a sym-bolic equation, one might say—from the penis to a baby. Her Oedipus complex culminates in a desire, which is long retained, to receive a baby from her father as a gift—to bear him a child" (ibid., p. 178). The impossibility of fulfilling this wish leads to a gradual abandonment of the Oedipus complex, but the wishes for a penis and a child remain strongly cathected in the unconscious, and play their part "to prepare the female creature for her later sexual role" (ibid., p. 179).

Using such arguments, Freud affirms the social hierarchy of the sexes, lending it scientific credence even when he admits in the end that his insights into female development remained "unsatisfactory, incom-plete and vague" (ibid., p. 179). Correspondingly, this is the point at which the criticism which started with Karen Horney and has lasted for decades begins, with the imputation of "inferiority" and the girl's unconscious efforts to compensate for it.

But let us first glance at the second of Freud's articles, "Some Psychical Consequences of the Anatomical Distinction between the Sexes" (1925j). Here one finds a reformulation of Freud's notions about the psychology of women, which he uses to systematically link to several earlier obser-vations. Of particular importance in this article is the (just as frequently criticized) thesis of the dual change in women's sexual development. One is the shift from the clitoris to the vagina as the pre-eminent sex organ, and the other is the shift in the sexual object away from the mother, as the primary reference person, to the father.

Freud regards the turning away from the mother as a result of penis envy. The girl makes the mother responsible for her own "disadvantage" and for equipping her with "inferior" genitalia, and in her disappointment turns away from her mother and towards her father. Freud also regards the shift in the pre-eminent sexual organ as a precondition for mature female sexuality: "the elimination of clitoridal sexuality is a necessary precondition for the development of femininity," because "masturbation, at all events of the clitoris, is a masculine activity" (1925j, p. 255). In that respect, there is often a strong counter-current against masturbation following the emergence of penis envy, which leads Freud to the conviction that "masturbation [is] further removed from the nature of women than of men" (ibid., p. 255). In this essay, Freud also discusses the difference between boys and girls with respect to the fading away of the Oedipus complex. The most important difference probably lies in the estimation that among boys, the Oedipus complex completely dissolves, smashed by the shock of the castration threat. The libidinal cathexes are abandoned and desexualized so that "in ideal cases, the Oedipus complex exists no longer, even in the unconscious; the super-ego has become its heir" (ibid., p. 257). Even though, at the end of the essay, Freud points out "that all human individuals, as a result of their bisexual disposition and of cross-inheritance, combine in themselves both masculine and feminine characteristics, so that pure masculinity and femininity remain theoretical constructions of uncertain content" (ibid., p. 258), his views have had a lasting effect not only on psychoanalytic theories about masculinity and femininity, but also on notions of what men and women actually are, and what they are like. This, too, has given rise to massive critique.

As one of Freud's first critics, Karen Horney reacted to his persistent failure to understand her approach, a failure that is quite clear in the two essays already noted, though in the latter he specifically refers to her. In her subsequent essay, "The Flight from Womanhood" (1926), Horney reacts in a manner one can read as sharply polemical: the

> "psychology of women hitherto does actually represent a deposit of the desires and disappointments of men. ... The present analytical picture of feminine development (whether that picture be correct or not) differs in no case by a hair's breadth from the typical ideas which the boy has of the girl" (ibid., p. 326).

She presents a table in which she compares the ideas a boy has of womanhood during the phallic phase with the ideas current in psychoanalysis, and comes to the conclusion that to a large extent, they overlap:

> "Further, we observe that men are evidently under a greater necessity to depreciate women than conversely. The realization that the dogma of the inferiority of women had its origin in an unconscious male tendency could only dawn upon us after a doubt had arisen whether in fact this view were justified in reality". (ibid., p. 331)

With reference to Simmel, Horney examines the effect of a male-influenced culture on psychoanalytic theory construction, proposing a method repeatedly followed for many years in other studies of femininity (see Schlesier, 1981; Rohde-Dachser, 1991).

Beginning with the observation that to date only the genital differences between men and women had been taken into consideration and not their differing contributions to reproduction, Karen Horney formulated a thesis of motherhood envy on the part of boys—the male counterpart to penis envy in girls—and contends that it is too seldom acknowledged as a dynamic factor. In analyses with male patients, it was evident how intense this envy of pregnancy, giving birth, and motherhood could be, as well as the envy of having breasts and of breast-feeding. In contrast to the penis envy of the girl, male envy is apparently more successfully sublimated. According to Horney, it is a significant impulse behind the creation of cultural values. No similar compensatory efforts are forthcoming from penis envy, however, either because it is less strong overall or because it is "less successfully" processed. The more intense male envy can be traced back to the fact that the woman is anatomically at a disadvantage only in the pre-genital phase (see above), but not in genital organization, while her part in reproduction is clearly larger. By contrast, female envy "in the best case" largely merges into the desire for a man and a child, and in the process, loses a major impulse directed towards sublimation efforts. In less fortunate cases, female envy is burdened with massive feelings of guilt that block a constructive approach to dealing with it.

This idealization of motherhood, together with its biological presuppositions, has earned Horney criticism from many quarters (among others, Chodorow, 1978). In her basic biological orientation, she also opposed Freud, whom she accused of using the tender affection of the girl for her father "to explain psychologically the biological principle of heterosexual attraction" (Horney 1926, p. 332). This basic orientation also casts a different light again on the previously cited reflections on homosexuality, which now take on the character of the "unnatural". On this point, therefore, Horney falls short of Freud, who regarded both homosexuality and heterosexuality as in need of psychological explanation.

In this second essay, Horney (1926) expands on her views of the female castration complex. She agrees with Freud that in women, the development of object love is always the fruit of penis envy, though she also has a different idea about how this develops. At heart, masculine desires serve as a defence against libidinous aspirations regarding the father. Penis envy in that sense serves to suppress "female desires" or acts as a barrier to their being discovered. It mitigates the girl's guilty feelings arising from her incestuous wishes and alleviates her fears of the revenge her mother might take. Often, it is not only the father who is abandoned as a love object. The girl may also shy entirely away from taking on a female role, a reaction called the "flight from femininity". Horney also regards the girl's castration fantasies as a secondary development, a by-product of this flight. In fleeing, female genital fear is translated, as it were, into male language, with a castration fantasy expressing fear of vaginal damage. According to Horney, such a translation also has the advantage that a girl's insecurity with respect to her anatomical realities, which finds expression in similarly diffuse fears of punishment, is then transformed into a concrete idea.

A year later, at the Innsbruck congress, Karen Horney received support from Ernest Jones for her arguments. In his article "The Early Development of Female Sexuality" (1927), based on five long-term analyses with homosexual women, Jones rejects Freud's thesis of a phallic phase in girls; like Horney, he regards femaleness as primary, meaning innate: "Freud's 'phallic phase' in girls is probably a secondary, defensive construction rather than a true developmental stage" (ibid., p. 472). Furthermore, Jones points to a wide-spread misconception with respect to the meaning of castration. Castration, which by the way refers to the penis alone, does not mean the complete abolition of sexuality. In fact, some of his male patients desired castration for decidedly erotic reasons. Nevertheless, the fear at the heart of all neurosis centres on the permanent extinction of sexuality, of the ability to experience sexual pleasure. For this fear, Jones uses the Greek term "aphanisis". Clinically, it is often expressed as thoughts of castration or of death.

Following Jones, castration fantasy is a special case of aphanisis, one that is structurally similar in both sexes but can be expressed differently; among women, it can also be expressed in the fear of being abandoned. The non-gratification of sexual desires evokes the fear of aphanisis in the child, and thus is equivalent to the fear of failure. At the same time, it evokes feelings of shame, which Jones sees as coming more from "inner" than from "outer" prohibitions. Jones describes the little girl's fears that her Oedipal desires regarding her father will incur her mother's rivalry. Like Horney, Jones assumes that vaginal sensations are already present very early in the life of a girl.

In a further conference paper about the "Early Stages of the Oedipus Conflict" (1928), Melanie Klein also noted early vaginal sensations among girls, on the basis of analyses involving children aged three to six. They respond directly to the loss weaning represents with an Oedipal shift towards the father. The withdrawal of the breast at the end of the first year of life, or at the beginning of the second, triggers Oedipal strivings. These are reinforced by anal "losses" or "frustrations" in the course of toilet-training. The anatomical difference between the sexes determines the subsequent course of sexual development. The boy moves from the oral and anal to the genital stage, and to the penetration aim connected with the penis, in the course of which he changes both libidinal position and aim, and as a result can retain the love-object. The girl, when shifting to the genital libido position, by contrast retains the receptive aim carried over from orality, which previously led to una-voidable disappointment with her mother. Hence, the girl inevitably feels a desire to receive her father's penis. At the same time, the onset of these Oedipal wishes leads to guilty feelings and the fear of castration. Melanie Klein, in these reflections, agrees with Ferenczi and Abraham, who, using concepts such as "sphincter morality", move guilt feelings into the pre-genital phase as well, unlike Freud, who places the forma-tion of conscience at the end of the Oedipus complex. Klein, however, also regards these pre-genital expressions of guilty feelings as effects of the Oedipus conflict, which presuppose the introjection of the Oedipal objects, that is, the creation of the superego. For Klein, the need to move the Oedipus complex forward from the first years of the child's life was a consequence of childhood fantasies expressed by children who were her patients, fantasies that could not be plausibly explained with exist-ing theories. Thus, it is not comprehensible to her, for example, that a four-year-old raises the phantasm of "devouring, cutting, castrating parents", though such a phantasm is characteristic of a one-year-old.

Remarkable in this argument is that Klein enlists neither the psychoanalytic concepts of regression nor those of *Nachträglichkeit* to explain her findings, which would have made such an extensive shift forward in time unnecessary. The central difference with Freud's concept of sexuality, however, lies in her merging desire, from the beginning, with feelings of guilt. She assumes every loss or frustration—prototypical are oral and anal frustrations—is understood as punishment, which perforce results in guilty feelings and hatred.

Melanie Klein also hypothesizes a developmental phase in both sexes, the essence of which is early identification with the mother. In this "femininity phase", anal-sadistic fantasies of acquiring the contents of the womb dominate. In addition to the wish for a child and the fantasy of robbing, there is also jealousy of anticipated siblings and the wish to destroy those siblings in the mother's womb. With respect to the desire for a child, the boy feels deprived and attempts to compensate for that deprivation. In the process, the special combination of the wish for a child with the drive to acquire knowledge allows him to engage in a "displacement onto the intellectual plane". The fears associated with the feminine phase drive him to identify with his father. For Klein, a favourable course for the boy in this phase is to successfully distance himself from femininity and suppress or over-compensate for "female desires", decisive for reaching "full potency" and the "genital position". The dichotomy between the sexes dominates Kleinian conceptualizations as well, and traditional gender role stereotypes are supported by the existence of anatomical potential, such as the ability to give birth. The notion of letting go of femininity was later recapitulated by Ralph Greenson (1968) in his much-cited concept of "dis-identification". Also noteworthy is Melanie Klein's assessment— not further supported—that it is only the suppression of femininity that allows for an unimpeded sexual functioning of the man. I see this exactly the other way around, as I show in terms of the integration of inner and outer genitality.

Like Helene Deutsch (1925) before her, Melanie Klein also starts with the assumption of a shift of oral libido to the genitals as the completion of female genital development. Unlike Deutsch, she does not see the girl's turn to the penis as paving the way to the vagina, but just the reverse. The turn to the father is a result of the oral, receptive aim of the female genitalia. As a further reason for turning to the father, Klein sees the girl's envy and hatred of the mother, because she possesses the penis of the father. In the girl, these fantasies of robbing and destroying also accompany identification with her mother. The strength of her fear of her mother then determines whether the identification can be maintained or must be abandoned in favour of identification with the father. The girl's castration complex is activated by the connection between the Oedipal conflict and the drive for knowledge. The absence of a penis is experienced as punishment and leads to a renewed hatred of the mother, which in turn is accompanied by feelings of guilt.

In his essay on the "Phallic Phase", Jones (1933) tried to summarize the central lines of argument in the controversy over female sexual development, and in the main he supported Melanie Klein's line of thought. Jones sees the key conflict of the boy's phallic phase as the desire to be a woman, which is unavoidably connected with castration anxiety. The "feminine stage" is alimentary and originally oral: wish gratification at this stage precedes male development. Frustration and loss leads to a fixation on the female at the oral or anal level, and "although originating in anxiety (it) may become intensely eroticised in perverse forms" (ibid., p. 11). Jones draws attention to the important point that in the imagination of the pre-Oedipal child, the parents are not yet separated into father and mother. In Melanie Klein's formulation, there is a "combined parental imago". In this phantasm, features of mother and father are combined and only later become separated into "male/masculine" and "female/feminine". It is at this point that the phenomenon of *Nachträglichkeit* can be seen most clearly.

According to Jones, "the typical phallic stage in the boy is a neurotic compromise rather than a natural evolution in sexual development" (ibid., p. 15). In this phase, the boy gives up the masculine aim of penetration, including his interest in the interior of the mother's body, and puts all his energies into securing the existence of his penis or of the mother's penis. Karen Horney also emphasizes the boy's inhibited desire to penetrate, seeing it as an important clue to his wish to be female. In her view, aside from this inhibition, the fear of the vulva is characteristic: the major source of this fear is the threat posed to the boy's sense of self by the feeling that his penis may not be large enough to satisfy his mother. He believes that is reason for her rejecting him. The fear of ridicule, the deep feeling of humiliation and inadequacy, leads him back to the "female desires", which are in turn connected to castration anxiety. Jones, by contrast, regards the feelings of inadequacy and the associated feelings of shame as secondary: to a greater degree, the boy fears the revenge of his mother for his alimentary sadism. This is a projection: the mother wants to have everything that is important and now wants to rob him, as she was robbed by him previously.

In the girl, by contrast, the early fear of her mother and the hatred directed at her mother are now transferred to her father; there these feelings are concentrated in the notion of the penis. A projection takes place, as in the boy's case, with the girl's sadism directed at the male sex organ. Jones, like Horney and Klein before him, assumes that the female/feminine and alloerotic is primary (in contrast to the male/masculine and autoerotic), and dominates in this early phase. Thus, Jones also casts doubt on Freud's conviction that clitoral sexuality is a form of male sexuality.

At this point I want to only briefly sketch the position taken by Helene Deutsch and subsequently by Marie Bonaparte as well; both endorse Freud's views in the main and cite their own experiences in conducting analyses as supporting evidence. For both, "female masochism"—following Deutsch, "the most elementary force in feminine mental life" (Deutsch, 1930, p. 60)—plays a central role in connection with sexuality. As a result of this masochism, in the view of both Deutsch and Bonaparte (1953) women endure rather than enjoy coitus. In addition, such masochism also serves to prepare women for the pain to be suffered during childbirth.

Freud (1924c) had already linked masochism with femaleness, distinguishing three types: erogenous, feminine and moral masochism. The first, pleasure in pain, forms the basis for the other two. The last, the most important form, is also described as an unconscious feeling of guilt. Masculine masochism, by contrast, is the most accessible through observation, and provides the fewest puzzles, according to Freud. In his exposition, Freud refers to fantasies of male patients that often correspond to a real staging of masochistic perversions. The "manifest content is of being gagged, bound, painfully beaten, whipped, in some way maltreated, forced into unconditional obedience, dirtied and debased" (1924c, p. 162). It is not a large step to then suggest that the masochist wants to be treated like a small, helpless, dependent child, especially one who has misbehaved. In cases where the masochistic fantasies are subject to a stronger psychic processing, one can observe that the person in these fantasies is set "in a characteristically female situation; they signify, that is, being castrated, or copulated with, or giving birth to a baby" (ibid., p. 162). It was for that reason Freud chose, as he says, the designation "feminine masochism", although it exhibits considerably more elements from infantile sexual life.

Another characteristic of feminine masochism, according to Freud, is passivity. In the Oedipus complex, the girl adopts a passive sexual attitude towards the father. In the article "A Child is Being Beaten" (Freud, 1919e), Freud regards the girl's wish to be beaten by her father as a defence against her desire for such a passive sexual relationship. The sexual wishes directed at the father lead to feelings of guilt, which are tempered through regression to the anal-sadistic, punitive form of eroticism. With this argument, Freud makes clear that he does not regard submissiveness and passivity as the actual Oedipal goals of the girl, but rather sees them as a reaction to guilt feelings that are prompted by sexual desire (Benjamin, 1986). With this reflection, Jessica Benjamin takes the wind out of the sails of critics of the Freudian perspective. As there is no plausible reason why girls should be more inclined to feel guilt than boys, one must assume passive sexual goals in both sexes, as well as non-gender-specific ways of processing the guilt feelings associated with these sexual goals. Comparison of submissiveness/masochism and castration anxiety as psychically equivalent ways of processing guilt feelings shows that such processing need not be gender-specific. One can observe castration anxieties in girls and women as well as masochistic wishes for subservience in boys and men.

But back to Deutsch and Bonaparte. Both take Freud's considerations a step further, as they also noted extensive fantasies of submissiveness and rape in their female patients. They attempt to account for these fantasies by resorting to an explanation based on penis envy. The wish for a penis is at the heart of submissiveness fantasies, they contend. The decisive step to masochism is taken by the girl, by contrast, if she relinquishes this desire and the active-aggressive sexual attitude associated with it. The wish for a penis is transformed into the wish to be castrated by the father through penetration.

Helene Deutsch's implausible and much-criticized conclusion with respect to female masochism—that women derive masochistic pleasure from the pain of childbirth—results, according to Jessica Benjamin (1986), from inadequate differentiation between actually experienced pain and the symbolic meaning of the fantasy of pain (on Benjamin's conceptualization of female masochism, see below).

Also heavily criticized are Helene Deutsch's notions of female pleasure. In her view, "woman's sexual life (is) characterized by frigidity without entailing any such consequences as would upset her mental balance and give rise to neurosis" (1930, p. 60). This is possible as a result of the complementarity of sexuality and motherliness: A large part of genitality is absorbed by reproductive functions and thus sublimated, as it were. However, Deutsch emphasizes that the type of woman in whom this form of sublimation is successful is gradually disappearing; the "modern woman", by contrast, is neurotic if she is frigid.

Another, far more differentiated picture of Deutsch's thinking is provided by her studies of female adolescence (1944). While she accepts the controversial Freudian notions of womanhood, she also examines the conflicts connected with adoption of the culturally ordained female gender role. Unlike a number of explicit critics of the Freudian position, such as Marie Langer (1992), Deutsch also avoids the danger of an uncritical idealization of fertility and motherhood as the fulfilment of womanhood.

The contribution to the psychoanalytic discourse on *Weiblichkeit* made by the Hungarian analyst Lillian Rotter was more marginal—wholly undeservedly, for in her essay "A Contribution to the Psychology of Female Sexuality" (1934), published in German in the *Internationale Zeitschrift für Psychoanalyse*, she embarked on a highly original, self-confident, and helpful critical examination of Freud's idea of femininity. At the centre of her argument are the two Freudian theses of the change of object and the change of primary erogenous zones. Lillian Rotter ties two different observations together in her argument: On the one hand, the girl, disappointed by her mother through unavoidable frustrations and losses (brought about by weaning, toilet-training, sibling envy, etc.), tries to invest her libido elsewhere. In that process, the interest of her father, brother, or playmates fits with her wishes. On the other hand, during the phase of infantile sexual curiosity, she discovers—while "playing doctor" or in similar games—conspicuous changes in the penis of her male playmates. This often takes place under circumstances that led her to conclude that she herself has caused the erection. The fantasy of having brought about this change in a magical fashion—through touching or just by being present—leads her also to think the penis belongs to her and is within her sphere of influence. Furthermore, she probably senses the arousal of her clitoris at the same time, which may cause her to fantasize that her own sensation is producing such conspicuous changes in the outside world. She then regards this part of the exterior world as something that belongs to her own ego, say, in analogy to the unity of mother's breast and nursing infant, because the equating of breast and penis is familiar to the unconscious. In this way, the penis, as a mental image, enters into the girl's sphere of influence, like a machine that she can steer and that is subject to her will: "The penis would thus actually be the visible executive organ of her feelings and her will" (1934, p. 24, translation for this edition).

According to Rotter, seduction situations of a clearly sexual nature are therefore not necessary for a little girl to become aware of her effect on the opposite sex. The two- or three-year-old child can already recognize by various signs whether father, brother, or grandfather is turning his interest towards her. Thus everyday situations, such as crawling into her parents' bed in the morning, sitting or riding on her father's knee, and similar games let her observe "that the closeness of her body to her father or grandfather evokes various signs of pleasure or arousal: loud laughter, blushing, shining eyes—all of that is directed at her" (ibid., p. 26, translation for this edition).

Rotter sees this as the path that leads the girl from the mother who has disappointed her to the father, that is, to the opposite sex. The girl's behaviour, however, is far from passive here, as Freud assumes, but instead decidedly active. Further, that can also find expression in her extending her phantasmal power of control to the entire individual, rather than confining this fantasy only to his penis: "My penis is my father or brother, I can do whatever I want to with it" (ibid., p. 26, translation for this edition).

The fantasy that the penis actually is made part of the female body can, in adult sexuality, be translated into reality during coitus. The fantasy makes clear, additionally, that the aim of the woman's drive, as with the man's, is an active one, and—among other things—consists in a kind of force of attraction or suction that acts to draw the penis into her body.

These considerations cast yet another light on the much-discussed topic of penis envy. For example, they make understandable what is often observed in clinical practice: female patients' tenacious clinging, in their unconscious, to the idea that they have a penis. Previous theories always left unclear where they actually keep this penis. Following Rotter, one could say that its locus is in men close to them, and also describe how that comes about. Thus, it becomes more understandable why the loss of the father or the man in general means "real castration for the woman" (ibid., p. 27, translation for this edition).

This illuminates a further phenomenon: women often interpret the impotence of their lover as their own failure, or react with a feeling of being profoundly narcissistically wounded. They regard impotence, so to speak, as proof of their own insufficient seductive powers, from which the feeling of being "inferior" and "castrated" can arise. Conversely, one observes a narcissistic confirmation of their powers of seduction lightly veiled in the "typical female day-dream of the man who is ready to do anything for her" (ibid., p. 27, translation for this edition). This day-dream, which leaves out the seduction scene, has the additional advantage that it spares the woman guilty feelings that are often the dark underside of seduction. Rotter illustrates these feelings of guilt with a sequence from an analysis in which the female patient remembers a long-forgotten scene that is typical for such situations:

> She sees herself lying in bed with her little brother, they are alone in the room, the mother has gone out. In play, she touches the penis of her brother; suddenly, she is stricken with great fear, she cries and calls out, but no one comes to her aid. So she crawls out of bed and climbs onto a chair in order to touch, with her hand, the holy scroll (the Jewish mezuzah) nailed on the doorframe. Her father had sometimes lifted her up to it and claimed that touching this holy scroll would heal everything. (ibid., p. 23, translation for this edition)

This patient felt guilty towards her brother all her life, and rationalized it in every possible way, but without ever remotely connecting it with a seduction scene.

The obverse of these scenes—being seduced—is often found in analysis with male patients. Rotter formulates it as the impression that "all analyses of men abound with accusations of being seduced by the woman, but that far too often was interpreted as a projection of the wishes of the patient" (ibid., p. 28, translation for this edition). The little boy undoubtedly feels that something is happening to his body without his doing anything, often even against his will, and ascribes it to the magical, uncanny effect of girls and women, something that is a recurring theme in fairy tales and myths as well. Particularly during adolescence, the male feeling of being able to do almost nothing about the obvious visibility of their sexual arousal is often accompanied by considerable shame. The feeling of powerlessness, of being completely at the mercy of women, often leads to massive anger and desperation. Rotter wonders whether behind the complaints "that women cannot love, are mendacious, and are baffling—is concealed, in the final analysis, in the doubt expressed by one boy in analysis: 'What do women feel with, or can they feel at all?'—that is to say, if they have no penis and he thus can see no feelings, meaning no erections" (ibid., p. 29, translation for this edition). It is remarkable, despite all the obvious changes in the relationship between the sexes, how little has changed in the last seventy years: these are the same complaints that can be heard in analyses even today.

Lillian Rotter makes a final interesting observation about women's passivity. In her view, when women remain passive, it is evidence of a congenial ability to empathize, expressing the sentiment: "Look, I'm the weak one, I flee from you; you're the strong one, the seducer—don't fear me!" (ibid., p. 29, translation for this edition). She sees this as a very effective way of allaying the man's fears of the woman.

Taking stock

To provide an overview, I have summarized the differences of opinion about female and male sexual development in the following table.

Both empirical and theoretical arguments are marshalled in the debates over such issues, but in this case they cannot be decided empirically. Neither direct observation of children nor indirect analysis of adults can yield criteria that would show the soundness of one or the other position. Far more decisive, as is true of many other theories, is the plausibility of the assumptions and whether internal coherence exists, whether the individual assumptions cohere into a consistent theoretical structure. Unfortunately, there seems to be no comprehensive counter-proposal to the Freudian theory of psychosexual development.

Freud, Deutsch, and others	Horney, Jones, Klein (in part), and others
Concept of a constitutional bisexuality:	Concept of an unambiguous, innate sex:
– early "masculine phase" in both sexes – femininity arises from the perception of sexual difference, that is, of castration	– early feminine phase in both sexes – femininity is regarded as primary and innate
Conceptualization of female genitalia:	Conceptualization of female genitalia:
– clitoris as a "masculine" organ – vaginal sensations only become significant with onset of puberty – the primary erogenous zone needs to shift from the clitoris to the vagina	– clitoris as an integral part of the female genitalia—existence and significance of vaginal sensations since early childhood – no shift is necessary, as the vagina is significant to begin with
Pre-genital development in boys and in girls:	Pre-genital development in boys and in girls:
– identical in both sexes – castration complex and penis envy as a necessary part of development	– sex/gender-specific – castration complex and penis envy as a secondary development or defence mechanism
Penis envy in the girl:	Penis envy in the girl:
as unavoidable envy due to "inferior" anatomical equipment	a defence against the incestuous love for the father or rivalry with the mother
Castration complex:	Castration complex:
Results, in both sexes, from the perception of "inferior" genitalia	In the boy, the result of a "wish for femaleness" or "female wishes"; fear of castration in both sexes as a special case of "aphanisis"

(Continued)

Continued.

Freud, Deutsch, and others	Horney, Jones, Klein (in part), and others
Conceptualization of the Oedipus complex:	Conceptualization of the Oedipus complex:
– begins in the phallic phase with the perception of castration	– begins in conjunction with oral refusal (e.g., after weaning)
– the girl's turning away from, or hatred of, her mother because she has "poorly equipped" her daughter	– diffuse hatred of the mother, which seeks expression through the wish for a penis
– the girl's turning to her father is the result of disappointment with her mother	– the girl's turning to her father is seen as the reason for the desire to have a penis, which serves as a defence against this incestuous love
– the wish for a child can be understood as a compensation for the lack of a penis	– the wish for a child as an expression of the "normal" female wish to incorporate the penis and transform it into a child
– significance of the fear of castration: in the boy, the Oedipus conflict is resolved via castration anxiety; in the girl, it is the prerequisite for the onset of the Oedipus complex	– in both sexes, the fear of castration triggers the Oedipus complex

His contemporary critics appear, in the main, to have worked doggedly and persistently on Freud's concepts, and in most cases their critique focused only on individual aspects rather than the whole edifice.

In reading these early texts, one is especially struck by the efforts of critics to distance themselves from Freud. Zenia Odes Fliegel (1973) investigated the significance, in the psychoanalytic community of the 1920s, of the debates over sexual development, and the controversy regarding female sexual development certainly appears to have helped create an independent psychoanalytic movement in London. Jones, in particular, kept emphasizing the differences between London and Vienna analysts. He also supported Melanie Klein, who became prominent through her observations and analyses of young children. This effort at distancing may also be at the basis of the overemphasis on hatred and on the sadistic in Kleinian psychoanalysis, in an effort to set an independent, dark image of how children develop against the libidinous development of the child that was Freud's focus.

Also noteworthy in this controversy, in my view, is that closer examination reveals almost no differences concerning the clinical findings. Rather, the disagreements result from the interpretation of those findings. The common empirical ground, however, is barely noted by the participants, which is indicative of the efforts by the one side to mark themselves off and by the other side to protect their theoretical system. It also is unclear what "observations" mean when the reference is to unconscious fantasies, or what counts as "clinical evidence". Beyond the fact that nothing generated in analyses speaks for itself but needs interpretation, all participants in this debate legitimate their findings with reference to clinical material. Kohut, decades later, justified Freud's refusal to change his views on female sexuality as "much more likely due to his reliance on clinical evidence—as it was then open to him" (Fliegel, 1973: 398 footnote, citing Kohut). Quite apart from the problem whether competing conceptualizations could be "proven" and thereby resolved through clinical findings, the question is what certain assumptions mean for psychoanalytic theory as a whole. Despite all the criticism of Freud's assumptions, their consequences for psychoanalytic theory as a whole have received almost no attention thus far. In my view, this is most likely a key reason for the unrelated juxtaposition of the most diverse concepts and theoretical approaches. Rohde-Dachser (1991) convincingly demonstrated that Freud's patriarchal definition of femininity influenced all of psychoanalytic theory and that the notion of *Geschlecht* embedded in it was subsequently reproduced in the most varied theories. However, it cannot be assumed that changes in the conceptualization of the sexes and genders had no effect on overall theory. Beyond doubt, comprehensive, systematic thinking remains to be done in this regard.

I would like to use two of Freud's conceptualizations—monosexuality and bisexuality—to illustrate how significant such carefully considered thinking about the entire theoretical edifice would be. Much criticism of Freud focuses on his monosexual conceptualization of the phallic stage, one characterized by the existence of a single sex—namely the male. Misunderstandings may have arisen in the reception of this notion. Thus, the alternative confronting the child in this phase is not the choice between penis and vagina, but between having a sexual organ and not having one, meaning being castrated. Therefore, the contrast is not between two anatomical realities, such as penis and vagina, but between the presence and the absence of such a reality. The structuring function of the phallic phase is of utmost importance, and is lost if this phase, as Horney, Jones and Klein argue, is regarded merely as a secondary defence mechanism. Laplanche and Pontalis (1973) point out that in Freudian thought the "phallus" is a detachable, changeable object that can be found in differing, metaphorical transformations. Thus Freud (1917c), for example, suggests a number of symbolic equivalences in which the individual terms are interchangeable (penis = faeces = child = gift). What they have in common is that they are detachable from the subject and can pass from one person to the next.

I also regard the implicit abandoning of the concept of (constitutional) bisexuality, in the course of the criticism of Freud's notions of *Weiblichkeit*, as being of considerable importance. Evidently, it stands in the way of conceptualizing an independent *Weiblichkeit*, or at least it seems to make it more difficult. Though it may sound paradoxical, critics have not addressed cultural heteronormativity and the hierarchy of the sexes, but have instead reproduced and promoted these views. Freud's primacy of the male is merely countered by a primacy of the female, and nothing is gained by it. The interrelation between male and female development is then lost, something at least discussed in the old concept of bisexuality. Noteworthy also is that anatomy, or the emphasis in psychoanalytic discourse placed on anatomical distinctions between men and women, paradoxically became genuinely significant only in the course of the feminist critique. Until Horney criticized it, Freud assumed a symmetrical development of infantile sexuality, oriented of course to the infantile sexual development of the boy. It was only afterwards that anatomy became destiny. Psychoanalytic authors thereby reversed the trend of feminist perspectives in other areas that had seen *Geschlecht* not as "innate" but instead as socially produced.

I regard a further aspect of the aforementioned critique of Freud's ideas as problematic as well, namely that it addresses only specific or individual aspects but has yet to produce a systematic, coherent account of female and male sexual development. In the essays discussed above, female development is basically seen as unrelated to male development, and one is often left in doubt whether a particular assumption is meant to apply to both sexes or not. This is not insignificant, for when one examines, say, Melanie Klein's argument that the trauma of weaning leads a girl to turn her attention to her father's penis, one can ask whether the same would also be true of her brother. Under such an assumption, sexual desires directed at the father, such as the "fellatory fantasy", would be seen as an integral part of male development. As logical as this may sound, it is not explicitly described, as far as I can discover, either in Klein or in her successors. It also remains unclear whether it makes sense to describe increasingly backdated experiences of a child as the model for later experience, or whether the idea of *Nachträglichkeit*, which plays a role neither for Klein nor for Jones, would not provide a more suitable conceptualization.

New wine in old bottles? The resumption of the discussion since the 1960s

The animated debates of the 1920s and 1930s were followed by a decades-long hiatus. Jewish analysts were persecuted and driven out of Germany and Nazi-occupied Europe, and during exile and while psychoanalysis was being (re-)constructed, discussion of femininity and masculinity subsided in psychoanalytic discourse. Other topics grew in importance. For the most part, Freud's views were embedded in mainstream psychoanalysis, while feminist critiques came more from outside, and were directed against affirmation and stabilization of traditional gender roles. It was only at the end of the 1960s that the discussion resumed, in the context of the second women's movement. Many of the old positions and arguments were "reopened" in the course of these debates.

An inventive and valuable reading of penis envy can be found in Maria Torok's work (1964). She sees this envy in conjunction with autonomy and dependence with respect to the child-mother relationship. She points out, both simply and convincingly, that it is not very helpful to the analytic process to take a symptom, such a manifest expression of envy, at face value. Doing so, in her view, blocks all prospects of gaining access to the unconscious wishes and fantasies that underlie it. The task of analysis, which "is to bring back to light a genuine but forbidden desire lying buried beneath the guise of envy" (1994, p. 42), cannot be addressed by referring to some kind of "constitutional inferiority". Torok comes to the conclusion that "though a seeming paradox at first, the fact is that in 'penis envy' nothing matters less than the penis itself" (ibid., p. 44). The "penis" in this case is "invented to camouflage a desire", and to the degree that the deficiency that caused it is resolved, penis envy also recedes. What is characteristic of a girl's envy is the idealization of the "penis", which encompasses all that is desirable and worth attaining, all that she herself does not possess, as well as its inaccessibility. On this point, Torok follows the Freudian notion of the "phallus". The penis, the hallmark of the other sex, appropriately enough symbolizes what is unattainable for the girl. To avoid misunderstanding: Torok in this context is not discussing projection processes; a girl does not ascribe to a boy or a man that which she cannot attain. The "penis" stands primarily for itself and is not regarded as the possession of another. The excessive cathexis of the desired object corresponds to the original value of the abandoned desire: "A complex, unconscious speech is concentrated in 'penis envy' and this speech is addressed to the maternal imago" (ibid., p. 49). According to Torok, this discourse is about hatred and anger, about dependence and devaluing the self, about unbearable affects towards the mother that must be denied to avoid losing the loved object. The envy of the idealized penis functions as a "loyalty oath" on the part of the daughter, and in the end serves to quiet the maternal imago. The daughter's aggression is disavowed, so there is nothing that could endanger the mother-daughter relationship.

At the same time, Torok sees penis envy also as an effort by the girl to camouflage her own pleasurable genital experiences. The discovery of the other sex is often connected with a suppressed memory of an orgasm or an orgasmic experience. Though a little girl is always latently occupied with her sex, which is certainly not unknown to her, she must repress it out of concern to please her mother. Through masturbation, she frees herself from her dependence on her mother, who to that point either has granted or denied the child pleasure at will. While Torok argues here at the level of unconscious fantasies, projections, and prohibitions, one can interpret the pleasurable mother-child interaction in a much more concrete manner. In terms of the general theory of seduction, I would like to emphasize that it is not only a matter of "granting" or "forbidding" but rather one of unavoidably, albeit unintentionally, inducing pleasurable genital experiences, such as in the context of infant care. It is significant that these actual experiences are connected with fantasies and thus contribute to an imago of an "all-powerful mother" to whose whims the child is subjected. Torok reports interesting passages from her analyses in which the hand of the female patient plays an important role, a hand experienced as cold, unusable, or not belonging to her own body. Here, too, Torok makes the rather abstract assumption that the hand "represents a means of introjection into the primal scene and always represents the genital organ of the opposite sex" (ibid., p. 49).

In my view, though, it could also be the hand of the mother with whom the female patient fails to identify. Correspondingly, I regard the child's identification with the caring, pleasure-bringing hand(s) of her mother as a pre-condition for satisfactory masturbation. Turning away from the mother through masturbation, like every other step toward autonomy, is an "act of aggression" that triggers guilt feelings in the child. Defining that as the origin of the widespread, unconscious guilt feelings associated with masturbation, which is still seen in many patients, both female and male, strikes me as more convincing than seeking an explanation in some kind of external ban.

According to Torok, the path to genital sexual maturity is already laid out in the orgiastic play of early childhood. In conjunction with orgasm, the child discovers "the power to fantasize our identity with our parents and the power to picture ourselves in all the positions of the primal scene, in accordance with the various levels at which it is apprehended" (ibid., p. 50). If such an experience is inhibited, it results in an "incomplete 'body of one's own' (some might say Body Image) that has as its corollary a world peopled with fragmentary realities" (ibid., p. 50).

That shows how decisive the conflict over autonomy is for sexual experience. The frequently noted connection between sexuality and a sense of guilt does not emerge just from religion or morality but also derives from the child's search for pleasure and gratification, resulting in its increasing independence from its mother.

According to Torok, the unconscious discourse on dependence and autonomy, which is summarized in "penis envy", is structurally relevant both for girls and for boys. A boy also tries to withdraw from his mother's control through identification, though not with his mother, as the girl does, but instead by relying on his father, who "owns" the "phallus". His father becomes his accomplice, while his mother is not yet the desired genital object she will become in the later Oedipal phase. In this manner, a boy can avoid making the anxiety-inducing connection between identifying with his father and being his father's rival during his efforts to loosen the maternal bonds. The impossible wish for gratification, for possession of the "phallus", crystallizes in both sexes in the desire for the same illusory object, the "penis". Torok points out that this desire is independent of genital differentiation and is exclusively connected with the un-integrated anal relationship. Torok's emphasis that the "penis" is inaccessible to both sexes seems important to me because what she means by it is the "phallus" that the father possesses. "Penis envy" hence plays a significant role in establishing the differences between the generations as well.

The controversies over the question of "penis envy" are not only a matter of academic interest, but also have direct effects on psychoanalytic therapy. Freud was the first to note the limits of psychotherapy in his late, oft-cited study *Analysis Terminable and Interminable*: "We often have the impression that with the wish for a penis and the masculine protest we have penetrated through all the psychological strata and have reached bedrock, and that thus our activities are at an end. This is probably true, since, for the psychical field, the biological field does in fact play the part of the underlying bedrock. The repudiation of femininity can be nothing else than a biological fact, a part of the great riddle of sex" (1937c, p. 252).

With Maria Torok, by contrast, one can show that neither penis envy nor the repudiation of femininity among female patients ought to be regarded as "bedrock"; rather, they are symptoms that need to be analysed (see the cases cited in Blum, 1977 as well). Though the psychoanalytic literature, from Karen Horney to Judith Kestenberg, repeatedly treats the connection between penis envy and repudiation of femininity as a self-evident theme, I do not see this connection as obligatory in any way. For only from the perspective of a dichotomous heteronormativity are maleness and femaleness mutually incompatible, irreconcilable opposites. Envy of the opposite sex, whether penis envy in girls and the analogous vaginal or womb envy in boys, offers a reading common to both sexes, in my assessment: Envy is the effort of the child to rebel against a fact of life, namely that a boy or a girl must accept that he or she has only a single sex, putting an end to any bisexual fantasies of omnipotence.

I regard this reading, one that applies the envy to both sexes, as very significant. Yet some critics of the Freudian view reject it out of hand. Thus, Zenia Odes Fliegel, referring to findings from empirical developmental psychology, notes "these findings also challenge the concept of a negative Oedipal phase as regularly preceding the positive—the centrepiece of the old controversy" (1982 p. 11). Though Freud's model of femininity is wholly unsatisfactory and must be modified, it is nevertheless imperative to develop a comprehensive alternative line of argument rather than to pick out individual aspects of the theory at random and question them. It is probably pointless to refute the idea that the Oedipus complex has its origin in the castration complex. For the assumption of a regularly occurring reversed Oedipus complex is not based at all on the "masculinity of the girl" and also is not a "normative concept" (ibid., p. 11). Instead, it enables an understanding, for example, of the "normal", "non-neurotic" development of female homosexuality. In addition, the conceptualization of a simultaneous, bipolar desire is of far-reaching importance for the entire theory.

Inner and outer genitality

The distinction between an outer and an inner genitality is the most important aspect of Judith Kestenberg's approach (1968). For her, the basic biological difference between the sexes is established through this differentiation. Her reflections lead to interesting and productive insights, even though she tends to repeatedly support cultural gender stereotypes with biological arguments. Psychobiologically based studies of female sexuality such as those she and Mary Jane Sherfey offer (see below) are based in a biological and medical stance, and reflect on the psychic consequences of anatomical differences. Unfortunately, such studies are too seldom found in psychoanalytic discourse, for despite all the criticisms that can be levelled at them, they fill an important gap in psychoanalytic theory. They give a precise view of the anatomical structures and physiological processes that not only serve as an independent basis for psychosexuality but also are crucial to its formation. From the point of view of the general theory of seduction, these processes themselves are also shaped by the early parent-infant relationship and the corresponding fantasies.

Judith Kestenberg's perspective encompasses both masculinity and femininity, though she devotes decidedly more space to the latter. Evidently, she, too, sees female development as still being in greater need of explanation. According to Erik Erikson (1964), a woman's identity is based on her inner genital core, the generative inner space that, regardless of culture, ensures both collective survival and individual fulfilment. Kestenberg takes up this idea, seeing in the "inside genital the core of the feminine body ego" (Kestenberg, 1968, p. 481).

With reference to Karen Horney's assertion of a "flight from femininity", Kestenberg regards the rejection of femininity common to both sexes as traceable back to fear of inner genital sensations. These are visceral sensations from the body's interior that can lead to overwhelming, inundating arousal, and therefore they need to be externalized. A man can more easily externalize such sensations because of his "greater" anatomical differentiation, connected with the increased size of his exterior genitalia and his greater muscle development.

Against the controversy over the primacy of vagina or of clitoris that has lasted for decades, Kestenberg argues that female sexuality "depend(s) on a specifically feminine integration rather than on simply quantitative variations in the importance of one organ or another" (Kestenberg, 1968, p. 460). Characteristics of mouth, anus, urethra, penis and phallus are blended in a mental representation with which the vagina is endowed in the individual's fantasies. Any excessive emphasis given to one or another of these elements leads to an imbalance in female integration. In the course of normal female development, clitoris and vagina are integrated into an overarching experience in which the inner genital is dominant. However, the vagina cannot achieve dominance in the same manner as the clitoris or the penis, because of the way it is anatomically equipped: it has far less sensitive nerve endings than either of the other organs.

Acceptance of the vagina as a source of pleasure without fear, according to Kestenberg, is important; but it is not the only factor in adult feminine integration. Throughout development, the girl goes through sustained phases of vaginal sexualisation and desexualisation, of shifts in cathexis from inside to outside and back again. All this creates an overall representation of the genitals in which the individual parts work with one another in harmony, though they participate differently in the release of sexual tension and in reproduction. As a "middle" organ between the proximal ovaries and Fallopian tubes and the distal clitoris, the vagina serves two functions: de-sexualization, when it is involved in expelling and sexualization when it performs a receptive role. In a unique manner, and at the same time, it is oriented both to externalization and to internalization, to arousal and to reproduction.

With this, Kestenberg counters the thesis of a one-time shift in the primary erogenous zone from the clitoris to the vagina, as Freud and others had argued. It is, in fact, a continuous shift in cathexis, not a one-time occurrence during adolescence. While this conceptualization seems very plausible, Kestenberg's suppositions about the relationship between the sexes are much less so. Thus, she argues that "in order to achieve an adult feminine orgasmic discharge, woman is just as dependent on man's performance as teacher and organizer of her sexuality" (1968, p. 482). Together with her dependence on him for reproduction, this "dual dependence" in her development calls for various preparatory phases in which she looks, while still a girl, for external helpers to free her from her genital tension.

One can regard this as an example of the way cultural heteronormativity and the primacy of heterosexuality seep into psychoanalytic theory. In addition, this perspective influences therapeutic practice. It starts with discriminating against homosexual women, who are implicitly denied the possibility of reaching genital maturity, extends through the notion that masturbation in girls generally promises less success than in boys, and ends with the cementing of gender hierarchy.

Against this background, I suggest replacing the idea that the woman is dependent on the man with the idea of a general dependence on the Other, and equally so for men and for women. If one pursues this thought, one can formulate a thesis of a general heteronomy of sexuality: the sexual is evoked by the Other and structured by the Other. With this, I build on the considerations in Chapter One. regarding the constitution of sexuality through the unconscious seduction of the infant by adults. With respect to sexual arousal, this thesis might still appear broadly acceptable; though probably it better supports the ideal of the autonomy of the modern subject to assume an endogenous source of arousal that is the body's own. Its seat would be in the genitals or in the pituitary, which apparently function independently and according to their own regularities, and are not influenced by the environment. One would then be aroused not by the Other but as a result of autonomous vegetative processes. So though it is inaccurate from a biological perspective to assume that hormone production is isolated or sealed off from the environment, this notion remains tenaciously anchored both in everyday understanding and in the law. Sex offenders, for example, are released even now on condition that they take "drive-reducing" or "drive-inhibiting" medications (Beier, 2007; see also Sigusch, 2001).

If one accepts the thesis of the heteronomy of sexuality for sexual arousal, then one would have to next examine to what extent the very structuring of sexuality can be regarded as heteronomous. One form of such heteronomy seems to be the constitution of the erogenous zones, which come about through parental care and which are inscribed in the body. With the ability of these areas of the body to be aroused, the sexual takes on concrete forms of expression and is structured at the same time. This structuring comes from outside, from adults, and is brought to the infant's body.

A further example of the heteronomous structuring of sexuality can be seen in the Oedipus complex, a universal structure existing prior to the subject that constitutes infantile desire and gives it form. Auto-eroticism and masturbation do not contradict this thesis of heteronomous determination in any way, as they are grounded in identification processes: in fantasy, the subject places himself or herself in the place of the Other. The heteronomy of sexuality is revealed not least in its being dependent on an object, even if imaginary, and on the specific "compulsive" quality of the sexual experience.

The externalization process can be observed not just in the development of female but also of male sexuality. According to Kestenberg (1968), men tend to equate the internal areas of the body with female-ness, and for that reason, project fear-inducing representations of their own inner bodies outwards. Correspondingly, they rarely perceive inner sensations in their own genital areas, reflected clinically in the fact that men rarely talk about their testicles or their prostate, other than in cases of illness. The nature of the fears and fantasies as well as the false notions about the internal genital structure of the man lead Kestenberg to argue that even in early childhood, diffuse, indeterminate sensations emanate not only from the testicles but also from the general pelvic area. For the entry into the phallic stage, the externalization and denial of the "inside" are thus just as significant for the boy as for the girl. Even if the libidinous cathexis of the penis is dependent on the success of such externalization, it is decisive for male development that the projection of the "inside" onto the woman is rescinded and integrated in the man's own body image. Only in this way can he gain access to his own inner sensations and tensions, and to the fantasies that accompany them. The penis plays a central role in the internalization process as a transmitting and transforming organ. Judith Kestenberg does not describe this process in greater detail, but the penis presumably contributes to internalization through its penetrating function, as it then becomes a part of the (woman's) inner body. In addition, one can assume that in the man, too—analogously to female development—externalization and internalization processes do not occur once and for all but continuously alternate throughout life.

Clinical observations indicate a complex organization of defences used by men to keep from becoming conscious of inner genital sensations. Kestenberg (1968, p. 484) notes a number of defensive processes, appearing in isolation or in conjunction, such as the regressive shift of cathexis from the testicles and other parts of the internal genitalia to nearby, pre-genital erogenous zones like the anus and urethra; the externalization of "inner" tensions and impulses to the penis with the consequent shift in the significance of castration anxieties; the equation of the inner genitalia with femininity or immaturity; and the extension of the phobic avoidance and isolation of the internal male genitalia to the female genitalia. These defence mechanisms protect men from the danger of being overwhelmed by genital-visceral sensations. Like other defence mechanisms, they are part of the development of every man. They become pathogenic in nature only when they lose their flexibility and substitutability and, given particular circumstances, become fixed and chronic. Kestenberg's stance is the exact opposite of Melanie Klein's, who was of the opinion that "to obtain full potency" a man has to give up what is female in him, which is equated with inner genitality. Yet both sexes must integrate inner genitality, and to the same degree.

Scientific research also shows how inner male genitalia are denied. Kestenberg complains of finding hardly any studies of internal male genitalia in the early 1970s, and that very little was known about erectile dynamics in childhood. The state of research, at least with respect to adult men, has changed in recent years, as more intensive study has been devoted to "erectile dysfunction" (see Porst, 2001). However, the knowledge of infantile sexual function remains minimal.

According to Kestenberg, such research is made more difficult by the fact that children seldom pose direct questions about what is inside their own bodies. Instead, they usually explore their bodies on their own and draw conclusions without talking to adults and sharing their observations, fears, or anxieties. It is only in analysis that one hears children's suppositions or fantasies, such as: "What is in the scrotum that makes it move? Is it full of urine, live worms (…) or faeces? Will it go away when you have a child? Does it steer the penis and make it move? Why is one side lower than the other? Are testicles pulled up by cords inside the body? Are they weights to keep the penis in place?" (1968, p. 496). Eich

(2005) comes to a similar appraisal of children's explorations of their own bodies. In addition to whatever pleasure such exploration brings, it serves to develop theories about the body's interior and the function of various body parts.

In Kestenberg's view (1968), representations of internal organs are connected with early objects, much like external body parts stimulated by parental touch. This fusion of the representations of organs and objects is also the origin of the fear that what lies inside the body will be attacked. Since the inner sensations from the midsection and pelvic area are closer to the primary than to the secondary process, the anxiety-inducing images and structures are more likely to be found in dreams, in (psychosomatic) symptoms, or in acting-out in transference than in verbal descriptions.

Kestenberg reports, for example, on male patients who express, in the way they badger or constantly nag others, that something (physically) inside them is bothering them. Though these men are often intensely concerned with the inside of their bodies, they never trace their unease back to genital sensations but only to gastrointestinal or anal sensations. Kestenberg ascribes the minimal success of these analyses to a (common) omission. She acknowledges that though she had analysed the male patients' fears of the female inner body, she had not addressed their fears and fantasies about their own inner bodies. With this omission, she simply repeats the externalizations and projections of her patients, at least to some degree, rather than helping them abandon them.

In a different analysis, in which Kestenberg treated a successful veterinarian for "marital discord" (1968, p. 498), it proved worth pursuing her focus on inner sensations and the anxieties emanating from them. Though her patient's low sperm count was the reason why his marriage was childless, he did not suffer from it subjectively, because he did not like children. However, his wife's frigidity had driven him to engage in a strictly sexual relationship with another woman. He complained about his wife because she was boring, a know-all and conceited. He acted out his revenge fantasy by denying her his semen during the sexual act—he experienced his orgasms with her without ejaculation. By contrast, he "fed" his girlfriend his ejaculate and expected her to swallow it. The analysis revealed a complex inner control system by which he tried to limit and control his diffuse inner sensations. However, he had not been successful at extending this control to his penis. Unconsciously, it had remained a dangerous organ that evaded all outside control. To the degree to which he was able to scale back the (projection or) externalization onto his wife and the splitting between wife and girlfriend, his wife became more important to him and he could discuss with her what his sexual expectations of her were. This process was accompanied by temporary erectile dysfunction, because he transferred his fears about his inner body to his penis for a while. In addition to these changes, it became increasingly possible for him to imagine having a child, and over time, he was able to take increasing pleasure in his contact with children, including during consultations in his veterinary practice. In this context, his sperm count also increased, so that he no longer had to feel infertile and had no need to withhold his semen from his wife. To the degree to which his penis increased in importance vis-à-vis his inner body, his drive to masturbate also decreased and his erections became more reliable. The patient also gained self-confidence, became braver and more competitive with other men, and his fear of hurting himself or others, by allowing his aggression free rein, was considerably reduced.

This convincing case makes it clear how important the analysis of inner genital sensations is among male patients. As in the past, this apparently continues to be the case. However, what has changed since Kestenberg's time is the assessment of masturbation as an immature form of sexuality that primarily acts as a substitute. Because it induces an orgasm, masturbation is now regarded as a fully-fledged form of sexuality.

For Judith Kestenberg, withdrawing the projection of internal male genitality onto the woman is linked with the goal of understanding how the man's own inner body functions. By accepting that knowledge, he can re-project it and thereby act as organizer of the needs of the woman's inner body. In contrast to this view, I think it makes sense not to assume a renewed re-projection onto the woman. Instead, I understand inner genitality as a genuine part of male sexuality, a part that must be accepted and integrated in the course of development. It is only the integration of inner genitality that makes possible the phantasmal, carefree alternation between externalization and internalization in sexual experience. This integration also forms the basis for establishing a creative inner space, as Vera King (1995) convincingly shows for female development.

MASCULINE—FEMININE   113

In order to integrate inner genitality into male development, it is necessary to separate that genitality from the mother. The major obstacle for boys in accepting their inner genitality, I believe, is that internal genitalia are indissolubly associated with their mothers and thereby seen as equivalent to femininity. While the girl can appropriate this location through identification, the boy must first free himself of femininity in order to integrate it into his male body image. This is made more difficult by the fact that inner genitality can be much less influenced by targeted action than can outer genitality. At least, people seem to be far more subjected to inner than to outer genital sensations, which is why this form of "passivity" also needs to be integrated.

The tendency to block out men's inner genitality is noted in passing by Mary Jane Sherfey (1972) in her psycho-biological investigations of female sexuality. It can already be seen in every day, and incomplete, notions of the male genitals: "Almost everyone thinks of the penis as simply the pendulous shaft hanging free in front of the scrotum, but this is only one half of it. The other half, containing the powerhouse for the orgasm and ejaculation, is hidden from view (I call it the cryptic portion)" (1972, p. 146). Regardless of whether the entire inner anatomy of the penis really serves the sexual act and not other functions as well, in her anatomical study, Sherfey draws attention to the important fact that the male abdominal cavity, lower abdomen, and pelvic area—unlike the analogous area of the woman—seem to have far less sexual significance both in everyday understanding and in traditional scientific understanding. Instead, the penis is most commonly understood as an external organ; there is scant awareness of its embedding in the abdomen and connection to other structures.

Sherfey tries to show in her study that the penile and clitoral systems exhibit homologous structures; each part has an exact equivalent in the other sex. Drawing on the empirical studies by William Masters and Virginia Johnson, she formulates her central thesis about female sexuality: "Females do possess a fundamentally 'masculinelike, sexual drive based on a highly effective clitoral erotism" (ibid., p. 53). Sherfey criticizes the widespread failure to give due consideration to the clitoral deep structures, unlike the vaginal one. As in the case of the male genitalia, that is true not just in everyday understanding: "there is still a widespread tendency to forget that the clitoris is not just the small protuberance at the anterior end of the vulva" (ibid., pp. 57–58), but also in anatomy and physiology textbooks, which often attach absolutely no importance to the hidden clitoral structures either. However, like the analogous penile structures, the clitoral structures have very important functions with respect to orgasm. Against this background, it is also understandable that most doctors regard vaginal orgasm as "more normal" than clitoral orgasm, though Kinsey, Pomeroy and Martin (1948) regarded the former as a biological impossibility. From her study of anatomy, Sherfey by contrast concludes that "it is a physical impossibility to separate the clitoral from the vaginal orgasm as demanded by psychoanalytic theory" (ibid., p. 85) because clitoral and vaginal structures are connected and cannot be stimulated separately. In addition, the contractions that lead to orgasm do not stem from the vagina but rather from extra-vaginal musculature. However, even though the penile and clitoral systems exhibit homologous structures, it is orgasmic ability that constitutes the clearest distinction between male and female sexuality, according to Sherfey, because in the female structures greater vasocongestion and engorgement in the pelvic area can be achieved. While women, when fully aroused, normally can experience multiple sequential orgasms, a refractory period occurs in men after orgasm, a (resting) phase of complete inability to become aroused that, depending on a variety of factors, can last from ninety seconds to several days. These physiological findings are not only interesting for the formation of psychoanalytic theory but also are directly relevant to therapeutic practice. For example, in an earlier era, multiple orgasms among female patients were often regarded as a sign of sexual immaturity (Deutsch, 1944).

In this context, Masters and Johnson (1966) also noted that the anatomical and physiological reactions during orgasm always occur in the same manner and are independent of the various types of arousal: "From an anatomical point of view, there is absolutely no difference in the responses of the pelvic viscera to effective sexual stimulation, regardless of whether the stimulation occurs as a result of clitoral-body or mons area manipulation, natural or artificial coitus, or, for that matter, specific stimulation of any other erogenous area of the female body" (Masters & Johnson, 1966, p. 66). Sherfey also adds fantasy to the aforementioned sources of arousal. Even if the invariant physiological course of orgasm can reveal nothing about the quality of the subjective experience (see the critique in Tiefer, 1995), it is significant nevertheless.

It could, for example, be used to weaken the normative hierarchy of sexual forms or the dominant view that coitus is the "correct" or "proper" form of adult sexual expression.

Beyond this, Sherfey contradicts Freud's thesis of a constitutional bisexuality. According to (what were then) the latest embryological studies, all human embryos are initially female, and additional endocrinal processes trigger male development only after about six weeks of embryonic life. Female structures, by contrast, develop independently, without the aid of hormonal differentiation.

While Sherfey initially claims that Masters and Johnson's studies of human sexuality called for fundamental reorientations of psycho-analytic theory, her judgment in the end is more moderate: "Other than concepts based on innate bisexuality, the rigid dichotomy between masculine and feminine sexual behaviour, and derivative concepts of the clitoral-vaginal transfer theory, psychoanalytic theory will remain what it has been" (Sherfey, 1972, pp.144–145).

Not just in psychoanalytic circles but beyond, particularly in the course of the second women's movement, the question of vaginal *vs.* clitoral orgasm was again hotly debated during the 1970s. Even now, the debate does not appear to have really ended, and it is one that reveals a rather inappropriate and mechanistic understanding of sexuality (Nieden, 2004). According to Volkmar Sigusch (1970), the concept of two different modes of female orgasm did not even originate with Freud, as commonly alleged. Freud certainly refers to the vagina as women's primary erogenous zone, but does not identify specific anatomical areas as decisive for orgasm. In contrast, subsequent analysts (including Deutsch, 1925) regarded "vaginal" orgasm as a sign of "mature" femininity, though others like Horney (1933) and Sherfey (1972) reject this view. Sabine zur Nieden draws attention to the fact that the question of potential vaginal sensitivity, in what is often an ideologically encumbered debate, is equated with the ability to achieve coital orgasm. Fundamentally, at issue is the assumption that coitus is the only normal sexual practice (see Schwarzer, 1977). This assessment is supported by empirical work like that of Masters and Johnson (1966) who found no evidence at all of differing biological modes of orgasm among women. Sigusch (1970), finally, provides an argument as simple as it is plausible: an orgasm cannot be "dissected" either anatomically or physiologically, as no organ, neither vagina nor clitoris, can react separately from the rest of the body. An orgasm is hence a complex reaction of the entire organism as well as of the psyche. Despite these unambiguous findings, the discussion continued in the 1980s. In a widely read popular science book, the existence of a "G-Spot" was asserted as well, a bean-sized area on the anterior vaginal wall which, when sufficiently stimulated supposedly swells up and triggers an orgasm (Kahn-Ladas, Whipple & Perry, 1982). As implausible as the G-Spot seems to me, it is noteworthy that the authors extend their concept to the male sex: a vaginal G-Spot orgasm supposedly has its equivalent in an orgasm triggered by the prostate, one in which the ejaculate is expelled less convulsively and powerfully. The ideology of traditional masculinity, at least, is obviously not advanced by such conceptualizations, given their simplistic nature.

According to Nieden (2004, p. 80), this discussion actually bundles together three distinct questions: the question of vaginal sensitivity, the question of differing modes of orgasm, and the question of an ability, often lacking among women, to achieve coital orgasm. The studies cited to answer these questions arouse great doubt, on the whole, and also seem rather inconclusive. The neurophysiological bases for sexual reactions remain, as before, inadequately clarified. This is particularly true for women, and that is why Sabine zur Nieden feels compelled to take the few studies of men and apply them to women, though with the unconvincing argument that, on grounds of physical development out of the same embryonic structures, one can find an equivalence. Still, one can agree with her that the real problem in this debate is the dualistic perception of the female genitalia: "The tip of the clitoris is not a stunted version of the male structure, nor is the vagina the other, genuinely female organ" (ibid., p. 86, translation for this edition). Finally, we "will never be able to confine sexual experience, the intensity of desire, or the degree of gratification to the sober, dry, measurable facts of sexual physiology" (2004, p. 89, translation for this edition).

Nevertheless, Judith Kestenberg and other authors have tried, using elaborate arguments, such as differentiating between discriminatory and visceral sensitivity—the former emanating from the sensitive nerve endings, the latter decisive for sensations in the inner genitalia—to find proof for a shift of the primary erogenous zone from the clitoris to the vagina. The problem with this line of argument is the need to demonstrate why there should be a shift away from the clitoris at all, as it is an organ with sufficient nerve endings at its surface, to an organ that has hardly any such nerve endings, namely the vagina. Regardless whether this assertion still corresponds to the current state of physiological knowledge, the question here is whether it makes sense to tie the emergence of sexual arousal primarily to the presence of nerve endings. If one assumes that arousal, as described in Chapter One, is shaped to a decisive degree by memory and fantasy, even if unconscious, then the question which organ is physiologically more strongly excitable plays a rather subordinate role. Experiences during infant care suggest that the sensation of the outer genitalia—clitoris and vulva—predominate to begin with. Pleasurable vaginal sensations, by contrast, set in only later. It seems to me that in the process (unconscious) fantasies play quite decisive roles.

I see these fantasies as a conglomerate of various ideas about the different erogenous zones, which may alter in the course of psychosexual development. Thus they include phantasmal representation of the vagina—following Kestenberg—including the most varied modes of pleasure and gratification during the individual developmental phases. Among these modes are the devouring or biting mode found in orality, the retaining or expelling mode of anality, and the penetrating or receiving mode of genitality. In this way, the vagina becomes a kind of "projection surface", a place where the individual partial drives are integrated. Here one hears echoes of the Freudian notion of integrating partial drives under the primacy of the genital. In contrast to Freud, though, I am not speaking about subordinating or even replacing the partial drives, as at least some reviews of his work have suggested. Instead, I assume that the vagina does not independently produce any relevant arousal. Rather, the ability of the vagina to become sexually aroused stems primarily from an unconscious, phantasmal interaction of the oral, anal, urethral, and clitoral modes of pleasure and gratification. This integration is not a one-time event but takes place continuously during psychosexual development. Decisive to it is the mode of *Nachträglichkeit*. The representations of the individual modes of gratification are reinscribed according to the latest level of development (see Chapter One). The transitions between the individual phases constitute junctures or nodes of sorts, where these reinscriptions are bundled together. The Oedipus complex and adolescence are particularly important nodes, for it is at these junctions that a fundamental restructuring and new structuring take place, in the case of the latter, the shift from infantile to adult sexuality. This is accompanied by a fundamental change in the meaning and function of the vagina.

The decisive point in my argument is that this integration and reinscription of the modes of gratification takes place permanently, in each developmental phase, and not just during adolescence. The modes—just like the fantasies and the representations of the body, especially of the genitals—are subject to a continuous alteration, which accelerates at certain times, such as during adolescence, or proceeds more slowly.

The same integration, in terms of structure, also takes place in men. Here it is the penis that serves as a "projection surface", as the place where the individual pleasure and gratification modes are integrated. This thesis with respect to men may appear even stranger than for women, because the functioning of the penis certainly does not seem in doubt. In contrast to everyday understanding, however, an analogous, permanent alteration of meaning and function takes place, arising from continuous re-inscriptions. In analogy to the vagina, that means the penis is also phantasmally equipped with oral, anal, urethral, genital-receptive, and genital-phallic pleasure modes. In the associations, fantasies, and dreams of certain patients, a phantasm, with oral overtones, of a sucking or devouring penis may appear, or the anal play of retaining and expelling sperm, or a receptive pleasure at being penetrated may be expressed.

I regard this complex interaction of the various pleasure and gratification modes as an appropriate way to conceptualize the genital primacy of adult sexuality. Here the genital does not replace the pre-genital modes but rather serves as the place where they were projected and bundled together. This bundling enables other feelings of pleasure, both qualitatively and quantitatively different from those experienced in infantile sexuality, as can be seen with the experience of orgasm. In addition, internal and external genitality are integrated in both sexes. Owing to menstruation and (potential) pregnancy, this psychic developmental task is more obviously for women than for men. However, the price for a lack of integration in a man is to remain confined to phallic sexuality.

While psychoanalytic theory in the last few years has been strongly focused on biological, and in particular, neurophysiological concepts, it has clearly distanced itself from psychobiological studies of the kind conducted by Judith Kestenberg or Mary Sherfey, when it comes to gender research. As the overview article by Zenia Odes Fliegel (1982) shows, there has been a remarkable shift in emphasis: the conceptualization of femininity and masculinity in psychoanalysis is increasingly divorcing itself from sexuality. The focus, unlike in Freud, is no longer on the various modes used in searching for pleasure and gratification but is instead on the development of object-relations, a largely de-sexualized discussion. The theory of drives has surrendered its promi-nent position to object-relations theory and to self-psychology. Today, it is no longer about pleasure and refusal but instead about autonomy and dependence.

Sexuality and reproduction

Technical developments in the last decades both in contraception and in reproductive medicine have increasingly weakened the close connection between sexuality and pregnancy that still existed in Freud's lifetime and in the early days of psychoanalytic theory. Yet in the unconscious life of many women, sexuality remains closely associated with repro-duction (Schlesinger-Kipp, 2002, p. 1022). One should probably also add the unconscious life of men, though there are hardly any studies of it, and in their conscious self-perception, men would likely reject the idea. In psychoanalytic understanding, conscious and unconscious fan-tasies of pregnancy and the ability to conceive and bear children should be distinguished from the real experience of pregnancy, conception and the desire to have children. Thus the desire for pregnancy does not nec-essarily also mean the wish to bear a child. This is probably clearer in the male procreative desire than in the female wish to give birth. If one wants to avoid normative over-determination, the distinction between fantasy and actual implementation is significant. It is precisely in the writings of earlier analysts that the birth of a child is ascribed particular importance for developing female identity. Some were of the view that only in bearing a child—preferably a son, of course—could a woman be reconciled with the "inferiority" of her genitalia, and other strange notions were current as well. In the following, and to avoid an over-emphasis on reproduction, which in the relevant literature is always exclusively of psychic importance for the woman, I confine my remarks on the significance of reproduction in sexual life primarily to the level of fantasy and the unconscious.

Menstruation and pregnancy

Therese Benedek (1950) argued that the female body, in every cycle from menarche to menopause, is preoccupied with the possibility of conception, or with its absence, namely menstruation. In addition, she saw a correlation between preconscious emotions and the ovarian hormonal function. However, this connection is usually hidden from conscious experience. In her view, women respond pre-consciously to follicle ripening with increased activity and sexual desire shortly before ovulation. The increased influence of progesterone prepares the uterus for implantation, and the woman withdraws into herself in preparation for pregnancy and bearing a child. However, one can object that numerous women experience their greatest sexual desire just before and during menstruation (see Sherfey, 1966, among others), suggesting that women's female sexual desire is probably largely independent of their hormonal state, or that if this connection exists at all, it is likely individual rather than common to all women.

Still, when Benedek emphasizes that a woman must engage in a psychosexual integration of emotions and hormones in every cycle, then—regardless of the hypostatization of "hormones"—this points to an important aspect: the menstrual cycle, the monthly recurrence of readiness to conceive or the lack of conception, needs to be worked through and integrated. Such integration is not achieved once and for all during adolescence but instead accompanies female development from menarche to menopause, in the sense of a continuing reinscription.

Though menstruation plays a very large role in the life of a woman, it is accorded practically no attention in psychoanalytic discourse. Helene Deutsch (1944) was one of the first analysts to address it, specifically in the context of female puberty. The most important element of this developmental phase, in her view, is menarche: "The intermingling of biologic hormonal events and psychologic reactions, the cyclic course of the somatic process, and the periodic return of menstruation, make it one of the most interesting of psychosomatic problems" (1944, p. 149). Deutsch points to the close connection between menstruation and the female castration complex, as well as between menstruation and all reproductive functions, in the fantasy life of the young girl. Psychoanalytic findings had shown how the threatening vision of bleeding genitals shifted to the interior of the body. The content of these visions, following Melanie Klein, is of being torn and cut into pieces, and in them, infantile castration fears are conjoined with ideas of giving birth—a frightening juxtaposition of both giving and exterminating life. These two principles, Klein says, are unconsciously connected with a woman's biological functions. Based on case histories, Deutsch describes, in an impressive way, how an individual woman's experience of menstruation is shaped by her personality structure, and the unconscious conflicts associated with it. Thus, each phase of puberty has its typical response to menstruation, one often maintained into adulthood. If genital bleeding begins in pre-puberty, for example, it is treated as though it were a new excremental function like urination or defecation, frequently triggering feelings of shame and a wish to keep the bleeding secret. In some women, menstruation unconsciously triggers a tendency to "lock away the self" and withdraw from social contact. Alternately, monthly "indisposition" can also activate the unconscious longing for the tender care of one's mother. An increase in depression or aggression during and shortly before menstruation is also often observable. With menarche, for the first time in a girl's development, the dual function of a woman as both "a sexual creature and a servant of the species" manifests itself. After this point, her fantasy life is strongly preoccupied with procreative functions. Deutsch believes that together with the first menstruation comes the fear that unconscious infantile fantasies of pregnancy and giving birth will be realized. This lends menstruation the character of a refusal of what is simultaneously both wished and feared. The anxieties often observed in this context, as well as neurotic pregnancy symptoms, might be understood as a girl's attempts to find expression for her disquiet about her hard-to-fathom, elusive, sexual arousal. Following Deutsch, cornerstones are laid during puberty and particularly during the first menstruation for later experiences of the body and of sexuality. It is precisely in the realm of sexual functions that the varied reciprocal effects of bodily and emotional processes are particularly pronounced. Deutsch emphasizes the influence that emotional arousal has on the organs in general and on the female sexual organs in particular: there is hardly any neurosis that fails to trigger a reaction in genital tract processes and in the menstrual cycle in particular.

Such extensive treatment of the psychological significance of menstruation as is found in Helen Deutsch appears only rarely in psychoanalytic discourse, and when it does appear, it is largely confined to the early years of the field. Mary Jane Lupton (1993) addresses this lack of attention to menstruation in her monograph *Menstruation and Psychoanalysis*, tracing this back to the many cultural and social taboos on the topic. In her view, however, traces of menstruation-related topics can be found in the earliest psychoanalytic theories, and they influenced Freud's dreams as well as his thought. In addition to finding evidence for these traces in Freud's oeuvre, Lupton also draws attention to Claude D. Daly (1928), a now largely forgotten analyst. Largely on the basis of anthropological studies, Daly sought to demonstrate that a "menstruation complex" existed, and that it provided the primary motive both for prohibiting incest and for menstruation taboos. This complex has the same significance for women and men, girls and boys. For the small boy, his sexually arousing, menstruating mother is the first object of desire from whom he has to free himself. The sexual wish for a bleeding vagina is suppressed. Daly saw in this the primary reason for the fear of castration: its key source is the mother and not the father, as in the Freudian conceptualization. However, one can agree with Lupton's observation that newer studies contain hardly any psychoanalytic material on menstruation, either in terms of treatment or in theoretical reflections.

In the German-speaking discourse, Ruth Waldeck (1988) has addressed menstruation as a central aspect of adolescence, and following Deutsch, sees menarche as the most dramatic experience in this phase of female development. Her central thesis is that menstruation taboos, with their concomitant effects on a woman's attitude toward her own sexuality, effectively fix dependence on a man more strongly than does the possibility of a pregnancy. At this juncture, I do not want to go further into the relationship between the sexes, though I regard the connection between menstruation and sexuality as quite significant. Waldeck draws attention to the experience of menstruation as a self-regulating cycle, as it performs an important stabilizing function in the physical life of a woman, and can give her a basic feeling of security and trust in her own bodily functions. However, negative feelings often predominate, and the first menstruation, in particular, is often linked to hygienic concerns and the danger of pregnancy. Pleasurable desires and sexual arousal in conjunction with menstruation seem to remain taboo and are rarely addressed, even by feminist authors. Mary Sherfey (1966) is an exception, as she delineates the capacity for greater sexual arousal during menstruation, when pelvic and genital vasocongestion is maximal. What phantasmal meaning menstruation has for sexual life is a topic future psychoanalytic study should address, and in my view, it is a question that is of interest with respect to the experience of both women and men.

Another important aspect in connection with sexuality and reproduction is pregnancy itself, in particular the first one, as many psychoanalytic authors regard it as a key turning-point in the development of female identity. Whether carried to term or interrupted, it means the beginning of an irrevocable, unalterable, mother-child relationship, through which a woman ceases to exist as an independent individual (see, among others, Deutsch, 1944; Caplan, 1959; Erikson, 1959). For a woman expecting her first child, pregnancy is proof of her sexual identity as well as a visible signal to the surrounding world that she has had a sexual relationship (Pines 1994). According to Helene Deutsch (1944), the tasks associated with pregnancy include the psychological and physical integration of the imago of the sexual partner. This requires a fusing of new libidinous and aggressive strivings with infantile strivings emerging from her relationship to parents and siblings. In addition, pregnancy activates earlier psychosexual conflicts and anxieties (see e 2002). In this context, the mother-daughter relationship takes on particular importance. The identifications of early childhood are reawakened, and the current relationship with her mother can develop further and its ambivalences can be softened at the same time. According to Therese Benedek (1950), pregnancy is libidinous fulfilment for the mother, as she replays her own psychosexual development in her daughter and becomes more independent. Each child offers her a new hope of better resolving her own conflicts. Janine Chasseguet-Smirgel (1986) likewise assumes such a libidinous fulfilment through the pregnancy and the early phase of the mother-child relationship. This fulfilment results from identification with the child during pregnancy and after the birth. Phantasmally, a woman can relive her own earlier situation with her mother. Yet there are not just happy experiences of fusion and the experience of fulfilment. We also know of women who experience this fusing as extremely threatening and who develop strong symbiotic fears, such as the fear of being devoured by the baby. These anxieties are often expressed as panic over the health of the unborn child or of the baby, as well as in postpartum depression. These findings also are confirmed in newer studies conducted by Elina Reenkola (2002). In the potential ability to become pregnant, she sees the "veiled female core", which decisively determines a woman's life experiences as well as her particular anxieties and her desires. In reference to Freud's insight, she emphasizes the importance of body experiences and that the ego is primarily physical. Thus, a woman's anxieties are not, as assumed in classical psychoanalysis, focused on a deficiency but are directed far more at her potential, namely her hidden reproductive core.

Dinora Pines (1994) also suggests an important differentiation. While the unborn child denotes an extension of self-representation on the part of the pregnant woman, motherhood is a form of object relation that begins only after birth, as soon as the infant separates from the body of the mother. Like Caplan (1959), she distinguishes between three phases of pregnancy. The first phase, which lasts until quickening, is characterized by an awakening of adolescent body sensations and fantasies, accompanied by an increase in libidinous cathexis of the self, a withdrawing from the object world, and an increasing passivity. Toward the end of this phase, a marked regression to the oral phase can be observed, including nausea and vomiting as well as a ravenous appetite for certain foods. In the second phase, the perception of foetal movement makes unavoidably clear that the child is a separate, independent being over whom the mother cannot entirely exercise control. These perceptions are accompanied not only by happy feelings but also by fears of separation and castration. According to Pines, in analysis the emergence of intense regressive fantasies is particularly noticeable. These can be traced back to an increase in ego-stability brought about by the unborn child, and this increase permits access to consciousness of what are otherwise repressed, archaic fantasies. For example, conscious and unconscious fantasies from early childhood are reinscribed, including those associated with orality, such as that the foetus could become a voracious, destructive creature, or associated with anality, such as that the foetus is something dirty and indecent that has to be expelled by the mother. Anal aspects can be seen also in the widespread significance ascribed to magical notions about what is good or bad for the foetus. In particular, toward the end of this phase, men often are regarded as intruders who might harm the foetus. Such notions permit old fantasies of the harmfulness of sexuality to re-emerge, and often lead women to forgo sexual intercourse, though they desire it. In the third phase, oral wishes to be cared for and be mothered often predominate. Furthermore, there are pronounced mood swings as well as fears; a woman wonders whether the child will be born healthy, or whether she herself will survive the birth unscathed. After the actual birth, a mother's body image must be readjusted, including filling the emptiness where the child previously was. A mother has to perceive herself again as whole, and not as emptied, before she can accept the child as an independent being.

Elina Reenkola (2002), in contrast to the earlier notions of Helene Deutsch (1944) and others, emphasizes that pregnant women can certainly profit from psychoanalysis, and are capable of establishing stable transference relationships. In fact, the emotional imbalance during pregnancy even brings otherwise deeply buried conflicts to the surface and makes analytic work easier. A woman's experience of the earlier relationship with her own mother, along with the associated disappointments and conflicts, is refreshed in such work. In this context, Ingrid Möslein-Teising (2007) emphasizes the particular importance of the separation conflict during pregnancy. On the one hand a daughter separates herself from her mother, while at the same time she herself becomes a mother. According to Reenkola, Oedipal conflicts, too, are reinvigorated. For example, the dreams of pregnant women, together with a core fear that the baby might be harmed, also contain indications that the pregnancy may be experienced as the fulfilment of forbidden Oedipal wishes. These dreams are accompanied by massive guilt feelings. Unfortunately, even Reenkola's extensive study contains no remarks about sexual experience and sexual fantasies during pregnancy. The converse question—how the possibility of pregnancy is expressed in sexual experience and in the (unconscious) sexual fantasies of both women and men—is a desirable topic for further research.

In a recent collection of essays about motherhood in the twenty-first century, Alcira Mariam Alizade (2006) draws attention to the fact that new forms of motherhood, such as single mothers or lesbian pairs, as well as technologically assisted reproduction, not only decouples sexuality from reproduction but are sources of new, phantasmal and symbolic scenarios both conscious and unconscious. These innovations also pose new challenges both for psychoanalytic theory and for clinical work. The classic psychoanalytic idea of "primary motherliness" as the core of every woman's identity is countered by newer studies that explore its many associated pathologies, which are often connected to a wish for children. They emphasize the significance of a woman's psychic organization, which is structured independently of her maternal functions. The dissociations of the sexual, previously noted with reference to Volkmar Sigusch's work, can be expanded by a dissociation derived from Alizade's attention to social and technological changes: the dissociation of femininity from motherliness. If one takes this idea to its logical conclusion, it means that motherliness in the future will no longer be confined to women but will become open to men as well, at least after the child is born.

After many years of treating women with unfulfilled desires to have a child, Ute Auhagen-Stephanos (2005) formulated the psychoanalytic thesis that—regardless of the presence of somatic disturbances—a psychic refusal can have the effect of preventing impregnation, since mental prohibition programs the body to experience pregnancy as a danger. Auhagen-Stephanos points out that in psychoanalytic terms, far too little is currently known about the unconscious meanings of reproductive technology for the primal scene. However, an unavoidable de-sexualization of the act of generation is associated with it. Instead of experiencing a pleasurable sexual act, the woman must undergo technical fertilization procedures, while the man must waive his generative potency and surrender it to the doctor.

Not infrequently, however, experiences with female patients who seek to fulfil their intense wish for a child by using reproductive technology reveal that it is the pregnancy alone that is desired. The subsequent life with a child, by contrast, seems more threatening than appealing to these patients. Among such women, Giovanna Ambrosio (2006) observes an autopoietic and parthenogenetic self-representation in which the Other has no place. These women have unconsciously created themselves, on the one hand, thereby denying the primacy of their parents, and on the other hand, they also are bringing their child into the world without the help of an Other—in a type of parthenogenesis like with the Virgin Mary. One patient formulated it as a warning to her granddaughter: one can do anything to bear a child and take advantage of any sperm offered—but should be aware of the risk of having a father in the picture. The "third party" and the primacy of the Other are thereby negated. Reproductive technologies oblige such wishes for narcissistic omnipotence and also support the illusion that one has a right to a child.

Estella Welldon (1988, 2006) takes this pathologizing view of motherhood beyond the narcissistic pathologies, and regards it as an instrument that serves a perverse staging. The woman in question "knows" unconsciously that as a mother she has complete control over a being wholly at her mercy. Of course, such a mother may later have the feeling it is the other way round, that it is the baby who controls and persecutes her. Every notion of separation is unbearable to such mothers, and the infant often serves to compensate for a deep sense of inner emptiness. In other cases, a baby can function to correct a fragile sex identity on the part of the mother and to confirm her femininity. Important differential diagnostic indicators thus are raised by the question whether a woman merely wants to become pregnant or whether she wishes to have a child. The wish for pregnancy derives from a pre-Oedipal identification with the mother and sometimes only serves to assure the woman that her inner body is intact. Such pregnancies, according to Welldon, tend either to be interrupted after a short time, or the infant is given away soon after birth once the psychic goal of conception has been achieved. The assurance of an intact interior generally is only short-lived and therefore often leads to additional, closely spaced pregnancies. These types of pregnancies are illusory attempts by a woman to create for herself object relations that compensate for the early experiences of deficiency with her own mother, and for feelings of loss and emptiness. If motherhood is staged as the expression of a perversion, the infant serves—in Winnicott's sense—as a transitional object that can be imagined, manipulated, used and misused, idealized and harmed, all at once. This tendency is reinforced when the pregnancy is brought about with the aid of reproductive technology, because they support the mother's illusion that she alone and autonomously has the power to give life. According to Welldon, a further aspect of the desire to have children is the longing for intimacy that is to be fulfilled through motherhood, as a substitute for complex adult intimacy with a sexual partner. Welldon concludes that the new reproductive technologies call for an altered understanding of motherhood. Motherhood now is broken up into three separate areas that were once unquestioningly united: the genetic aspect, the pregnancy itself, and the realm of care after the birth. I would add that through these dissociations, motherhood moves closer to fatherhood: siring has always had the potential of being independent of a socially defined fatherhood. That fatherhood has always been in doubt is reflected in the Latin saying *pater semper incertus est* (the father is always uncertain). Its continuation, *mater semper certissima* (but the mother is certain), no longer seems tenable, however.

Though it seems indisputable that pregnancy and the birth of a child also have psychological significance for a man, little psychoanalytic literature addresses it. Freud himself confined his remarks about male fantasies of pregnancy to the negative Oedipal fantasizing engaged in by boys (see the case studies of Little Hans (Freud, 1909b) and of the Wolf Man (Freud, 1918b), as well as Boehm (1930) and Kestenberg (1956), while Ruth Mack-Brunswick (1940) and Edith Jacobson (1950) focused more on pre-Oedipal aspects. Wilbur Jarvis (1962), however, observed male patients during the pregnancy of their wives, and found that an initial disturbance of the husband's psychic equilibrium was brought about by the pregnancy. Jarvis believed that a close connection exists between the man's early childhood development, in particular the course taken by the castration complex, and his later behaviour during his wife's pregnancy, during which earlier, pre-Oedipal as well as Oedipal conflicts are reawakened. These infantile conflicts lead to regressive identification of two kinds: identification with the little boy who is in a relationship with women, and identification with the woman in an effort to stave off castration anxiety. During the pregnancy of his partner, these conflicts are repeated. In the case of the regressive identification, this is manifested in, say, the use of transitional objects, and in the case of identification with the wife, it is manifested, for example, in mothering, caring behaviour towards the pregnant wife. Jarvis emphasized that the nature of the reawakened conflicts always depends on the personality structure of the man.

There is consensus in psychoanalytic discourse as well about the significance of male envy of a woman's ability to give birth, which is in no way is inferior to female penis envy (see among others, Jones, 1942). However, very few psychoanalytic studies of masculinity exist, and when it is examined at all, the focus is usually on the phallic aspects (see Rose, 1961). This opinion seems not to have changed fundamentally over the last forty years, at least in terms of published reports of treatment. Gilbert Rose emphasizes that pregnancy fantasies not only derive from bisexuality (in the sense of sexual orientation) and passive homosexual wishes, but also encompass active, omnipotence and "hermaphroditic" strivings. Using case studies, he shows they can also serve as a defence against death wishes and separation fears. One should also emphasize their close connection with creativity.

Menopause

The last few years have seen an increase in the psychoanalytic literature devoted to "menopause" as the ending of a woman's ability to give birth, which once again sheds an interesting light on the meaning of the procreative functions. The term "menopause" (from the Greek *pauein*, put an end to, terminate) refers retrospectively to the final menstrual period, diagnosed after 12 months of amenorrhea. In our culture, that occurs at about age fifty or fifty-one. The term "climacteric" designates the preceding transitional period, which lasts from two to ten or, in exceptional cases, fifteen, years; it is accompanied by many changes in body and psyche (Schlesinger-Kipp, 2002). A survey of the medical and psychological literature on the "menopausal years" published between 1988 and 1992 showed that the majority of the nearly 1,000 German and English studies were nearly exclusively concerned with questions of organic function and gynaecology, and especially with hormone replacement therapy. Psychosocial problems, women's major reason for seeking medical help during menopause, are largely marginalized in such studies (Sydow & Reimer, 1995).

Helene Deutsch (1944) was one of the first analysts to address meno-pause, and in the climacteric, she saw a narcissistic injury that is very difficult to overcome, as it is an experience of partial death. Everything a woman has acquired since puberty drops away piece by piece, and this reduction in physiological functioning is often felt to be close to death. However, Deutsch admitted that a woman has a complex emo-tional life at her command that is not confined to motherhood, and that as a result she can find a way out of her biological complications.

Using the example of menopause, and in the context of the Freud-Klein controversies, Paula Heimann and Susan Isaacs presented their notions of regression, fixation, and the death wish (King & Steiner, 1991). In their view, women regress during the menopausal years, burdened by guilt feelings because they no longer have the possibility to "make up" for the sexuality they experienced through reproduction. That regression frees destructive impulses as well as fantasies about an evil, empty interior. The persecuting mother is made responsible for this. The genital level already achieved by the libido is threatened by cannibalistic impulses from early childhood. These destructive fanta-sies lie hidden behind a conscious fear of becoming old and unattrac-tive (see Schlesinger-Kipp, 2002).

Therese Benedek (1950) offers a less bleak view and emphasizes the developmental aspect of this phase of life. In her opinion, the strug-gle between the sexual drives and the ego that began in puberty weak-ens during menopause and frees a woman from sexually-oriented conflicts. The resulting excess of energy gives new stimulus to learning and socialization. Ruth Lax (1997), in her overview of issues in the menopausal years (Lax, 1982), by contrast emphasizes the emotional crisis of the climacteric, whose outcome depends on how women assess their self-image, their interests and mission in life, and their body's functionality. Dinora Pines (1994) prefers to see the menopausal years as an incentive to continue to develop and grow emotionally. Sexual life, in particular, can become freer and richer when the possibility of pregnancy no longer exists. She sees the depressions often observed in menopause as less rooted in the climacteric than in the children's moving away from home, which frequently also occurs at this time.

Following Judith Kestenberg (1988), three successive phases in women's development need to be integrated into a complex feminine gender identity: the "maternal" phase, the phase of "phallic pursuit of achievement", and the "sensual-Oedipal" phase. Kestenberg emphasizes the connection with female cyclicality, which she sees as beginning already before menarche:

> "The ability to mother, to care for and to love sensually stands in a
> contrasting relationship to the female cycle, one that most likely starts
> during childhood and that becomes differentiated in later puberty.
> In some phases of adult life, certain feminine traits emerge more
> strongly than others". (1988, p. 361, translation for this edition)

During the different stages of a woman's life, these phases vary in importance. That is also true of the climacteric, when there is merely a change in how the individual aspects manifest themselves.

In the German-speaking psychoanalytic discourse, Andrea Hettlage-Varjas and Christina Kurz (1995) have addressed women's psychosexual development during the menopausal years. With respect to what is in any case a sparse psychoanalytic literature on the topic, they criticize the dominant view of the climacteric as a disease, disorder, or experience of loss. Common to more recent studies, they argue, is that revisions of the Freudian theory of femininity are not really brought in line with drive theory. Hettlage-Varjas and Kurz take this as a starting point for a conceptualization of menopause that does just that.

They define the menopausal years (climacteric) as "a significant developmental phase in the life of a woman, in which her bodily, psychic, and social identity is shaken by a crisis brought about by momentous bodily, psychic, and social events" (Hettlage-Varjas & Kurz, 1995, p. 906, translation for this edition). This crisis prompts the woman to question her prior understanding of herself and organize herself anew. Noteworthy in this approach is the interpretation of the crisis in normative terms. Other approaches, such as that of Sies and Nestler (1992), which see these years as less crisis-laden, stand accused of downplaying or denying this reality. At the same time, along with Betty Raguse-Stauffer (1990), the authors concede that the possible crisis of femininity in this phase depends primarily on what notions one has of femininity itself. In my view, women's interpretation of the actual ending of their procreative functions depends, for instance, on their particular psychic conflict structures and subjective life experiences. That includes, perhaps, a motherhood they have or have not experienced, and its accompanying conflicts and experiences. There is probably also room for interpretation with respect to physical attractiveness. Here, too, judgments differ widely, depending on how significant that attractiveness was up to that point for the self-image of the particular woman. These large differences between individuals, which incidentally are observable as well when one compares female patients in psychoanalytic treatment, speak against a normative conceptualization of menopause as a period of crisis. This has great practical relevance for psychoanalysis, because an imputed denial of this crisis (as in Hettlage-Varjas & Kurz, 1995) has a decisive influence on the course of therapy. At the same time, it is also theoretically significant, since taking crisis as the norm presupposes homogeneity in the life course of women that constructs women as members of a uniform group and makes them appear to be a "monolithic bloc". The point of view underlying that attitude is in fact biological, since the argument rests on somatic processes and reflects their effects on psychic processes. Thus, the absence of menstruation, which is accompanied by complex hormonal changes that in turn influence numerous other physical processes, is credited with a relatively uniform simple psychic importance: it is a crisis. One could just as well start the other way round, however, with psychosocial processes and focus on their somatic influence. For example, a woman's family or employment situation could be examined in terms of its effects on the aging process and on menopause, and on how these are processed. As psychoanalyses show, subjective experience varies quite widely, and a woman's self-image is by no means always shaken. In addition, one should not underestimate the decisive importance of unconscious fantasies in influencing psychic changes.

Hettlage-Varjas and Kurz's approach contains some other fundamental difficulties that emerge time and again in the psychoanalytic discourse on femininity, such as that a pregnant woman is regarded as representing female potency. Such a conceptualization is highly problematic, as it actually weakens the image of a potent woman: a pregnancy occurs far more seldom in the life of a woman, if at all, than for example an erect penis in the life of a man. Here the problem of a dichotomized construction of the sexes appears once again, in the stubborn struggle to define an idiosyncratic femininity that is separate from masculinity. Unintentionally, motherhood becomes idealized here, for if a woman's potency basically is evident only during pregnancy, then femininity again becomes marginalized.

If "potential motherhood (is understood as) the woman's sex-specific, libidinal possibility" (Hettlage-Varjas and Kurz, 1995, p. 927, translation for this edition), then in addition one remains, paradoxically, within the problematic context of the Freudian matrix of the "penis substitute". This imputation also sounds extremely laboured, since one can certainly ask where the modality of pleasure is located in potential motherhood.

The effort to ascertain a "distinct" femininity is difficult at other points as well. An idealization of motherhood inevitably also means devaluing women during their climacteric: "There is no question that women in the menopausal years embody a lost femininity par excellence" (ibid., p. 929, translation for this edition). Correspondingly, the idea is also expressed that "our culture ... offers no further social script for a woman after the menopausal years that would confirm her gender identity" (ibid., p. 930, translation for this edition). Astonishingly, the authors do not consider that this might be related to their idealization of the biological reproductive function. Overall, they provide an exceedingly dismal image of this stage of a woman's life: "Her attractiveness as a sexual partner fades away, motherhood with all its emotional and social significance belongs to the past, and her function as provider is at least reduced" (ibid., p. 930, translation for this edition). In my view, such assessments are cultural clichés whose sweeping form is not supported by any findings, and they are more apt to be detrimental to a well-founded psychoanalytic understanding of the menopausal years.

This problematic view persists with respect to sexuality. What is experienced sexually is an important organizer of gender identity, yet the woman must "forgo the claim of being openly desired". Such phrases leave the impression that the plausible feminist critique that women are treated as sex objects never existed. With respect to psychodynamic arguments, such views are of considerable significance; however, Hettlage-Varjas and Kurz derive from them the wholly unsubstantiated claim that "at the latest in the menopausal years ... a woman is confronted with the fact she is no longer desirable to most men on account of her age" (ibid., p. 932) and that the resulting narcissistic injuries and insecurities cast her back into Oedipal and adolescent situations. This is a highly questionable explanatory mode. The reanimation of Oedipal conflicts, at any rate, is not necessarily connected with narcissistic injuries in any way, as I will show in my later discussion of Gertraud Schlesinger-Kipp's work. In addition, Hettlage-Varjas and Kurz point out that the "solution" arrived at in the past—to delay Oedipal desire for the father until later—is no longer possible after menopause. This sorrow over what is now not possible anymore can lead a woman to have a deeper conflict with her father. But it can also lead to integration of her love, idealization, anger, rebellion, and sorrow with respect to him, in a solidly internalized, if ambivalent, father image.

While this is a fundamental critique, Hettlage-Varjas and Kurz do provide an interesting approach with respect to how the menopausal years are seen, because it rates the girl's relationship to primary objects and the re-evaluation of those objects as very significant for female development and identity in this life phase. Aside from the relationship to the father, this can also be seen in the rejuvenation of separation and individuation difficulties with the mother, which are further reinforced at this time. On the one hand, hatred of the mother is reactivated. So is an image of an aging, no-longer-desired, and abandoned woman, which the adolescent daughter had erected as part of her efforts at autonomy. On the other hand, the daughter also envied that image of a woman, her mother, who was equipped with a stabile identity and a full, rich life. To be able to part with an existence as a daughter and the associated existence of a desirable woman (though the mother is not master of her own desire), it is necessary, at the latest in the menopausal years, to construct ambivalently cathected parental imagos. Relationships between women, as during adolescence, take on increased importance, including in erotic terms, in the menopausal years.

Gertraud Schlesinger-Kipp (2002) regards this as a time, and an opportunity, for inner and outer changes, for necessary separation processes and for psychic restructuring. Since there are few explicitly psychoanalytic explanatory approaches to the climacteric, Schlesinger-Kipp tries to apply existing psychoanalytic theories of femininity, in particular those of Janine Chasseguet-Smirgel (1970), Marie Langer (1992) and Dinora Pines (1994), to this phase of life. Through liberation from the "physical conflict between the poles of child-bearing ability and independence", a woman can experience the climacteric both as crisis and as opportunity for a new stage of life after menopause (Schlesinger-Kipp, 2002, p. 1019, translation for this edition). If it is possible to (partly) resolve unconscious conflicts, and if the body remains healthy, greater amounts of psychic energy can be set free and a more intense experience of identity and sexuality realized. If conflicts are not resolved, however, it can lead to increased psychic problems which, if untreated, can also impair the later phases of life in old age (sixty to seventy-five) and in very old age (over seventy-five).

Schlesinger-Kipp identifies the following psychodynamically relevant areas of conflict that become virulent in menopause and call for (renewed) psychic processing: separation from the mother and her "late revenge"; the "empty" inner room; the "daughterly existence"; sexuality and desires for merging; and finally, the question of age.

The end of the ability to procreate also means renewed separation from the mother with respect to the inner and outer reality of being a woman. With respect to the inner reality, it is important that the fantasy of a merger of mother and child, which is linked with a potential pregnancy, can no longer be sustained. The loss of symbiotic mother-child experience must be mourned both from the perspective of the child and from that of the (potential) mother, so that a feeling of liberation and a consolidation of female identity can ensue. Working through loss and sorrow in this phase is often supported by outer reality, as through the possible illness and death of a woman's mother. Marie Langer (1992) focuses on another aspect of the mother-daughter relationship, according to which the climacteric is or can be unconsciously experienced as a "late revenge" by the mother for the feelings of triumph displayed by her daughter during puberty. The angry and destructive fantasies directed against the mother, the feelings of rivalry, and the idea of a possible Oedipal victory over the mother can no longer be compensated for by having a child. Therefore, on the one hand, those thoughts, which can change into Furies, who pursue and find their victim late in life, can bring about depression. On the other hand, the fantasy of having survived the revenge of the mother can also lead to reconciliation with her. After menopause, mother and daughter are "more alike" than at any time in the past. The Oedipal rivalry can thereby dissolve and allow for a new rapprochement with the mother, one without great guilt feelings, because the unconscious guilt has been atoned for by the daughter's suffering a similar fate. According to Melanie Klein, the destructive fantasies of a daughter vis-à-vis her mother is associated with the notion of an "evil, empty inner space". When the woman's feeling that she can bring a healthy child to term disappears at the time of menopause, her certainty of having a "good", healthy interior is also lost. The projection of a "bad" inner space is again turned against herself, and the loss of this security requires separation and grieving processes, so that she can again arrive at an integrated body image. It is particularly among women who have had hysterectomies that the unconscious guilt feelings associated with the surgery and consequent depressions are observed (Schlesinger-Kipp, 2002, p. 1024).

Menopause also marks the end of the daughter's Oedipal fantasy of being the better partner for her father and her being able to grace him with a child again. In abandoning this incestuous wish, finitude is accepted, and a woman can also cease her "daughterly existence", which is accompanied by the illusion of youthfulness and child-bearing ability. Separation from the father is far more seldom addressed in the psychoanalytic literature than separation from the mother. Yet it is of vital importance to a woman in the climacteric period, too, to prevent her "daughterly existence" from becoming fixed. The renunciation of Oedipal wishes directed at her father and of rivalry with her mother is therefore an important step in developing a woman's identity.

In addition, Schlesinger-Kipp notes that the oft-described increase in sexual desire during the climacteric calls for a psychodynamic explanation; the falling away of the fear of unwanted pregnancy alone is a not a sufficient reason. As described above, the regressive wish to merge can be present in the wish for a baby. As this is no longer possible after menopause, a woman can intensify her fantasies of merging with a man. A strengthening of homosexual tendencies is also possible, because the period of intensive mothering has passed and a man can no longer give her a child—again calling into question the heterosexual resolution of the Oedipus complex.

Finally, Schlesinger-Kipp points out the importance of coming to terms with one's own aging. In particular, an aging body is often experienced as alien and not really belonging to one's self. At the same time, that body plays an ever-increasing role in the life of the aging woman. Health, previously taken for granted, increasingly takes centre stage, and the body often (again) becomes the site where unconscious conflicts are carried out. In her own body image, the older woman frequently also recognizes the likeness of her mother, so her relationship to her mother takes on new significance. According to how loving or problem-laden that relationship is or was, a woman either treats her own body tenderly and lovingly or rejects it.

This psychodynamic line of argument underscores yet again the specific logic, spelled out in Chapter One, of psychodynamic development theory. Development, even in later phases of adult life, can be adequately described with and by specific constellations of the basic psychosexual conflicts. It would be contradictory, however, to understand the menopausal years as an independent phase of psychosexual development.

Sex and gender

Before reconstructing the discourse on gender from the perspective of object relations theory, which can be pointedly formulated as "gender without sex" (Reiche, 1997), a brief comment on the history and use of the terms "sex" and "gender" as understood in the English-speaking world is appropriate. The distinction between "sex" and "gender" has its origins in a differentiation made by the American sexologist John Money (1955) to describe how hermaphrodites, despite their unclear or contradictory physical sex, nevertheless are able to develop a clear gender identity. This distinction was introduced into psychoanalysis by Robert Stoller (1968).

In the context of translation problems, it is often noted that the German term *Geschlecht* does not differentiate between the meanings of "sex" and "gender", and that the physical aspect and the cultural aspects—the sex of the body and the psychosocial gender identity—coincide. Interestingly, it is rarely noted that the reverse is also true. The English term "sex" is not differentiated and in German translation is taken to mean both "gender" as well as "sex". Particularly in adjectival usages, translated texts (especially notable in Fast 1984 and Alpert 1986 but evident already in Greenacre 1968) thus often employ *sexuell* (sexual) where the context would call for *geschlechtlich* (gender, gender-related) would need to stand. This is not only extremely confusing or misleading, but also highly significant for the understanding of sexuality and *Geschlecht*, as well as for psychoanalytic theory. The issue of *Geschlecht* in psychoanalytic discourse takes on increased importance as well in the context of Gender Studies. At the same time, the sexual per se is evaporating from this discourse, a fact particularly criticized by European authors (Parin, 1986; Reiche, 1997; Green, 1995; Koellreuter, 2000). This evanescence also may be connected with the fact that in the traditional English-speaking discourse, the sexual seems inextricably linked to the physical, bodily, dimension in an essentialist, biologistic manner.

Stoller introduced the notion of a "core gender identity" to designate the child's conviction acquired early in life "that one belongs to one sex and not the other". This conviction is strongly influenced by the expectations and attitudes of the parents. At the age of about eighteen to twenty-four months, by current scientific consensus, a child is able to recognize itself as either a boy or a girl, (usually) in keeping with its biological sex. According to Stoller, the core identity develops largely unnoticed and free of conflict. In girls, it "instinctively", as it were, continues the primary identification with the mother; in boys, by contrast, it calls for a process of "dis-identification" (Greenson, 1968). To acquire a male identity, a boy must clearly and vehemently distance himself from his mother. At this point, one may already question whether this occurs in as conflict-free a fashion as Stoller assumes. Wholly dubious is his additional assumption that a transsexual core gender identity also can be acquired free of conflict, as it contradicts the many reports from clinical practitioners who work with transsexuals.

To the concept of core gender identity, Person and Ovesey (1983) later added the idea of gender role identity, to encompass social expectations and norms with respect to gender self-image. Stoller's idea of a core identity has been fittingly illustrated and extended by Reimut Reiche (1997) in a three-layer model, with two concentric circles surrounding the core identity. The inner core consists of the physical sex, though in contrast to everyday understanding, this is not monolithic but is rather constructed from various anatomical, morphological, and endocrinological factors. Around this is a layer that is either isomorphic or anisomorphic; that is, it either has or does not have the same form as the body. That layer in turn becomes a core, namely the core gender identity. Finally, this core is encircled by the gender role identity, which encompasses the diverse gender-related self-representations and object representations, as well as the social conventions and norms.

Stoller's model has influenced the psychoanalytic understanding of (the development of) gender identity for nearly forty years, so it deserves a critical examination. The starting point for core identity development is what Stoller assumes to be an initial state of primary femininity in both sexes—analogous to the approaches taken by Jones or Klein noted above. This assumption, however, appears just as questionable as Freud's androcentric view. Stoller also relies on biological processes, and assumes that the core gender identity is "imprinted" by a kind of "biological force". Without reservation, one can agree with Person and Ovesey that relying on "imprinting" is not necessary for a psychoanalytic theory of *Geschlecht*, as genuinely analytic concepts like identification or introjection are more suited for describing the acquiring of gender identity. Visible in the concentric layer model is the underlying structure of the concept of *Geschlecht*, with its three layers of physical, psychic and social *Geschlecht*. In German, these are summarized by only a single term—monolithically, so to speak—while the English differentiation between "sex" and "gender" draws attention to the fact that the three need not necessarily coincide. However, the metaphor of the three layers also shows its limitations, as the term "layers" gives the impression that the individual layers exist next to, and are independent of, one another. Interrelationships between them are difficult to illustrate in this model, so it is not discernible how relationship experiences are inscribed in the body, or how, conversely, experiences of the body are reflected in relationship experiences. In my opinion, it would aid in the understanding of sex and gender identity if such interactive relationships between the individual layers could be included in the model. In addition, I suggest that within the layers, one should posit various mixes of male and female elements in terms of anatomical features, specific hormonal levels, or contradictory "masculine" and "feminine" behavioural traits. With respect to *Geschlecht*, in my view it does not make much sense to try to create clarity through reduction. It would be more profitable to think of polymorphic mixes existing in as well as between layers. Thereby, the concept of *Geschlechtervielfalt*— sexual diversity or gender diversity—could become clearer, not as an "idealistic" category as is often alleged, but in a specific, material way that includes the body.

The critical analysis of Stoller brought Reiche (1997) to an interesting, productive perspective, in connection with the general theory of seduction, with respect to the development of *Geschlecht* identity. Like Person and Ovesey, Reiche criticizes Stoller's "biological" approach, but beyond that, he questions the assumption, which Person and Ovesey still found convincing, of a conflict-free acquisition of core gender identity. As noted above, the example of transsexuals/ transgendered and intersex peoples shows just how conflict-ridden establishing a *Geschlecht* identity can be. Similar conflicts often appear in psychoanalyses, though individuals who have an unquestioned, "inconspicuous" *Geschlecht* identity are usually unaware of it at that point. Yet they, too, face the task of integrating "masculine" and "feminine" parts of themselves and tying them together into a more or less consistent, non-contradictory identity. These clinical observations led Reiche to hypothesize the existence of a "universal, unconscious, core gender ambiguity". In so doing, he harkens back to the Freudian concept of "constitutional bisexuality", a notion that in the context of "gender" is increasingly being lost. Instead of the biological process of "imprinting" that Stoller posits, Reiche sees the genesis of *Geschlecht* identity in the context of the seduction situation involving adult and child. The specific sex assignment of a child—"it's a boy!" or "it's a girl!"—Reiche sees in Laplanchian terms as an "enigmatic message" that goes far beyond its factual meaning. Its unconscious purport instead encompasses an entire conglomerate of gender-related self-representations and object representations, which the child unavoidably introjects when it is referred to as a boy or a girl. These messages leave traces that cannot be assimilated and, as "unconscious objects", act as an organizing principle for both identity and object-choice. In this view, the primary object "imprints" the core gender identity and the sexual "core" object-choice at the same time. Reiche uses the term "imprinting" (*Prägung*) as well as "core" as metaphors. His concern is largely with the connection between *Geschlecht* identity and object-choice, a topic I will return to in Chapter Three, but in my view, the primacy of the Other is quite decisive in his approach, and the child responds to the Other's demand or claim by establishing its *Geschlecht* identity. In my view, the moment that a child is identified as a boy or a girl, prenatally or postnatally, it is confronted with all that being (or not being) a boy or a girl means unconsciously for its parents (and also at a particular point in history in a given culture). This meaning is a kind of foreign object in the psychic structure of the child, and persisting mental work on his or her part is required in order to come to terms, unconsciously, with these meanings. In the terms I use here, the traces of the assignment of sex, with its implications, are subjected to an on-going process of reinscription. Depending on the current cognitive, social, or affectual developmental state, sex and gender take on new meanings, and new unconscious efforts are undertaken to decode the enigmatic parental messages.

How parents pass on their unconscious messages can be seen in the name they give the child, as names often hold interesting messages about the meaning of *Geschlecht*. It often becomes evident in analysis how much the name also is the parents' *Anspruch* (in the word's dual sense of "mode of address" and "demand"). At the same time, names that do not clearly signal gender, such as Chris or Kim and that are used by both men and women, may sometimes reflect wishes for androgyny, or want to leave open the question of gender identity.

The English distinction between "sex" and "gender" is connected with another important topic: the relationship between *Geschlecht* and sexuality. Person and Ovesey (1983, 1993) assume that core gender identity can be acquired free of conflict, but their conceptualization of the relationship between sexuality and *Geschlecht* is also problematic. They believe psychosocial gender precedes sexuality developmentally and organizes it, not the other way around. Such theses go to the heart of the difference between conceptions based on object-relations and those based on drive theory. In terms of object-relations theory, Person and Ovesey reverse the Freudian assumptions. According to Freud, sexuality structures object-relations, but from the object-relations perspective (*Geschlecht*) identity develops through relationships, and that (or they) in turn organizes sexuality. From this perspective, in contrast to the Freudian view, the early object-relations of both genders, of girls and boys, differ. Children first must learn to which *Geschlecht* they belong, and identify with the corresponding parent, before they can enter the Oedipus complex.

This view is problematic for various reasons, but particularly because it remains unclear in which respects and especially at which level the object-relations of boys and girls differ. Even if it is empirically beyond dispute that adults, from the onset of life, respond to male and female infants in a gender-conscious and gender-specific way, this does not justify concluding that different forms or structures of relations also emerge in consequence. It only provides evidence for the importance of cultural heteronormativity as the main organizing principle for modern societies. As in other areas of experience and behaviour, one can assume here too that, statistically speaking, the variance of a feature, in this case, of the object-relations, is smaller between the genders than it is within a particular gender (see Nunner-Winkler, 2001).

More serious, though, is the relapse into a traditional, pre-psychoanalytic concept of sexuality. If sexuality only develops after gender identity, then the first year of life (at least) is free of any form of sexual expression. Thus, there is no need to assume that an oral sexuality exists, constituted in the first encounter between new-born and adult. The object-relations theory perspective hence lags behind Freud's path-breaking recognition of infantile sexuality. Through the focus on the Oedipal, sexuality is implicitly reduced again to the genital, and the partial drives—orality, anality, urethrality and phallicity—appear to no longer play a role.

Beyond geschlecht: transsexuality/transgender and intersex

In contrast to the gender discourse in the social sciences, in the psychoanalytic discourse on gender, the topic of transsexuality/transgender has received little attention, and intersex is marginalized as well. Nevertheless, the early studies of transsexuality are of considerable significance for psychoanalytic theory, as they have had lasting influence on the analytic discourse about gender issues. Thus, Robert Stoller's conceptualization (1968) of gender identity, and of perversion, was strongly influenced by his psychotherapies with transsexuals. For the purpose of my argument, transsexualism is an example that biological sex need not automatically coincide with subjective gender identification. Transsexualism thus contradicts the essentialist understanding of *Geschlecht*, one that regards the body as the natural, self-evident, basis for gender identity. In intersexuality, the problems created by cultural heteronormativity and the use of *Geschlecht* as a central organizing principle for society, are revealed in a drastic and particularly painful way. This shows the need to overcome the dichotomizing, polarizing construction of *Geschlecht*.

Transsexualism is a phenomenon that is indicative of deep doubts about anatomical sex, with men reporting that they "feel" they are women, and women "feel" they are men. These on-going, constant self-assessments are connected with displaying the corresponding behaviour of the desired gender, along with continuing efforts to change sex at the level of the body, society, and the law.

A brief note on language use is necessary here. I think it does not make much sense to adopt the English terms "trans*sexuality*" and "inter*sexuality*" in German usage, because these are not forms of sexuality but questions of *Geschlecht* that involve both sex and gender. However, the specialized literature uses the terms transsexualism and transsexuality as well as the more general medical term "gender dysphoria syndrome". In terms of the method of treatment, German calls it *Geschlechtsumwandlung* (literally sex transformation), a change that is undertaken at the hormonal, surgical, and legal or civil status levels. No adequate German translation exists for the English term "sex reassignment", though that more accurately captures the idea than "transformation" (*Umwandlung*). It better expresses the notion of an *Anpassung*, an "adaptation" describing the experience of many patients who have not been "transformed" into something else but instead have wanted their bodies to be better adapted to their own sense of *Geschlecht* (Pfäfflin, 1993, p. 5 et seq.; vivid self-portraits by transsexuals are provided in Kamprad & Schiffels, 1991; Ulrich & Karsten, 1994).

The diagnosis of transsexuality was first included in 1980 as a "psychosexual disorder" in the third edition of the DSM, the Diagnostic and Statistical Manual of Mental Disorders, published by the American Psychiatric Association. The WHO's classification of diseases and related health problems (ICD-10) has included transsexuality since 1987. The fourth edition of the DSM, published in 1994, no longer lists transsexualism separately, and instead includes it under "gender identity disorders", as does the ICD-10. In doing so, the inter-action between the phenomenology of a cluster of symptoms and the medical treatment options is particularly striking. A "gender identity disorder" is understood as the subjective suffering resulting from insecurity as to one's sex or gender, not knowing which *Geschlecht* one belongs to, or as the feeling of being stuck in the wrong body.

Friedemann Pfäfflin has provided the most comprehensive empirical study of the phenomenology and aetiology of transsexualism in Germany. Pfäfflin treated more than 600 transsexual patients from 1978 to 1993, of whom about 450 were primarily male and 170 primarily female. By the end of the study, about half had undergone surgery, about 200 had abandoned the desire for surgery they expressed at the beginning of treatment, and about 100 were still undecided. What is impressive in this study is its documentation of the enormous improvement in the overall situation of those affected, whether in psychic, occupational, or social terms, following the sex reassignment surgery. It also speaks clearly against over-emphasizing innate causal factors (in Stoller's sense; see the previous section) and speaks for the importance of developmental, psychological and interactional factors in the emergence of transsexual symptoms (Pfäfflin, 1993).

Before discussing the details of this study, I wish to briefly sketch the history of psychoanalytic theory in this area. The phenomenon of transsexualism has been known for a long time, though under other names (for a history of terms, see Sigusch, 2001). The first psychoanalytic studies of transsexuals are found in Otto Fenichel (1930), Helmut Thomä (1957) and Charles Socarides (1970). These classic case studies address the reconstruction of the pathogenesis of what was then still called transvestism. However, in the latter two studies, the analyses were soon broken off, and nothing more is known of the outcome of the treatment of Fenichel's patient.

The Daseins-analyst Medard Boss conducted fifty hours of therapy with a transsexual patient, whom he then referred for surgical treatment. This occasioned an extremely heated debate over basic issues, in the pages of *Psyche*, that is still worth reading (Mitscherlich, 1950/51; Mitscherlich et al., 1950/51a, 1950/51b—a summary is in Springer, 1981; critical remarks in Boller, 2000, p. 103 et seq.). Alexander Mitscherlich asked whether it didn't completely run counter to psychoanalytic thinking to undertake such an endeavour. Was it the doctor's role to lead a patient to accept "the unavoidable tragedy of his existence" rather than formulate the goal of therapy in opportunistic and pragmatic ways—and regard "mutilation" as healing? Similarly, Helmut Thomä (1957, p. 115) criticized Boss for orienting his treatment too much to his patient's narcissistic experiences and paying too little attention to the defensive nature of the illusion of narcissistic perfection, as found in perversions whose function is to ward off fear.

Following the highly publicized surgical and endocrinological sex change of an American in Denmark in the early 1950s, numerous "gender identity clinics" that concerned themselves with the phenomenon of transsexualism were founded in the United States during the 1960s. This was also the context for Robert Stoller's psychoanalytic studies postulating a basic difference between female and male transsexualism. He viewed the female version psychodynamically, hence oriented toward a model of conflict, but saw the genesis of male transsexualism as conflict-free and based in assumptions from learning theory. Central to his view was a differentiation between a "core gender identity" and a "gender identity". Only among male transsexuals could Stoller find a contrasexual "core gender identity", initially present in the preschool years and remaining steady throughout life. He traced this back to a "biological force" (see the critique in Pfäfflin, 1994, p. 912 et seq.).

In Adam Limentani's view (1979), by contrast, no valid evidence for a uniform pathogenesis exists. Instead, one finds highly differentiated development courses. Clinical observations speak for the view that transsexual symptoms emerge as a "common final stage" of quite varied psychopathological developments.

About thirty years after Mitscherlich initiated this controversy, Germany experienced, more or less, a new version of this debate, though with a remarkable shift in accent. Those like Eberhard Schorsch (1974) or Volkmar Sigusch and Reimut Reiche (Sigusch, Meyenburg & Reiche, 1979), who in other areas were extremely sceptical of pragmatic, technologically oriented "solutions" (see the critique in Schorsch (1988) of stereotactic neurosurgery to treat "perversions", for example) and were counted among the critics, now became proponents of surgical treatment. Though these founders of the "Frankfurt Model" for the study and treatment of transsexual patients have meanwhile distanced themselves from their earlier views (see Sigusch, 1992), the degree of polarization, and the hardened positions in this debate are noteworthy: "The pros and cons of surgical intervention became a shibboleth", Pfäfflin (1994, p. 908, translation for this edition) noted. In the meantime, somatically oriented ideas about hormonal and surgical treatment have prevailed for patients with transsexual symptoms. After clinical assessment, most decline psychotherapeutic treatment, and conversely, therapists frequently regard them as not very amenable to psychotherapy. Here Pfäfflin sees unconscious resistance mechanisms on both sides that can lead to an over-hasty agreement to engage in somatic treatment.

In dealing with transsexual patients, innumerable and massive reactions become apparent in terms of both defence and countertransference. Thus, these patients are often described, in a degrading manner, as "coolly distanced and affectless, rigid, uncompromising, egocentric, threatening, obsessive and narrow, remarkably uniform, normalized, stereotyped, monotonous, and superficial" (Burzig, 1982, p. 852, translation for this edition). Yet together with this, one can find descriptions of close, symbiotic therapeutic relationships. Burzig, for example, urges that patients who feel they do not really belong to either sex or feel they are in a "no-man's-land" be brought out of this state and that "their agony be ended by being in a different 'uniform'" (p. 854, translation for this edition). Similarly, Reiche (1984) describes falling into a backwash of empathy with a transsexual patient, who brought him to identify with his desire for a sex reassignment and support the wish for an operation. The effort to "pull the patient out" is expressed not just in approving the surgical intervention. It is expressed just as much in psychotherapists' over-estimation of their own powers, which is expressed in their firm belief that all transsexual patients can be cured through psychotherapy or psychoanalysis (Pfäfflin, 1994, p. 910). Something similar takes place not only in psychotherapy but also in the interaction with surgeons, where the transsexual patient's narcissism often corresponds to that of the attending surgeon: "The pathological narcissism of the transsexual corresponds to the grandiose wishes of those surgeons who harbour the illusion that they can operatively transform a transsexual man into a perfect woman" (Diederichs, 1993, translation for this edition). As a result, Ilse Rechenberger (1995) regards transsexualism as an interpersonal phenomenon, the expression of individual and collective unconscious fantasies, and wonders whether transsexual behaviour isn't even encouraged by society's delegating its unconscious wishes.

Newer studies of the development of *Geschlecht* identity (see Irene Fast's theory (1984) in the next section) emphasize the importance of the separation and individuation phase for the differentiation of the sexes: This phase is thought to be quite decisive for the aetiology of transsexualism as well (Pfäfflin, 1994). Explicit fears of loss and separation make themselves known, as do archaic defence mechanisms. The strong affects—in addition to anxieties, they include anger, hatred, shame, and envy—return in countertransference reactions. Reiche calls the characteristic transference and countertransference constellation with such patients an "alternation of fusional charging and discharging" (Reiche, 1984, p. 56, translation for this edition). With respect to early forms of resistance, Robert Stoller points to the role of splitting in the genesis and maintenance of transsexual symptoms. The symptoms of transsexuals also indicate that the "discovery" of sex difference is not a one-time occurrence, a moment when something already existing in a fixed form is discovered. Instead, this "discovery" is a process that stands in correlation to the further development of the self and accompanies such development (Pfäfflin, 1994, p. 915).

Burzig (1982) notes a further characteristic element in transference among transsexual patients, which he calls the demand for recognition of a self-chosen gender identity. Here he sees a simultaneous dependence on external assurance together with efforts to free themselves from this dependence. Burzig understands the transsexual yearning as a narcissistic effort at stabilization, one in which the Other, here the analyst, has to be negated in his Otherness. In the encounter, the transference hatred is split off and directed against the person (or rather the genitals) of the transsexual.

Reimut Reiche (1984) asks whether transsexuality represents a human mode of being, and whether a transsexual identity exists beyond all the pathologies, or whether the term merely stands for a multitude of different, clinically significant, gender-identity disorders. The basic challenge emanating from this phenomenon is the inner certainty on the part of the transsexuals that the gender with which they are physically endowed is the wrong one. This undermines a usually unquestioned and apparently "natural" implicitness of having a particular, predetermined sex. The connection between "sex" and "gender" is completely severed in this manner. However, the radical separation from biological sex leads just as radically back to anatomy. Using the phenomenon of transsexualism, Stoller shows that anatomy is not destiny, but that what humans make out of anatomy becomes destiny. Yet in the case of transsexualism, the disempowerment of existing anatomy does not lead to any increase in freedom.

Reiche follows Stoller in arguing that the possibility of a transsexual identity sui generis stands and falls with the idea of a "core gender identity" and the notion of a non-traumatic, anisomorphic, "transsexual" imprinting. In the previous section, I offered a basic critique of this notion, and it provides no greater illumination in the present context of transsexualism either. Reiche himself in the end has no answer to the question he poses at the outset.

Norbert Boller (2000) emphasizes there is an "obsession with surgical intervention" among transsexuals, and a "quasi-paranoid, obsessive fight for release through the knife" (2000, p. 98, translation for this edition), and, in distancing himself polemically from Pfäfflin's critique (1993, 1994), tries to allow a sense of the affected individuals' experience to shimmer through. But a theoretical understanding of this phenomenon is still lacking. The German Transsexuals Law, which came into effect in 1981, has given these patients the freedom to choose, and determine, the sex of their own bodies. If one sees that as the core of transsexuality, psychoanalysis can add nothing of substance to its illumination: no analytic relationship can breach the wall of this demand (ibid., p. 19). The obsession, paranoia-like, suggests rather an "abdication" on the part of psychoanalysis (in Boss's sense), which enables what seems strange in transsexualism to be kept at bay and prevents what seems strange from being made commensurable with the psychoanalytic cannon.

In a vignette of one case, Pfäfflin describes an analysis carried out with a younger patient, who at the beginning of treatment was wholly fixated on receiving an assessment he could use to obtain surgical treatment. In addition to massive resistance to psychotherapeutic treatment, strong and aggressive affects were evoked in transference and countertransference in this patient. Only after a severe depressive decompensation, which required in-patient treatment, did this patient's defensiveness abate and allow for sustained, intensive work. On the basis of this case, Pfäfflin tries to prove that transsexualism is primarily about identity as such and not so much about *Geschlecht* identity. Also evident in this case is how unhelpful it is to categorize transsexualism as one of the "perversions", as one repeatedly finds in the literature. The dimension of pleasure and gratification, a constituent element of perversions, is lacking. Pfäfflin (1994), by contrast, emphasizes the narcissistic dimension of transsexualism. He sees these symptoms as "creative defence mechanisms" against an earlier, archaic identity diffusion that emerged in the context of incomplete separation and individuation. In Anna Freud's sense, defence has a system-maintaining, regulatory function: it serves integrative purposes and helps maintain ego cohesion, and it prevents earlier traumatic experiences from being perpetuated by restaging them in a softened form. This connection between resisting and addressing an issue is also seen in the transsexual staging. Unlike in "perversions", for a staging to function, patients need to rely on others "participating" by providing attestations, operations, and so forth. In this context, Pfäfflin (p. 925) speaks appropriately of an "allo-autoplastic entanglement", which also leads to a transference-countertransference constellation of behaviour that is hard to endure and has elements of blackmail and coercion. The core of transsexual defence, Pfäfflin concludes, following Erikson's notions of "identity resistance", lies in the patient's fear that the weak core of his or her identity might be destroyed and then replaced by that of the analyst. Following Pfäfflin this identity resistance can become the chief problem in treatment, because the patient "sabotages" communication and insists that the therapist accept his or her negative identity as real and necessary. As with other patients who show identity resistance, such as anorexics, the symptoms are experienced as egosyntonic, which also explains why many do not regard themselves as "patients". In consequence, they do not want to take advantage of psychotherapy but instead want only the "service" of sex reassignment.

Over a thirty year period, Ilse Rechenberger (1995) observed the psychosocial aspects of transsexuals and intersexuals and noted a trend toward greater awareness at both the individual and the societal levels. In Christine Jorgensen's case, there was still talk of "effeminate homosexuality". Since 1951, castration has been a method of medical treatment, followed soon thereafter by penectomy in 1953 and neovaginoplasty in 1954. Germany's Transsexuality Law, officially called the "Law on Changing First Names and Establishing Gender Identity in Special Cases" went into effect in 1981, and the Federal Social Court ruled in 1987 that operations were necessary curative treatments for transsexuals, thus decreeing that their costs would be borne by health insurance. The number of transsexuals in Germany is estimated to be from 3000 to 6000. Even if the issues involved in transsexualism and intersexualism have nothing in common, they establish that dealing with intersexualism has brought the diagnostic and therapeutic view of transsexuals into sharper focus. While intersexuals as a rule evoke compassion and empathy, transsexuals are confronted simultaneously with both fascination and rejection.

Unlike transsexualism, a relatively new phenomenon that has received broad public interest, intersexuality is far less known, even though it has been described as hermaphroditism since antiquity. In these cases, such individuals have bodies that cannot be unequivocally assigned to either male or female sex, as attributes of both are present.

"Intersexuality" is a medical term coined in the early twentieth century, though it seems ill-suited. As with the term transsexuality, it has nothing to do with sexuality itself but only with the manifestation of *Geschlecht*. In addition, it gathers the most varied forms of the phenomenon under a single umbrella term that sets a particular norm (on the definitional problems, see Richter-Appelt, 2007). However, since the term "hermaphrodite" is just as inadequate (Bödeker, 1998), I use all three terms interchangeably and synonymously in this book. Over the course of time, hermaphroditism has been dealt with in ways ranging from killing children so born to the social display of one particular gender (up until about the eighteenth century) to today's accepted medical practice. This last typically involves assigning intersex children, after about the sixth week of life, to one unambiguous sex, underscored with hormone treatments and/or surgery (see Hirschauer, 1993). Characteristic of this medical practice is the following view, in which a doctor, after a digression about mythology and the godlike character of hermaphrodites, cursorily states that nowadays, such persons are unhappy: "the precondition for hermaphrodites to achieve an emotional balance, in our view, is to approximate their external appearance to the normal, meaning the surgical correction of the intersex genitalia as well as the precise adjustment or substitution for what is often a flawed endocrinal system" (Hecker, 1985, p. 2, translation for this edition).

In keeping with this widely-held medical view, doctors and psychologists nowadays almost exclusively concern themselves with the "correct" assigning of gender and the problems an "incorrect" assignment brings. Estimates suggest about one in 2000 persons is so affected, and that Germany alone is home to about 40,000 intersexuals (Lang, 2006).

The problem with such estimates is that no statistics exist on the number of intersexuals: Medical records do not specifically take note of them, and immediately after birth, as with any other person, sex is assigned in accordance with the laws on civil status. As a result, this is a largely invisible social phenomenon. The most common form of intersexuality is congenital adrenal hyperplasia (CAH), which results from a genetically induced enzyme deficiency in the adrenal glands. It is therefore usually medically treated as an endocrinal disorder, since the enzyme deficiency causes cortisol, an essential steroid hormone, to be produced in insufficient quantities. This leads to an overproduction of male sex hormones (androgens) in pregnancy, which can cause a masculinization of the genitals in genetically female individuals. Depending on the level of hormones produced, and on other factors, this can lead to clitoral hypertrophy or intersexual genitalia, or to the formation of what appear to be external male genitalia (see Richter-Appelt, 2004, p. 99 et seq.). Children with this condition are usually raised as girls, with the enlarged clitoris usually surgically corrected (in what is called "surgical feminization"). Hormone replacement therapy, administered later, is intended to prevent further virilization. Generally, these girls develop a female gender identity, though with a tendency to display masculine gender role behaviour.

Another form of intersexuality arises from an androgen receptor deficit that can lead to resistance or either partial (PAIS) or complete (CAIS) insensitivity to androgens. A female phenotype can then develop from a male set of chromosomes. Often the disorder is discovered only during puberty, because externally, female genitalia are clearly present. Those with CAIS (complete androgen insensitivity) usually have a female gender identity, live as adults in heterosexual partnerships, and are satisfied with their sex lives (Hiort et al., 2003; Wisniewski et al., 2000). Those with partial androgen insensitivity differ in external appearance, though at birth, ambiguous genitalia are often observed. In the past, the recommended approach was to operate on such children and raise them as girls, but this practice has come to be increasingly criticized.

Still another form of intersexuality involves a disturbance in the biosynthesis of androgens that impairs the transformation of testosterone into the androgen dihydrotestosterone, which can lead to insufficient masculinization of the genitals at birth. By contrast, a clear virilization can take place during puberty. Sex/gender change is frequent in this group, with children initially raised as girls not infrequently living as men after puberty.

Since the 1950s, Money, Hampson & Hampson (1955) have recommended three guidelines to be followed if ambiguous genitalia are observed: early assignment to a *Geschlecht*, operative adaptation to a particular biological sex, if possible in the first few months or years of life, and maintaining secrecy or providing no information about the surgery and about taking hormones for many years during childhood. The guidelines are based on Money's long clinical experience working with such children, as well as on the conviction that nurture plays an overwhelming role in the nature/nurture debate. In this case, the idea is that one can achieve the wished-for *Geschlecht* in every child if one only raises that child in a sufficiently unambiguous manner (see Richter-Appelt, 2004, p. 102 et seq.). In the last few years, such views have come under critique, not least in the wake of publicity about the sensational case of Bruce/Brenda (Colapinto, 2000). Especially criticized are medically unnecessary operations based on wholly unproven, problematic assumptions, such as that a boy with a too-small penis cannot pass through psychosexual development unscathed, that a boy must be able to urinate standing up, that it may be prejudicial if a girl has a too-large clitoris or, to ensure unimpaired development, that a girl must have a vagina built up as early as possible because the tissue is more malleable early in life. In point of fact, the elasticity of an artificially formed vagina can be maintained only with the help of regular, painful treatments. Richter-Appelt (2004, p. 104) summarizes these debates and critiques to argue that *Geschlecht* is determined by many different biological and psychosocial components. Generally, surgical sex reassignment is not an emergency measure. If possible, informed consent should be obtained from the person in question, and medically unnecessary operations should be undertaken only if one can include the person in the decision. Ambiguous genitalia, or genitalia that deviate from the norm, do not necessarily lead to a disturbed psychosexual development, and repeated operations and examinations in the genital area can be more traumatic than having unusual-looking genitalia. There are a variety of genitalia, not just two outward forms—and a variety of identities, not just two.

Such observations are a major rejection not only of the everyday understanding of *Geschlecht* in its dichotomized manifestation, but also of previous scientific conceptualizations of *Geschlecht*. This is also true of psychoanalytic understanding, where the dichotomy of masculine and feminine has heretofore been self-evident. In *Intersexualität: Vom Gen zur Geschlechtsidentität*, a Hamburg catamnesis study, Herta Richter-Appelt (2004) takes a new approach and deals among other things with the question of what significance treatment measures have for the development of *Geschlecht* identity, gender role, and sexual preference. She also examines how satisfied subjects are with their sexual experiences, and the behaviour of individuals who have varying diagnoses of intersexuality. In her study, twenty-nine adults were given extensive questionnaires. Given the extremely small sample, one can speak only of possible trends, but in this group, those with a disorder of androgen biosynthesis tended toward bisexuality or homosexuality, while those who suffered from CAIS or PAIS tended to live as heterosexual women. While the latter group had not been operated on, many in the former group experienced repeated surgery on their genitalia when they were growing up. Even those affected often underestimated the traumatic effect these operations had. Though too little is known today about intersexuals as a collective group to be able to make a decision about changing treatment measures—long-term studies, in particular, are lacking—there is a growing tendency to show more tolerance with respect to how external genitalia look, as well as with respect to a strict assignment of *Geschlecht* identity, gender role, and sexual orientation. As a result, intersexuals often cannot easily state what their "true" sex is. Sex-specific behaviour, such as reproduction, is often anatomically impossible, and in addition, many do not conform to the clichés in terms of gender-specific behaviour. One can see this as an enrichment in the variety human beings display, beyond the categories of "man" and "woman" (Richter-Appelt, 2004, p. 109 et seq.). A follow-up study was able to confirm the initial findings (Brinkmann, Schweizer & Richter-Appelt, 2007). In particular, the medical or surgical measures taken do not appear to have met expectations with respect to stabilizing *Geschlecht* identity and sexual functionality. The Hamburg researchers were also critical of the limitations of a notion of sexuality that in essence focuses solely on function and ignores subjective satisfaction.

Studies of intersexuality also permit deeper insight into the complex process of forming a gender identity. According to Richter-Appelt (2004, p. 95), the following aspects are decisive: *Geschlecht* assignment after birth; parental and societal attitudes; somatic and psychic predispositions and developments; body awareness; and interaction with peers. One also needs to distinguish gender identity from sexual identity, meaning the subjective experience a person has as heterosexual, homosexual, or bisexual. This feeling is determined by the idea of what can be arousing, and in her view, this is not pronounced prior to adolescence (see the extensive discussion of sexual orientation in Chapter Three). In taking this position, Richter-Appelt rejects all biologically based speculation, which is inclined towards a genetic predetermination of sexual identity. She also rejects psychoanalytic studies that locate sexual identity in the context of the Oedipus complex, which initiates such identity before—in the classical view—it is later consolidated in adolescence. On the other hand, sexual identity must be distinguished from sexual orientation or preference, which describes certain charms a person finds attractive or sexually arousing. Generally, sexual identity and orientation match, but in exceptional situations, such as homosexual behaviour among soldiers during wartime, sexual behaviour and sexual identity can diverge. A psychometric investigation of gender identity found no significant differences between heterosexual and homosexual men and women. However, they clearly differed in gender role behaviour, as measured on a scale ranging from "typically masculine" to "typically feminine behaviour". Thus, homosexual women displayed lower "femininity values" or higher "masculinity values" than did heterosexual women. Homosexual men displayed higher "femininity values" and lower "masculinity values" than did heterosexual men (Richter-Appelt, 2004). In light of the more general changes in gender roles and their current tendency to converge, or the broad variety now on display, these current findings are remarkable. Still, the question remains how to explain these differences.

What is indispensable is a clear differentiation between transsexuality and intersexuality (see Rechenberger, 1995). Thus a sex change that an intersex person undertakes as an adult cannot be regarded as transsexuality but instead is a correction of an assignment made in childhood without the consent of the person affected. She also notes that sexual transgression in our culture (almost of necessity) is socially stigmatized and ostracized, because it questions the dichotomized sexual order with its heteronomous basic suppositions.

Ambiguity in *Geschlecht*, however, is not an illness calling for treatment but must instead become socially accepted. Politically active intersexuals therefore regard themselves as neither man nor woman and reject any efforts to assign them to one particular *Geschlecht*.

The desexualization of the gender discourse

The starting-point for Judith Kestenberg and Mary Jane Sherfey's reflections on sexual development lies in biology or anatomy. Nancy Chodorow (1978), by contrast, begins with social relationships, and her viewpoint is that of object relations theory. She asks what psychological consequences follow from the fact that everyone's first love relationship is to a woman, namely to their mother. Though Chodorow is less concerned with conceptualizing the development of human sexuality than with motherliness and the social organization of the sexes/genders, a closer look at her approach to a theory of gender is worthwhile, as it represents a broad current in feminist and psychoanalytic discourse. It also exemplifies the beginnings of an increasingly desexualized discourse on gender.

Chodorow emphasizes the significance of the "earliest mother-infant relationship in the earliest period of infantile development. This early relationship is basic in three ways. Most important, the basic psychological stance for parenting is founded during this period. Second, people come out of it with the memory of a unique intimacy which they want to recreate. Finally, people's experience of their early relationship to their mother provides a foundation for expectations of women as mothers" (Chodorow, 1978, p. 59).

The most important aspects of the mother-child relationship, Chodorow believes, are protection and the possibility of growth, as well as the development of the self and the ego. She favours Balint's notion of "primary love" (1935) and Bowlby's attachment theory (1969) over Freudian drive theory. In her view, an infant has no sexual drives but instead an innate, primary need for human contact. The increasing tendency among very small children at about age two to busy themselves with their genitals is something she does not regard as sexual, in that it takes place because it is pleasurable, but instead as part of the development of the bodily self and of gender identity. Object-relations conflicts over such topics could lead to castration anxieties and penis envy.

This theory, in contrast to the general theory of seduction, accords no explicit significance to the unconscious, and to the unconscious sexual desire of the mother. In this, Chodorow lags behind Freud's late insight (1931b) that a mother is the first seducer of her child, though she does note the body contact children need with someone who is emotionally involved with them. Here one could surmise a connection with sexuality, as all this caring by adults contains unconscious sexual messages, but this level of unconscious meaning and unconscious desire in the parent-child relationship finds no place in her approach.

Instead, the core of her study is the differences rather than the commonalities between the sexes/genders. According to Chodorow, these differences are basically reproduced through gender-specific parental behaviour, because the fundamental attitude of a mother, how she treats her child to begin with as well as later, differs depending on the sex of the child (Chodorow, 1978). Gender stereotyping begins immediately, in the first hours after a child is born, as empirical investigations have shown. Correspondingly, differences in pre-Oedipal development can be observed in the mother-son and in the mother-daughter relationships. The emphasis in Chodorow's argument is that mothers do not perceive daughters as being sexually different from them. Here one also sees a deep ambiguity in the English text, since "sexual" could just as well mean "gender", which would carry a different meaning. Primary identification and symbiosis is therefore more strongly marked in the mother-daughter than in the mother-son relationship. Separation and individuation remain "particularly female development issues" related both to difficulties in boundary-setting and to an insufficient feeling of distinctiveness (1978). For girls, these questions are more significant, since as a rule they grow up in families in which women take on parenting functions:

"As long as women mother, we can expect that the pre-Oedipal period will be longer than that of the boy and that women, more than men, will be more open to and preoccupied with those very relational issues that go into mothering—feelings of primary identification, lack of separateness or differentiation, ego and body-ego boundary issues and primary love not under the sway of the reality principle". (ibid., p. 110)

One sees terminological vagueness in these formulations, and they persist throughout her entire work. Still, phrases such as "feelings of primary identification, lack of separateness or differentiation" do not seem to be genuinely psychoanalytical, at least, and thus render it more difficult to follow Chodorow's meaning. Perhaps it is a matter of making clearer at what level such differentiation should be sought. One can certainly agree with Chodorow when she writes: "Boy and girls experience and internalize different kinds of relationships, they work through the conflicts, develop defences, and appropriate and transform the affects associated with these relationships differently" (ibid., p. 114).

Plausible though her theses are at first sight, one has to ask whether the differences are genuinely larger between the sexes than they are within a given sex, or statistically speaking, whether the variance between the sexes significantly differs from the variance within a sex. No empirical studies, as far as I know, compare the sexes with respect to such unconscious processes. But even on the basis of clinical experience, one suspects the ways women and men unconsciously process conflicts and form corresponding defensive reactions differs as much among as between, and hence that no appreciable gender-specific differences exist in these realms. On this point, too, there is a lack of terminological clarity and conceptual precision, since conscious and unconscious processes are not clearly demarcated from one another.

In my view, a key problem lies in this haziness. Precisely in the conceptualization of the sexes/genders, it is of overriding importance to differentiate between conscious and unconscious processes, since both sexual/gender positions exist side by side in the unconscious of every person. As a result, no gender-specific differences in unconscious processes can result.

In addition, the unconscious is conceived as a category without any notion of order, either temporal or spatial, without causality, without negation, and so on (see Freud, 1915e). For that reason as well, gender differences cannot be reflected in the unconscious. In contrast, one can observe differences between men and women at the level of what is manifested in behaviour, attitudes, affect, and so forth. This may be the key or decisive reason why the unconscious plays so little part in gender research.

Chodorow's basic assumption that the family situation affects the inner psyche differently in girls than in boys can be put more precisely by saying that this is true only of phenomena accessible to observation, but not of the mental structure. It does not strike me as particularly sensible to assume differing female and male psychological structures, though I suspect the notion of such gender-specific mental structures is widespread, even (implicitly) in psychoanalytic thinking. I would rather locate cultural heteronormativity at the level of the secondary process, seeing it as a factor that imprints an ordering principle onto modern society—deeply influencing the behaviour and experiences of every person in that society.

Consequently, I also regard the notion of male and female Oedipus complexes, as suggested, by Chodorow and others, as not very helpful. Such a "sexualization" or "genderization" short-circuits the constitutive and structuring function of the Oedipus complex, which extends far beyond a mere pattern of interaction between parents and child. Instead, the Oedipus complex can be regarded as a triangulation site where individuals locate themselves within a social network, first within the family and later in wider social contexts. The core issue is to relate oneself to the (prior) Other, meaning to give recognition to the Other's primacy (rather than treating the Other merely as a different subject). In contemporary societies, two axes of difference are established in the Oedipus complex: the difference between the generations of the parents and of the child (diachronically), and the difference between man and woman (synchronically). On the one hand, the differentiation has the goal of bringing about a clear assignment, and on the other, a constituting of boundaries and limitations. What becomes established is the sure conviction on the part of the child, for example, that he is the son of this woman and not her husband, or that he is a man and not a woman.

Erecting these boundaries requires mental work, and stands in sharp contrast to the development of autonomy and narcissism preceding it. Barely acquired, that autonomy is challenged by the prior existence of the Other, and narcissism is challenged by the limitations of one's self. At the affective level, the Oedipus complex is about ambivalence: hating a person at the same time as one loves him or her. The Other, who must be accepted in her or his potency, cannot be clearly assigned a place because emotional reactions to that Other are concurrent yet contradictory. In addition, the Oedipal conflict is also a negotiation of object-choice. Like the concurrence of contradictory feelings, there is also a concurrence of homo-sexual and heterosexual orientations, meaning the love directed at the same time to both father and mother. The socially determined primacy of heterosexuality supplants this concurrence of the contradictory, and these developmental tasks are structurally the same for both sexes/genders.

But according to Jessica Benjamin (1986), whose approach is also oriented to object-relations, Chodorow's approach leaves "an unsolved problem: *women's desire*. The problem begins with the fact that the mother is not articulated as a sexual subject: she is the woman without desire. ... Mother is there to serve the interests of the child" (1986, pp. 113–14). Identification with her creates a problem for a girl with respect to developing a sense of sexual agency. Because, as Benjamin puts it, this "seems an ill-fated beginning. Whence, if not through the phallus, through masculine orientation, do women derive their sense of sexual agency? And what represents it? There is no equivalent symbol of female desire that, like the phallus, suggests activity and potency" (ibid., p. 114). Additionally, in the traditional psychoanalytic view, the mother's "emblem of power is the borrowed phallus that she loses when she becomes the Oedipal, castrated mother" (ibid., p. 114). But even the borrowed phallus does not make a mother an active, desiring being: Her power does not lie in sexual potency but at best in her control over others. The absence of an independent female desire leads women to submit themselves to an ideal male figure "in order to acquire vicariously something they have not got within themselves" (ibid., p. 114). Such masochism, particularly in the form Benjamin describes as "ideal love", can thus be understood as an alienated attempt to represent female desire, one located in a dual opposition "that arises out of the tension between identifying with and separating from a desexualized mother, and between wishing and being unable to identify with a father who stands for desire" (ibid., pp. 114–15). Benjamin concludes from this that, "unable to create a representation of desire based on maternal identification, a sense of sexual agency that is active and feminine, the girl turns to idealizing love for a male figure that represents desire" (ibid., p. 115).

Benjamin, in connection with Chodorow's theory, sees the female proclivity to masochism as based on socially-learned patterns of gender identification as well as grounded in the separation and individuation that emerge from a predominantly female parenting. At the same time, she regards this masochism as a "perversion of women's sexual agency, and as an alienation of sexual desire" (ibid., p. 116). For various reasons, however, I regard it as not very helpful to keep associating masochism with femininity without further ado, as Benjamin does here—though she stands in a long psychoanalytic tradition reaching back to Helene Deutsch. Thus, it is remarkable that the thesis of masochism always appears in conjunction with an alleged lack of female desire. It is not evident what advantage there is in theoretical terms to insist on a lack of female desire or a lack of active female sexual agency. This insistence seems all the odder when contrasted with the simple and plausible notion of female desire put forward by Lillian Rotter. It is probably a dead-end to try to conceptualize something like a "genuinely" female desire, meaning a desire conceived as wholly independent of male desire, or as fundamentally different from the male one. That seems, in turn, just as implausible as assuming a male desire independent of the female. Rather, desire obtains its force precisely from the tension between the sexes. Yet to prevent a misunderstanding of this in terms of a normative heterosexuality, it is worth reiterating that this tension between the sexes can exist within a person just as well as between two persons (see Reiche, 1990; this approach is presented more fully below).

A further argument against assuming a specifically female proclivity to masochism is the clinical observation that submission fantasies are as readily found among male patients. In my view, these fantasies result generally from the primacy of the Other, but are generally more strongly repressed or denied by men, so as to not too strongly conflict with social notions of masculinity. In addition, in masochistic fantasies, one can also see an initially gender-neutral processing of guilt feelings that accompany Oedipal sexual desire, as Freud, for example, describes in his essay "A Child Is Being Beaten" (1919e).

Beyond the problem of masochism, Benjamin's arguments provide an opportunity for examining the premises and implications of the approach used in object-relations theory. In its modernized version, this is addressed in terms of recognition. This approach, which emphasizes differences between the sexes/genders and thus supports cultural heteronormativity theoretically, has received much attention over the last twenty years in the gender discourse, and seems meanwhile to have become part of mainstream psychoanalytic theory. Tellingly, this line of argument begins with Stoller's theory (discussed above) of core gender identity. In it, Benjamin sees the key to a "reinterpretation of the association of masochism with female experience" (1986, p. 118). In this, masochism is the submission to an idealized Other—an "ideal love "rooted in the relationship to the father during the separation phase (from the mother) and during individuation. Disappointment and refusal at that time can lead, according to Benjamin, to an adult woman's search for ideal love becoming the basic content of maso-chistic fantasies. The French analysts Torok (1994) and Chasseguet-Smirgel (1970), as well as Dinnerstein (1976) and Chodorow (1978) in the United States, "concur that the power of the father and his phallus derives from the role they play in separating from the mother. Standing for difference and separation, the phallus becomes the desired object for children of both sexes, who wish to possess it in order to have that power" (Benjamin, 1986, p. 120). For Benjamin, the penis is "a symbol of revolt and separation", in particular to be free of the power of the mother.

The lack of differentiation between phallus and penis is found fre-quently in the gender research literature, which strikes me as problem-atic both for understanding desire and for understanding masculinity and femininity. The level of immediate, bodily, sexual desire thereby becomes mixed together with the symbolic level. The phallus stands for desire, symbolizing it regardless of gender, while the penis—analogously to the vagina, clitoris, and other erogenous zones—is only one of the possible locations where desire obtains a specific bodily form of expression.

In addition, one often reads that the phallus is regarded as free of con-flict of ambivalence, which seems quite implausible. What is overlooked is that support of the wishes for separation and difference simultane-ously threatens the wishes for unification and melding—a point often ignored in the object-relations theory view, or more generally in the high value nowadays placed on separation and individuation. Rather than speaking of conflicts between wishes to separate and wishes to unify, from this perspective one speaks of conflicts between self-assertion and fear of separation. The wish to merge is replaced by anxiety. In the case of the phallus, though, it is precisely the tension between difference and unity that is significant in my view because, in addition to separation and difference, it also stands for unification. The phantasmal posses-sion of the phallus, in the guise of the penis, supports the separation of the child from its mother in this manner, and in the same breath makes (re-)unification with her possible.

Stoller's theory of core gender identity points out that the acquisition of a gender identity, at an age of about eighteen to twenty-four months, occurs at the same time as the rapprochement phase, when the experience of the child as a separate being intensifies (Mahler, Pine & Bergman, 1975). According to Benjamin, it is just at this point that the paradoxical, tension-laden need emerges to be recognized as independent precisely by the person on whom one was formerly dependent. This wish is linked as well with the narcissistic vulnerability of recognizing one's own dependency. Yet the child not only loses faith in the omnipotence of the mother but becomes aware at the same time of its own will and ability to act. Through this, the child also becomes the "subject of its desires". In Chapter One, I already questioned this emphatic subject theory proposition of a "subject of desire". From the perspective of the general seduction theory and the primacy of the Other, the individual is regarded not as the "subject" of his desire but instead as subjected to this desire. Autonomy, as the embodiment of subjecthood, is thus hemmed in precisely by desire. Given the high cultural value placed on autonomy and subjecthood in modern societies, this is likely an unwelcome insight. While Freud placed subjecthood in the Oedipus complex, it is moved back into the pre-Oedipal phase in object-relations theory, reducing the significance of the Other. As a result, the object-relations approach is diametrically opposed to the "alterity theory" approach derivable from the general seduction theory. In both approaches, it is a matter of a shift in perspective. While in the one view, the desire of the subject is directed to the object, in the other view, the subject is subjected to the desire of the Other, and responds, through experience, behaviour, and its own desire, to this Other.

What far-reaching changes in psychoanalytic theory the shift in paradigm from the Freudian, drive-theory conception to object-relations theory or to relational psychoanalysis brings, is pointedly summarized in two sentences: "The child (as the subject of his desire, IQ) now wants not simple satisfaction of need. Rather, in each of these wants lies the desire to be recognized as a subject—above and beyond whatever is wanted, the child wants recognition of its will, its desire, its act" (Benjamin, 1986, p. 121). Recognition has now replaced pleasure and gratification. It is unclear in this perspective what has become of the unconscious: In these acts of will, is it a matter of conscious or unconscious will? This would be no trivial distinction for a psychoanalytic theory.

In Benjamin's formulation, we can recognize the cultural ideal of the autonomous individual, conscious of itself, though it stands somewhat at odds with the Freudian insight into the limitations placed on this autonomy by the unconscious.

Nevertheless, this paradigm of recognition has received much attention in the last years, not just in social philosophy but also in psychoanalytic discourse. "Recognition", however, is such a multi-layered concept with so many different meanings that one must carefully clarify in which ways this term can be usefully employed in psychoanalytic thinking. Precisely when unconscious processes are at issue, various ambiguities emerge. Thus, in Benjamin's comments, it largely remains open what it means in a psychoanalytic sense "to be recognized in one's own desire". This can be understood in many ways, such as that others regard, either consciously or unconsciously, the desire of the subject as justified, or that they grant it space in addition, or even are involved in the satisfaction of this desire. These interpretations go in quite different directions and, without further elucidation, lead to more confusion than illumination, in my view. This confusion arises, for example, when Benjamin separates recognition and gratification from one another. She regards the father as the "subject of desire" and writes "The other subject is not the object of gratification, the supplier of need, but the one who gives recognition" (1986, p. 123). But it is unclear to me why the father cannot supply the child with gratification and recognition at the same time. Separation of recognition and gratification is problematic in that it implicitly deprives the mother, too, of the status of subject. Following Benjamin, from the point of view of the child, the mother is the object of gratification and not the subject of desire. With this, we return to Benjamin's starting-point, namely the lack of sexual desire on the part of the woman (and mother) that Chodorow postulates. But in the case of the mother, as with the father, it is not clear why she cannot simultaneously be the object of gratification of the child and a subject of desire. Following Laplanche, one can use the general seduction theory to show how both aspects can be conceptualized as existing within a single person, and need not be split between father and mother, or between man and woman.

Benjamin bases her conceptualization of gender identity development on Abelin's concept of the father's significance during the rapprochement phase (see Abelin, 1980). In this phase, the father exerts more of a liberating influence on the boy than on the girl. He remains "exciting", "a stable island of practicing reality" (Benjamin, 1986, p. 122), while the mother, meaning her representation, "becomes contaminated by feelings of intense longing and frustration" (Abelin, 1980, p. 155). The father is the "knight in shining armour" and becomes a symbol of liberation, separation, and desire during the rapprochement phase. It remains unclear whether the father's unconscious meaning for the child is meant, or whether this ascription is due to his lack of participation in infant care. Regardless, the consequences for the child's development are considerable. In this reading of Abelin, "the identification with the father offers the boy toddler his first model of desire" (Benjamin, 1986, p. 122), meaning his sexual desire, and "the first symbolic representation of the object and the separate self, desperately yearning for that object" (Abelin, 1980, p. 154). Phantasmally, the son now takes the place of his father with the wish "I want Mommy", and with this, he, like his father, becomes the "subject of his desire". Through this identification, the boy can avoid feeling dependent: he has the fantasy, with respect to his mother, of being like his father and not being her helpless baby.

The recognition of the difference between the sexes during the second half of the child's second year of life allows the differentiation of father from mother. This differentiating is structurally tied to the conflict over separation and dependence. According to Benjamin, this phase is so important that it is almost as significant theoretically as the Oedipus complex, though she does not say why. In terms of theory construction, her thesis does not seem very plausible at first glance. Its basic function seems to be to increase the significance of sex differentiation. If, with Freud, one regards the Oedipus complex as the "core complex" of neuroses, then one arrives at an interesting reading. In the North American context, differing gender roles are regarded as an important factor in mental health (see Friedman, 1986, more fully described in Chapter Three), and in that context, recognition of sex difference would also have an important function in the aetiology of neurosis, analogous to the Oedipus complex.

But the connection Benjamin makes between the individuation-separation conflict and the recognition of sex difference, or differentiation between father and mother, creates a further problem. It is based on the traditional division of roles between man and woman, in which the mother basically takes care of the children and the father is largely absent. But if, ideally, both parents are equally involved in child-rearing, then the differentiation between father and mother, beyond mere externals, becomes much more complicated. Conflicts over separation and individuation are then not divided between the parents but instead conducted with both parents equally (for comparison, see the newer developmental psychology studies by Klitzing, 2002). The self-assertiveness of the child must therefore apply to both father and mother. By the same token, support of the child as an independent being must also come from both parents. These considerations are related to Chodorow's (1978) thesis, which sees one approach to overcoming polarization between the sexes as having both parents take on the tasks of "mothering". The consequences of such altered parental behaviour on a child's psychosexual development are as yet unknown, but it seems important to accord sufficient significance to the unconscious dimensions in addition to the actual behaviour displayed.

An analogous problem to mothering, largely ascribed to the woman in psychoanalytic discourse, exists conversely in the case of desire, which is largely taken to be "male". Under societal conditions of gender polarization, motherliness, in the sense of mothering behaviour and sexual desire are likely incompatible and hence need to be divided between both sexes. One could either wait until gender polarization changes, or conceptualize psychosexual development differently. If, for example, one ceases to assume that women suffer from a lack , then it ought to be unnecessary as well to question women's desire (as done by Benjamin, see above). Women's sexual desire would thereby be taken for granted, just as male desire is, and would not always need to be treated as a separate problem. However, there is a glaring lack of plausible conceptualizations of desire itself, be it male or female. The everyday understanding of male sexuality favours a kind of "boiler model": a muted energy emanating from inside the body needs, over and over again, to be discharged. Female authors mostly reject such a model as a description of female desire. Instead, it is often asserted that drive theory is particularly unsuited for describing female sexuality (Chorodow, 1978; Sydow, 1993). However, the view that female sexuality cannot be conceptualized as a "drive" is at heart based on a fundamental misunderstanding of the drive concept. That is what prompted me to reformulate this concept and give it a different name.

According to most psychoanalytic studies, the adoption of gender dichotomy largely takes place symbolically, hence is independent of a child's specific experiences or of a given family constellation (see, among others, Chodorow, 1978; Benjamin, 1986). The meanings of masculinity and femininity are therefore much more a matter of cultural transmission, and are correspondingly adopted by the child. However, Sonja Düring dissents, citing a case from her psychotherapeutic practice in support. Her example shows how the meaning of gender difference in its concrete form is based on role models of parents or other close persons and thus can also stand in contrast to prevailing cultural symbols:

> A female patient, who had grown up as the second of three daughters, described her mother as the dominant figure in the family. A number of aunts whose husbands had been killed in the war lived with them. Her father came back to the family, as an invalid, when the war was over. At around this time, the patient had taken a bath together with a boy for the first time, and thought he, too, was crippled because such strange parts hung between his legs. She felt pity for him and interpreted the sexual difference in line with the relationship between her parents. Since her mother regarded her father as an annoying troublemaker, and someone who in addition had to be supported, the daughter fantasized him as weak and genitally maimed. In the end, he was driven away when her mother, not least at the urging of her daughter, divorced him. (1993, p. 18, translation for this edition)

Though this view of the male genitals as maimed is a highly subjective exaggeration, likely grounded in the specific mental structure of this patient, this vignette underscores a family constellation that is not at all uncommon: a dominant mother and an absent or weak father. The specific images and experiences of maleness and femaleness that a child confronts in its own family often stand in clear opposition to the cultural significance of the sexes. In addition, masculinity and femininity have unconscious meanings for the adult care persons, and they confront the child with these meanings. Finally, all efforts at assigning meaning are subject to the principle of *Nachträglichkeit*, which leads to constant reinscription. Thus, one can note that the development of gender affiliation is not resolved once and for all in early childhood, as part of the Oedipus complex, or in adolescence, but rather remains a dynamic process extending throughout life. What is contradictory is processed into more or less consistent identity blueprints.

Maleness: a "dark continent"?

Though phallocentrism, beginning with Freud and lasting well into the 1970s, dominated psychoanalysis, and psychosexual development was conceived in terms of an ultimately male-oriented, mono-sexual model, masculinity seems to have remained a "dark continent" in psychoanalytic theory right up to the present. Femininity, at least, has had somewhat more light shed on in it over the years.

The neglect of masculinity could have many causes. One might be a socially-determined gender hierarchy, where an unequal distribution of power gives the privileged gender few reasons to investigate itself, but by the same token makes it more attractive to research the subordinated gender. It could also be due to the fallacy that because of an implicit orientation to the male, which was generalized in psychoanalytic theories, this would result in insights into the specifically masculine. Or it could simply be due to a lack of interest. Whatever the case, the difference in the scope and type of research on femininity as opposed to masculinity is substantial. This is particularly true for studies taking a critical stance toward conceptions of maleness. Heinrich Deserno has categorized psychoanalytic studies about masculinity (following Fogel, Lane & Liebert, 1996) into four realms of relationships:

– the relationship of the man to the woman as *object* (of his love, his aggression, his envy, and his identifications),
– the relationship of the man to the woman as *self* (to the feminine, or to the female in the man)
– the relationship of the man to the woman as representation (usually of the infantile, immature, and archaic in the man)
– the relationship of the man to other men (which the woman can interfere with, because she embodies the female aspects in the male relationships, whether they are fended off or acted out). (Deserno, 1999, p. 81, translation for this edition)

Most striking in this summary is the extent to which the man is defined with respect to his relationships to women. This stands in sharp contrast to the definitions of femininity that have been offered, where the effort is often to define a femaleness that is independent and separate from the male. In the previous sections, which have focused largely on female development, there were repeated discussions of male development and masculinity, and these will not be repeated here. Instead, I want to select a few topics that illustrate the particular conflicts of, or in, maleness.

One can find a wealth of insights into the pathological limitations of masculinity in the discussions of the "negative" Oedipus complex. In the 1930s, these limitations were subsumed in the concept of the "femininity complex" (Boehm, 1930). Boehm conceptualized the immediate precursor to the Oedipus complex as an "early, feminine, phase of development, in which the boy's feelings are very much like those of a girl. … In this phase the oral zone and the region of the perineum play a larger part as erotogenic zones than the penis" (Boehm, 1930, p. 465). The boy is passive in his relationship to his father, desiring to lean on him in a tender, girlish fashion, and seeks his protection.

Feelings of hatred for his father are not yet manifested in this phase. In the course of the Oedipus complex, this feminine phase of development can be regressively strengthened and connected with guilt feelings, though it never entirely ceases to play a role throughout a man's life. Boehm, in his deliberations, allows himself to be guided by everyday speech. One says a boy still has very maidenly features, or is a girlish creature, or that an aged man acts like a woman. The fixation of the feminine developmental phase or the regression back to this phase shows itself in the most varied forms, in envy of the woman's ability to give birth and to nurse, in envy of her body characteristics, as much her vagina as her breasts, or also in anger, for example, at a sister given preferential treatment by their father. The fixation extends into expressing a more general attitude of disdain, disparagement, and oppression of women, as well as overt and exaggerated displays of masculinity.

In the context of the Oedipus complex, the regression to feminine wishes serves as a kind of distraction: the father is meant to be distracted from the mother so that the path to the mother is clear for the son. Here one sees the unquestioned primacy of heterosexuality. The "negative" Oedipus complex is understood as a distraction and not as an expression of male desire that is just as valid as the desire for the opposite sex. Boehm also draws attention to the fact that along with the regression, a genitalization of the pregenital developmental stages inevitably takes place: "The sense of guilt is 'shunted' along with the regression, just as railway-carriages are shunted from one set of rails to another" (1930, p. 463). The feelings of guilt prevent working through and integrating these feminine wishes, and during analyses a particularly stubborn resistance to bringing these wishes to awareness often develops. Particularly intense feminine tendencies, tenaciously held in the unconscious, not only are reflected in difficulties with potency, of whatever form, but also frequently keep a patient from achieving any real success as a man in life. As I understand it, some difficulties in working life such as mysterious breaks in a career can be understood in conjunction with such tendencies. Analyses frequently fail because of insufficiently working through these "feminine" wishes; they were noted already in Boehm's day and likely still persist.

Pieter C. Kuiper (1962) asks a question similar to Boehm's, though in different terms. He discusses the meaning of the passive-feminine stance of the man, as an expression of the negative Oedipus complex, in the analytic process. These passive wishes generally evoke a great deal of anxiety in male patients, and not infrequently lead to a "healing born of resistance" (p. 326, translation for this edition). The wish to be a woman, that is, to be "castrated", reinforces the fear of castration and impairs the sense of self. One finds "pseudo-masculinity or masochism, the sense of always being unlucky or the victim" (p. 327, translation for this edition) as forms of defence against the tendency to become passive, and Kuiper regards both the negative Oedipus complex as well as passivity wishes as regressive. For defensive reasons, both oral and anal sexual gratifications once again become important. They serve to ward off an activity that is aggressively taking over, a pleasure in controlling the situation. Kuiper formulates the goal of analysing male patients as follows: "The goal of a man's development is attained when he can work, when he does not fear a fight, when he has a healthy ego-ideal and a not-too-punishing superego, when he is capable of heterosexual pleasure—which includes that the partner's needs are taken into account as well—and when he can use his passive-feminine needs for purposes other than the merely sexual" (p. 344, translation for this edition).

In such goals, and patients, one can see problematic limitations on masculinity. The objective is not integration but rather resistance of receptive, "feminine" wishes, though expressed here in a sublimated, de-sexualized form. Just how widespread Kuiper's views were at the time can be seen in Margarete Mitscherlich-Nielsen's response (1962) to Kuiper's talk. She, too, sees the passive-feminine orientation of the boy closely connected to his passive-infantile attachment to his mother; if the castration anxiety is too great, it hinders masculine-active development.

Ralph Greenson points to a particular circumstance in the development of sex identity in boys: "I am referring to the fact that the male child, in order to attain a healthy sense of maleness, must replace the primary object of his identification, the mother, and must identify instead with the father" (1968, p. 370). This "dis-identification" perspective remains wide-spread in psychoanalytic discourse today and seems to largely determine the psychoanalytic understanding of masculinity. According to Greenson, the particular problems boys and men have with gender identity results from this necessary "ending of identification". He is convinced that men are far more insecure in their masculinity than women are in their femininity.

Both kinds of identification, the dis-identifying with the mother and the counter-identifying with the father, are established in chronological order, meaning the dis-identification with the mother is also a precondition for identifying with the father. With the help of the famous case study of the five-year-old "transvestite-transsexual" boy Lance, Greenson tries to show how necessary dis-identifying is for the creation of a male gender identity. In Lance's case, his mother "hated and disrespected her husband and men in general" while his father "was absent … and had little if any pleasurable contact with the boy" (ibid., pp. 371–72). As a result, his development was made difficult by an extremely intrusive, possessive mother and a weak father. Describing the development of gender identity, Greenson wrote, "I suggested three factors which play a role in this process: (a) awareness of the anatomical and physiological structures in oneself, primarily the face and the genitals; (b) the assignment to a specific gender, done by the parents and other important social figures, in accordance with the overt sexual structures; (c) a biological force which seems to be present at birth" (ibid., p. 372). A fourth factor needs to be added in the case of boys: the ending of identification with the mother and the development of a new identification with the father. This process is particularly difficult because a boy must do without the object that provided security in order to identify with the object less accessible to him. In addition, a mother must be ready to allow a boy to identify with his father. An important motivation for a boy to do so is the love and respect his mother shows his father. How this dis-identification process can be conceptualized in detail, however, or whether this might also be a "reversal of identification" or a "counter-identification" remains, for Greenson, something for future research to determine. To date, that research has not been forthcoming. As I point out at other junctures, the postulated necessary dis-identification appears to be a central problem in the psychoanalytic conceptualization of masculinity. In my estimation, such a dis-identification leads to a reduced, even a halved, masculinity, while the integration of feminine identification, or identifying with the (representation of the) mother and her desire, is what enables a stable construction of a male gender identity.

Robert May (1986) has suggested a somewhat different image based on the fact that the first and most important person providing care for a boy is of the opposite sex/gender. Rather than speaking of a necessary dis-identification, May speaks of the hurt and envy of the boy. When he discovers he cannot be a mother, he turns away from her. In many men, this leads to the development of a character style that denies this hurt, compensates by asserting its own power, and rejects any "feminine" characteristics such as tenderness and attachment.

The psychoanalytic musings about the meaning that identification with the father has for the development of a male sex identity can take on some decidedly bizarre hues. Until a few years ago, for example, "upright urination in identification with the father (was) considered an early step in assuming a male gender role" (Tyson, 1986, p. 7). Beyond that, Phyllis Tyson, in an approach based on developmental psychology, summarizes the main psychoanalytic notions of the development of male gender identity, and these continue to dominate the understanding of masculinity. The main task during the phallic-narcissistic phase, from this perspective, lies in consolidating a narcissistic and "sexually" differentiated and intact body image, and in adopting a male gender role. As soon as this is adequately consolidated, a boy wants a different relationship to his mother. He no longer wants to remain in an anaclitic dependence on her but instead wants to be the man in her life. Using the term "sexual" above to refer to the body image again shows again the difficulty in translating the English gender discourse into German, for it does not make sense to speak of a "sexually" differentiated body image but only one that is differentiated in terms of *Geschlecht*, a term that in German encompasses both sex and gender.

In contrast to a girl's development, the Oedipal phase in a boy, according to Tyson, is no longer tied to a switch in object. However, the fantasies about the love object have changed: "The ego ideal now holds winning, protecting, and providing for a woman a valued aspect of masculinity" (ibid., p. 12). In masturbation fantasies, it is often the case that a boy wants to be as big and strong as his father, or to have his father's large penis replace his own, small one. Castration anxieties in this phase correspondingly focus on the father and no longer on the mother. Because of the content of his masturbation fantasies, however, a boy feels guilty and fears his father might in some magic way damage the organ of his pleasure and the source of his arousal. But he may also fear damaging his own genitals by masturbation. In both cases, he repeats masturbation to reassure himself that his penis is still intact and functioning properly. Castration anxiety also leads the boy's negative Oedipal constellation to be only weakly developed. In addition, he has to fear that in case of a rivalry with his mother, he might lose her basic emotional devotion to him. Tyson concludes from this that "Generally, therefore, the boy repudiates any female identifications or transsexual wishes and turns his attention ardently to his phallus, and finds more and more ways in which he can identify with his father" (Tyson, 1986, p. 16). Tyson's approach makes clear that, as before, dis-identification with the mother is a necessary step in the development of masculinity, and that the emphasis lies on demarcation and rejection, not on integration.

The integration of inner and outer genitality is a key psychological challenge for male development as well, which basically, but not exclusively, takes place during adolescence (Kestenberg, 1968, see above). This stepwise acquisition of a sexually mature body develops in the course of dealing with different aspects of male and female identification, as well as with body-related images and fantasies. On the basis of a case history, Heinrich Deserno (2005) describes a conflict-laden developmental process in which the psychic representation of the prostate becomes the locus of an unresolved conflict between active and receptive wishes. Accepting both inner and outer genitality takes place in a particularly dramatic fashion during adolescence because it is tied both to the loss of a child's body and to separation conflicts. One also suspects that a particular closeness to his mother as well as identification with her genitalia is preserved in a man's representation of his inner genitalia. Such female identifications may come to the fore in an unconsciously and compromised manner in symptoms such as prostatitis.

In conjunction with erotic transference, Ethel Person (1985) addresses the tendency of a man to split the nurturing object from the erotic object. As is the case with girls, boys too must give up libidinous attachments to their mothers. According to Freud (1920g), the boy gives up his mother not just out of fear of retaliation from his father but also because of a massive narcissistic injury: he is not in a position to replace his father. This narcissistic injury remains and permeates the most varied areas of life. One manifestation, in Person's view, can be seen in continuing anxieties about the size of the penis and its ability to function. In adolescence, this narcissistic injury is heightened. A typical experience in male adolescence, Person states, is being continually sexually aroused without having adequate opportunity for release. The extremely unsatisfactory situation of the Oedipal phase repeats itself here, as do feelings of inferiority vis-à-vis other men. Fantasies serve as compensation, as do wishes to split sexual desire among multiple women. In this way, the adolescent can, on the one hand, keep the sources of sexual arousal and satisfaction under control; on the other hand, should a woman turn away from him, she can immediately be replaced.

I see another form of processing this narcissistic injury in "erectile dysfunction", currently the most widespread male disorder of sexual functioning today. The continued worry about the ability of the penis to function, as an expression of the early narcissistic injury, can lead to taking potency-boosting medicaments like Viagra on a prophylactic basis. Patients not only complain of complete impotence, but often say that their penis "is not stiff enough" or "doesn't stay stiff long enough". These formulations point to a sense of being inadequate, potentially reinforced by unconscious Oedipal fantasies, as noted above (see also Quindeau, 2007).

Separating a nourishing object from an erotic object, or separating being nourished from having Oedipal desires, as Ethel Person suggests, can also be revealed the other way round. The passive position may be retained as the exclusive condition for love, as Wilfried Wieck put it in his aptly entitled book *Männer lassen lieben* (1987) about "men allowing themselves to be loved". What is lacking is an integration of active and passive wishes. A bridge between the opposite tendencies in a boy's relationship to his mother, and one which helps promote this integration can be provided by a favourable, protective, father-son relationship. This allows a son to have Oedipal desires without being too directly rejected and aggrieved (Deserno, 2005). This fathering function stands in clear opposition to the punishing, "castrating" father of traditional psychoanalysis, and calls for a father who allows the desires of the son but who also absorbs the rejections and affronts that then arise. It remains an open question whether such a confident position on the part of the father really is less problematic, especially if it means not taking a son seriously as a rival, quite apart from the fact that a father, himself emotionally involved in the Oedipal drama, would hardly be able to sustain it emotionally.

In the "negative" Oedipus complex, a passive-genital goal for his drives develops in the boy. He fantasizes himself in a "female position" by wanting to replace his mother as his father's lover (Freud, 1918b). This receptive goal of the drives can be shown to be extremely conflict-laden for male development or male self-image. "In the receptive position, a man encounters his own denied femininity, his envy of women, and finally also his fear of his own undeveloped drives, which, in an unconscious resistance, he would like to identify with the feminine and keep at bay" (Deserno, 2005, p. 232, translation for this edition). This defensiveness is reflected in resistance to the inner genitalia, unconsciously treated as the site of threatening "feminine" aspects such as arousal, receiving into oneself, and bringing forth. Deserno, using an example from analysis, shows how such resistance can take the form of a conversion and how the receptive goals of the drives are shifted to other organs like the bladder, intestines, or pelvis. The arousal and satisfaction that come from the original goals of the drive are expressed in a transformed manner through anxiety and painful cramps.

These conflicts in men with regard to accepting and integrating their outer and inner genitality are seldom mentioned in psychoanalytic discourse. For the man, in keeping with prevailing cultural norms, the notion of masculinity and its significance appears to focus exclusively on appropriating the outer genitalia, and then largely only one part, namely the penis. Inner genitality, as a locus of receptivity, passivity, or procreative ability, is given very little attention. In this problematic and unnecessary abbreviation, as the studies discussed show, one can find, in my view, the key reason why male gender identity is regarded as less stable and more insecure than female gender identity. Rather than postulating that dis-identification with and rejection of feminine aspects are particularly important for the emergence of masculinity, it seems important to emphasize that these parts need to be integrated in order to establish a less limited and more stable male identity.

From geschlecht dichotomy to geschlecht tension

In Freud's psychoanalysis, "constitutional bisexuality" plays an important role: "In human beings pure masculinity or femininity is not to be found either in a psychological or a biological sense. Every individual on the contrary displays a mixture of the character-traits belonging to his own and to the opposite sex; and he shows a combination of activity and passivity" (1905d, p. 219).

Freud employs the concept of bisexuality to account for this mix of masculine and feminine traits in the individual. This concept was of core importance to him: without it, he wrote, "it would scarcely be possible to arrive at an understanding of the sexual manifestations that are actually to be observed in men and women" (ibid., p. 220). I continue to regard this insight as fundamental. Freud adopted this notion of a biological, constitutional bisexuality from his friend Wilhelm Fliess. The theory is based, first of all, on anatomical and embryological facts: "a certain degree of anatomical hermaphroditism occurs normally. In every normal male or female individual, traces are found of the apparatus of the opposite sex. (…) These long-familiar facts of anatomy lead us to suppose that an originally bisexual physical disposition has, in the course of evolution, become modified into a unisexual one, leaving behind only a few traces of the sex that has become atrophied" (ibid., p. 141).

This biological bisexuality needs to be distinguished from the psychological bisexuality that emerges from the existence of male and female traits in the mother and father with which the child identifies. At the same time, bisexuality is also reflected in the desire for a sexual object, that "combines the characters of both sexes; there is, as it were, a compromise between an impulse that seeks for a man and one that seeks for a woman" (1905d, p. 43). The significance of bisexuality can also be seen in Freud's tracing the outcome of the Oedipus complex back to it: "In both sexes the relative strength of the masculine and feminine sexual dispositions is what determines whether the outcome of the Oedipus situation shall be identification with the father or with the mother. This is one of the ways in which bisexuality takes a hand in the subsequent vicissitudes of the Oedipus complex" (1923b, p. 33). Though Freud always emphasized the importance of bisexuality, he never provided a systematic exposition of the concept. Even in 1930, he regretted in *Civilization and Its Discontents* that "The theory of bisexuality is still surrounded by many obscurities and we cannot but feel it as a serious impediment in psychoanalysis that it has not yet found any link with the theory of the instincts" (1930a, p. 105).

Constitutional bisexuality not only affects identification with a gender but also shows itself in object choice, as will be discussed below (see Chapter Three). While I regard this concept as indispensable for understanding sexuality as well as gender identity, bisexuality is accorded hardly any attention anymore, particularly in the English-speaking world, with the exception of authors like Otto F. Kernberg. How could it have come to this?

In *Gender Identity: a differentiation model* (1984), Irene Fast presents an interpretation of the acquisition of gender identity that has received wide recognition in psychoanalytic discourse, and it is a conceptualization diametrically opposed to the idea of bisexuality. The author follows the paradigm of differentiation that has proven useful in other contexts of development, such as in distinguishing self from object, or separating subjective from objective reality. The differentiation paradigm assumes an undifferentiated state with respect to sex. Thus, the earliest childhood experiences are not yet differentiated in a gender-specific way. Rather, at this early stage, children are within "an undifferentiated and overinclusive … matrix" (Fast, 1984, p. 13). Only at about age two do they become aware of differences between the sexes. Irene Fast sees this as a ubiquitous and injurious experience that calls for an intense confrontation with the limitations of one's own sex. Envy of the other sex became a constitutive element in the development of gender identity. The egocentric position, the illusion that everyone must be shaped the same way one is shaped oneself, must be overcome. After becoming aware of sex difference, experience correspondingly must be re-categorized with respect to gender. Gradually, the ideas of masculinity and femininity begin to be differentiated, and are first formulated and then developed with respect to the child's father and mother. In the process, the perception of the parents also changes.

According to Fast, in realizing this difference, typical difficulties become evident. First, the transition from the undifferentiated experience of unlimited possibilities to the realization of sex difference is experienced as loss or deprivation. This can be manifested in varying ways, for example, as an utter loss (if I am not omnipotent, then I am powerless) or as a personal divestment not affecting others (1984, pp. 24–44). Normally, these difficulties are only transitory. In their place, a feeling of personal uniqueness arises: "When the girl becomes aware of sex differences she develops a complex sense of femininity and herself as feminine in relation to a concurrently developing sense of masculinity attributed to males and experienced in relation to them" (ibid., p. 26). While Fast only suggests but does not explicate this wide-ranging thesis, in doing so, she presents a very plausible way of understanding penis envy. The oft-observed wish of a girl for a penis is not at all the wish to be male, but rather the narcissistic wish to return to an earlier inclusiveness.

In Fast's model, the genital sexuality of a girl is decisive for the development of her femininity. In a 1937 publication, Edith Jacobson (1976) already argued that a girl's discovery of her own genitality allows her to give up her desire for a penis, and Judith Kestenberg (1968) suggests that a girl has the feeling of having a "productive inside". They thereby contradict, in my view correctly, the Freudian notion that the vagina is given no significance before puberty, and that female genitalia in childhood are reduced, essentially, to the clitoris.

However, Fast's critique of the Freudian approach is very harsh, and she rejects drive theory and the idea of bisexuality lock, stock, and barrel. Not infrequently, however, her objections are based on a simplistic reading or on misunderstandings of Freudian thinking. Among other things, she reduces the concept of a "constitutional bisexuality" to a simple biological bisexuality, and rejects this as untenable (1984, p. 37). This has far-reaching consequences for her theory of gender identity development. Thus, she is of the opinion that children, as soon as they become aware of sex difference, deny the earlier representations and identifications that transcended gender and see them as no longer compatible with their own sex. Donna Bassin (1996) criticizes this view for taking the rich representations that transcend gender and replacing them with a simple acceptance of the limitations of external reality. What is lost here, in Fast's epigenetic developmental model based on Piaget, is that the denied and discarded representations remain active in the unconscious. Fast's concept of "gender appropriate self-definition (both bodily and social)" (1984, p. 77) is also arguably problematic. Even though she draws attention to the developmental appropriateness of the masculine phase of the girl and the feminine phase of the boy in the context of the differentiation paradigm, she clings to the notion that these phases must be abandoned in favour of a gender identity more in line with reality (ibid., p. 78 et seq.). This description gives the impression that it is always completely clear what is deemed gender-appropriate or inappropriate; on-going cultural change is wholly disregarded. The cultural and individual conflicts, whether in personal development or in analysis, are inevitably associated with such efforts at determination and thereby resolutely ignored. Despite all assertions to the contrary, this approach in the end understands sex in a biological or essentialist manner.

The reception of this theory is made more difficult by Irene Fast's misleading, ill-founded critique of Freud. She alleges that the assumption of the boy's early identification with his mother is incompatible with Freud's theory: "Every major tenet of that theory is called into question by it" (Fast, 1984, p. 51). But the opposite is the case: Freud's concept of bisexuality is based precisely on these early identifications, which he calls introjections. Fast's supposed "new formulation" is thus based on false imputations. A closer look is nevertheless worthwhile. According to Fast, in the phallic phase, the boy is aware not only of his own, male, sex but also of the other, female sex, which he admires. His anxiety is thus not only about the possible loss of his penis but also about the loss of the potential of having female characteristics, a potential he believes he has. Beyond this, the Oedipal phase is not only about male rivalry for his mother; the boy must understand himself as masculine vis-à-vis both parents, too.

With these considerations, in my view, Irene Fast sheds an interesting light on the Oedipal triangle, in which a boy must assert himself as masculine, and on his fear of castration, which is overlain by the psychic confrontation with the painful fact of his possessing only one sex. In light of the need to renounce bisexual omnipotence, he feels robbed, reduced in his sexual possibilities, and curtailed in his sex and gender. In a manner similar to female development, the body, particularly the genitals, in Fast's approach, also plays a central role in acquiring male gender identity: "The boy elaborates masculinity within himself, centred on his male body. Femininity is attributed to members of the other sex, centred in their female bodies" (ibid., p. 53). The feminine is increasingly seen by the boy as something not part of himself or in his possession, but instead accessible to him only in the context of relationships. In other words, the development of masculinity and femininity is not a further narcissistic development within the self but instead a development in the context of object-relations.

One can note that while this perspective appears constructive, such differentiations take place in the form of projection processes. It is characteristic of such processes that they shift what is incompatible with the self to the outside world, to other people. Unavoidably, this involves a kind of devaluation, since what is moved to the external world is generally experienced as alien, and not infrequently is even fought against.

The process of projection turns the earlier admiration and valuation of a characteristic into its opposite. Fast's thesis that the boy, for example, regards the ability to give birth as feminine, then excludes that from his self, and then ascribes it to women and admires them for it, may seem morally desirable but also does not seems very plausible in psychological terms. In the course of the differentiation process, the Other appears as the negation of the self; in this manner, polarities are generated and established. Probably against her own intent, Fast thereby conceptualizes a dichotomous relationship between the sexes, one unavoidably determined by polarization and mutual devaluation. In my view, it can be expected that a boy, in particular, is put in a precarious psychological situation by this mode of acquiring gender identity, because the love he has for his mother comes into irreconcilable conflict with his narcissistic tendencies.

In addition, Fast's approach reveals a fundamental problem in the "difference discourse". The difference between the sexes or genders becomes inappropriately reified and essentialized. At first glance, the differentiation paradigm evokes the impression that it involves a continual process of creating difference. Yet according to Fast, that is true for an only limited period. The goal of development is to acquire an (externally) predetermined difference, which is then established and fixed. This approach differs diametrically from Derrida's notion of *différance*, which describes a continual creating (and annulling) of differences as the central mode of the psyche. I regard it as extremely beneficial to use this concept of *différance* for the psychoanalytic conceptualization of the sexes, to avoid linking differences with anatomy in an essentializing manner.

In contrast to Irene Fast, Donna Bassin (1996) provides arguments against gender polarization. Her goal is a reconciliation of the masculine with the feminine. As I regard this approach as one of the most interesting current psychoanalytic conceptualizations of the genders, I would like to explore it at somewhat greater length than other approaches discussed previously. A broader discussion is also necessary inasmuch as Bassin's approach is grounded in a paradigm different from my own. Like Irene Fast, Jessica Benjamin and others, she advocates an intersubjective, relational psychoanalysis based on a paradigm of recognition. My own thinking is based instead on the primacy of the Other, and follows theoretical approaches emphasizing alterity, such as the general seduction theory. Though the different ways of conceptualizing the relationship of subject and Other, and of subject and subject, have an effect on notions of gender, Bassin suggests a number of concepts that are also useful for my own approach.

Bassin replaces the dichotomy of *Geschlecht* with the proposition that diverse "sexual" (though she probably also means "gender") identities exist in the psyche, mixes of active and passive, masculine and feminine, and subject and object. However, one can take issue with her critique of the one-sided assigning of the idea of the phallic to male genitalia, and noting the limitations the phallic order has for both sexes, as it reduces the variability within a sex and creates a normative gender identity through polarization and suppression. Phallicity ought to be contrasted with an understanding of genitality "as the provocative and rather utopian culmination of psychosexual development" (1996, p. 181), one allowing for a genuine relationship between the sexes/genders. In the classical psychoanalytic view, the dissolution of the Oedipal stage goes hand-in-hand with the end of a gender polarization that separates humanity into the phallic and the castrated. The genital character is marked by the capability for object-love, which, by largely transcending narcissism and ambivalence, makes it possible to place oneself in relationship to the Other (Abraham, 1925). The libidinous cathexis is extended to the entire beloved person. In particular, the ambivalence toward the Other's genitalia, which in earlier developmental stages still evoked fear and curiosity, is overcome in the genital stage of development. Sexual impulses are connected with tender impulses. This by no means original but continually obscured notion of genitality rather than phallicity seems constructive and helpful to me, though for a different reason. In my perspective, genitality introduces not so much a "genuine relationship between the sexes/genders" or the ability to place oneself in relation to another, as the ability to tolerate the Other as Other and not allow the alienness and unfamiliarity of that Other to vanish. This includes one's own alienness, which is manifested in the sexual realm and in the respective subjective modes of pleasure and gratification, and is accessible, and "controllable", only to a very limited extent.

In the conventional psychoanalytic view (up to Irene Fast), the representations of the other sex in the genital phase are also ascribed to the Other, in order to maintain gender consistency. According to Otto F. Kernberg (1991), this loss of representations of bisexuality is mitigated by pair formation, whose function it is to transcend the barrier between the sexes and discover in the other what has been repressed in one's own sex. In his view, however, the potential problem in such cases is that each partner only relates to his or her own projected identifications, rendering mutual understanding of the Other impossible. With a similar aim, Jessica Benjamin (1988, 1993) argues that the Other cannot be loved as a subject if he or she is to provide the Other with the sense of completeness. Key in her approach, by contrast, is to not think of difference and otherness as opposite or as a polarity. Bassin employs these considerations to argue that female genitality can be understood as a way of overcoming the "either/or" of phallic logic. To this one can add, in my view, that this is not only true of female genitality but ought to be equally applicable to male genitality.

The reconciliation of masculinity and femininity in the genital phase, according to Bassin, depends on the self's being able to open a transitory space and use symbolic representations of the other sex/gender as symbols. The symbolic representations serve to overcome the dichotomy between the sexes/genders. Such an integration of the representations of the other sex/gender clearly differs from the problematic "ideal of unlimited possibilities" that Blos (1967) draws attention to in the context of bisexuality. Instead, in Bassin's approach, the representations of the other sex/gender serve ego-development purposes and support it in its function of "inner and outer control". At this point, I wish to emphatically point to an essential shift that the intersubjective, relational approach in psychoanalysis has undergone with respect to classical psychoanalysis: representations of the other sex thus are to be understood less as unconscious (drives or) wishes or as a mode of desire, and far more with respect to the ego functions they serve. According to Bassin, they promote the ability of the self to recognize the Other as a "subject on equal terms". The assimilation of the Other into the Self enables the recognition of the Other. But as long as a woman is determined solely by her vaginal world, her inner generative space, and finds no access to her earlier, over-inclusive body-ego experiences, she cannot engage in a genuine object relationship to a man. Again, this is also analogously true for a man.

Even though I regard these individual aspects of Bassin's approach as quite telling, at this juncture I want to again point to the differing paradigms underlying our approaches. While the theorem of recognition is aimed at acknowledging the Other as a *subject on equal terms*, as a subject like myself, from my "alterity theory" viewpoint the issue is acknowledging the Other *as Other*. One could put this trenchantly: I am interested in the recognition of the obverse of the subject, thus precisely not the area over which the subject has autonomous control and of which he or she is aware (which is how the German Idealist tradition understands the subject) but rather the alien, the Other, the inaccessible, unconscious. With respect to the generative space of woman and man, this means I do not emphasize the enabling of an object relationship as Bassin does. I see this space instead as a place where bisexual, homosexual and heterosexual representations, as well as the most varied modalities and fantasies of pleasure and gratification, can continue to coexist. The space so provided does not reject or ostracize the alien and the different, for the purposes of an unambiguous, dichotomous gender or sexual identity. The generative space stands for the recognition of the alien in oneself. This makes it possible to deal in a more relaxed manner with the alien aspects both in oneself and in other persons, and to not devalue or combat them.

Recognizing differences in *Geschlecht* and differences in reproduction is regarded as an important part of the construction of reality (Chasseguet-Smirgel, 1981; McDougall, 1985). As wholeheartedly as I agree on the one hand, the normative implications for psychoanalytic thinking strike me on the other hand as problematic, particularly when it is a question of psychic reality, of unconscious processes. Yet both authors, for example, regard the unconscious denial of a difference between the sexes as pathological, in a normative sense, and as a key marker in the aetiology of perversions and postulate on the other hand that its unconscious recognition is indispensable for mental health. As I previously noted, such a notion of unconscious recognition is extremely questionable, especially as—at least in the Freudian conceptualization— sex differences can play no role in the unconscious either, because the unconscious has no concept of order. More fruitful, it seems to me, is Bassin's notion of a polarity of *Geschlecht* as a necessary phase in development, needed temporarily to form self-identity and object bonds and giving them the necessary stability and consistency, but afterwards needing to be transcended. Bassin compares this process with musicians who can learn how to improvise only after they have mastered the basic musical techniques and rules. Once the reality principle has been established, it then becomes possible to effect subtle differences between the sexes and genders without immediately succumbing to bisexual omnipotence fantasies or exposing oneself to the suspicion of perversion, as Chasseguet-Smirgel, in particular, emphasizes.

This becomes especially clear in the psychoanalytic process, where it becomes apparent in transference that many and various gender and sexual identifications are possible, among patients and analysts alike. One can agree wholeheartedly with Bassin here, though less in her emphasis on an "empathetic understanding of the Other", promoted through identification with the cross sex/gender: "Over-inclusive body-ego representations afford the raw material, or foundation, for the imaginative elaboration of the Other" (1996, p. 158f). While Bassin is concerned with an understanding of the Other that in the end leads his or her Otherness to disappear, the point to me is to be able to let Otherness stand and tolerate it without transferring it into one's own system of understanding and meaning.

But aside from that, Bassin has a further interesting conceptualization: the female body-ego. Though Freud's separation of sexuality from biological sex was very helpful for the understanding of human sexuality—and here I wholly agree with Bassin—in that context, his failure to address the organization of the female body-ego poses a problem. Freud's critics did describe a specifically feminine body-ego, but rescinded the separation of sexuality from biological sex.

The notion of a genuinely female subjectivity was introduced together with the concept of a primary femininity by Horney, Jones and others, and was theoretically elaborated in the 1980s (among others by Bassin, 1996, Bernstein, 1983, and Irigaray, 1985). As useful as these new conceptualizations of a femininity that develops out of a specifically feminine physicality, independent of masculinity, might be, they are also constricting. On the one hand, they help understand how women perceive and deal with their inner genital space, and the particular anxieties, wishes and conflicts associated with it, but they are problematic on the other hand owing to the newly created normativity for women's experience and behaviour patterns. Such "politically correct" norms for women's behaviour basically have just as destructive an effect on psychoanalytic theory formation as similar norms had in Freud's lifetime: they create—and here I fully agree with Bassin—a mere reversal, a "female version of a phallocentric theory" (Bassin, 1996, p. 176).

Bassin does not see an insurmountable contrast between the classic stance and its revision. In her view, one can understand the overlap in the two positions as a "duality at the heart of the feminine" (ibid., p. 176). One can also readily agree with her that the experience of "positive femininity" and the experience of a deficit in consciousness can coexist in a woman. Thus, the feminine organization of consciousness is divided into two developmental strands:

> "one moves toward firm gender identity based on anatomy, iden-
> tification with the same-sex parent, and resolution of the positive
> Oedipal drama; simultaneously, another allows the psyche to move
> away from the comforting but containing limitations of gender
> based on early over-inclusive body-ego experience with non-geni-
> talized parents, identifications with cross-sex parents, and resolu-
> tion of the negative Oedipal in adolescence". (ibid., p. 176f)

This, too, seems to me to be as true of male as of female gender identity.

The paradoxical conceptualization of simultaneous identity and multiplicity, according to Bassin, finds support in developmental psychology. Girls simultaneously create a specifically female body-ego and include the multiplicity through employing symbols of a remembered earlier body-ego that transcended the sexes. Unfortunately, the author does not elaborate these promising thoughts. In particular, the "remembering symbolization" is worthy of further consideration. In addition, over long stretches in Bassin's approach, the complex relationship of conscious and unconscious with respect to sex or gender identity remain unclear and call for greater specification.

An expansion and clarification of the concept of the body-ego, by contrast, is given more space and Bassin ascribes two functions to it: as the origin and source of metaphoric and symbolic representations, and as the receptacle for experiences. The body-ego represents the symbolic or metaphoric relationship to one's own body and, following Lacan, can be described as "imaginary anatomy". It is not a matter of a precise, "realistic" image but instead of interpretations that are dependent on object relationships and representational abilities. As a limiting and containing structure, the body-ego organizes drive activity. A well-developed body-ego also permits children to recognize themselves as the initiators of action, and that recognition contributes to their development of intentionality, instrumentality, and proficiency in handling themselves.

The body-ego incorporates representations of sex and gender norms as sources of symbolic content that can be both differentiated (especially with respect to anatomy) and undifferentiated (e.g., transcending the sexes). Though the body is an important source of experience and can serve as a model by which experience can be understood, the body-ego is by no means restricted to the body and its anatomy. It can also incorporate aspects of the outer world, as well as project aspects of itself onto that world. Anatomy is not a barrier to creating representations of the cross sex/gender and representations that transcend sex: "The physical impossibility of cross-sex behaviour does not prevent the mind from playing with reality" (ibid., p. 178). This is all the more true of the unconscious, in my view.

In this context, Bassin points to the important factor that the outer world increases in familiarity to the degree it is processed by the self. In this manner, cross-sex representations also become more familiar. On this point, Bassin is diametrically opposed to Fast, who emphasizes the ostracizing and rejecting of those very representations. I think it important not to apply this exclusively to the female body, as Bassin does, but to see it as an equally appropriate model for a male body-ego.

Finally, I would like to mention those assumptions in Bassin's approach which relate to symbolization theory and are particularly helpful for understanding the clinical implications of her conceptualization of the sexes. One can illustrate this with a short case vignette. Her note that, in the context of gender representations, symbols function as links between opposites and as mementos of lost objects, strikes me as particularly important. One can also agree with her that imaginative configurations of cross-sex identifications can serve as a way of mourning for the lost (conscious) bisexuality. In this symbolization, Bassin sees a possibility for "mastering the loss" rather than suppressing it. It is also important for the subject to know that she generates the symbol herself, and that the symbol must be differentiated from what is symbolized. For example, a penis can take on a metaphorical meaning and thereby lead a woman to relate to her earlier bodily experiences that transcended her sex. Such symbolization needs to be distinguished from a fetish, which implies lack or castration.

Bassin makes these distinctions clear with two clinical vignettes that are based on dreams (ibid., p. 108 et seq.), one of which I will sketch here: It reveals an interesting aspect of the phenomenon traditionally described as penis envy. A female patient suffered from a fear of penetration during heterosexual intercourse—her lover asked much too much of her, she thought—and intense fear while driving, especially that she might cause an accident in which someone would die. In the course of the analysis she gradually sensed her envy of her boyfriend and her aversion towards him, as well as anger at his invasion of her body. In numerous dreams, according to Bassin, an unconscious masturbation fantasy could be discerned. The patient ascribed a penis to herself and identified with a representation of the other sex. In the view of her analyst, this female patient can use this symbolically to represent her ability to advance into areas of her consciousness that were previous inaccessible. Bassin differentiates this from a concretistic reading of the wish for a penis, which would express a desire for this actual body part. This distinction is an extremely constructive, fruitful way out of the entrenched discourse about "penis envy" noted above. The insight that she herself was the one who created this symbolization and thereby gave her experience a particular meaning was of decisive importance for this patient. The identification with the cross-sex representation permitted her to represent her own penetration wishes, and in the further course of the analysis to gradually accept and experience that it belonged to her. In this context, one can agree with Hanna Segal (1991) that as soon as the subject recognizes a symbol as his or her own creation, that symbol becomes freely usable—in contrast to a symbolic equivalence.

I want to emphasize that this case reveals the way in which sexuality takes on a subjective meaning, one that fundamentally determines sexual experience. This meaning is independent of actual anatomy and gender roles, and is neither given to nor taken away from the individual, even if it subjectively is often experienced this way, or is imputed in the discourse about the absence of female desire. Instead, it develops during the life span, in various relationships, in the mode of on-going reinscriptions.

In a different vignette, Bassin shows how such symbolization can fail, and how an appropriated penis can also serve as a fetish to mask deficient ego functions. The development of a stable body-ego is the precondition for integrating over-inclusive body representations. In a fragmented body-ego, there is a danger that body parts may take on meanings of the self, such as the warding off of anxieties. Thus, the representation of a penis can serve to address castration fears or the fear of losing control over one's own body. In such cases, the penis is not used as a symbol but instead, concretistically, as a wished-for body part. This is often connected with false hopes that are directed at the penis, for example that it is an object that stands for power, influence, and activity and is able to compensate for a deficiency. This concretistic usage also shows the influence of a phallocentric culture.

In addition to Donna Bassin's conceptualization of the sexes and genders, Reimut Reiche's (1990) approach also seems extremely fruitful to me for a psychoanalytic understanding of gender and sexuality rooted in the primacy of the Other—even though Reiche demonstrates as little support for an alterity-based theoretical paradigm as Bassin. With his notion of gender tension, Reiche, unlike Bassin, emphasizes the unconscious dimension of sex identity and the relationship between the sexes, and thereby also emphasizes a core aspect of psychoanalytic theory. Reiche occupies a special place in the psychoanalytic discourse on gender, not only as one of the few men in a discourse largely carried out among women, but as one of the first in German-speaking Europe to question sexual dichotomy: "Already the designation 'two sexes' is incorrect, and seduces one into thinking in bipolar opposites and binary models. The correct formulation is this: sex/gender appears in two forms (meaning: dimorphously)" (1990, p. 46, translation for this edition). With this, he emphasizes the differentiation in what is unity. Unlike his female American colleagues, his questioning of gender polarity is based not on sociological critique of concepts of the social order but largely on biological arguments. Reiche's approach fundamentally differs from my own, but interestingly enough, and for completely different reasons, he arrives at similar conclusions. In addition to his consistent consideration of the unconscious, what is particularly important to me is his basic understanding of bisexuality.

Reiche is not referring to interpersonal relationships when he uses the term "gender tension", but instead to the tension-laden relationship *in* a man or *in* a woman resulting from the dual forms of sex and from the difference between masculinity and femininity. The relationship of man and woman is determined by four relations: "by *differentiation* in sex; by *inequality* in the distribution of social and economic positions of dominance; *struggle, violence* and *reconciliation* in the relations between the sexes; and by *equality* in the id, in the drives with their lack of direction (ibid., p. 8, translation for this edition; italics in the original). To depict biological differentiation, Reiche relies on Max Hartmann's (1943) genetic theory of a general, bipolar gender dichotomy. After a discussion of phylogenesis, Hartmann formulates three laws of sexuality. These are the "law of general bipolar gender dichotomy", the "law of general bisexual potency" antithetical to it, and the "law of the relative strength of masculine and feminine determination", which gives the impression that it neutralizes the polarization of the prior two laws. The first law states that that reproductively relevant functions and structures are distributed between two sexes ("polarity"); the second law formulates the force ("potency") opposing this polarization; and the third stipulates that the realization of the "masculine" or "feminine" type depends on the relative valence of the self-determining factors (ibid., p. 10). In biology, therefore, one finds a flexible and less well-defined determination of sex, in the sense of either more or less. By contrast, a dichotomous, mutually exclusive, conceptualization of sex in terms of a rigorous either/or corresponds more to a societal need for order that wants to see unambiguous conditions that can be interpreted in a binary, bipolar fashion. Reiche revisits Ferenczi's (1924) genital theory, generally rejected as mythological and speculative, as well as Balint's (1935) attempt to formulate psychosexual parallels to a "biogenetic basic law". In the differentiation of the phylogenetically developed sexual functions into two actions—copulation and fertilization—and into two action modes associated with it—draining (expulsion, separation) and union (merging)—he sees psychoanalytic conceptualizations of sexual arousal and of the connection between pleasure and procreation that have not been addressed thus far. In the case of the latter, Balint sees it as unity in contradiction, and thereby confronts ideologies of highly diverse provenance and the conservative moral notion that copulation and fertilization must belong together, as well as the progressive critical variant insisting the two must be separate.

To substantiate the thesis of sexual equality in the id, Reiche refers to a differentiation Morgenthaler makes when he speaks of the sexual as the "aimlessness of the ... instinctual impulses" (ibid., p. 106), as opposed to sexuality, which functions as a dictatorship ... established by the instinctual and ego developments by means of the events in the secondary process" (ibid., p. 110), and indicates what the secondary process has made out of the drive activities. Morgenthaler assigns sexuality to a biological space. Extremely fruitful is his thought that the sexual is organized through the secondary process and thereby becomes sexuality. This organization begins with the cathexis of the erogenous zones, moving through orality and anality in the phallic-narcissistic phase to the genital organs, which then constitute their permanent "home". In my view, one can object to this limitation to the genital, as there is no doubt that the pre-genital erogenous zones continue to remain erogenous. From the point of view of genitality, there are—and here one can agree without reservation with Reiche and Morgenthaler—certainly differences between men and women. For Reiche, the question poses itself whether it makes sense to assume only male and female sexualities (in various historical and cultural patterns), or whether one should also take as starting point a sexuality whose origin, ultimately biological, is to be found in different masculine and feminine forms (ibid., p. 23). This question seems to me of eminent importance for the connection between gender and sexuality, and for psychoanalytic conceptualizations, it emphasizes the importance of the unconscious. One can answer this in different ways.

If one examines the category of gender primarily (in its sociological function) as a structure that orders society, one would have to distinguish gender-specific sexualities that one could be conscious of from a gender-unspecific understanding of the "sexual" that is unconscious. If one instead views *Geschlecht* as a biological predisposition, one would have to assume not only that different sexualities are developed in a gender-specific manner, but the underlying "sexual" as well.

In the Freudian conception of the id, there are no contradictions but only "movement". "Identifying" characteristics of specific individuals as masculine and feminine, for example, is differentiation achieved by the ego, and the moulding of gender identity results from such ego achievements. However, Freud emphasizes the free mobility of the libido:

> We have called the motive force of sexual life "the libido". Sexual life is dominated by the polarity of masculine-feminine; thus the notion suggests itself of considering the relation of the libido to this antithesis. It would not be surprising if it were to turn out that each sexuality had its own special libido appropriated to it, so that one sort of libido would pursue the aims of a masculine sexual life and another sort those of a feminine one. But nothing of the kind is true. There is only one libido, which serves both the masculine and the feminine sexual functions. To it itself we cannot assign any sex. (1933a, p. 131)

Freud's view here is fundamental to my own understanding of human sexuality; I do not want to subdivide it into a male and a female sexuality but instead understand sexuality as something that transcends gender. This gender-neutral character strikes me as particularly necessary for locating the *Geschlecht* tension that manifests itself in every form of human sexuality, both individually and in relationships.

The similarities and differences between the sexes and genders, the struggle between and the reconciliation of the masculine and feminine, is reflected in an impressive manner in the orgasm (Reiche, 1990, p. 19). Following Reiche, it makes little sense to speak of a vaginal or clitoral orgasm, as the location of the orgasm cannot be anatomically specified (see the discussion above in the context of inner and outer genitality). To Reiche, it makes no sense to speak of a male or a female orgasm: instead, one finds the expression, in Hartmann's sense, of a "bisexual potency". It reveals itself in the melding of the representations of both subject and object. At the moment of orgasm, representations of the "masculine" and the "feminine" dissolve and are formed anew, regardless of which manifested object relationship (heterosexual, homosexual, auto-erotic, or with a fetish object) it takes place in, in which bodily organs it is triggered, and which fantasy images that are capable of becoming conscious are associated with it. In this respect, no primacy of heterosexuality is connected with this perspective. What is far more significant for Reiche in this context is the primacy, or specifically human omnipresence, of the primal scene and the Oedipus complex. Independently of the manifested object choice, the child must come to terms with father and mother and can do so only on the basis of its bisexual identifications. Seen psychoanalytically, the orgasm is a "multi-person phenomenon" that consists of the acting ego as well as the entire subject and object representations that merge at the moment of orgasm. The dissolving of the polarities between these representations is regarded as so marvellous because it is accompanied by a symbolic new beginning, in Balint's sense. At the same time, the dissolution of "feminine" and "masculine" makes reference to the pre-genital backdrop of sexual activity in the breastfeeding process. The experience of dissolution, fusion, and melding goes back to the time predating the formation of object representations: "In the end, it is probably always the internal image of the mother and the child who falls asleep at her breast after being nursed or fed that fuse together in the moment of orgasm" (ibid., p. 21, translation for this edition). In the "alimentary orgasm" posited by Sándor Radó (1928), we find the beginnings of such ideas as well. Eventually, one finds gender-specific, fully differentiated images of man and woman laid onto this background image in later life. In my vocabulary, I would call them on-going reinscriptions which emerge from the general seduction scene and the infant's primary experiences of satisfaction (see Chapter One).

In the sense of a "multi-person phenomenon", Freud writes in a letter to Fliess: "I am accustoming myself to regarding every sexual act as a process in which four individuals are involved. There is much more to be said about this" (Masson, 1985, p. 364). In this offhand remark, Freud makes reference to bisexuality, but unfortunately does not expand on it. If one follows this line of thought, however, it casts doubt on the general notion of homosexuality and heterosexuality: in every sexual act, at least phantasmally, both sexes and both forms of object choice are present. This thought allows the phantasm of the primal scene to be linked with orgasm: the primal scene is woven together, as it were, with the breast-feeding scene and appears—a paradox, but only at first glance—also as a reinscription.

In conclusion, I want to return to Laplanche's considerations of the general seduction scene, as noted in Chapter One and link them with Judith Butler's (1993a, 1993b) gender theory. Drawing on Foucault (1977a, 1977b), Butler regards gender and the dichotomous heteronormativity of humans primarily as a structure for ordering society. One might call the general seduction scene the locus at which gender, in the manner Butler describes, is constituted (see Quindeau, 2004b). In my view, Butler provides a theory of gender that can be connected to psychoanalytic theories of sexuality, desire, and the development of gender, and though she does not do so explicitly, one could say that she draws on the approaches taken by Irene Fast and Donna Bassin. In "Melancholy Gender/Refused Identification" (1997), Butler formulates a core thesis that belonging to a particular gender is accompanied by a kind of melancholy. Understanding the self as male or female can be understood as the result of a melancholy process. Butler, like Irene Fast, focuses on the loss implied by insight into the limitations of one's own sex. Giving up fantasies of bisexual omnipotence calls for a specific form of grieving, which she conceives of as melancholy.

Melancholy represents an incomplete grieving process. While grieving, according to Freud, leads to a complete separation of the libido from the object that has been lost, and the now freed libido is available for new object cathexis, in the case of melancholy, it is taken back into the ego: "Thus the shadow of the object fell upon the ego, and the latter could henceforth be judged by a special agency, as though it were an object, the forsaken object. In this way an object-loss was transformed into an ego-loss and the conflict between the ego and the loved person into a cleavage between the critical activity of the ego and the ego as altered by identification" (1917e, p. 248). In this view, melancholy is thus an impoverishment of the ego. In "The Ego and the Id" (1923b), Freud returns to the process of melancholy, calling it a common and typical psychic process that plays a large part in the construction of the ego and of that which one calls character. The reason for this revision of views lies in a changed understanding of the meaning of identification. Identification now is seen as a stage prior to object choice, namely as an early designation of an object. The object, in accordance with the phase of libido development, is to be incorporated or eaten. In that sense, identification represents an enrichment of the ego. Through identification, the lost object is resurrected in the ego. The ego partly changes following the model of the lost object. The note that there is identification in the case of a retained object is also important, as it means the object need not be given up.

The melancholy mode thereby has an important meaning for structuring the ego. With regard to the development of gender identity, one can observe that identification with both parents, hence with both masculine and feminine parts, takes place. As Irene Fast also writes, these identifications are independent of, but also transcend, gender. Girls not only identify with their mothers but also with their fathers, much as boys not only identify with their fathers but also with their mothers. In psychoanalytic theory, identification with both parents is situated at the level of character (that is, at the "gender" level). In her argument, Butler goes a step further and relocates the identification process to the level of the body (the "sex" level). In so doing, she focuses on a level less considered in Laplanche's general seduction theory but important for a theory of sexuality. Butler draws here on the Freudian thought that the ego is primarily a "body-ego" (1923b, p. 27). As something physical, the ego takes on a gender-specific morphology. The early form of identification, understood as a form of incorporation, one can now say, constitutes the body and constitutes the gender-specific morphology. The assumption that the body is brought forth by object relations or by the impact of such relations, is a strong challenge to our conventional understanding, which sees the body as something given or natural. To avoid misunderstandings, I want to point once again out that the "forming" of the body is meant in the sense of bringing forth, of performance, and not, for example, in the sense of manufacture. However, by "forming" I do not mean only the psychological appropriating and forming of the body. As the example of the erogenous zones (addressed in Chapter

One) indicates, relationship experiences are directly inscribed in the body and are what first elicits its arousal.

Judith Butler links yet a further line of argument to the mode of identification. She points out that identification, the internalizing of the object, goes hand-in-hand with non-recognition of the loss: when the lost object is internalized, there is nothing else that might be lost. By becoming, through identification, a part of one's own psychic structure, the lost or renounced object is preserved at the same time. Identification is, following Butler, thereby a magical, psychic way of preserving the object: what is supposed to be given up is simultaneously retained. In consequence, melancholy is an extremely productive, "clever" mode of processing losses that makes object cathexes available for ego formation. Yet all this has its drawbacks, too: the loss, the giving up, of object cathexes that are the precondition for identification. The important point in Butler's argument is that identification with the same-sex parent presupposes relinquishing her same-sex desire: a girl becomes a girl by giving up desiring her mother and instead identifying with her. The cathexis of the mother as love object is replaced by identification, which in turn is necessary for forming the ego and gender position.

In Butler's terminology, the development of the masculine and feminine position occurs through prohibitions that call for the loss of certain sexual attachments and that also prohibit any grief over these losses (Butler, 1993a). These prohibitions are a result of the heteronormativity in our society, which rejects homosexual attachments. In her opinion, heterosexuality arises not only through the prohibition of incest but primarily by enforcement of the ban on homosexuality. This perspective is highly questionable in my view, in particular because Butler refers only to the girl's development, and ignores the relationship of the boy to the mother, which is a heterosexual one from the outset. Nevertheless, the connection she suggests between giving up desire and identification seems very important to me for understanding the development of gender affiliation, under current cultural conditions. However, I want to emphasize that the psychodynamic mode she describes is by no means necessarily so, or is necessarily the result of psychological processes, but goes back exclusively to heteronormativity and the associated rejection of homosexual attachments.

Butler reconstructs the emergence of gender affiliation against a backdrop of the dominance of the heterosexual order. In this, she relies on Foucault's theories (1977a, 1977b), which see gender as a structure for ordering society. The gender positions are subject to a binary logic: a person is either male or female, and the assignment to one position or the other is compulsory at birth, if not already prenatally. In Butler's theory, however, neither femininity nor masculinity are biological dispositions but instead are developed, "achievements" that arise simultaneously with the acquisition of heterosexuality. This means that the development of masculinity and femininity—gender identity—takes place simultaneously with object choice.

Butler goes a step further. Our cultural logic calls for a close association between gender affiliation and heterosexuality, so a threat to heterosexuality—such as by rejected homosexual tendencies—also threatens gender affiliation. Masculinity and femininity, affiliation with a sex/gender, become basically stabilized, in her view, by the heterosexual order. Butler's thesis is an effort to explain the strong social acceptance of bans placed on homosexuality, which persist despite all efforts at liberalization. At the same time, she offers a reason for many heterosexuals' widespread fear of homosexual strivings; to them, homosexual desire unconsciously represents an attack on gender identity. Butler herself admits that the supposition of such a close connection between gender identity and sexuality is exaggerated. But it is one she regards as necessary to emphasize the problem of the loss and grieving that accompany the development of gender affiliation.

By reconstructing a girl's development, one can show that gender identity is at least in part accomplished through rejecting homosexual attachments: "The girl becomes a girl by being subject to a prohibition that bars the mother as an object of desire and installs that barred object as a part of the ego, indeed, as a melancholic identification" (1993a, p. 169). The identification thereby preserves the ban on homosexual attachments and homosexual desire, while incorporating the unmourned loss at the same time. So far, so good. What cannot be sustained, however, is the thesis that "heterosexuality is cultivated through prohibitions" (ibid., p. 169). It is then incomprehensible why a girl should love her father, for in my view, the reasons cannot be solely the prohibition against continuing to love her mother. Instead, it lies in a father-daughter relationship independent of the mother.

Without going into the details of problems with the psychoanalytic theory of a change of object (see above, as well as Chapter Three), Butler's argument, in light of a dichotomous relation between the sexes, would need to be augmented by an aspect of Irene Fast's (1984) approach: the girl also becomes a girl by abandoning her identification with her father. If the assumption is true that a child bisexually identifies with both parents, gender identity development then must consist in repudiating identification with the opposite sex in order to arrive at one's "own", unambiguous, gender. This appears, in my view, to be the main effect of the cultural dominance of heterosexuality. This is less a matter of object-choice, hence of homosexual or heterosexual attachments, than one of the binary coding of sex, which leads to an unambiguous assignment—male *or* female—and thereby forces the exclusion of the other. It is only in modern times that the binary coding of sex has taken on the exaggerated importance it now enjoys. What is interesting, therefore, are the processes of exclusion and rejection at the psychic level which are compelled by the binary coding, and which presumably lead to multiple unconscious conflicts and symptom formation.

In her article "Melancholy Gender—Refused Identification", Butler addresses not just the development of the girl but also that of the little boy. In the cultural logic of heterosexuality, becoming a man entails rejecting femininity, which nevertheless, and at the same time, is a precondition of heterosexuality. The heterosexual desire of a man is rooted in the rejection of femininity: "He wants the woman he would never be" (1993a, p. 170). The early identification with the mother is rejected (in Lacan's sense of foreclosure), yet persists as desire. The problem with this argument is that the desire predates the identification. The little boy loves his mother and identifies with her in order to maintain the love relationship (this is the melancholy identification mode). Thus "from the beginning", a heterosexual object-choice or identification exists that the boy must give up in order to become a man. To resolve this aporia of desire, identification and rejection that exist in Butler's argument, one would need to adduce the identification with the father and with his desire, too, to explain the development of manliness, and thus start with a bisexual identification. At the same time, it is significant that the rejection of femininity and of identification with the mother is regarded as a prerequisite for the development of manliness. This rejection, too, means a loss impossible to grieve over.

Butler uses the term "foreclosure" (*forclusion*) from the Lacanian tradition to describe the process of exclusion. She distinguishes it from repression, which presupposes an already formed subject. Foreclosure, in contrast, is an act of negation that founds and forms the subject itself. Because the genesis of gender identity is meant to be interwoven with the constituting of the subject, this use of the term seems conclusive to me.

These "foreclosed" identifications, the losses that are unconsciously experienced and cannot be mourned, and that take place in the process of acquiring *one* gender, are expressed in specific settings. Butler calls them performances, and illustrates this by pointing to transvestism. The term performance, as used in the philosophy of language, plays a key role in Butler's argument, where it means not only production but also execution.

The term describes the connection between speaking and showing. Utterances are, on the one hand, regarded as rule-governed executions of a particular programme (as in a grammar), and on the other hand as acts in the sense of performances or productions. While the execution of a speech act can be understood wholly through knowledge of the given programme and its goals, the performance of an utterance is characterized as an event that always contains more than can be understood with the help of the rules that govern speech. This excess of meaning is not to be understood as deviation or fault; instead, it calls into question the system of order itself. The performative character of speech both creates and at the same time changes reality. This can be seen in simple examples such as a wedding at the registry office, a letter of dismissal, or a court case. With words, acts result at the same time: the signing of the marriage contract has multiple consequences for the real lives of the participants, the dismissal turns an employee into an unemployed person, and a court decision may make a free man into a prisoner. By analogy, one can also understand the assigning of individuals to a gender as a performative act that turns individuals into girls or boys, men or women.

In her book *Gender Trouble* (1990), Butler presents a theory of gender identity in which she describes gender as performance. In this understanding, gender identity is not understood as a fixed core that is "expressed" through language, actions or gestures. Instead, the performance of belonging to a gender evokes retrospectively—*nachträglich*—the illusion of an inner core gender. In addition, gender affiliation is evoked through ritualized repetition of conventions: this ritual is partly socially compelled by the dominant matrix of heterosexuality. In her later essay (1993b), noted above, Butler concedes that it is not enough to think of gender merely as performance, or to derive its significance from its performance. Here she has recourse to the category of the unconscious in psychoanalysis, which makes clear that there are modes of action in gender identity that are not revealed in what is performed as gender. In that respect, what is expressed, the performance, always needs to be understood in relation to what is excluded from it, what may not be shown. Butler explains her thesis of gender performativity using the example of transvestism, and in the process makes an analogy between the performance of transvestites and the performance of gender. If a man, as transvestite, wears women's clothing, then it is in imitation of femininity. Traditional gender theories do not see this femininity, which the transvestite is imitating, as imitation, at least not if femininity is conceived of as an inner core that is expressed through a particular behaviour, a particular clothing, etc. But if one understands femininity—as Butler does—as something acquired in the course of childhood development, as the result of identifications, then gender identity, too, is always about imitation. Butler comes to the following conclusion: "drag imitates the imitative structure of gender, revealing gender itself as an imitation" (Butler, 1993a, p. 176). To formulate gender as "imitation" may seem strange, for gender identity, in particular, seems to us to be a fixed, nature-given core of our identity. The deconstructionist argument, however, aims precisely to question this seeming naturalness and reveal that it is socially constructed.

What remains open is through which forms of exclusion and "foreclosure" the performance of gender occurs. How is the phenomenon of gender melancholy connected with the practice of gender performance?

To answer this question, Butler has recourse to the psychoanalytic category of "acting out" (*agieren*). In transvestism, she states, an unfulfilled longing is reflected in the mimetic annexation of the gender identity of the other sex. For that reason, one suspects it is precisely this longing that is acted out in the transvestite performance: the repudiated (foreclosed) identification with the opposite sex/gender. As acting out, this performance in turn points to the problem of the unacknowledged, unmourned loss. The transvestite performance incorporates this loss and takes the place of the grief.

In her gender theory, Judith Butler focuses less on the acquisition of one's own gender and much more on the reverse, the repudiation of the opposite sex/gender associated with that acquisition. Both "masculinity" and "femininity" are formed and consolidated through identifications. Starting from the bisexual identification with both parents, affiliation with a particular sex is acquired at the cost of giving up the other sex. This loss cannot be mourned, however, and must therefore be "foreclosed". Since this is a form of grieving that does not, and cannot, achieve closure, one can speak of a melancholy process. Heterosexual identity is achieved through a melancholy incorporation of a love that it denies at the same time. A heterosexual woman will, for example, say of herself that she has never loved another woman and consequently has also never lost another woman. This is a dual denial: never having loved and never having lost. The heterosexual subject—and of course the homosexual subject as well—is grounded in this dual denial, and in the impossibility of admitting the lost attachment. Following Butler, the result is a culture of gender melancholy, in which masculinity and femininity both have traces of a love that is not mourned and that cannot be mourned.

Yet if one surveys the psychoanalytic discourse about "femininity" and "masculinity", one is somewhat perplexed. The discourse is strangely at odds with the significance these categories possess in the social order, in our self-understanding, and in our understanding of the world. Yet psychoanalysis seems incapable of defining what masculinity and femininity are with any great precision, or how it develops over the course of a life. This tension could be due to the specific logic of psychoanalytic thought, which has little use for dichotomized oppositions and tries instead to bring together, in overarching concepts, what appears contradictory or mutually exclusive.

Robert May (1986) illustrates these difficulties with the example of gender *identity*. This term refers to the understanding of the self, self-definition as either male or female, and to the behaviours, attitudes, fantasies or desires regarded as male or female or ascribed as appropriate to a man or a woman. The term "identity" demands that all these differing levels be brought together into a coherent whole.

As has been noted in the various explanatory efforts, discrepant self-representations of the other sex/gender need to be abandoned in the process of forming a gender identity in order to arrive at an unambiguous gender identity. This development is deemed as accepting "reality". Conflicts that arise in this process are regarded as transitory and as to be overcome. Such a homogenized, unifying identity construction, which excludes the Other and the contradictory, can be regarded as an impoverishment and a fixing of the subject. For it is only from disparate and inconsistent wishes, fantasies, behaviours, and inner images that one derives the possibility of development and change. To be sure, giving up aspects of the other sex and gender does not mean these representations disappear. Instead, they persist in the unconscious and continue to have multiple effects. For there is no negation in the unconscious, contradictions exist side-by-side, and in that sense, no dichotomous differentiation of masculinity and femininity exists there either.

Instead, psychoanalytic thinking allows for a notion of gender that is not dichotomous, and sees masculinity and femininity as existing, in differing mixes, in a complementary manner in each and every one of us. The notion of interplay of masculine and feminine in a person can be found in many of the approaches discussed. However, when examined more closely, it frequently proves to be mere rhetoric. For it is often left open what these "masculine" or "feminine" parts might be and how they stand in relation to one another. The continuing conflict between these constellations, which is the rule rather than the exception, is addressed only by Reimut Reiche, pointedly so in his notion of gender tension. This is a conceptualization that by far has yet to be exhausted in its significance for psychoanalytic theory.

Though sexuality appears ever more rarely in gender discourse, there seems to be widespread consensus that sexuality can be thought of only as masculine or feminine. The trendy, plural, term "sexualities" takes away the apparently monolithic stature of the artificial term "sexuality", with which disparities are inappropriately unified. If it is indisputable that there are innumerable forms, rather than just one form, of sexuality, then it is not evident why there should be only one unitary female or male variant of it. If one takes the significance of conscious and unconscious fantasies in sexual experience seriously, then sexuality, seen psychoanalytically, can only be conceptualized as transcending sex and gender in terms of gender tension. Perhaps one can even say that what is sexually experienced is constituted, in every person, precisely by this gender tension.

Consensus about a gender-differentiated sexuality exists, however, not only in psychoanalysis but also, remarkably, in the field of sexology. Thus, in the German sexological discourse Sonja Düring writes: "Sexuality is no longer conceivable as a single sexuality, but must be seen in the context of the cultural difference between the sexes" (1995, p. 166, translation for this edition). Volkmar Sigusch also accepts the feminist challenge: "To think about the *differentia sexualis* is one of the urgent tasks in our rich countries," in combination with the concern that sexology will hurt its critical and emancipatory reputation "if it shows itself unable to meet the feminist challenge, that is, if it fails to question its andromorphic viewpoint, and to think, painfully and critically, about the relationship between *sexus* and *genus*" (1993, p. 49, translation for this edition).

It is certainly not unproblematic to step outside this broad, cross-disciplinary consensus by using a psychoanalytic approach to contradict the postulate of a female and a male sexuality that is influenced by the cultural gender dichotomy. But as I have tried to show, it is not backsliding with respect to feminist accomplishments if the concept of a differing male and female sexuality is questioned. On the contrary: I think such a position which countermands the fixed opposition of the sexes and genders, and which, instead of speaking of a gender polarization, starts from the position that a tension between the sexes exists within each one of us furthers the feminist agenda, as such a notion is less reductionist and limiting. It also commits an individual less, in a normative sense, to being (sufficiently) masculine or feminine, and instead supports the diversity of what we associate with sexuality and gender.

CHAPTER THREE

Homosexuality, heterosexuality, perversion

Object-choice and the phantasmal conditions for love

"*In fact it is always in the form of desire that Freud identifies infantile sexuality in psycho-analysis: as opposed to love, desire is directly dependent on a specific somatic foundation; in contrast to need, it subordinates satisfaction to conditions in the phantasy world which strictly determine object-choice and the orientation of activity.*"

—Laplanche and Pontalis, 1973, p. 421

In differentiating sexuality from love and need, a boundary is set for sexuality at the psychic level that separates it from love, and at the somatic level that separates it from need. In the process, object-choice is emphasized, and this concept is therefore very important for the analytic understanding of (psycho-) sexuality. With its help, one can explain the origin of differing forms of sexuality, such as heterosexuality, homosexuality, and "perversions", and conceive of them as psychically equivalent. In so doing, one can avoid the popular normative hierarchization of sexual forms, which is not confined solely to everyday understanding. Yet, in psychoanalytic theory, just as in its institutional history,

199

there is an entire array of normative judgments, right up to blatant homophobia, and they are in considerable tension with this theoretical conceptualization.

Freud differentiates between two types of object-choice, each of which has two forms. One form is narcissistic, while the other, the *Anlehnungstypus*, is the anaclitic or attachment type; both have an infantile and pubertal variant, with the former preparing the way for the latter. Actually, neither "object-*choice*" (*Objektwahl*) nor "*choice* of neurosis" (*Neurosenwahl*) really signifies an ability to choose one of numerous possibilities. In the *Three Essays*, Freud speaks more accurately of finding an object: "There are thus good reasons why a child sucking at his mother's breast has become the prototype of every relation of love. The finding of an object is in fact a refinding of it" (1905d, p. 222).

In object-choice, therefore, memories and images from the earliest mother-child interactions play a role. At this point one finds a remarkable change in Freud's theory. In the *Three Essays*, he emphasizes the sexual dimension of this relationship:

> "A child's intercourse with anyone responsible for his care affords him an unending source of sexual excitation and satisfaction from his erotogenic zones. This is especially so since the person in charge of him, who, after all, is as a rule his mother, herself regards him with feelings that are derived from her own sexual life: she strokes him, kisses him, rocks him and quite clearly treats him as a substitute for a complete sexual object". (ibid., p. 223)

In a footnote, Freud adds that "anyone who considers this 'sacrilegious'" will find a similar description in one of Havelock Ellis's publications (1903). In his *On Narcissism: An Introduction* (1914c), by contrast, Freud de-sexualizes this relationship. With the conceptualization of an object-choice of the anaclitic type, he argues that "persons who are concerned with a child's feeding, care, and protection" (ibid., p. 87) serve as a model for the later, sexually gratifying object. Sexual arousal and gratification through the primary reference person no longer play a role in this conceptualization. Rather, Freud emphasizes the gratification of the "self-preservation instinct", to which the sexual drives are first attached. Only in later writings, such as the *New Introductory Lectures on Psycho-Analysis* (1933a) or *Female Sexuality* (1931b), does Freud return to the constitutive sexual dimension of the mother-child relationship.

I have noted previously what importance these early experiences with the mother have with respect to the development of the erogenous zones as well as the gratification modes, or what in Freudian terminology are called the sexual goals (see Chapter One). If this is to apply to the choice of the later love-object as well, then in a culture in which the infant is primarily cared for by its mother, one would expect to see a heterosexual object-choice only among men. Among women, by contrast, the more likely in psychic terms would be a homosexual object-choice. That a heterosexual relationship prevails in most cases, however, Freud ascribes to the "change of object" accomplished by the Oedipal girl (see Chapter Two)—as well as to the cultural primacy of heterosexuality. As described above, the girl withdraws her libidinal cathexis from her mother and turns to her father instead. However, Freud is imprecise and vague on this point, as he ascribes this switch to disappointment and desires for revenge on the part of the girl. In my view, it is instead the incest taboo that plays the key role in this withdrawal of libidinal cathexis. It calls for the withdrawal of cathexis from the mother's body, and in this context, the actual somatic dimension is far more relevant than the psychic aspects noted by Freud: love, revenge, and disappointment. Even after the withdrawal of cathexis under the pressure of the taboo, desire remains: the longing for the original sexual object remains operative in the unconscious. However, Freud relocates the establishment of the incest taboo in puberty. The diphasic nature of sexual development is significant: "But, by the postponing of sexual maturation, time has been gained in which the child can erect, among other restraints on sexuality, the barrier against incest, and can thus take up into himself the moral precepts which expressly exclude from his object-choice, as being blood-relations, the persons whom he has loved in his childhood" (1905d, p. 225). The incest barrier is primarily a "cultural demand society makes", but psychoanalytic investigations show how intensely individuals wrestle, in their developmental phases, with the temptation of incest, and how often they violate that prohibition in fantasy—and not infrequently in reality as well. Incest fantasies and experiences, often involving siblings, also surface in my own therapeutic practice and analyses, and these have a serious impact on the subsequent love life of patients both male and female. It is remarkable that barely any discussion of this exists in the psychoanalytic literature.

According to Freud, overcoming and rejecting incestuous fantasies, together with separating from one's parents, is one of the most significant, if most painful, psychic accomplishments of puberty. If this psychic detachment is only partly successful, it has a detrimental effect on later sex life. Thus, girls who "to the delight of their parents, have persisted in all their childish love far beyond puberty (become precisely those) girls who in their later marriage lack the capacity to give their husbands what is due to them; they make cold wives and remain sexually anaesthetic" (1905d, p. 227). From this, Freud concludes that sexual love has the same origins as infantile love. Even if the infantile libido does not remain fixed, object-choice follows the models provided by the parents. This should not be understood in quite so concretist a way as is ordinarily the case. Rather, object-choice is guided by memory traces that are revived in puberty; there is a complex psychic processing in the sense of a reinscription (see Quindeau, 2004a).

> "A child's affection for his parents is no doubt the most important
> infantile trace which, after being revived at puberty, points the way
> to his choice of an object; but it is not the only one. Other starting-
> points with the same early origin enable a man to develop more than
> one sexual line, based no less upon his childhood, and to lay down
> very various conditions for his object-choice". (1905d, p. 228f)

With this formulation, Freud makes clear that object-choice is by no means clearly predetermined, as the quote from Laplanche and Pontalis's *The Language of Psycho-Analysis* at the beginning of this Chapter seems to suggest. As the concept of trace and reinscription makes clear, it is not a matter of deterministic processes that fix an object-choice for life but rather of biographical experiences and conditions that show object-choice to be neither random nor arbitrary. Freud reminds us of the "innumerable peculiarities in human love-life" and of the obsessive aspect of being in love, which can be understood only with reference to childhood or as vestiges of its impact.

In *On Narcissism: An Introduction* (1914c), Freud contrasts this anaclitic type of object-choice with narcissistic object-choice. For Freud, the strongest motive for adopting the hypothesis of narcissism lies in the discovery that certain subjects "are plainly seeking themselves as a love-object, and are exhibiting a type of object-choice which must be termed 'narcissistic'" (ibid., p. 88). In addition, "A person may love: According to the narcissistic type: (a) what he himself is (i.e. himself), (b) what he himself was, (c) what he himself would like to be, (d) someone who was once part of himself" (ibid., p. 90). Laplanche and Pontalis (1973, p. 259) point out that "These headings cover very varied phenomena. The first three instances concern the choice of an object resembling the subject's own self, but it must be stressed, first, that what serves as model for the choice is an image or ideal, and, secondly, that the similarity between the object chosen and the model may be quite partial, amounting to nothing more than a few common traits. Under (d), what Freud has in mind is the mother's narcissistic love for her child, who was 'once part of herself'. Here the situation is very different, for the object chosen does not resemble the subject as a unified individual but is, rather, the thing that allows the subject to rediscover and restore his lost unity".

Finally, in this essay Freud compares the object-choice of men with that of women. Characteristic for men is a complete object-love of the anaclitic type, which is reflected in conspicuous sexual over-estimation. This derives originally from primary narcissism and is transferred to the sexual object. In the case of women, by contrast, a narcissistic object-choice usually results from the increase of narcissism in puberty: "Women, especially if they grow up with good looks, develop a certain self-contentment which compensates them for the social restrictions that are imposed upon them in their choice of object. Strictly speaking, it is only themselves that such women love with an intensity comparable to that of the man's love for them" (1914c, p. 88 et seq.). Freud himself recognizes that this stereotyped contrast is too schematic and notes that women also experience the anaclitic type of love and men also the narcissistic, from which he concludes that "both kinds of object-choice are open to each individual" (ibid., p. 88), and can alternate or be combined with one another. This seems to still be the case, even if gender-specific differences continue to be postulated in the discourse on gender. In this context, Freud also makes a significant observation about the sexual objects that children or adolescents distil from their gratification experiences. Humans initially have two sexual objects, "themselves and the woman who nurses them" (ibid., p. 88). From those sources, through countless reinscriptions and surrogates, evolve the love-objects of adults, which preserve their origins in the original models. Interesting in the Freudian formulation is that one finds "the woman who nurses them", namely the wet nurse, where today one would expect instead to read "the mother". This indicates the special significance of the interaction with the child. For the choice of sexual object, that the person is related, or male or female, is less important than what the person does with the child. This consideration opens a new sphere of activity for the father as well: it is by no means inevitable and immutable that the mother serves as the primary love-object for the child.

The Oedipus complex, which Freud formulates in "positive" and "negative" variants, performs the central function in structuring object-choice. The terms "positive" and "negative" are oriented to the normative cultural ideal of heterosexuality, and it is therefore reasonable to replace them with other terms. Such attempts are now discernible occasionally in the psychoanalytic discourse—though I find none convincing thus far. Provisionally, one could speak of same-sex and opposite-sex Oedipal constellations, but even that is so cumbersome that I generally prefer to set "positive" and "negative"—as well as the term "perversion"—in quotes here. Having variously discussed the Oedipal constellations in Chapters One and Two, I wish only to outline its functions briefly here with respect to the choice of love-object. In Freud's view, sexual orientation becomes fixed at the time when the Oedipus complex is resolved; the way for this orientation is paved in childhood and is conclusively defined in puberty (Freud, 1905d). A heterosexual object-choice therefore comes about through a fixing of the opposite sex Oedipal constellation, a homosexual one, correspondingly, by a continuation of the same-sex Oedipal relationship. Reimut Reiche (1990) correctly criticizes the notion of a lifelong fixation and notes that the Oedipus complex remains dynamic throughout life. Sexological findings also support this argument, as they show a change taking place in sexual orientation, in principle, at any age (see Düring, 1994).

Apparently, this need not necessarily be ascribed to the fact that those in question have concealed their "true" object-choice up to this point. In the psychoanalytic view, it is plausible to see this as a further processing, a fresh reinscription of the Oedipus complex. This change in sexual orientation is made possible through the bisexual object-choice in early childhood, one of whose variants continues to manifest itself while the other is suppressed, though still operative in the unconscious. Under certain circumstances that call for a fresh reinscription, the repressed orientation also can determine the new choice of love-object. Unfortunately, there is virtually no psychoanalytic research on such changes in sexual orientation. Case studies are less suited because, in keeping with the genre, they usually depict the change of love-object in the context of overcoming a neurotic conflict. One example of a non-pathological conceptualization can be found in Ulrike Schmauch (2004), though more from the viewpoint of socialization theory than from a psychoanalytic perspective. In one of the *Contributions to the Psychology of Love—A Special Type of Choice of Object Made by Men* (1910h), Freud asks which "love prerequisites" influence the object-choices people make, and how people are able of to reconcile the demands of their fantasies with reality. In his view, love life is primarily determined by fantasies, which are expressed through a particular configuration of reality, and which "succeed in dominating the man's love in real life" (ibid., p. 172). This central insight of the psychoanalytic understanding of sexuality remains valid, in my view. Both conscious and unconscious fantasies thereby acquire a constitutive function, as it is through them that reality is constructed. Fantasies in that sense are not just decorative details, though they are often regarded as such in everyday life. Instead, they are fed by unconscious wishes and—like dreams—have the function of representing these wishes as having been fulfilled. In this essay, Freud lists various fantasies that function as "love prerequisites" for men for a particular type of object-choice. These fantasies can either merge or just be developed separately in a given person, and they appear not only in the love life of neurotic men but in non-neurotic men as well, though in differing gradations. Freud's depiction by now seems quite antiquated if not obsolete, though his discussion of these fantasy-based "love prerequisites" addresses fantasy patterns or structures that continue to be observed today, albeit in a different, more contemporary form. What is decisive is that these fantasies play an important role in the structuring of relationships and in the choice of specific love and/or sexual partners. With respect to disorders of sexual experience and function, these patterns are highly significant, in my view.

Following Freud, to these fantasy "love prerequisites" of some men one must add the feeling of being an "aggrieved third party". Such a man experiences women who are already attached to another man as particularly desirable. A second, allied, prerequisite can be that the woman must evoke an impression of being "sexually disreputable", as Freud puts it, and must generate doubts in the man about her faithfulness and reliability. Freud pointedly calls this prerequisite "harlot love". Today, such a label probably would not be used, though such a love prerequisite continues to be observed. What is important, following Freud, is that this gives the man every reason for jealousy, and yet such a woman appears to him to be a "highly desirable love-object". Love relationships of this kind are maintained only with the highest psychic effort, and not infrequently to the exclusion of all other interests. The man in this love relationship often strives to "save" the loved one. Contemporary versions of this phantasmal love prerequisite can be found, for example, in psychoanalyses with men who keep falling in love, unhappily, with married, "inaccessible" women, as well as in patients who quite consciously select drug-dependent women or prostitutes as lovers, and do their utmost to try to rescue them from their milieus.

Freud sees all the markers of this particular form of object-choice as deriving from an infantile fixation of feelings of tenderness on the mother. While the first love prerequisite, the attachment of the woman to another man, seems quite evident in the case of the mother, the second prerequisite—"harlot nature"—is much less clear. On the other hand, aspects often coincide in the unconscious that in reality are in sharp contrast and separate. The impression of motherly infidelity, incidentally, derives from the Oedipal experience, from the rejection of the son in favour of the father. In masturbation fantasies, according to Freud, the mother's infidelity is a frequent theme, and the lover with whom she engages in this infidelity not infrequently bears traits of her son's ego. The rescue motif can be interpreted as derived not only from the mother fixation but also from the parental complex, the complex used by the son to escape from them. To rescue the mother, can also mean, at the same time, to bestow a child on the mother; hence to be one's own father. In this rescue fantasy, the son completely identifies with the father.

In the next essay in this series, *On the Universal Tendency to Debasement in the Sphere of Love* (1912d), Freud addresses the consequences of fixation on the infantile sexual objects. Thus, an incestuous fixation on mother or sister that a man has not overcome can lead to psychic impotence as well as to a splitting of sexuality into "sensual" and "tender" aspects. Freud understood "psychical impotence" to mean partial erectile dysfunction that occurs only at particular times, with particular persons, or in conjunction with particular practices, and not at other times: "If the practicing psycho-analyst asks himself on account of what disorder people most often come to him for help, he is bound to reply—disregarding the many forms of anxiety—that it is psychical impotence" (ibid., p. 179). It is noteworthy that this is the most frequent reason men give nowadays for seeing a urologist (see Quindeau, 2007).

Following Freud, an incestuous fixation impairs the further development of the libido, and prevents connecting the tender and the sensual aspects of sexuality. While the tender aspect is the older and corresponds to the primary infantile object-choice, which is in turn derived from the survival instinct and is directed at early caregivers, the sensual dimension is added during puberty and now invests the infantile objects with far higher degrees of libido. In that process, it comes into conflict with the incest taboo, which as a rule leads to the subject's turning to other, unfamiliar objects. Under certain circumstances, libidinal cathexis can remain fixed on the incestuous objects and become fixated on unconscious incestuous fantasies. Absolute impotence can be the consequence. In the case of psychic impotence, by contrast, only some but not all of the sensual aspects are reserved for the incestuous objects. The sexual activity of these persons does not utilize all their libidinal energy, but is erratic, easily disturbed, and not much enjoyed. Object-choice is limited, because all objects that serve as reminders of the taboo incestuous object must be avoided. Love life is then split in two directions: "Where they love they do not desire and where they desire they cannot love" (ibid., p. 183). One way to address this split is to demean the sexual object while continuing to esteem the incestuous object. Given the prerequisite of humiliation, sensuality can develop freely. Furthermore, the split leads to retention of perverse sexual goals, whose non-fulfilment is experienced as a grave diminution of pleasure.

Against this background, the abovementioned unconscious fantasy of "harlot love", a phantasmal debasing of the mother as whore, is an effort to overcome the splitting of the man's love life, and by humiliating her, to win her over as an object of sensual aspirations. A central function of this debasement is to find a defence against anxieties. Nitzschke (1980, p. 95) suggests that as a result, a great deal of fear lies behind the devaluation of women. Following Freud, these fears and devaluations go back to incestuous fixations. Ethel Person (1985), by contrast, distinguishes among several developmental levels at which these men's fears of women originate, and points as well to "the male propensity to split erotic longing and sexual longing" (p. 177). She also distinguishes between the pre-Oedipal fear of the mother who deserts or devours the child and the Oedipal fear of the mother who cannot be satisfied, who rejects, or who perfidiously seduces.

In his exposition, Freud goes a step further and asserts that the incestuous fixations not only evoke anxieties and devaluation, but also manifest themselves in a psychic impotence that is more widespread than one might think. If one looks at the flood of Internet advertising for potency-enhancing medications like Viagra® or Cialis®, and adds observations from psychoanalytic treatment, it seems to continue to be true, though this is not evident from published psychoanalytic case studies. Freud pointedly notes that: "we cannot escape the conclusion that the behaviour in love of men in the civilized world to-day bears the stamp altogether of psychical impotence" (1912d, p. 185). Thus, this impotence does not refer only to failure during coitus but should be extended to a more generally reduced sexual pleasure, one in which the same etiological factors can be found. Aspirations to tenderness and sensuality are, as a rule, combined extremely poorly: "It sounds not only disagreeable but also paradoxical, yet it must nevertheless be said that anyone who is to be really free and happy in love must have surmounted his respect for women and have come to terms with the idea of incest with his mother or sister" (ibid., p. 186). The great significance of unconscious incestuous fantasies is often noticeable, then as now, in psychoanalytic treatment, especially among patients with erectile dysfunction, the current jargon for Freud's "psychical impotence". Erectile disorders can be understood as a return of the repressed, in this case of the desire to commit incest. Like identification with the opposite sex, these incestuous longings also need to be psychically integrated and cannot merely be rejected. This integration is carried out in the context of the Oedipus complex, which aims to establish differences and draw clear lines between the generations. The less stable these lines are, the sooner the unconscious incestuous fantasies must be rejected. The increasing spread of erectile dysfunctions therefore points as well to less sharp generational boundaries or to their increased porosity.

According to Freud, a comparable need to denigrate the sexual object does not exist among women. This opinion, however, seems to me more due to the hierarchy of the sexes than corresponding to the psychic reality of women, at least as manifested in psychoanalytic treatment. The forms of denigration vary a great deal, to be sure, and may be manifested more, for example, in the form of contempt. In the requirement for what is prohibited and secret, Freud sees among women a parallel to the "love prerequisite" of debasement among men; it psychically replaces the linking of the sensual aspirations and the ban on incest. If women hold on to this connection for too long, however, it can also lead to psychic impotence and frigidity. Freud understands these requirements for love as a consequence of the long delay between sexual maturity and sexual activity, which the upbringing of girls, for cultural reasons, promoted in his day. This is largely no longer true, though there are more and more girls today who, for the most diverse reasons, wish to preserve their virginity until marriage. Both love requirements among women, the maintaining of secrecy as well as the staging of the "forbidden", are efforts to ease the collision between the desire for tenderness and the desire for sensuality, thus warding off psychic impotence. From this perspective, I regard the increasingly common phenomenon of "sexual lethargy" among women (see Lange, 1994) as the obverse of the so-called sexual liberalization, in which everything appears possible and open, and where it seems no more secrets and bans exist.

In the last section of his *Contributions to the Psychology of Love*, Freud (1912d) turns to the antagonism between sex life and culture. Regardless of all the efforts at imposing cultural restraints, the impossibility of complete gratification is inherent in the sex drive itself. On the one hand, this results in the diphasic onset of object-choice, with the interposition of the incest taboo. The original love-object remains inaccessible and is replaced by an endless series of surrogate objects none of which fully satisfies, however. This could explain the volatility in object-choice and the "craving for stimulation" so frequently seen in the love life of adults.

On the other hand, the sexual drive is composed of elements that are subjected to repression in various ways. Coprophilic and sadistic aspects, for example, are affected to a far higher degree by such defence mechanisms. And yet they remain active in the unconscious: "The excremental is all too intimately and inseparably bound up with the sexual; the position of the genitals—*interurinas et faeces*—remains the decisive and unchangeable factor" (p. 189). With the development of culture, such aspects have been largely excluded from gratification, however, and these unused stirrings are reflected in sexual activity as insufficient gratification.

In the third of the *Contributions to the Psychology of Love*, Freud addresses *The Taboo of Virginity* (1918a). Although sexual initiation, the *first time*, by now no longer carries much significance in the experience of youth (at least from the point of view of empirical sexology: see Helfferich 2005), it remains interesting with respect to unconscious dimensions of meaning. It is remarkable, however, that there is barely any psychoanalytic literature on the subject, especially recently, for either the male or the female experience. In the matter of sexual initiation, the historical change is of particular consequence, and Freud's reflections exclusively focus on women. While virginity until marriage was still the norm for women at the turn of the twentieth century, the age at first coitus for both sexes has been dropping steadily, albeit with variations by social class and levels of education (Helfferich, 2005). Thus, one can no longer assume that a woman's defloration brings about "sexual enslavement", as a rule, and that the "first time" binds her steadfastly to a man.

Interesting nonetheless are the ethnological findings that defloration in traditional, indigenous societies was ritually performed, perhaps by a clan elder, and was not reserved for the future husband. Such rituals were intended to avert the danger associated, in animistic thinking, with defloration: "The danger which is thus aroused through the defloration of a woman would consist in drawing her hostility down upon oneself, and the prospective husband is just the person who would have every reason to avoid such enmity" (1918a, p. 202). Reasons given for this antagonism were seen in the immediate bodily pain, and in particular, the narcissistic injury that accompanies the tearing of the hymen.

To this often is added disappointment with first coitus, in which expectation and realization do not coincide. The disappointment also results from the fact that sexual intercourse was to that point associated with a strict prohibition; a woman possibly draws less pleasure from now-permitted intercourse. Following Freud, this is why young women often keep love affairs secret, in particular from their parents, even if they expect no objection. More significant, is another aspect, grounded in the evolution of the libido: sexual wishes from childhood that were directed at the father and brother. In this respect, the husband is always only a surrogate. The more intense this fixation is, the less satisfactory adult love life is felt to be. A woman's frigidity, like the psychic impotence of the man, can be traced back to such a fixation, and can solidify into a neurotic inhibition or supply the basis for the emergence of other neuroses. As I described with regard to male development, a woman's sexual experience also calls for psychic integration of unconscious incestuous tendencies. Finally, Freud believed that other unconscious tendencies, in particular castration desires and penis envy, become virulent through defloration. In the dream of one newlywed woman, Freud detected a wish to castrate her young husband and to keep his penis for herself as a reaction to her defloration. Myths, too, provide numerous examples of this motif, as in the story of Judith and Holofernes. The man who breaks the taboo of her virginity in deflowering her is decapitated, with his severed head, following Freud, serving as a symbolic replacement for castration.

Heterosexual desire

In the *Three Essays on the Theory of Sexuality* (1905d), Freud describes the independence of sexual desire from the object:

> Psycho-analysis considers that a choice of an object independently
> of its sex—freedom to range equally over male and female objects—
> as it is found in childhood, in primitive states of society and early
> periods of history, is the original basis from which, as a result of
> restriction in one direction or the other, both the normal and the
> inverted types develop. Thus from the point of view of psycho-
> analysis the exclusive sexual interest felt by men for women is also
> a problem that needs elucidating and is not a self-evident fact based
> upon an attraction that is ultimately of a chemical nature. (p. 144)

Following this, heterosexuality is just as much in need of explanation as homosexuality. Nevertheless, this was barely addressed in subsequent psychoanalytic theory formation. Of course, there are numerous publications about homosexuality, but one seldom finds works that explicitly deal with the psychodynamics of heterosexuality. Apparently, in psychoanalysis heterosexuality has been regarded as so self-evident, or so culturally unquestioned, that it rarely became an object of study. A less pleasant side-effect of its being taken for granted was revealed at a 1983 meeting of the American Psychoanalytic Association, when the assertion was made that because it permitted reproduction, heterosexuality was "normal" sexuality while homosexuality was "failed heterosexuality" (Friedman 1986). Why women desire men and vice versa, which fantasies, wishes, and fears a body of the opposite sex sparks, has—remarkably—not been systematically investigated from a psychoanalytic perspective thus far and obviously remains a desideratum for further research.

Given the independence of object-choice from the sex of the object, as Freud puts it, one can in my view also draw the reverse conclusion that, with respect to the subject, one should strictly separate *Geschlecht* identity from sexual orientation. Unfortunately, it is not only in psychoanalysis but also in the widest variety of other discourse settings that the two are repeatedly conflated. For example, Peter Fiedler (2004), an academic psychologist, claims in his theory of sexuality that such a deep connection exists. In his view, the development of *Geschlecht* identity can be broken down into an inner-psychic aspect and an interpersonal aspect; the former refers to femininity and masculinity, the latter to heterosexuality, homosexuality, or bisexuality (p. 53). Thereby, and in a manner not further elucidated, far too strong a connection is made in my view, and particular significance is ascribed to sexual orientation in shaping the sense of identity. That abets popular prejudices of the "masculine lesbian" or the "effeminate homosexual man". The postulated significance of sexual orientation for a sense of identity arises, in my view, less from sexuality than from the cultural primacy of heterosexuality. That primacy forces a close connection to be made between *Geschlecht* identity and sexual orientation. Also noteworthy in my view is the increasing emphasis on sexual identity rather than sexual orientation.

Though this shift can be found even in the theories of some homosexual authors. I suspect it too is a consequence of heterosexual primacy. To ascribe an identity-creating function to sexual activity is the unavoidable result of making heterosexuality the norm and excluding all that deviates from that norm. Finally, I also want to draw attention to a translation difficulty in this context. While German draws a distinction between *geschlechtlich* (that which is related to the gender or sex of a person) and *sexuell* (sexual), the two notions are conjoined in the English term "sexual". Possibly, the two identities distinguished in German are regarded as similar simply because they are not linguistically differentiated in English (and in translation into German, the undifferentiated English usage is adopted).

Heterosexuality is rarely discussed not just in psychoanalysis but in the sexological discourse as well and when it is, then the focus is largely on its problematic aspects. During the 1990s, the discourse hence was dominated by the issue of sexual violence. Carol Hagemann-White (1995, p. 156 et seq.), for example, emphasizes one cannot separate sexuality from violence. The "feminist formula" of regarding rape as a crime of aggression rather than as a sexual offense is "a defense of heterosexuality", she argues, but it seems in the end naïve. Hagemann-White assumes that sexuality is "naturally" free of violence, or that sexually satisfied people no longer have any need for violence, but in the end this assumption is only a variant of the "boiler" theory. At the same time, research on perpetrators shows male desire to most certainly include violence. Even if this is incontestable, seeing the relationship between the sexes as a battleground leaves little room for reciprocity, spontaneity and pleasure. Under these conditions, heterosexual relations appear instead to be highly pathological.

A different discourse, which may be more relevant to questions of heterosexuality, is concerned with psychoanalytic views of love. Here, too, countless publications exist, though the sexual aspect is addressed at most in the margins. Otto F. Kernberg's work (1995, 2011) is an exception. Owing to his concept of psychic bisexuality, and in particular his thesis that every person has both "masculine" and "feminine" desires, he plays an important role in my argument.

In his study *The Sexual Pair* (2011), he formulates the following characteristics of erotic desire: the first characteristic is the striving for pleasure, always directed at another person, at an object that can penetrate or be penetrated, or an object to endeavour to penetrate or be penetrated by. This desire for closeness and merging contains elements of both forcible boundary transgression and unity with another person. It is important to understand that penetration or reception is not a characteristic either of a man or of a woman. It is instead a fluid interplay of penetration and reception at both the phantasmal level and the actual somatic level. Thus one recognizes "fantasy of active incorporation and passively being penetrated together with active penetration and passively being incorporated" (p. 225). At the level of the body, this interplay is reflected in "the relation between bodily protrusions and bodily openings: penis, nipple, tongue, finger, faeces on the penetrating or invasive side; and vagina, mouth, anus on the receptive or encompassing side" (ibid., p. 225). Kernberg regards psychic bisexuality, as revealed in sexual experiences, as universal among both men and women: "Bisexuality is first of all a function of identification with both participants of a sexual relation, or with all three in the triangulation of sexual experience" (ibid). Much as I share the notion of a universal bisexuality, the cultural norm of heterosexuality, which even here is unthinkingly applied, strikes me as problematic. According to Kernberg, a child identifies with both members of the Oedipal pair, hence with the father as the person who desires the mother and is also the object of the mother, and conversely, with the mother who desires the father and is desired by the father. This identification provides the elementary frame of reference for psychic bisexuality, and solidifies the triangular situation in the unconscious fantasy of the child. Yet, in my understanding, these Oedipal identifications are not so much a basic frame of reference as a reinscription of the earlier, pre-genital identifications with both parents.

The second characteristic of erotic desire Kernberg lists is also subject to the primacy of the heterosexual. It is the gratification that arises from identification with the opposite sex, or more precisely, from identification with the sexual arousal and orgasm of the sexual partner.

In this, two complementary experiences of interconnectedness fuse. One is the pleasure taken in the desire of the other and the ecstatic, ego-transcending experience connected with it. The other is the feeling of becoming both sexes at the same time, and for a short time transcending the separation of the sexes. This occurs together with the feeling of mutual complementarity in the pleasure at penetration and incorporation or at being penetrated and incorporated. This aspect of erotic desire, too, can be formulated without necessarily having recourse to the premise of heterosexuality: one can locate sexual tension and identification with the opposite sex not only in the partner of the opposite sex but in each participant individually.

The third characteristic, finally, is the sense of transgressing and transcending prohibitions. These are thought to be implicit in all sexual encounters, because they go back to the Oedipal structuring of sexual life. The transgressions can take the most varied forms. With respect to rapid social change (see Chapter One), Kernberg's reference, originally published in 1994, to transgressing conventional morality, namely "the ordinary social constraints that protect the intimacy of body surface as well as the intimacy of sexual excitement from public display" (2011, p. 225), is interesting. Today, this could hardly be regarded as transgression; as such intimacy has long since become public. However, Kernberg also includes unconscious prohibitions in his considerations, pointing to the transgressing of the Oedipal ban on sexual intimacy with the parent of the opposite sex, connected both with a challenge to the rival and with a triumph over him. This thought, while certainly correct, also applies to the same-sex desire existing in the "negative" Oedipus complex, in my view, so that here as well one need not necessarily assume that the cultural norm of heterosexuality is at work. A further dimension of transgression is directed at the sexual object itself, simultaneously experienced as seductively attractive and reserved. In this context, Kernberg emphasizes the connection of desire to aggression. What is constitutive for sexual experience, perhaps particularly for sexual arousal, is the feeling of overstepping the boundary of the Other. Both penetration and engulfing are seen as a violation of the Other's boundary. Such a transcending of the boundaries of the self reveals itself especially in orgasms. The pleasurable satisfaction of the desire for aggression—the ability to evoke pain in the other and to identify, in this pain, with the erotic desire of the Other—is also supposedly arousing, and permits the Other to take pleasure in the pain. Kernberg refers to the superego as the "border guard" over this fusion of desire and aggression.

For sexual experience, the Oedipal constellation is significant not only in the aforementioned sense of identifications. A further significant aspect is the transcending of the Oedipal prohibition on sexual union with the loved and idealized object. While Kernberg limits this union to an object of the opposite sex, in my view this is true of both variants of Oedipal desire. Beyond this, Kernberg raises a central issue: "Behind this oedipal father, a woman's lover represents the preoedipal mother as well, satisfying her dependency needs while expressing tolerance of sexual intimacy with a symbolic oedipal object" (ibid., p. 231). This thought—that the mother, in her unconscious fantasy, tolerates the love relationship of her daughter to another—seems of eminent importance to me. It is here one finds, without doubt, a gateway for manifold disorders of sexual experience. Thus, for example, the sexual lethargy women increasingly complain about (see Lange, 1994) could be related to an insufficiently developed unconscious representation of a "tolerating mother", as often appears in conflicts over individuation and dependency. Similarly, this conflict dynamic might also be expressed in male erectile dysfunction. With respect to same-sex and opposite-sex Oedipal constellations, one might ask whether, in addition to a representation of the "tolerating mother", a "tolerating father" would also be significant in the sexual experience of a daughter or a son.

Triangulations in various forms, according to Kernberg, are the most frequent and characteristic scenarios that both threaten and consolidate the sexual pair's cohesion. Thus, every man and every woman, consciously or unconsciously, fears a third party exists who might be more satisfying for their sex partner. This third person, male or female, is on the one hand a reason for emotional insecurity in sexual intimacy, and on the other hand a reason for jealousy, acting as an alarm to protect the pair's integrity.

Kernberg describes the converse triangulation as a revenge or compensation fantasy in which one becomes sexually involved with a person other than one's own partner. This idealized member of the opposite sex stands for the desired Oedipal object, and establishes a triangular relationship. The subject is thereby being wooed by two members of the opposite sex rather than competing with the Oedipal rival of the same sex for an idealized Oedipal object of the opposite sex.

Kernberg connects these two universal fantasies in an interesting thesis that at the level of unconscious fantasies, "six persons are always in bed together: the pair, their respective unconscious Oedipal rivals, and their respective unconscious Oedipal ideals" (ibid., p. 234). If one adds Freud's notion that each member of the sexual pair consists of four persons because of their dual bisexuality, then one arrives, in a phantasmal manner, at the conclusion that every sexual act between a pair involves fourteen persons.

Kernberg, referring to the work of Didier Anzieu (1986), draws attention to a further, interesting aspect of this relationship. In the unconscious choice of love-object, Anzieu sees a homosexual and/or a heterosexual augmentation of the self. In this case as well, the dimensions of homosexuality and heterosexuality are limited to heterosexuality, but in my view, one could extend many aspects to the homosexual couple as well. A homosexual augmentation, in Anzieu's sense, would mean that the heterosexual partner would be used as a mirror of the self. In this, everything that did not fit into this pattern of augmentation would be excluded. If this intolerance is applied to the sexuality of the Other, it can lead to severe sexual inhibition. Following Anzieu, this intolerance is often based on a narcissistic envy of the opposite sex. If the partner is unconsciously perceived as a twin, then a fantasy of combining both sexes into a single one can arise. The two models of object-choice as a complementary augmentation or as a doubling of the twin doubtless illuminate important aspects of the sexual couple. On the basis of the double bisexuality and sexual tension in both partners, one can postulate that this exists in the same measure in both homosexual and heterosexual pairs.

Homosexual desire

As previously noted, one finds a plethora of studies on homosexuality, in comparison with the sparse psychoanalytic discourse on heterosexuality. While Freud's conceptualization of homosexuality is regarded as a pioneering theory that has lost none of its topicality (Gissrau, 1993, p. 171; Dannecker, 1993, p. 165), more conventional views pathologizing homosexuality soon came to dominate psychoanalysis (see Rauchfleisch, 1994, 2002; Lewes, 1988, provides an overview of the American discussion on homosexuality and psychoanalysis). Here I present the varying lines of argument in chronological order, separating the discussions of male and female homosexual development. This corresponds to the extant research literature, in which some authors emphasize that they can speak only about male homosexuality and not at all about female homosexuality. Without providing any justification, they call the latter fundamentally different (see Friedman, 1988).

In the *Three Essays on the Theory of Sexuality*, Freud refers to homosexuality as "inversion" and distinguishes among the "absolute", the "amphigenic", and the "occasional" invert. Surprisingly, these forms are based on behavioural criteria, which otherwise are not accorded much importance in psychoanalysis. While the sexual object is exclusively of the same sex in the case of the "absolute invert", the sexual object can be of either sex in the case of the "amphigenic invert". "Occasional" inversion, by contrast, occurs as a result of external conditions, whenever, as during war or imprisonment, objects of the opposite sex are not readily available. Differences also exist with respect to time. Thus, some date their inversion back to their earliest childhood memories, while others place its origin at a later date, such as during puberty. However, Freud correctly points out that this kind of memory probably is not exactly reliable because it tries—*nachträglich*—to connect a particular current behaviour with a plausible story about its origin. The time span of inversion also differs. For some, it lasts a lifetime, while in others it recedes for a time behind a heterosexual orientation or emerges only late in life. In these formulations, one already hears precursors of a concept discussed in sexology during the last years: the idea of a "sequential" homosexuality or heterosexuality. This questions the traditional notion of sexual orientation as a lasting characteristic, as an exclusive, "true", and persistent entity (see Düring, 1994). In searching for an explanation for inversion, Freud discusses the opinion common in his day, and focuses on two aspects: degeneracy and innateness. He rejects both because they do not aid in understanding inversion itself. The notion of an innate attachment of a person's libido to a particular sex object is a "crude explanation", he contends. While the notion of degeneracy has become uncommon in the meantime, the search for the "pink gene" (Müller-Jung, 2005) has yet to be abandoned despite its limited chances for success.

To explain inversion, sex researchers at the end of the nineteenth century looked to bisexuality as well as to psychic and somatic hermaphroditism. While inversion and somatic hermaphroditism proved largely independent of one another, Freud tends to assume the existence of a degree of psychic hermaphroditism among inverts, though only among women: "But it is only in inverted women that character-inversion of this kind can be looked for with any regularity. In men, the most complete mental masculinity can be combined with inversion" (1905d, p. 142). Freud does not explain why this rather implausible gender-specific difference should exist, and it is only in a later essay that he once again addresses the psychodynamics of female homosexuality (1920a, see below).

Freud concludes his etiological considerations as follows: "Nevertheless, two things emerge from these discussions. In the first place, a bisexual disposition is somehow concerned in inversion, though we do not know in what that disposition consists, beyond anatomical structure. And secondly, we have to deal with disturbances that affect the sexual instinct in the course of its development" (1905d, p. 143f). With the second remark, Freud reveals his ambivalent stance. On the one hand, his theory attempts to remove homosexuality from the realm of the pathological, but on the other hand he regards it in the same breath, following convention, as a "disturbance".

Furthermore, with his theory of homosexuality, Freud upholds the cultural primacy of heterosexuality. Thus, he assumes that the inverted man, like other men, is seeking not masculine but feminine psychic features in his sex object. In support, Freud refers to pederasty in antiquity:

> "It is clear that in Greece, where the most masculine men were numbered among the inverts, what excited a man's love was not the masculine character of a boy, but his physical resemblance to a woman as well as his feminine mental qualities .... In this instance, therefore, as in many others, the sexual object is not someone of the same sex but someone who combines the characters of both sexes; there is, as it were, a compromise between an impulse that seeks for a man and one that seeks for a woman, while it remains a paramount condition that the object's body (i.e. genitals) shall be masculine. Thus the sexual object is a kind of reflection of the subject's own bisexual nature". (1905d, p. 144)

Beyond dissenting from the unquestioned primacy of heterosexuality, I regard Freud's observation that both gender positions are combined in the sex object as extremely productive. It takes into account the bisexual identifications with both father and mother, and thus also reflects the individual's own bisexual constitution. At the same time, it preserves the original bisexual object-choice with respect to both parents.

From this, I conclude that in every love relationship, be it manifestly homosexual or heterosexual, a same-sex object-choice is combined with an opposite-sex object-choice. By taking this perspective, I want to dissent from the assumption there are two sides of object-choice, one that, for example, is heterosexual and conscious, and another that is homosexual and has, by contrast, become unconscious. Such a conceptualization appears problematic because it makes object-choice appear to be a unified whole, a kind of "monolithic block" which ascribes exclusively same-sex or opposite-sex aspects to the object of love. I suggest instead that one regard object-choice as a conglomerate of various same-sex and opposite-sex aspects, and that these can be just as much conscious as unconscious. For a love-object blends feminine and masculine features together, not just at the psychic level but at the physical, bodily level as well. This blending need not be as blatant as among androgynous women with muscular upper bodies or deep voices, or androgynous men with delicate features and soft skin. In one's subjective estimation of another individual, it is often the small and seemingly insignificant details that are linked to gender characteristics, such as a particular shape of the hands, ears, or eyes. On the other hand, owing to social pressure (or constraints) for unambiguous assignment to a particular sex/gender, this blending usually takes place less at the level of the physical body and more in the psychic dimension. But the physical dimension of the androgynous is of incomparably greater significance for sexual experience and the unconscious fantasies associated with it.

Male homosexuality

Robert M. Friedman (1986a) presents a historically based and theoretical critique of the widespread pathologizing of homosexuality. He objects to regarding homosexual men as narcissistic or as suffering from a disturbance of ego structure, and also opposes the assumption that homosexuality exclusively and necessarily emerges as a result of a particular family dynamic (an intrusive mother; a weak father). Friedman first draws attention to how remarkably few fundamental concepts for understanding sexual orientation have been developed in psychoanalysis since Freud. His arguments are based exclusively on male homosexuality, "because there is no reason prima facie that male and female sexual preferences would have similar meanings or developmental roots" (1986, p. 82). However, this assumption of such a difference in male and female development is merely postulated and not further justified.

This dichotomous view of masculinity and femininity is of a piece with the rejection of the Freudian theory of constitutional bisexuality, a critique one can trace back to the work of Sándor Radó (1940), who regarded Freud's conceptualization as ambiguous because it was "based on long-outdated embryological facts ... and had ceased to generate any useful empirical hypotheses" (Friedman, 1986, p. 68). Radó (1949) instead develops a new notion of homosexuality, which thenceforth has been regarded as the "classic" psychoanalytic stance. In it, he rejects the idea that homosexual desire has a biological basis. Instead, exclusive homosexuality is a reparative substitute for an anxiety-ridden heterosexuality that originates in parental pressure or intimidation with respect to sexual behaviour or male self-confidence. Radó also holds that the original desire for a woman survives among homosexual men, behind all the rationalizations. Therefore, homosexual couples simulate male and female role models, and in this counterfeit manner, find orgiastic gratification through an unconscious illusion of heterosexuality.

During the 1950s, Radó's interpretation was subjected to comprehensive clinical and empirical scrutiny. Most influential was a clinical study conducted by Irving Bieber (1962) that, over a period of nine years, compared about 100 homosexual patients in psychoanalytic treatment with 100 heterosexual "control patients". Though the very idea of "control patients" in psychoanalysis seems quite strange, Bieber's conclusions solidified the psychoanalytic view of homosexuality as a psychopathological disturbance that requires treatment, lending this conceptualization new authority. Bieber followed Radó's lead, seeking empirical evidence to prove the biological primacy of heterosexuality and the reparative character of homosexuality. In his view, "pre-homosexual boys were all said to have had normal erotic attraction to females that had been inhibited as a defence against anxieties generated within the nuclear family. More specifically, Bieber described a "classical" triangular constellation in which the pre-homosexual son was chosen unconsciously as "the interactional focal point upon whom the most profound parental psychopathology was concentrated" (p. 310). The most typical mother of a homosexual was said to be "close-binding," that is, overly close and possessive, as well as emotionally over-intimate and sexually seductive. The typical father, in turn, was found to be openly or covertly hostile—as shown by cruelty, humiliation, and rejection—or else he was simply detached and/or absent. The marriage itself was unusually poor, with the mother contemptuous of her husband. In other words, the mother preferred her son, whose father treated him as a hostile rival. These family dynamics all served to bind the boy to his mother, inhibit his masculine assertiveness, and thus steer him toward effeminacy and homosexuality" (Friedman, 1986, p. 69). In criticizing these assumptions, Friedman points out that such a family aetiology is inadequate to explain homosexual development. While Freud acknowledged and accepted the limitation of family aetiology as an explanatory model, this was apparently no longer the case for Bieber and his associates. In examining Bieber's data, Friedman concluded they could account for the postulated differences between homosexual and heterosexual patients only to a limited degree statistically. Bieber also sought evidence for the thesis of a reparative function homosexuality performs by citing his patients' memories of sexual arousal in early childhood brought about by women—another highly questionable approach, as it proves nothing more than the universally acknowledged positive variant of Oedipal desire. A further problematic view of homosexuality in psychoanalysis can be traced back to Charles Socarides (1968, 1978), who was the first to assert a primary, pre-Oedipal aetiology. He, too, based his ideas on observations of homosexual patients, whose severe psychopathology he regarded as the expression "of an early developmental failure to separate from the symbiotic mother" (Friedman, 1986, p. 73). He summarized this in terms not commonly found in scientific discourse: homosexuality is "filled with aggression, destruction and self-deceit. It is a masquerade of life" (Socarides, 1968, p. 8). In cases of "exclusive male homosexuality, consequently, there exists a core identity disturbance manifested by sexual deviation, marked effeminacy, and a host of major psychiatric symptoms" (Friedman, 1986, p. 73). Socarides's approach shows a close connection between sexual orientation and gender identity in a particularly drastic form, a postulate I have criticized above. According to Socarides, because of the structural ego-deficit these men behaved in a homosexual manner in hopes of being able to narcissistically stabilize themselves. Though Socarides identified further types of homosexuality in which more neurotic personality structures developed, he "classified approximately half of his homosexual patients as suffering from serious borderline and psychotic-like conditions" (Friedman, 1968a, p. 73). He thereby succumbs to the grave logical fallacy of positing sexual orientation as the basis and precondition for the severe psychic disorders of his patients—an approach that presumably would meet with considerable dismay if one were to argue the same for heterosexual patients.

After lengthy debates in the American Psychiatric Association, homosexuality per se was removed from the DSM-III in 1973, and instead of being classified as a mental disorder was now put in the category of "sexual orientation disturbances". In the discussion, leading analysts such as Charles Socarides and Irving Bieber were staunch opponents of the efforts to de-pathologize homosexuality (see the critical remarks in Lewes, 1988).

Martin Dannecker (2001) concludes that despite diverse efforts on the part of sexology and sociology, as well as by sections of the "enlightened" public, to have it be treated as a "normal aspect of sexuality" in discourse, it has not been possible to de-pathologize homosexuality. In Dannecker's view, that continues to be the case in psychoanalysis down to the present. He offers as evidence the successive editions of renowned German psychoanalytic textbooks (such as Loch, 1967), which reflect the successive, and contradictory, psychoanalytic views of homosexuality. In the 1989 edition, another textbook author, Peter Kutter, still places homosexuality in the category of "other psychiatric conditions" (1989, p. 262), but at least provides a 'liberal' preface, owing either to the zeitgeist or to the critiques within psychoanalysis regarding its pathologizing. However, this caution is not sustained: in the text itself, Kutter holds firmly to the view already expressed by Socarides: that homosexuality is grounded "at least in a narcissistic personality structure" (ibid., p. 263). A decade later, in a newly written chapter authored by Kutter and Thomas Müller titled "Psychoanalysis of Psychoses and Personality Disturbances", homosexuality is no longer mentioned at all.

To Dannecker, however, this is no reason to assume that a permanent change in the perspective on homosexuality had taken place in the psychoanalytic discourse. For in this Chapter as well, the necessary critical confrontation with the past problematic view is still lacking, leaving an impression of having "left something undone" (2001, p. 106). This impression is reinforced by a new chapter in this edition by Alex Holder that addresses psychoanalytic pathology among children and youths, and it returns to the pathologizing conceptualization of homosexuality. As to why this approach is so widespread precisely in the psychoanalytic literature, Dannecker points to the sociology of knowledge. Of all the schools of psychology, psychoanalysis has the "most elaborated corpus of psychopathological theories of homosexuality" (ibid., p. 106), though it is one that perpetuates itself.

Thinks that a major problem in the psychoanalytic account is its oversimplified understanding of the parent-child aetiology of male homosexuality, which for most authors is a

> "combination of (a) close-binding mother and a hostile-detached father". According to such theories, this "causes both the sexual deviation proper and the emasculation of the pre-homosexual boy. It is the father, in particular, who plays 'an essential and determining role in the homosexual outcome of his son. ... We have come to the conclusion that a constructive, supportive, warmly related father precludes the possibility of a homosexual son' (Bieber, 1962, pp. 310–311)." (Friedman 1986, p. 74).

Friedman notes that the assumption of a

> "simple causality between the parenting and the associated homosexuality and effeminacy" of the son ignores the complexity of the interactions and mutual influences. Thus, much of what Bieber and his associates list as causes of homosexual behaviour could just as well be its effects, and reflect, for example, the inability of some fathers to accept their homosexual son or the inability of some sons to accept their father. A further fundamental problem, as variously noted, is the "persistent confounding of homosexuality as an atypical object-choice with the phenomenon of male effeminacy". (1986, p. 74)

Such effeminacy is repeatedly claimed without any genuine proof being provided.

This problematic view is brought into sharp focus in a quote from Stoller: "The relationship between femininity and male homosexuality has been known for thousands of years, so those of us working on this subject are probably only tightening the fit of this observation. Here is the hypothesis updated: the more feminine the boy, the more likely will he desire someone of the same sex, the earlier will overt homosexuality begin, and the less likely either the femininity or the homosexuality can be reversed by psychoanalysis" (cited in Friedman, 1986, p. 75).

Here again one sees the importance of American gender norms, the devaluation of the feminine mixed together with the homophobic. In this context, Robert Friedman notes an interesting historical and culturally specific phenomenon, namely that "since the 1930s, psychological tests defined personality norms for men and women, that is, distinctive sex roles that were deemed essential for mental health. By the 1950s it was further theorized that the male sex-role identity was particularly vulnerable because of the boy's initial identification with his mother" (ibid., p. 71). From pioneering work by John Money (Money, Hampson & Hampson, 1955; Money & Ehrhardt, 1972) on gender identity, psychoanalysts often derived "experimental confirmation of gender acquisition as a psychological product of social learning, and surprisingly independent of physical determinants. Spurred by this research, ... psychoanalysts focused attention on the developmental line of gender formation and on gender disturbance" (ibid., p. 72).

Some time later, Richard C. Friedman (1988), one of the few analysts in the International Psychoanalytic Association to have disclosed his homosexual orientation, took up the issue of gender identity again and proposed a "modernized" psychoanalytic theory of homosexuality. This model is often referred to in the discourse, though it is quite problematic in certain aspects, which is why I wish to discuss it in greater detail. Friedman has further developed the so-called "biopsychosocial" model, linking the theoretical aspects of clinical psychoanalysis with research results from other fields, including biologically oriented psychiatry, neuropsychology, sociology, and anthropology. He regards homosexuality as a window onto psychoanalytic theory in general, making evident what needs to be critically examined. In his view, what needs revision in particular is the "psychic determinism" of psychoanalysis, the inadequate conceptualization of gender differences, which, in their full significance, are far from being discerned. Also requiring revision is the psychodynamic perspective, which he wants to replace with a "bio-descriptive view" along the lines of the DSM-III. In my estimation, Friedman's understanding of Freud is characterized by a number of fundamental misunderstandings, some of which lead to glaring errors of judgment. Thus, for example, he regards Freud's concept of inversion, as presented in the *Three Essays on the Theory of Sexuality*, as a medical-pathological model (1988, p. 54), though he provides no justification for assuming so. He also rejects the assertion of a universal, unconscious, homosexual object-choice, though it is a constitutive pillar of the psychoanalytic theory of sexuality (ibid., p. 56). Instead, he cites empirical studies showing that disturbances in gender identity or gender roles predispose men to homosexuality (ibid., p. 60). It has apparently escaped the author that theories of this kind attest to the very psychic determinism that he is at pains to criticize. On closer inspection, what Friedman extols as a general modernization of psychoanalytic theory falls short of Freud's own efforts—which, admittedly, were not sustained—to differentiate and de-pathologize homosexuality. This problematic line of argument is pursued in an analysis of sexual orientation against the background of character or personality disorders. It reveals a mundane understanding of sexuality largely restricted to genitality that has little in common with the sweeping psychoanalytic understanding of psychosexuality shown by Freud. Though Friedman takes an explicit stand against pathologizing homosexuality, he nevertheless believes that among some men, homosexual phenomena should be regarded as symptoms, especially if those men have not "always been" homosexual (ibid., p. 201).

Richard Friedman regards "effeminization" in a boy in early childhood as a decisive marker of subsequent homosexual development. A number of empirical studies, he argues, concluded that those who were largely or exclusively homosexual had experienced disturbances of gender identity in childhood. These could be divided into three main groups: "1. exceptional femininity in childhood, 2. mild to moderate femininity in childhood (thus, a subdued or less strongly articulated form of femininity), and 3. unmanliness" (ibid., p. 212), whereby the last of these was demonstrated by avoidance of physical confrontations ("playful scuffles") in the latency period.

Richard Friedman's argument is problematic for a variety of reasons: He assumes a dichotomous, polarized relationship between the sexes, manifested in sharply separated gender roles. A closer look at the—only rudimentarily cited—empirical studies, however, shows the difficulty of trying to operationalize this "feminization". The rather unsophisticated understanding of masculinity he propounds gives physical aggression a normative character. Conversely, femininity is negatively connoted and devalued. The suggested connection between homosexuality and disturbances of gender identity in effect means a pathologizing of homosexuality, even though Friedman at other points clearly criticizes this. Finally, the close connection made between sexual orientation and gender identity does not seem very apt: As Freud already remarked, "full masculinity" can certainly be compatible with a homosexual object-choice.

Martin Dannecker (2001) provides a far more differentiated, non-pathological concept of a "feminization phase" among homosexual boys, though the choice of this term seems somewhat unfortunate, given its unavoidably pejorative connotations. With this term, Dannecker by no means refers to unmanliness in the sense of "early faggishness" but rather to an integration of feminine aspects into an unimpaired masculinity. Through this integration, the Oedipal boy tries to attain the love of his father by becoming like his mother in some aspects. The father is the primary love-object of the homosexual boy, following Dannecker; homoerotic fantasies are already present as of about age four or five (see also Isay, 1989). In contrast to these observations, psychoanalytic conceptualizations generally evoke more of an impression of a wholly desexualized father-son relationship (see, for example, the case studies in Socarides, 1968). Instead, traditionally, the emphasis always is on the mother-son relationship, depicted as so over-powering and monstrous that the son can free himself neither from his identification with her nor his desire for her. If, however, one also considers the father, then the entire Oedipus complex, in its negative and positive forms, becomes apparent. But Dannecker criticizes, with justification, the notion that the boy desires his father only in a "feminine" manner, meaning he passively subjects himself to his father. Even if not much is known thus far about the negative Oedipal wishes of a boy, one needs to assume that phallic strivings vis-à-vis the father also play a role. This interpretation, in my view, should be accepted without reservation. Tender and feminine sentiments vis-à-vis their fathers can also be observed in heterosexual boys, but solidify among homosexual boys and become more visible over time to others as well. The reactions of others, as well as same-sex sexual fantasies that are increasingly capable of becoming conscious, in the end shape the growing homosexual boy's feeling that he is different. Nevertheless, and despite that confusing feeling, there is affirmation of the boy's own body and own sex. Masculine gender identity is by no means called into question by same-sex desire. As a result, Dannecker also does not see the wearing of women's garments during the Oedipal phase as the expression of a boy's fantasy of being a woman, but rather as an attempt by the boy, by wearing them, to seduce his father.

The scattered feminine traces from the Oedipal phase persist even among grown homosexual men, without producing the impression of unmanliness. For various reasons, however—homophobia as well as the gender hierarchy—these men have learned to distance themselves from their feminine introjections. A careful reconstruction of the life histories of homosexual men makes their specific form of masculinity evident, and it is one that encompasses femininity.

Such a non-pathological conceptualization of the integration of feminine aspects within male gender identity seems to me not just appropriate to the description of homosexual development. Starting from the concept of a complete Oedipus complex, I suspect far more that such integration—possibly with differing accentuations—is part of the development of every man.

In addition to connecting disturbed male gender identity with homosexuality, Richard Friedman (1988) also hypothesizes that the crystallization and differentiation of erotic fantasy prior to adolescence affects sexual preference. Friedman cites findings from his own empirical investigation of homosexual and heterosexual subjects not in psychotherapy. The subjects were asked, retrospectively, about their first sexual stirrings and fantasies that accompanied erections. As expected, the homosexual subjects remembered being sexually interested in men since earliest childhood. But prior to adolescence, many of them had not understood this as an indication of their possible homosexual orientation. However, they had felt themselves to be "different" and were embarrassed by their homosexual fantasies. The findings of this study are generally extremely vague and therefore not very meaningful. Nevertheless, from them Friedman derives a far-reaching theoretical model, arguing that insecurity with respect to male gender identity is reinforced by homosexual fantasies. Among pre-homosexual boys, he says, there is a mutually reinforcing spiral of feeling one does not belong, threats to self-esteem, and consolidated homosexual fantasies. It is possible to represent, as a kind of closed loop, how sexual fantasy influences representations of the self and is itself influenced, which in turn has an effect on social interactions and again affects self-representation (ibid., p. 219). This loop, too, strikes me as extremely problematic, as its orientation is fundamentally pathologizing: it is insinuated that the development of positive homosexual self-esteem is well-nigh impossible.

Finally, Richard Friedman is of the opinion that male sexual orientation begins with sexual fantasies prior to puberty and persists throughout life (ibid., p. 221). Accordingly, the images that fix sexual orientation, much like core gender identity, are firmly rooted in the specific representation of the human body. Noteworthy here is that Friedman apparently assumes the existence of congruence between sexual fantasy and sexual behaviour. Psychoanalytic experience suggests that in general this is not the case. Thus, Freud conceived of homosexual fantasies as an expression of an underlying universal bisexuality—and incidentally, in analyses with men and women, both heterosexuals and homosexuals, one still encounters such fantasies.

Reimut Reiche, in a variety of publications (1970, 1990, 2000, 2001a) has provided a non-pathologizing psychoanalytic understanding of homosexuality and pointedly summarizes his experiences with homosexual patients in analysis: "The more one understands about the structure of the personality and the more the symptoms fade, the less one understands the psychogenesis of homosexuality—if there is one" (2000, p. 360 translation for this edition). His view of male homosexuality is based on two fundamental assumptions: 1. The sexual object-choice that is the core of homosexuality does not come about as a result of a pathological defence mechanism. Just as there is normal, healthy heterosexuality, there is also normal, healthy homosexuality. 2. "One has always been homosexual or heterosexual, and then one formulates one's always-been-like-this and being-thus, as one's essence. The core of *Geschlecht* identity and the core of object-choice develop concordantly together, synchronously and not diachronically" (2001a, p. 288, translation for this edition). While the first assumption would likely find wide assent, the second is less evident and is at odds with current psychoanalytic doctrine holding that sex identity comes first and only then does object-choice become established (see Person and Ovesey, 1983; Tyson, 1991). Reiche's thesis of synchronous development does have the advantage that homosexual development can no longer be regarded as the result of an impaired gender identity, as in Socarides's (1968, 1978) or Richard Friedman's (1988) approaches.

Like Kernberg (1995), Reiche begins with the Oedipus complex, which fuses the development of the self with that of the drives; the child develops by commencing an intense love relationship with his or her primary object. "To develop and to develop a love relationship are one and the same" (2001a, p. 291). Of central importance in Reiche's argument is the focus on the unconscious determinants of gender identity and object-choice, in contrast to received doctrine, which in his view is too strongly oriented to self-perception and perception by others. This developmental process is long-lasting, a process in which various stations are reached from which no turning back is possible—comparable to Morgenthaler's "setting of the switches". In Reiche's view, one also needs to take account of the mutual influences exercised on one another by the proto-*Geschlecht* identity and the proto-object-choice. As primary socializers, the parents not only designate the *Geschlecht* of their child in abstract terms but also equip that child at the same time with certain conscious and unconscious tasks and expectations: "This is who you are for me. You are John and this is how you are supposed to love (me)" (ibid., p. 293). The child serves as a container for the dreams and traumas of the primary objects (see also Benedek, 1959), just as, in reverse, the primary objects serve the child as a container for what cannot be assimilated. Reiche makes reference in his considerations to Jean Laplanche's general seduction theory. In Reiche's context, I interpret *Geschlecht* identity and object-choice as reinscriptions of the "enigmatic messages" of the adults.

Less convincing, however, is why Reiche sees these reinscriptions as settings of the switches leading to what was "always there", to *either* heterosexuality *or* homosexuality. In this approach, the process of reinscription seems needlessly rigid and deterministic. In contrast, I find it more sensible, in these messages and in their subjective processing, to see both forms of object-choice, the homosexual and the heterosexual, as side by side and simultaneous. Over the course of life, this object-choice manifests itself then in one way and/or the other. This interpretation has the advantage that it does not need to have recourse to possible biological (pre)determinants of sexual object-choice. It presents both object-choices as part of "normal" psychosexual development, as well as psychically equivalent, and is able to accommodate possible changes in object-choice later in life.

The thesis of a simultaneous establishing of *Geschlecht* identity and object-choice in the context of the general seduction scene doubtless has a certain attractiveness. It is problematic, however, in that at the same time, it ascribes to object-choice the character of a setting of switches that is just as irreversible as *Geschlecht* identity. Possibly, this problem is the inevitable result of the notion of a *simultaneous* development of both aspects. Beginning with the primacy of the Other, however, I would like to suggest placing the emphasis as well on a diachronic developmental course, though in reverse order in comparison to orthodox psychoanalytic doctrine. The relationship of the Other to the child is, in my view, the decisive condition for the child's development. In other words, the relationship precedes the subject. Therefore, it makes sense to assume that the love relationship of the child precedes the establishing of the child's *Geschlecht* identity. One could object that the relationship of the Other to the child "always" is with a child whose *Geschlecht* is specified. But at this point, it is necessary to distinguish the level of a manifest, usually unambiguous, sex from the level of the manifold unconscious ascriptions with respect to that sex, which by no means must always proceed in the same direction (see my comments on Reiche's approach in Chapter Two). In the classic psychoanalytic view, identifications are ways of overcoming losses. A child identifies with the lost object and re-establishes the desired aspects of the object within his or her own ego. In that respect, identification, or introjection as its precursor, is accorded great significance in the creation of the psychic structure. Because the child establishes relations with both parents, it also identifies with both sexes and/or genders. In my view, this is how one can understand Freud's description of bisexuality as "constitutional": the bisexual identifications are what constitute the psychic structure. It is only later, *nachträglich*, that the sexes and/or genders are differentiated and a categorizing, by the self or by others, into one or the other *Geschlecht* takes place.

Reiche correctly points out that the "enigmatic message" of the parents is contingent. In my view, this is quite decisive for a theory of homosexuality, because it makes clear that there is and can be no parental message that forcibly leads to homosexual development, as other, aforementioned, psychoanalytic theories suggest. Thus, various psychoanalytic theories, each with consistent rationales, reach contrary conclusions about the love relations and identifications of the pre-homosexual boy. While Morgenthaler (1988), for example, assumes that the pre-homosexual boy, like all other boys, primarily loves his mother but unconsciously equips her with a penis, Dannecker (2000) and Isay (1989) hold the opposite view that the father is the primary sex object. I personally agree with Reiche that a psychoanalytic theory of homosexuality must try to accommodate, in a single model, these differing developmental paths. The model of reinscription I suggest, under the primacy of the Other, provides such a possibility, in my view. It avoids being fixed to a particular aetiology, such as a specific, characteristic, parent-child relation for a homosexual development, and instead describes, at the structural level, the more general development of sexual orientation. This takes into account the realization that there is neither an unambiguous nor a necessary path to heterosexuality or homosexuality. Renouncing a psychosocial aetiology does not mean by inference that sexual orientation is innate, but rather that its development is simply more contingent and more strongly influenced or determined by cultural factors (such as the normative primacy of heterosexuality) than one might assume. For that reason, the development of sexual orientation, just as with other behavioural characteristics, can only be reconstructed, *nachträglich*, in each individual case. As before, there is a limitation: "It is not for psycho-analysis to solve the problem of homosexuality" (1920a, p. 171). That is just as true for the problem of heterosexuality, with the emphasis on the aspect of a *solution*. Unaffected by that is the task still facing us: the psychoanalytic conceptualization of the various forms of object-choice.

Female homosexuality

After the unsuccessful treatment of a female homosexual patient, Freud addresses the problem of female homosexuality in an essay (1920a), which contains an oft-cited observation: "One must remember that normal sexuality, too, depends upon a restriction in the choice of object. In general, to undertake to convert a fully developed homosexual into a heterosexual does not offer much more prospect of success than the reverse, except that for good practical reasons the latter is never attempted" (1920a, p. 151). This insight led Freud to break off the treatment, which was initiated not at the behest of the eighteen-year-old patient but at the insistence of her father. The girl's love for a "courtesan" ten years her senior had aroused her parents' concern, and in particular unleashed the anger and embitterment of her father, who was determined to fight this love affair with every means at his disposal. After the father had met the two by chance on the street and glared angrily at them, the girl had impulsively tried to commit suicide by throwing herself over a wall into a ditch. Half a year after this accident, the parents turned to Freud. As in hardly any other case study, Freud elaborates on his uneasiness with her treatment, as in his view, it lacked the key preconditions for a psychoanalytic process (1920a): There was no inner conflict suffered by the patient; the girl was not ill and had no deep wish to change, but simply wanted to spare her parents any further distress. Freud's assessment that this patient was not ill strikes me as of special importance, given the later psychoanalytic pathologizing of homosexuality.

Freud describes the development of his patient as largely unremarkable; he could find no particular events or incidents. He did regard a renewed pregnancy of the mother, when the girl was sixteen, as a key moment in the aetiology of this particular case. The love for an older woman would in this case be seen as a replacement for the mother. In addition, the woman his patient loved had characteristics of her older brother, so the chosen object would have corresponded not only to her female but also to her male ideal. Freud saw this as confirmation for his theory that in the love-object, the gratification of the homosexual wishes is linked to the gratification of the heterosexual wishes, and again emphasized the significance of the fundamentally bisexual object-choice: "In all of us, throughout life, the libido normally oscillates between male and female objects" (Freud, 1920a, p. 158).

If that oscillation is interrupted, according to Freud, it points to a particular factor favouring one side or the other. Such a factor, in the one case, is likely the cultural primacy of heterosexuality. In the case of homosexuality, specific other factors can be assumed. In his patient, in Freud's view, it was probably the particular processing of her mother's pregnancy that had come into conflict with the daughter's Oedipal desire for a child, a desire revived during adolescence. Unconsciously, the daughter wanted a child from her father and was vehemently disappointed when her mother, her rival, actually had a child. Because of this failure, the daughter, following Freud, rejected her femininity and sought to accommodate her libido elsewhere.

Freud at this point emphasizes again that his patient was "in no way neurotic" (1920a, p. 158), to avoid engendering a misunderstanding of the psychodynamics in this case. I would like to underscore that point: with her same-sex object-choice, the patient finds a way of "resolving" the unconscious conflict by permanently accommodating her sexual desire in a person of the same sex. To avoid possible misunderstandings: from the psychoanalytic perspective, these unconscious conflicts are ubiquitous. They exist in everyone; it is merely a question of how these conflicts are addressed, how they are "defended against", which varies by individual. These defence mechanisms can be brought into play both intra-psychically and interpersonally, and under certain conditions may take on a neurotic or even psychotic character (Mentzos, 1982).

For Freud's patient, psychodynamically speaking, this means she accommodated her libido in a manner that was just no longer able to lead to a neurotic way of dealing with this conflict. If one looks at this aspect, namely an accommodation of the libido that is at least potentially permanent, then the immutability of sexual orientation seems extremely plausible. Put the other way around, if the desire on the part of the patient is directed at an object of the opposite sex, the unconscious conflict will again flare up. One may conclude from it that once sexual orientation has been established in one way or another, it presumably can be changed only if, in the course of life experience, unconscious conflicts are refreshed in a way that calls for a new manner of overcoming the conflict. In my view, a change in sexual orientation in later years can thus be understood in psychodynamic terms as a reinscription, as a way of overcoming unconscious conflicts, and should neither be regarded as regressive nor be called a late "coming out", a disclosure of what was repressed for many years.

My conceptualization, in particular, challenges the widespread notion, one which also exists in psychoanalysis, of a "critical period" in which sexual orientation is determined. John Money (1988, p. 129) suggests this as a compromise answer to the old nature vs. nurture controversy, but in my view it is better suited for describing grey goose goslings in Konrad Lorenz's ethology than for psychoanalysis. If one understands sexual orientation as the reinscription of the child's bisexual love for its parents, then one can grasp the psychodynamic connection between early-childhood love life and adult love life—a connection that is lost in the more recent notions of different or varying "sexualities". From a theoretical perspective it is less than satisfactory merely to descriptively array, side by side, various "homosexualities" and their respective development, for example, putting a man who had always known he was homosexual next to another whose homosexual orientation became evident only in the course of adolescence, and placing the latter beside someone who, after decades of heterosexual life, has turned his affections towards a man (see, among others, Isay, 1989). This descriptive disparity strikes me as less than helpful either for a psychoanalytic theory of sexuality or for clinical treatment. Though it is a great step forward, in comparison with earlier theory formation, even to distinguish between differing forms and cease to present "homosexuality" as a monolithic entity that leads to a particular psychic structure, or is the result of such a structure, as is just as untrue in the case of "heterosexuality".

But for all the advantages of a non-pathological aetiology, one can also discover a number of problematic assumptions in Freud's case study, such as that the patient has rejected her femininity. As already noted in the context of male homosexuality, one finds an overly close connection between *Geschlecht* identity and sexual orientation here as well. Freud initially notes that:

> What is certainly of greater importance is that in her behaviour towards her love-object she had throughout assumed the masculine part: that is to say, she displayed the humility and the sublime overvaluation of the sexual object so characteristic of the male lover, the renunciation of all narcissistic satisfaction, and the preference for being the lover rather than the beloved. She had thus not only chosen a feminine love-object, but had also developed a masculine attitude towards that object. (1920a, p. 154)

Yet Freud then takes this, in an unnecessarily inclusive manner, to be a rejection of her femininity. Here, again, one sees the problematic, ambiguous use of the terms "femininity" and "masculinity", which Freud uses in equal measure to describe unconscious positions and empirical *Geschlecht* identities. I think many of the misunderstandings and criticisms of his theories rest on this permanent commingling. Eva Poluda-Korte (2001) raises another point of critique as well: Freud, she believes, was unable to recognize that the girl's original love was for her mother. Thus, he was forced to assume that in this case, too, the patient in early childhood had switched her object-choice to her father and that it was only disappointment and a desire to exact revenge on her father that had led her back to her mother. Poluda-Korte is unquestionably correct that the same-sex desire of the daughter came from her own self, in other words, without any disappointment engendered by her father. The plausibility of such psychodynamics was realized by Freud himself some years later (1931b). Still, and taking the bisexuality of desire as a starting point, I would nevertheless assume the existence of disappointment brought about by the father in this case, creating a double disappointment for the daughter, which can also explain the deep despair that led to her suicide attempt.

While Freud's conceptualization of female homosexuality, even more clearly than his delineation of male homosexuality, avoids any pathologizing and develops non-neurotic, largely "unobtrusive" psychodynamics for this sexual orientation, this is distinctly not the case for Freud's successors. Joyce McDougall (1970, 1980), for example, and Elaine Siegel (1988), like Bieber and Socarides, describe female homosexuality as the result of a highly pathological development. One should note, though, that McDougall (1995) has since distanced herself from her earlier views. Yet the earlier conceptualizations seem to have remained firmly ingrained in the minds of many analysts. A systematic revision of notions of female homosexuality has not yet, at least, been undertaken (see Poluda-Korte, 2001).

Following the Freudian assumption of bisexuality, McDougall (1970) suggests the odd thesis that the homosexual woman is unable to integrate her homosexuality but must instead act it out in an obvious way, which is why she also suggests that the homosexual woman does not have an active fantasy life. By contrast, the heterosexual woman accommodates her homosexual libido through friendships with other women, in motherhood, and in her profession or creative activities. The inadequate integration of homosexuality leaves a gap evident in identity disorders, in anxieties during relationships to others, and in serious inhibitions of the ability to sublimate. These observations, like those reported by Bieber and Socarides, are based on McDougal's experiences with evidently seriously disturbed female homosexual patients, whose pathology she quite incorrectly traces back to sexual orientation.

Elaine Siegel (1988), too, who repeatedly cites Socarides with approval, bases her views on homosexuality on her experiences treating neurotic women. She finds—unsurprisingly in the case of neuroses—disruptions in individuation and separation, as well as fixation and regression back to the earliest stages of the mother-child relationship. Same-sex love, following Siegel, in the end is a narcissistic love in women as well, based on a fundamental deficiency. In homosexual relationships, a woman seeks confirmation for her femininity, which she experiences as forbidden, as well as completion of her body image through a deferred integration of the vagina.

The genesis of female homosexuality, like that of male homosexuality, is ascribed to a specific typical family constellation. Hence McDougall (1980) sees as characteristic of homosexual development as largely unavailable father who brusquely rejects his daughter's love. As a result of this disappointment, the daughter turns again to her mother, though her mother, too, treats her with little affection and similarly disappoints. The girl responds to this with increased idealization and tries to win her mother's love by acting like a man. For her mother's sake, this also includes relinquishing her love for her father.

Ruth-Jean Eisenbud (1969, 1986), taking a feminist psychoanalytic perspective, regards the lesbian object-choice as adaptive, a positive accommodation of the ego in its struggle for fulfilment (1986, p. 229). She, too, revises her earlier insights into female homosexuality, which she regards at its core as a "fear of heterosexuality", meaning a defence against Oedipal desires. Contrary to this assumption of regression, she instead locates the idea of a primary lesbian object-choice at the pre-Oedipal stage, and regards the daughter's early directing of sexual arousal towards her mother as the result, not the cause, of longing on the daughter's part for secure attachment. She also criticizes her own earlier conviction that lesbian relationships are fundamentally structured by a (phantasmal) staging of being a heterosexual pair. That view was influenced by heteronormativity, and she now emphasizes instead the self-willed orientation of the relationship, one that is not centred on a man.

In an original, constructive, and helpful way, Eva Poluda-Korte (1993, 2001) suggests that female development can lead equally to a homosexual or a heterosexual orientation, and she thereby avoids the problem of pathologizing female homosexuality. The "lesbian complex", traditionally referred to as the negative Oedipus complex, plays a special role in every female's development. Like Melanie Klein, Poluda-Korte distinguishes between the earlier and the "proper" Oedipus complex, with the earlier form being associated with processes of differentiating self and object in the first year of life. In the early Oedipus complex, the love of a daughter for her mother is massively frustrated both by the taboo on homosexuality and by the daughter's observation that her mother does not love her exclusively, but also loves her father. This repudiation is experienced as devaluation and betrayal, and can lead love to turn to hate, sexual wishes to be transformed into murderous impulses, and guilt feelings to become suicidal tendencies. The massive narcissistic and Oedipal aggression linked to the lesbian complex is integrated into a rigid, early superego. Disappointment and the homosexual taboo arising from heteronormativity prompt the daughter to shift her object-choice to her father. In addition, there is an erotic identification with the mother that is part melancholy, part sublimation, and it transforms the primary homosexuality of the daughter into motherliness. Poluda-Korte sees in this transformation, in the production of motherliness, a key function of the taboo on homosexuality. "Out of love for the mother emerges the wish for a child, through which this love is expected to be restored" (2001, p. 83, translation for this edition). The girl turns to her father with this wish, and he is blamed for the destruction of the mother-daughter dyad, for which he can make amends by fulfilling her desire for a child.

In a lesbian development, the taboo on homosexuality is not accepted. The anger over it is not bound to the superego but instead remains in the ego, so that the desire for the same sex can continue to be asserted and upheld. In Poluda-Korte's observations lesbian women develop a specific relation both of identifying with and loving their mothers. This relationship stands intermediate between those existing between heterosexual woman and men. Thus, less transformation of object-love into identification occurs among lesbians than among heterosexual women, but more than among men. At the same time, lesbian women develop a stronger identification with fatherly potency than do hetero-sexual women, though this identification is less strong than among men. These considerations aid Poluda-Korte in explaining the role shift in conquest and surrender that both homosexual women and men practice (see Morgenthaler, 1980). However, such a role shift can also be assumed among heterosexual pairs, at least at the level of sexual fantasy. With this, I want to point out that the ratio of object-love to identification is not simply distributed along the traditional gender roles but is instead a highly complex conglomerate of levels and aspects in every individual.

Poluda-Korte (2001) correctly emphasizes how important the creation of a vaginal representation is for female development. In her critique of Janine Chasseguet-Smirgel's (1974) conceptualization of female sexuality, she sees the absence of such representation, in the theoreti-cal formulations as well, as a reason for the devaluing and pathologiz-ing of female homosexuality. Such a representation of the vagina also comes about when the depressive position, in Melanie Klein's sense, is achieved. With it, not only is the division between "good" and "bad" nullified through the integration of libidinous and aggressive drives, but so is the sexual monism of the primary dyads. It becomes possible in this way to recognize the existence of two sexes and their differences. Following Chasseguet-Smirgel, for the daughter to be able to develop, she must flee the power of her mother. Poluda-Korte by contrast, tak-ing a position I wholly support, emphasizes that the integration of the vagina into the body scheme of the daughter calls for a mother-daughter relationship based on desire rather than hostility. Only in this manner can a positive female self-image and body image develop.

In her conception of a "lesbian complex", Poluda-Korte is inspired by the Freudian Oedipus complex, expanding on its 'negative' variant to explain female development. Together with Freud, she also asserts the universal validity of this complex, one that exists in equal measure among homosexual and heterosexual women. Though I agree with her observations, by and large; calling it a 'lesbian complex' is unfortunate. Freud already rejected Jung's suggestion that the female variant of the Oedipus complex be called an 'Electra complex', as such a sex-specific separation might obscure the significance of the universal, structuring function of the Oedipal. This argument strikes me as still valid. Still, the normative connotations of designating a 'positive' and a 'negative' Oedipus complex in the context of heteronormativity are problematic. Despite all the difficulties associated with changing entrenched terminologies, I would nevertheless like to suggest abandoning such linguistic short-cuts and instead referring, with greater precision, to a same-sex or a cross-sex Oedipus complex, Oedipal relationships and constellations, and so forth.

Addressing psychoanalytic studies of male and female homosexuality raises the basic question how useful it is to categorize heterosexuality and homosexuality as separate categories. The case studies, as well as the theoretical conceptualizations, result in such a variety of individual manifestations that one clearly can speak as little of one homosexuality as one can speak of one heterosexuality. What has never been suspected of heterosexuals seems now to be clear in the case of homosexuality as well: it is not a monolithic entity, and cannot be defined as a particular, specific type of psychic structure. In consequence, there is already widespread talk of (homo- or hetero-) *sexualities* (see Braun and Otscheret, 2004). However, I agree with Reiche (2005), who criticizes this usage, and hold to the comprehensive, systematic, collective singular.

Freud begins his psychoanalytic discourse on sexuality by speaking of "perversions" and "inversions" to make clear the connection between human forms of sexuality. As noted above, this line of argument was lost in the course of subsequent psychoanalytic theory. Conventional value judgments also play a role, and with the increasing turn to the medical, pathology has come to play a large role. As with the categories "masculinity" and "femininity", the categories of homosexuality and heterosexuality at heart serve an ordering function for society, and the valuation that inescapably accompanies this classification is due to the cultural primacy of heterosexuality (see Poluda-Korte, 2001).

Such categorization is not very helpful to psychoanalytic thinking. In the case of gender, this was already evident in Freud's highly differentiated definitional efforts, in which he regarded "masculinity" and "femininity" as positions and not as terms to describe the identity of individuals. However, he did not uphold this differentiation in his later work (see Chapter Two). Similarly, in the case of sexual orientation, one finds in Freud a psychic equivalency of the different sexual forms. One can thus ask whether a unifying category such as homosexuality or heterosexuality really describes essentially common ground, or whether it is not more the case that the differences are subsumed, and smoothed away by being included under a single, comprehensive, term. The designation "homosexual" is used simplistically, to construct a type that, as we have seen, evidences neither a specific psychic structure nor a particular life history and development, nor (presumably) a specific genetic predisposition. For that reason, the attempt to create a psychoanalytic theory of *homo*sexuality ultimately fails, and one cannot identify any specific differences between male and female homosexuality, either (see Rohde-Dachser, 1992).

Hence I argue that one should abandon the fruitless search for differences, and give up the conventional differentiation in psychoanalytic discourse between homosexuality and heterosexuality. In this sense, one can follow Eva Poluda-Korte (2001), who, along with Freud, assumes the most variable aspect of drives to be the object itself. A concept of sexuality is needed that has differing, polarized dimensions, such as one with homosexual and heterosexual, or one with masculine and feminine, endpoints. This conceptualization emphasizes the connections between different forms of sexuality and tries to avoid conventional valuations. The continua of the different dimensions are to be found both within an individual as well as distributed between the persons in a sexual relationship.

The "Dictatorship of sexuality"

Fritz Morgenthaler (1988, p. 105 et seq.) draws an important distinction between the sexual and sexuality. His reflections play an important role in my approach, because he consistently takes the unconscious into account and avoids pathologizing as well as conventional valuations. In his view, the sexual is an unfocused, energetic potential that follows the primary process. Through the development of libido and ego, it has experienced a priming that subjects it to sexual goals, transforming it into "organized sexuality": "When we speak of the sexual, in contrast to organized sexuality, we mean by that the instinctuality of the id, that is, an energetic potential that gives experience in general an urgelike dimension" (ibid., pp. 106–07). Morgenthaler speaks of a "dictatorship of sexuality" (ibid., p. 110) and compares it "to a society ruled, for example, by a military power" (ibid., p. 111). He goes on to note that "the comparison of the dictatorship of sexuality with that of a military junta seems justified, in view of the hostility of our industrial societies towards instinct" (ibid., p. 112). In these pointed formulations, though, he seems to be throwing the baby out with the bathwater. Reimut Reiche (2006) justly criticizes them, correspondingly, as a dualistic, schematic opposition of good and bad, and as a vitalist revision of Freudian drive theory or anthropology. Lost in Reiche's critique, however, is Morgenthaler's helpful contribution. By questioning "the harmony between instinct and sexuality", he makes it clear that both are far from having "a simple, smooth" relationship and instead "oppose each other in a ruptured relationship from the very beginning" (Morgenthaler ibid., p. 112). Additionally, Morgenthaler takes up an idea Freud raised in the *New Introductory Lectures on Psycho-Analysis*, and investigates how the drives serve sexual functioning, and what changes the drives undergo under the influence of the organized ego.

Freud describes the connection between the drives and repetition compulsion in *Beyond the Pleasure Principle*, "ascribing it to the conservative nature of the instincts" (ibid., p. 112) that in Freud's terms is "an urge inherent in organic life to restore an earlier state of things" (1920g, p. 36). One recognizes a similarity here to the concept of the wish, a terminological predecessor to the drive as it was formulated in the *Interpretation of Dreams*. Nonetheless, Morgenthaler criticizes this notion of Freud's, arguing that compulsive repetition is always determined by the secondary process, because the primary process is wholly aimless. In the compulsion to repeat, Morgenthaler instead sees one of the two organizing principles of sexuality, which ensue from the channelling of the primary-process drive impulses into attachments to sexual objects. The compulsion to repeat the sexual object-cathexis is called forth by the "dictatorship of sexuality" and established through the organization of the ego. Insurmountable conflicts are tied to this repetition compulsion, "because the sexual development, no matter what type it may be, necessarily induces dependency on the sexual object" (1984, p. 114).

This dependence, in turn, goes hand-in-hand with regression, softening the organization of the ego. In this way, drive impulses from the ego are again permitted and can serve sexuality. Such a dynamic leads to permanent transformations and further development of sexuality, in the sense of a convergence with the aimless aspect of the primary-process instinctual impulses. The emotional agitation from the primary process can thereby be linked to sexuality. What is achieved through this is a capacity to love, which is independent of any individual sexual organization, whether homosexual, heterosexual, or perverse.

In setting this goal, which echoes the polymorphously perverse aspect of infantile sexuality, Morgenthaler moves diametrically away from Freudian assumptions about sexual development that culminates in the establishment of genital primacy and a heterosexual orientation. In the course of further development, this sexual organization is shaken in adolescence, with one result a reformulation in the direction of genital sexuality. Following Morgenthaler, sexual development is not concluded in adolescence or later in adult life. Instead, it continues to develop to the degree that it can accommodate new impulses from the id. The primary process, finally, links sexuality to the adult capacity to love, a capacity developed in adolescence as a new point of reference. This adolescent experience differs fundamentally from childhood experience, when despair and helplessness influenced the unconscious sexual imaginings, and neither object-fixation nor the satisfaction of needs was secured as yet. If the development of the capacity to love is successful, sexuality increasingly falls under the primacy of the primary process "which asserts its influence without direction, aimless, timeless, without conditions, and unconsciously creates new aspects of experiencing, and knows no repetition" (ibid., p. 122).

Morgenthaler's concern is to relate heterosexuality, homosexuality, and perversion to differing drive destinies, in order to make clear that they lead to different sexual organizations, which are not, however, intrinsically pathological. For that reason, there are both neurotic and non-neurotic forms of homosexuality, heterosexuality, and perversions. Morgenthaler regards the markers of pathology in a sexual organization as torpidity and rigidity, the immutability of the connection between sexual cathexis and dependence on the sexual object. He describes a vicious circle which this link can become when the drive towards sexual cathexis becomes a compulsion, and the dependence becomes a form of bondage or enslavement. Under these conditions, a curtailment of the ego results, with a loss of autonomous functions, because the sexual attachment intensifies the dependence, and the dependence on the sexual object in turn activates the sexual attachment. Thus, the emotional stirrings of the primary process are blocked, promoting the development of aggression. In such neurotic developments, the love relationship has a symptomatic character; an oscillation between dependence, regression, and incorporation of new id aspects is no longer possible or is possible only to a very limited degree. These considerations make clear that difficulties and conflicts are not caused by sexual organization, thus are not induced by homosexuality, heterosexuality, or perversion, but rather are due to "a capacity to love that is restricted or deprived of its potential" (1988, p. 126).

This conceptualization of pathogenesis in connection with sexual life seems extremely constructive and helpful to me for the psychoanalytic understanding of illness. Though the question whether homosexuality should be regarded as an illness can by now be regarded as resolved, in psychoanalytic discourse, and the diagnosis of "homosexuality" has been removed from the international classifications of psychic disorders, one can still see similar questions raised with respect to the perversions. Here too, Morgenthaler's reflections would seem to provide sensible criteria for a differentiated diagnosis: what constitutes illness in this context is not a particular sexual behaviour or experience but rather its absence of flexibility and its inalterability, or the psychic function it could possibly have.

Morgenthaler seeks to describe this psychic functioning by using a now much-cited concept of a sealing plug or a filling (*Plombe*). Though developed to describe the perversions, one can use it for all forms of sexual orientation. It is an important diagnostic criterion not only for perversions but also for homosexuality and heterosexuality, because it permits assessment of a possible pathological function performed by any sexual behaviour: the question of the pathology of a particular behaviour is not posed from the start. The concept of the *Plombe* is described in greater detail in the discussion of "perversions" in the next section.

Morgenthaler differentiates between the various sexual orientations of heterosexuality, homosexuality, and perversion with respect to how each handles the vicious circle of the cathexis of sexual object and dependence on that sexual object, as well as to each orientation's differing perception of the disharmony between the primary-process impulses and organized sexuality. He places the desire for identity, the desire to know who one is, at the centre of the development of a heterosexual orientation. One's sense of identity plays a leading role in shaping a harmonious sexual life that tries to reconcile the physical, psychic, and societal dimensions. An over-cathexis of identity is thus viewed as the psychodynamic precondition for a fixed heterosexuality. This over-cathexis is regarded as necessary so that the polar opposition of male and female gender roles can overlay the disharmony between the primary process and organized sexuality, and thereby make the disharmony unconscious. If both love partners are successful in liberating the long-term cathexis of the sexual object from an obsessive dependency, then an over-cathexis of gender polarity is no longer necessary; heterosexuality loses its ideological character; and sexual behaviour, which remains heterosexual, is allowed greater variation.

In a homosexual orientation, the wish for autonomy is in the foreground, and is over-cathected. Autonomy finds its precursor in autoerotic activity, which provides a child very early with a possibility to maintain sexual cathexis, and to eliminate object dependency by making oneself one's own sex object. Every love relationship activates the danger of dependence on the object, and the vicious circle develops more rapidly and clearly than among heterosexuals, as there are also fewer societal institutions for delegating dependence that are available for overcoming it. A promiscuous sex life can be understood, for example, as an effort to protect oneself from a dependence regarded as threatening, and that is as true of homosexuals as of heterosexuals. The fear of dependence blocks the development of the capacity to love, and the connection of emotional involvement with the partner and thus with a primary-process exchange.

In contrast to this, perversion is characterized by extreme object dependence and rigidity in object attachment, which, detached from what is emotionally experienced, acts like a foreign object in the personality. Morgenthaler notes that "the form of deviation from the normal sexual life cannot be the fundamental issue. In fact, it becomes evident that the instinctual gratification, which perverted patients seek in peculiar rituals and arrangements, while indeed representing a regressive formation of a striving for pleasure and gratification, is in itself subject to a change of function" (1988, p. 13). This function Morgenthaler tries to describe with his "metaphor of a filling, a plug—that is, a connecting or bridging structure" (ibid., p. 14).

In the perversions, following Morgenthaler, one sees in its most extreme form the vicious circle between the repetition compulsion of sexual cathexis and the dependence on the sexual object. As much as Morgenthaler tries to depathologize sexual variants, one must nevertheless conclude he is not really successful at doing so in the case of perversion. This is also evident in the imagery used to make this sexual organization, at least in its pathological versions, clear: The dictatorship of sexuality has been given an island on which it can indulge itself and thereby leave the rest of the country in peace (a similar thought can be found already in Glover, 1933). The formation of a perversion functions in such a way as to fix in place one of the polymorphously perverse partial drives "like a bridge pier" and thereby make permanent access to experience available to the primary-process impulses. The disharmony between primary process and sexual organization is not repressed. Rather, and in contrast, it is expressed in an exaggerated manner by the staging of a sexuality that is experienced as alien and often does not match the personality. Object dependency, unlike in the other sexual organizations, is not fought against. However, communication with the primary-process aspects carries the price of devitalizing the sexual objects. When dealing with other people, the perverted patients shy away from object attachment and object dependence. In the analytic process, the point is to disrupt the compulsion to repeat object attachment and dependence in such a manner that object cathexis seems possible without sliding into compulsive dependence. The perverse sex organization is not thereby changed, but the dictatorship of sexuality is brought back from the island to the mainland, and the primary-process impulses are thereby granted broader and freedom to experience once again.

'Perversions,' 'paraphilia', 'inverted love'?

> In view of what was now seen to be the wide dissemination of tendencies to perversion we were driven to the conclusion that a disposition to perversions is an original and universal disposition of the human sexual instinct and that normal sexual behaviour is developed out of it as a result of organic changes and psychical inhibitions occurring in the course of maturation. (1905d, p. 231)

The contribution of Freudian sexual theory, which remains important, consists of seeing the "perversions" in the context of "normal" sexuality, rather than excluded as "completely different". It remains—as before, in my view—an

> "unavoidable task to give a complete theoretical account of how it is that these perversions can occur and of their connection with what is described as normal sexuality". (1917, p. 307)

Freud successfully conceptualizes this connection via infantile sexuality and argues "that perverse sexuality is nothing else than a magnified infantile sexuality split up into its separate impulses" (ibid., p. 311). This once again shows the vast importance of the concept of "infantile sexuality" for the entire theoretical edifice. The evidence of childhood sexuality is not only significant empirically and in terms of developmental psychology, but also underpins the entire theory of sexuality. Without it, one could hardly make a connection between the different forms of sexual objects and sexual goals, and therewith the notion of psychically equivalent sexualities. The psychoanalytic theory of sexuality remains in addition the only such theory that asserts this equivalence and underpins it theoretically.

In his work "Fetishism" (1927e), Freud describes the psychic mechanism of "splitting", a side-by-side perception of what is wished and what is real, as prototypical for the development of perversions. Thus, when the boy sees the absence of a penis on a woman, making him fear for his own penis, he creates a fetish. By phantasmally attaching it to the woman, he employs the fetish as a replacement for the penis, and in this manner moderates his castration anxieties. With the fetish, perception again is reconciled with what is wished: the woman has a penis and is not castrated, and his own penis thus is also not endangered. The fetish signifies both a triumph over the threat of castration as well as protection against it. With the fetish, the infantile belief in the phallus of the woman can be both preserved and at the same time abandoned. However, this (fantasized) penis is no longer the same as it was prior to the perception of a difference between the sexes. Rather, much more interest is paid to the replacement, the fetish, because the fetishist has memorialized his abhorrence of castration in the fetish. The alienation from actual female genitalia also points to this abhorrence, one absent in no fetishist. It is through the fetish that a woman becomes bearable to the fetishist as a sexual object. Not only objects and organs that are generally recognized as penis symbols serve as fetishes. In fact, introducing a fetish seems like stopping the memory in the case of traumatic amnesia: "the subject's interest comes to a halt half-way, as it were" (1927e, p. 155). Thus the foot or the shoe is the last impression that still records the phallic fantasy before the boy, looking from below, espies the "castrated" female genitalia, or thus the moment of disrobing is preserved in undergarments. The tenderness, and the hostility, in the treatment of the fetish betray the ambivalent attitude of the fetishist toward the castration of the woman, both the denial as well as the assertion of the castration.

Using fetishism as an example, Freud discusses the psychodynamics of the castration complex. This psychic issue remains to this day the core of the modern psychoanalytic understanding of perversion (Reiche, 2005). Reimut Reiche (p. 139) sees castration as metaphor, and conceptualizes three phases of threatened obliteration. In the first, oral, phase, it is about fusion and merging, and about extinction and the fear of obliteration; in the second, anal, phase, it is about narcissistic integrity and the denial of one's own autonomy (characteristic is the "intrusive mother" of the subsequent perverse individual); in the third, genital, phase, it is about possession and loss of "whole" objects (fear of loss). The object threatened with castration is not the penis, however, but phallic-narcissistic integrity at all three stages, so this correspondingly applies to both sexes. As helpful as this suggestion seems, with respect to extending the notion of castration to both sexes, it also narrows or intellectualizes the perspective by abandoning the concrete reference to the body that is present in the Freudian notion. That notion seems, in my view, far from being as "concretist" as Reiche charges. To be sure: this is not about the actual removal of penis or testicles (or the fear thereof), but most assuredly about a specific location of bodily pleasure, and the fear of losing this location and hence this pleasure. This aspect was already considered by Jones in his reading of castration anxiety as the fear of 'aphanisis', meaning the loss of the ability to experience pleasure (see Chapter Two). Here I see an appropriate extension of Reiche's phased conceptualization of the castration complex.

Such an extension could also shed some light on the question of sexualization, which Reimut Reiche (2005) regards as a still-unresolved puzzle in perversion. This assessment is surprising. Amidst the great diversity of perverse sexual forms, it is precisely sexualization as the constitutive characteristic of perversion which strikes one as probably the only common feature. One would have thought that long since resolved, but Reiche tries to show that this is not the case with a complex argument—wrongly, I would argue. For sexualization can be used to show, admirably, the differences between a conceptualization of sexuality that is biologically based and one based on the primacy of the Other. Hence, I will briefly sketch out Reiche's line of argument, but not just to discuss the problem of sexualization. Rather, I wish to present an explicitly constructive psychoanalytic theory of perversion, one in which various strands of earlier theories are incorporated.

Morgenthaler's "filling" or *Plombe* stands at the centre of Reiche's theory. It is trenchantly summarized in a manner rare in psychoanalytic discourse: "Perversions are (…) primarily function. This function can be best described as a filling, a plug, a heterogeneous creation that fills the gap created by a narcissistic development which is going astray. Thanks to this "filling", it is possible to create and maintain homeostasis in the narcissistic sphere" (1974, p. 1081, translation for this edition).

Even though this functional definition of perversion is well-founded and convincing, Morgenthaler, of all people, in whose writings the sexual plays such an important role, has reduced the notion of perversion to the narcissistic dimension. The dimension of pleasure is largely ignored, which Reiche appropriately criticizes. In justifying his own conceptualization, Morgenthaler does not refer to Freud's *Fetishism*, with its notion of splitting and projection, and thereby creates for himself the problem of having to explain the sexualisation of the "filling".

Such a model did not originate with Morgenthaler but can be found in other, earlier authors. Phyllis Greenacre, for example, published five significant works on perversion between 1953 and 1970, and suggested the model of the "necessary prop" (1971, p. 314). Masud Khan referred similarly to the "collated internal object" and Joyce McDougall to "neo-sexualities" (see Reiche, 2005).

According to Reiche, and here I agree with him, it seems neither sensible nor necessary to draw up a catalogue of sexual acts or fantasies to which the term "perversion" applies. Instead, in the sense of a Weberian ideal-type, Reiche (1990; 2001b; 2005, p. 143 et seq.) suggests five criteria that must be met if one is to speak of perversions.

First, all perversions, following the criterion of the necessity of a fetish, are dependent on a fetish, whether overtly or covertly. All possible inanimate objects and/or those appurtenances connected with them, as well as bodily parts, though the latter are perceived as detached from it, can serve this purpose. These are sexually highly charged and function in the sense of a "triggering stimulus".

Second, the criterion of a perverse setting dictates that all these fetish objects and actions need to be brought together in a scenario indispensable for sexual arousal to occur. This scenario can be implemented by the individual alone or can call for a partner, either male or female. In Reiche's view, the central inner object relationship that had led to the "gap" and the ensuing creation of a "filling" is externalized in this scene. With this, Reiche distances himself from theories that postulate a specific family dynamic or constellation as being responsible for the genesis of the perversion. At most, based on his clinical experience, one can observe increased traumatization in these patients due to over- or under-stimulation in early childhood. The compulsion towards periodic externalization differentiates perversion from a mere sexual fantasy, merely having fun, or a hobby.

Reiche has in the meantime revised his third criterion, namely orgasm. This criterion does not apply to all perversions: sexual arousal can occur even in the process of setting the scene, without leading to a sexual discharge in the form of an orgasm. Morgenthaler has already made clear that "the change in function that underlies the drive activity of the perverse individual (...) stands so much in the foreground, that the satisfaction of the drive is not only secondary but in most cases is remarkable weakly cathected" (1974, p. 1080; translation for this edition). Despite this, the orgiastic discharge, in the sense of a temporary "deliverance", is in many other cases an indispensable part of the scenario.

The fourth criterion—behaviour indicating addiction or compulsion—refers to the compulsory nature of the periodic repetition of the scene, experienced as a physical addiction. If the possibility of externalizing the inner object relationship on an external stage is interrupted, it can lead to massive psychic crises and forms of decompensation ranging all the way to suicide and acts of violence.

Under the fifth criterion of the (wooden) doll-inside-another-doll, Reiche sees the structural creation of a perversion in which every manifested perversion contains a further perversion that has been fended off. In a crisis, or during psychoanalytic treatment, the outer doll, or filling, can collapse and a new one, perhaps only temporarily, come to the fore.

Unlike Robert Stoller (1975), Reiche accords no particular significance to hate and aggression in perversion, because his model is constructed more from the perspective of the psychic surface than from that of psychodynamics. Reiche's question goes more in the direction of how hate is eroticized, thus in the direction of its sexualisation. In my view, he refers here to Morgenthaler's neglect of the pleasure dimension in his conceptualization of perversion, which may derive from Morgenthaler's theoretical orientation to ego psychology. In Morgenthaler's view, the fetish closes "a gap in the self" that is evoked by the sight of the penisless mother. But can one really assert that a gap in the self is caused by this sight? Freud says merely that this sight triggers fear, anxiety about a narcissistic injury to the body, and anxiety about losing the pleasure-giving organ. This fear, however, leaves no "gap" behind. Such a gap comes about, in my view, only if the castration threat is too massive and the narcissistic equilibrium can no longer be maintained. While Freud focuses in this context equally on narcissism and desire, Morgenthaler looks solely at the formation of the ego and the self. The sexual dimension, the sexualization, is thereby constitutive of and contained in Freud's concept. The pleasure-giving organ, the penis, is symbolically replaced by the fetish, with the fetish itself (as described above for the fetishist) evoking even greater pleasure. From this perspective, I do not understand why Reiche regards this sexualization as an unresolved problem and needs to turn, in his argument, to the analogy of the transitional object in the manner that Phyllis Greenacre (1971) already suggested as a way for better understanding the fetish.

However, if one regards the fetish "as a triggering cue created by the subject", as Reiche does (2005, p. 148; translation for this edition), one which fills the gap caused by man's delivery from instinct, both in phylogenesis and in ontogenesis, then the sexualisation does in fact become a puzzle requiring explanation. Reiche, put simply, poses the question why that which fills the gap and "actually" serves the formation of ego and self should have an arousing, sexual effect. In explanation, he suggests the concept of a "triggering cue", which he does not want to have understood only as a contingent link to a biological program but also as something created by the "subject". Sexual arousal is initiated through this "triggering stimulus". In the classic behaviourist understanding of Pavlov and Skinner, such triggers arise through simple conditioning, but in Reiche's interpretation, the "subject" has a decisive significance in their genesis. However, what remains unresolved is whether such a model isn't inevitably bound to the amply problematic notion of a conditioned sexual reaction released by the triggering stimulus. Introducing additional concepts such as the triggering cue is also unnecessary if one returns to Freud's initial concept, which links desire and ego-formation from birth in the process of constituting the psychic structures. These structuring functions, which Reiche assigns to sexualization and desexualization, are already contained in the Freudian conceptualization. There is a final argument, in my view, that speaks against burdening such a concept of sexualization with this meaning. Reiche describes sexualisation as a process that originates in the "subject" and decidedly emphasizes that subject's autonomy. This is particularly clear in his notion of unconscious fantasies: "Unconscious 'sexual' fantasies are, by definition, always incestuous. They must be linked to the autonomous gesture of the subject: I know the object that arouses me; I can steer the arousal myself through the subject; with this knowledge, I can use an object to gratify myself. I regard as mistaken the psychoanalytic doctrine according to which incestuous fantasy *eo ipso* is arousing. Put in other terms, the unconscious (=incestuous) fantasy *must be sexualized*" (2005, p. 149, emphasis in the originaltranslation for this edition).

This emphatic focus on the "autonomous subject" certainly stands in some tension with the concept of the unconscious and in diametric opposition to the assumption of a primacy of the Other, as I have suggested in my approach grounded in the general theory of seduction. In my view, sexualisation is precisely not an autonomous gesture on the part of the subject but is rather the reverse, a process that originates in the Other. As described in Chapter One, in the seduction scene, the enigmatic messages from the (sexual) unconscious of the adult are intromitted into the child, inscribed in the developing child's structure. In this manner, the child is unavoidably confronted with the unconscious sexual desire of the adult. As an answer to this message, an unconscious, sexual desire is constituted in the psychic structure of the child. In this view, the unconscious incestuous fantasies, as the fallout of the seduction scene, are very probably *eo ipso* arousing and need no subsequent sexualisation by the subject.

There is also controversy over whether perversions are a "male domain" (Reiche, 1986, p. 90), and whether there are "no perversions without a penis" (McDougall, 1995, p. 80) or whether perversions among women, to be recognized as such, do not need to be conceptualized differently than among men. Estela Welldon (1988) has offered a theory of "female perversion" that opposes the "pathological privilege of the man" (Becker, 2002, p. 282). This formulation seems odd, but it points, especially in light of the considerable resonance her theory has had, to the evidently attractive aura of perversion as norm-breaking sexuality, tied to the hope for recognition and valorization of female sexuality and aggression (see Becker, 2002). In her theory, and like other authors, without giving any reason for it, Welldon starts from the assumption of basic differences in the psychopathology of men and women. She then tries to conceive of perverse behavioural forms among women "according to a separate, completely different psychopathology which originates from the female body and its inherent attributes" (1988, p. 5). Her main thesis is that perversion is a particular form of motherhood: "Odd though it may sound, motherhood provides an excellent vehicle for some women to exercise perverse and perverting attitudes towards their offspring, and to retaliate against their own mothers" (ibid., p. 63). With this focus on motherhood rather than on sexual desire, I believe Welldon follows the cultural model of a desexualized mother whose power lies not in sexual potency but in power over others (see the critique of this cultural cliché in Benjamin 1986, discussed in Chapter Two). In Welldon's aetiology of perversion, the early mother-child relationship plays the decisive role. Here the father becomes significant only in adolescence (Welldon, 1988, p. 11). Like Helene Deutsch, Welldon notes that "women frequently act as if their whole body were a sexual organ" (ibid., p. 12), and the child—in the case of "perverse" motherhood—as "extensions of their own bodies" (ibid., p. 16).

Abusive mother-child relationships are without doubt repeatedly observed, but I regard categorizing them under the term perversion as problematic for a number of reasons. Welldon's notion of perversion is unrelated to sexual lust, or at least it is not evident from her clinical examples what pleasure is to be gained in cases of "perverse" motherhood. As a result, she also criticizes the limiting of the psychoanalytic understanding of perversion to sexuality. In her efforts to define perversion, she uses it in the sense of "deviations of instinct", in this case deviation from the "maternal instinct" (ibid., p. 64). Welldon's biologistic basic orientation focuses particularly on the woman's reproductive function, and distinguishes between genital sexuality, seen "as a living—or loving—force" and "what appears to be sexual, but actually corresponds to much more primitive stages where pregenitality pervades the whole picture" (ibid., p. 7). Such a distinction betrays a narrowed view of sexuality which normatively makes genital sexuality oriented to procreation equivalent to "sexual emotional maturity" (ibid., p. 11). In so doing, she dismisses as only "apparently" sexual that which is particular to the psychoanalytic understanding of psychosexuality, namely the myriad pregenital possibilities for pleasure and gratification.

In contrast to this desexualized notion of perversion, Lorenz Böllinger (2005) provides a brief vignette of the case of a young woman with a clearly masochistic perversion that is distinctly pleasurable and sexual in nature. The patient outlined the "indescribable pleasure in the feeling of being so utterly at someone else's mercy that he can resolve over my death and I no longer have any influence at all on it" (2005, p. 45; translation for this edition). Böllinger, with reference to psychodynamics, notes the "phallic cathexis of one's own body", which interacts with societal attributions of sadomasochistic experience and behaviour as well as with an external social reality in which a "multiplicity of sadomasochistic institutions" can be observed. Böllinger unfortunately does not pursue these promising thoughts leading towards a psychoanalytic theory of perversion.

Sophinette Becker (2002) also draws attention to other manifestations of female perversion: inducing or even forcing gynaecological operations to be performed. As in Welldon's conceptualization, in these cases, too, it is not about gaining pleasure. However, it does seem quite plausible to see the perverse element, particularly in a highly instrumental, abusive, and destructive treatment of one's own body. In these cases, the body does not serve to sexually arouse, but the reverse: it is damaged in this function. Pleasure is perverted into injury. According to Becker, this is not only specifically true for gynaecological operations but also for cosmetic surgery, because the woman's sexuality is not so focused on one organ as in the case of the man, and the entire body of the woman, in Helene Deutsch's and Estela Welldon's sense, can serve as a sexual organ.

Following Welldon, Becker sees a fetishizing of the woman's own body in many cases of female perversion. This idea of a fetishizing strikes me as less plausible, however, because the aspect of sexual arousal in this conceptualization of perversion has largely receded into the background. In this de-sexualized notion of fetish, which now focuses only on its function as filling (*Plombe*), the fetish seems to have lost its "actual" or "original" function as pleasure-inducing. Nevertheless, I agree with Sophinette Becker that knowledge of the polymorphous nature of female perversion could shed light on other clinical symptoms such as anxiety and acting out with respect to contraception and pregnancy, as well as disorders in sexual function, behind which a repressed perversion may lie hidden. In the sense of the defence against pleasure and sexual arousal noted above as a possible function of female perversion, one can perhaps regard these symptoms not only as a warding off of a perversion but perhaps also as the reverse: as the expression of a perversion.

The connection between sexuality and hate or antagonism can be seen most clearly in sadomasochism, which did not take root only recently in today's broad and diverse SM scene but was the most widespread form of perversion even in Freud's day. One of the first to draw attention to this connection was Robert Stoller (1975), who regards perversion as an eroticized form of hatred. It is a notion deeply at odds with the romantic, everyday understanding that sexuality is inextricably entwined with love or at least with attraction and longing. In hatred and antagonism, Stoller (p. 26) sees the central aspect of perversion, namely the wish to do harm to another person, to be superior to or triumph over him or her. In this, the perverse individual seeks revenge. Perversion serves to transform a childhood trauma into a triumph for the adult. To call forth the highest arousal, perversion also must be portrayed as a risky enterprise. According to Stoller, all perverse actions—sexual practices as well as phantasms—are based on hate or antagonism and their object is to dehumanize the sexual object.

Stoller's theory of perversion resulted from his earlier work on masculinity and femininity. From this work, he also came to the conclusion that perversion arises from an attempt to come to terms with threats to one's own gender identity, that is, to ideational realization of masculinity and femininity. In this point, it is interesting to observe how the original Freudian concept of castration fear has changed: identity has replaced desire. It shows how strongly, particularly in the English-speaking world, the categorization of masculinity and femininity influences theory-building.

Following Stoller (ibid., p. 17), perversion is a fantasy that is transformed into action, a gradually constructed defence system for the purpose of keeping erotic pleasure safe. The wish to preserve this gratification comes from two sources: first, from the highest physical pleasure, which calls for repetition; second, from the need to maintain identity. Stoller emphasizes how significant fantasy is in the aetiology of perversion, and of sexual arousal more generally. He follows Freud in arguing that sexual experience is just as strongly determined by fantasy as by physiology and the environmental factors that sexologists emphasize (ibid., p. 83): "Pleasure is released only when fantasy—that which makes perversion uniquely human—has worked." This estimation of the constitutive significance of fantasy also is at the heart of my own understanding of sexuality; it is noteworthy that very little psychoanalytic literature exists on sexually arousing fantasies. Stoller's argument is thus ideally suited to illuminate the functions of fantasies, and not just those connected with perversion.

Stoller chooses the example of pornography to illustrate the function of fantasy. He does not use the term pornography in its everyday sense, but instead regards it as a complicated "daydream, which translates activities that are usually, but not necessarily, openly sexual into written, visual, or acoustic form in order to create genital arousal in the observer" (ibid., p. 93, translation for this edition). In this understanding, nothing is pornographic per se, but becomes so only through the fantasy the observer adds to it. Pornographic fantasies always contain perverse elements. What cannot be gratified in a real sexual act with another person can be gratified through this fantasy, for example, in the case of masturbation. Masturbation thus should also not be regarded as a substitute but instead as an independent sexual act, with its own specific impulses and energies (1975, p. 79 et seq.). Pornography too, like every perversion, "has as its basis a fantasized act of revenge, one which concentrates the sexual history of the person concerned—his memories and fantasies, dreams, frustrations, and joys" (1975, translation for this edition). Correspondingly, there is always a victim to whom amends are made by means of the pornographic fantasy. Following Stoller, the use of pornographic material is a perverse act with three components. The most obvious is voyeurism. The second, more veiled, that comes to light is sadism (that is, if it is not manifested sadism), and the third, the most obscured, is masochism (also with the exception of manifested masochism), in the unconscious identification with the victim. In the conscious fantasies expressed through pornography, one finds the actual sexual history, the unconscious remembering of real, previous events. Here Stoller draws attention to a clinically highly significant aspect, and shows what valuable potential the analysis of sexual fantasies holds for understanding the psychic structure.

In my view, what is important to emphasize is that these fantasy constructions are unconscious memories. What actually took place is not faithfully reproduced, but is instead processed psychically and transformed into scenes. These scenes thus do not depict actual events but instead express what was subjectively experienced. That, in turn, should not be identified as what was experienced "back then" but instead as a multi-layered conglomerate, a constellation that incorporates both "outer" realities and psychic processing at various points in time (more extensively discussed in Quindeau, 2004a). Even if these fantasies have no proportional relationship to what actually occurred, they nevertheless provide important clues, not just to subjectively significant pleasure and gratification modes, but also, and at the same time, to the context of their origin in the individual's life-history as well as to their psychic function. Yet as little as the conscious sexual fantasies depict what actually occurred, they do reflect what is "really" wished for. The psychic contribution of fantasy is evident at this point, as it serves to express precisely what has no place in "real life". In this manner, sexual wishes that are not given manifest form, whether for moral, ethical, aesthetic, practical, or even neurotic reasons, find a way to be staged and (at least partly) gratified.

In an aside, Stoller draws attention to the remarkable and still valid fact that thus far only the physiological process of sexual arousal—as in Masters and Johnson's research—has been explored. Little is known, by contrast, about the psychic process of arousal, what triggers and maintains it, how it subsides, returns, or leads to boredom. That is true not just for perversion but for sexual arousal more generally.

In the case of perversion, Stoller provides information about the emergence of sexual arousal based on the example of perverse, arousal-inducing transvestism. Using the example of a male patient, he describes how a fantasy—in this case, of being humiliated by hostile women who had forced the patient to put on women's clothing—can have a sexually arousing effect. Based on this example, one would have to explore the extent to which one can generalize—going beyond perversion—about criteria for the phantasmal inducing of sexual arousal. Stoller's first explanation is that the patient only identifies virtually with the pornographically depicted experience, and is additionally aware that it is a fantasy. At first glance, this differentiation may seem trivial, but it is certainly not so. I consider knowing the difference between fantasy and reality to be of decisive importance in the widespread rape fantasies among women, a phenomenon repeatedly described as enigmatic (see Lawrenz & Orzegowski, 1988; *vs.* Sydow, 1993). The enigmatic quality disappears when one sees the fantasy as an instrument with whose help incompatible sexual wishes can coexist. In this case, it is wishes from the realm of anality, that is, wishes both for power and autonomy, and for powerlessness and submission, simultaneously.

This becomes clearer in the second explanation Stoller offers for understanding sexual arousal. In the pornographic scene, arousal is linked by narrative device to exoneration from guilt. In the example, one cannot accuse the man forced to wear women's clothing of having wanted to do so. Such exoneration can be found as much in pornography as in humour. Only parenthetically does Stoller note how highly significant the sublimation of hostile components is, "as, for example, for the theatre, fine arts and 'normal' sexual relationships ... Imagine, if heterosexual intercourse were regarded as 'sublimated activity'!" (1975:). I do not regard this last thesis as unfounded at all. On the contrary: is it of a piece with Freud's psychoanalytic understanding of a polymorphously perverse sexuality which—as I have noted repeatedly above—is not, as in traditional psychoanalysis, confined to childhood but instead is inscribed and reinscribed throughout life. Heterosexual intercourse, too, should be regarded as such a reinscription, one in which the hostile components, as a rule, are no longer visible. "As a rule" of course means there are certainly forms of this practice in which hostility is sublimated only to a limited degree or not at all—as in the case of rape. The key point in Stoller's suggestion, however, lies in the view, one that still is not self-evident in psychoanalysis, that an apparently so "natural" heterosexual practice, oriented to reproduction or at least potentially so, is not to be understood as the genuine expression of sexual lust but rather as its sublimation.

In his further explanation of the perverse scene, Stoller describes the life history, in great detail, of this man who was in analysis with him, trying to piece actual events together like a mosaic in order to understand the arousal. Thus, he thinks this man, for example, really had been forced by women to engage in such dressing up. Efforts such as Stoller's to explain through history this close dovetailing of biography and pornography are not very useful, I find, even if the life-history events used to explain the perverse scene are quite plausible.

They take the genuinely psychic dimension—the subjective psychic processing of the events—too little into account, or accord it too little importance. In addition, I regard such actual instances of dressing up neither a necessary nor a sufficient condition to explain the development of transvestism. In analyses with patients who showed transvestite symptoms of sexual arousal, at least, I was able to find completely different aetiologies, in which, say, the processing of (other kinds of) traumatizing experiences or of genetically determined physical deformations played a role.

How far newer psychoanalytic conceptualizations of perversion have now moved away from older efforts at causal determination can be seen in Fritz Lackinger's (2005) theory defining perversion as a psychopathological structure to be understood in the context of earlier disorders. Freud used the example of perversion to demonstrate the variety of human sexuality, beyond all pathologizing. He questioned the prevailing categories of "normal" and "deviant" sexuality by conceiving of perversion as sexuality with a "perverted" sexual goal, meaning one that had become distanced from reproduction.

Stoller, and others, have moved away from this broad notion of sexuality, and understand perversion, often including that going beyond the boundaries of pleasure and gratification, basically as a threat to *Geschlecht* identity. Seeing perversion as a psychopathological structure extends the argument noted at the outset about desexualization: 'sexualization' now serves only as a defence mechanism. Following Lackinger, it is a pseudo-genitalization of oral and anal partial object relations l, as a defence as well as an expression of pre-genital aggression. Perversion, as a psychopathological structure, consists of a constellation of persisting pregenital conflicts, a premature or pseudo-Oedipalization, a defective triangulation of object relationships, an inadequate mentalization of affective experience, and the employing of sexualization as a favoured defence mechanism. Such conceptualizations also have a not unproblematic effect on the psychoanalytic understanding of sexuality more generally. Thus, a polymorphously perverse sexuality, for instance, is regarded and described as typical for patients with borderline personality organization (Lackinger, 2005, p. 1111). There is some tension between that and the suggestion made here that polymorphous sexuality is precisely one of the key characteristics of human sexuality. Lackinger continues, noting that "even normal adult sexuality (…) can contain perverse elements"

(2005, p. 1113, translation for this edition), though these elements can be kept under control or, in the sense Wilfred Bion meant, "contained" by a mature genital relationship. In the perverse parts of the healthy person, Lackinger identifies "benign perversions" that are psychopathological aberrations, though they do no harm to other people. In addition, however, there are also perversions that involve an attack on the sexual self-determination of others. He calls "transgressive" perversions those which involve trespassing without body contact, or which involve sexualized touching with very limited effects. If, by contrast, the realization of sexual wishes is brought about by force or violence, then "malign" perversions are present. Lackinger claims he is formulating a structural model of perversion, but its descriptive character seems to predominate. In addition, the normative implications of the individual categories are not very helpful for a well-founded understanding of perversion. Quite devastating effects on the persons concerned can result from such assessments: "malign perversions, as a rule, lead to serious, repeated, sexual crimes" (2005, p. 1116). Even if such assertions probably ware meant as a plea for psychotherapeutic treatment, they are also likely suited to encourage populist prejudgments of sexual offenders. The case history Lackinger cites in support presumably hardly serves to counter this, either, as it offers evidence of the possibility of a favourable course of events: the therapeutic transformation of a malign paedophilic perversion into a benign form in which the paedophile fantasies continue to play a role, to be sure, but the paedophilic impulses can be securely controlled.

The term paedophilia leads to a more general problematizing of the use of terms in this area. Thus, Sigusch suggests speaking not of pae-*dophilia* but rather of paedo*sexuality*, because the suffix "-philia", meaning affection, attention given, love shown to the child, euphemistically downplays the set of facts to be characterized (2001, p. 202). In my use of terms, I also agree with a further argument Sigusch makes that the term "perversion", with its proximity to affects and stereotypes, is more appropriate than the Latinate technical term "paraphilia" to describe the psychosocial situation of people whose sexual life is characterized by addictions and compulsions (on the psychiatric classifications of perversion and objections to them, see Sigusch 2001, p. 206 et seq.).

Wolfgang Berner (2000, 2005) differentiates paraphilia from perversion, though following a different criterion. For him, the organization of the personality and the preferred defence mechanisms are the *differentia specifica* of perversion. Berner suggests reserving the term perversion, used psychodynamically, for cases "when the extent of the splitting is small and limited to individual symptoms, and when, besides, one finds a neurotic structure that can also be accessed with classical psychotherapeutic techniques" (2005, p. 173; translation for this edition). Paraphilias in the sense used in the DSM IV and the ICD 10, by contrast, point to a borderline personality organization and a very pronounced splitting mechanism, in both of which the aspect of hostility towards relationships plays a large role.

Ruth Stein (2005) points out that even the "polished" term paraphilia, with its prefix meaning "beyond" or "to one side of", has the connotation of the marginal and deviant. On the other hand, like Fogel and Myers (1991), she is of the view that perversion is the latest frontier for psychoanalysis, superseding borderline and narcissistic disorders, and is where the most interesting developments in clinical and theoretical knowledge are taking place. Perversion confronts us with the paradox that it is precisely where deviation from the normal—reproduction—occurs that the genuinely "human" becomes apparent, the biologically un-programmed, varied, changeable. To differentiate "colourful, challenging, subversively polymorphous sex, the essence of eroticism, and perversion or perversity proper" (Stein, 2005, p. 795), she suggests, following Donald Meltzer, the term polymorphism. Perhaps she means something akin to what Berger means by the term perversion; by using this term, one could avoid confusion and misunderstandings and approach a broad concept of sexuality in the psychoanalytic discourse.

CHAPTER FOUR

Conclusion: the 'suspension' of *geschlecht* difference. Highlighting the psychoanalytic theory of sexuality

In hardly any other realm is the difference between the sexes seemingly manifested as clearly as in sexuality. At first glance, it seems completely self-evident that there is a masculine and a feminine sexuality. This intuitive clarity, however, vanishes upon closer examination, so that in concluding my line of argument, I would like to speak of a "suspension" or "sublation" of *Geschlecht* difference in psychoanalytic sexual theory. By that, of course, I do not mean negation or denial of existing differences; I mean it more in the Hegelian sense of the dialectic, whereby the difference of man and woman is both preserved and abolished, and thus transcended, elevated to a higher level. Though, unlike Hegel, we are not dealing with the philosophy of history in the present context, I do associate with this the expectation, that the *Geschlecht* dichotomy will be superseded and that the notion of gender will gain a new quality and become more relaxed and less intent on demarcation.

I am led to this view by a wealth of studies and issues, which I would like to highlight once again, to single out the most important aspects of my psychoanalytic understanding of human sexuality.

The crucial aspect of a psychoanalytic theory of sexuality, in contrast to other theories of sexuality, is that it gives unconscious processes the decisive weight. From this perspective, the cornerstones of our everyday understanding of sexuality—the gender dichotomy and the primacy of heterosexuality—appears by no means self-evident, and actually thwart a psychoanalytic understanding, though they are often found in psychoanalytic theories as well. With respect to the emergence of sexuality, too, I do not agree with the common assumption of a biological program that gradually unfolds, dependent on genetic predisposition and maturation. Instead, I take account of an interpersonal relationship, that of the infant to an adult, and one in which sexuality is generated through seduction. Generally, the early parent-child relationship is such a place of unconscious seduction and elementary gratification. If one understands seduction as a basic socialization structure, then one obtains a concept of human sexuality whose origins are to be found in the Other. My vantage point turns the currently dominant developmental theory on its head. In that child- or subject-centred view, the child is the "producer of his or her development"; in my view, one starts with the primacy of the Other. In a modification of the Cartesian "cogito ergo sum" (I think, therefore I am), which emphasizes the importance of autonomy and self-determination in the self-understanding of the modern subject, I wish to give the Other priority in the process of constituting sexuality and suggest "desideratus ergo sum" (because I was desired, I am). The—unavoidably sexual—desire of the adults becomes the condition for the psychic existence of the child. Those who find this thesis disconcerting should recall the undisputed consensus that has existed for decades in developmental psychology, according to which the survival of a child requires not just nourishment, sleep, and warmth but just as importantly, bodily contact and attention. And this care for the child has both conscious and unconscious elements, which, in Freudian understanding, are irreducibly sexual. Unconscious desire, in the universal seduction situation, is thus inscribed in the nascent psychic structure of the child. Coping with this "enigmatic message" forms the core of the child's unconscious. In this way, I understand every desire as a response to being desired. In this responsive relationship to the Other, human sexuality not only comes into existence: even in adulthood, sexual desire responds to these scenes of early childhood socialization, of being desired by one's mother, father, or other reference persons.

Instead of the oft-misunderstood Freudian term *Trieb* (drive, instinct), I use the term "desire", as it seems most suited to me to incorporate the key determining elements of the original Freudian concept. My intent in using a different designation is not to abandon the original Freudian concept, which remains very important, but rather is an effort to rescue it by using new terminology, and embedding its origin explicitly in socialization theory. As noted, human desire originates in a social, intersubjective space under the primacy of the Other.

As a liminal concept between the somatic and the psychic, desire is inscribed in the body. This can also be seen in the erogenous zones, which I understand as memory traces of earlier gratifications. Sexual arousal is grounded not only in specific physiological conditions of individual locations on the body but also in unconscious memories. These memories can be activated during stimulation of the erogenous zones, though they do not necessarily require this perceptual stimulation. In the basic independence of sexual arousal from sensory perception, in the fact that the former can be evoked equally by (unconscious) fantasies and (unconscious) memories, lies the central criterion for human sexuality.

A universal expression of sexual fantasy lies in the primal scene, which serves as a prototype from which, in the course of life, quite diverse variations develop. Like all fantasies, it too is based on specific perceptions and is a way of processing memory traces. Against the backdrop of the general seduction scene between adult and child, I see it at heart as a processing of this seduction that is organized in a predetermined societal scheme—the triad of father, mother, and child. The primal scene becomes the organizer, helping to structure the "enigmatic messages" by bundling these messages as in a prism and giving them, *nachträglich*, a form. Similar to memories, these primal scene fantasies are also subject to a permanent process of reinscription, *nachträglich*. In this process, they are both adapted to the current stage of cognitive and affective development, and changed to reflect the needs and conflict constellations of the respective present. Sexual fantasies are, accordingly, not only fantasies with explicitly sexual content but fantasies that lead to (sexual) arousal.

In the sexual fantasies, one finds a condensation of the gratification modes of the various psychosexual developmental phases. These phase-specific dominant modes of orality, anality, urethrality, phallicity, and genitality can be understood as subsequent (*nachträglich*) inscriptions and reinscriptions of the infantile experiences of gratification. Particularly characteristic here is the tension between the permanent formation and revision of sexual fantasies, on the one hand, and the immutability of the unconscious infantile wishes on the other hand. In the concept of *Nachträglichkeit*, in my view, lies the crucial point of the psychoanalytic theory of sexuality. Thus, experiences, impressions and memory traces are adapted at a later point in time, based on new experiences or newly achieved developmental stages. With this reworking, the earlier experiences simultaneously receive new meaning and new psychic effectiveness. Of particular importance here is the dissolution of linear notions of time. Earlier experiences are, accordingly, as important for later experiences as the reverse. Such a notion of time as "constellation" (in the sense of Walter Benjamin) seems to make sense, particularly for the understanding of human sexuality. Every sexual activity is a constellation of numerous experiences that have been gathered at different times in life, and they are processed in a new inscription.

The concept of infantile sexuality has constitutive significance for the psychoanalytic theory of sexuality. This does not describe childhood per se; rather, the infantile, and that means the "polymorphously perverse", is the key characteristic of adult sexuality as well. The notion of infantile sexuality puts the behaviour and experience of the child and of the adult in the same category. What becomes visible is not only its continuity but especially its manifold forms. Sexuality is not reduced to a biological reproductive function but expresses itself in differing, psychically equivalent forms. This applies to both heterosexual and homosexual object-choice as well as to the so-called perversions. Thus, a normative valuation and a hierarchization of sexual behaviour does not take place. The question of pathologizing, too, can be posed differently. As is true more generally of the psychoanalytic understanding of illness, it is not a specific behaviour that should be regarded as pathological, but instead it is the function that this behaviour plays that at heart determines whether or not there is an illness. Correspondingly, the border between so-called normal and deviant or pathological behaviour can be established only in the individual case and not in a general or abstract manner.

I have described the different varieties of infantile sexuality as reinscriptions of gratification experiences in personal history. The infant's primary experience of gratification—as Freud designed it in the *Interpretation of Dreams*—stands as an unequalled model for every later sexual gratification; in the course of life, it will be altered and replaced in many ways. It is a further important characteristic of human sexuality, that any desire remains unquenchable, yet unequalled and out of reach … Freud aptly expressed this in his notion of *Trieb*, and this is carried forward in my notion of desire. Gratification, then, always can be achieved only partially and temporarily. While Freud called autoerotism a key marker of infantile sexuality, I would like to emphasize the primacy of the Other. In my view, it is not that the new-born seeks pleasure at the breast but that it is the "breast" (which stands for the nursing, feeding mother) which first evokes pleasure and sexual desire. Pleasure is created or emerges from the memory of gratification; that is, the gratification precedes the pleasure. Autoerotism is in that sense a secondary manifestation, a response to being desired and to the loss associated with it due to the repeated necessity to be separated from the breast.

Oral eroticism remains to the end of life, in various, more or less altered, forms. Central to these feelings of pleasure is, for one, the stimulation of the mouth or the mucous membranes, such as in kissing, eating or drinking, or smoking. For another, the incorporation of objects is also pleasurably cathected, and this applies to both swallowing and breathing. The example of biting makes clear that this early form of oral sadism is not about aggression. The infant does not bite because he or she is angry or frustrated, but instead out of pleasure. This differentiating of oral sadism and aggression contradicts everyday understanding. It is not about the pleasure to be gained from inflicting pain; pain is far more a by-product that results from the search for pleasure. Sadomasochistic practices as found in the "perversions", therefore, can be reinterpreted again, when one connects them not with aggression and pain but instead with modes of pleasurable gratification early in life. The interweaving of desire and prohibition, too, can be made clearer by using the example of biting. The infant's biting during nursing leads the mother to pull away and interrupt the pleasurable game. The pleasure is not dissipated thereby; rather, the state of tension and arousal is maintained. Postponement means the prohibition intensifies the pleasure.

Such a delay is still more marked in anal eroticism, which is characterized by anticipatory tension. It is not just the elimination processes themselves that are experienced as pleasurable, but also their delay and retention. This intensification of pleasure through retention is true of all forms of putting off pleasurable sensations. Generally speaking, the anal pleasures are more affected by repression and recasting than are the oral modes of gratification. As there is a general cultural ban on taking pleasure in the eliminatory process and its products, one unavoidably passes on this ban even in the most liberal of toilet training. Therefore the child experiences an environment opposed to its modes of gratification, and is forced to control them. In conjunction with anal eroticism, the boundaries between the self and the Other are further constituted in the process of individuation, as are the boundaries between inside and outside with respect to the body. Retention allows an intensification of the perception of the inner body, and the elimination process makes it possible to experience the transition from inner to outer, thereby consolidating the body's boundaries. A specific gain in pleasure is associated with relinquishing of parts that to that point had been experienced as belonging to one's own body.

Urethral eroticism plays a particular role in the context of the pleasure taken at excretion, though it is barely still perceived as a separate mode of sexual expression. This is regrettable because focussing on the sexual aspect can provide a deeper understanding of chronic urinary tract illnesses, or also of transference manifestations in which the urgent need to urinate plays a role. If this is, as usual, interpreted solely as a form of resistance, one then overlooks the more important aspect of (distorted) pleasure and gratification.

Pleasure in contact or touch, in its active and passive manifestations, is one of the most elementary means of experiencing pleasure and gratification. Skin is the largest erogenous zone of the body, but its pleasure-giving function receives little attention in recent psychoanalytic works. Instead, the communicative or ego-forming aspects of the skin, as well as its limitations due to disease, as in the case of eczema, are far more frequently emphasized. The sensory modalities of hearing, smelling, and tasting are similarly desexualized. So, too, is the kinaesthetic mode, whose sexually arousing effect is well-known in everyday as well as clinical experience. It plays a role in transference and counter-transference, but tends to be neglected in theory formation. The modality of pleasurable incorporation connects the eroticism of skin and sight. Ironically, taking visual pleasure, a form of gratification that is decidedly excluded from analytic settings, has received some theoretical attention particularly in the realm of psychoanalysis of the cinema.

Genital eroticism starts not first in the phallic or infantile-genital phase, but can already be observed in the first half of the second year of life, and it shows an unambiguous connection with the unavoidable sexual stimulation of the genitals during infant care. The central task of infantile genital organization for the child consists in dealing with its fantasies of bisexual omnipotence, the unquestioned conviction of being able to be both sexes, and the necessity of coming to terms with the loss, and fact, of being limited to being only one sex. This task is shared equally by both boys and girls. By the primacy of the phallus, therefore, I also do not mean some type of male superiority but instead the child's perception of having a sex at all. The contrast, as a result, is not between having a penis and being "castrated", but rather between having a *Geschlecht* and not having one. The child becomes aware of having desires rather than being passively exposed to desires, as has been the case up to that point. The fear of castration is then directed at the anxiety of losing this *Geschlecht* and thereby also losing the ability to experience pleasure, and to understand oneself as the subject of this desire. Masturbation contributes significantly to this process of becoming a subject, and with its help, the child can become independent of its—pleasure-providing—mother. In this sense, seeing masturbation as an autoerotic activity falls short, as the child, in striving for pleasure, remains oriented to the Other. Rather, masturbation serves an important function precisely with respect to the interaction of adult and child. The function of masturbation in promoting autonomy remains present in later life: conflicts over masturbation often reveal themselves, in clinical analysis, to be conflicts about separation and autonomy. This makes understandable the feelings of guilt that are not infrequently associated with masturbation. Psycho-dynamically speaking, they result less from moral sanction than from the effort to free oneself from one's mother. Beyond masturbation, this is more generally true for the linking of sexuality with feelings of guilt. In addition, I see a form of memory in masturbation, one that preserves the gratification of the infant which can never again be achieved. Though masturbation repeatedly revives the loss anew, it simultaneously overcomes the separation. This occurs not just phantasmally but also in terms of action and body. What was passively experienced by the infant while being cared for and given affection by its parents is expressed in masturbation as an active structuring and restructuring. Masturbation thereby is a form of reinscription, through which the child continues the parental activity, and in turn helps to develop its sexually arousable body. In addition, these considerations, especially with respect to the function masturbation plays in overcoming loss and separation, make clear an important psychoanalytic insight: what is apparently sexual in everyday understanding does not necessarily primarily serve the purpose of pleasure and gratification. Conversely, many aspects of behaviour and experience that do not appear to be sexual certainly have pleasurable functions. A further important aspect of phallic sexuality is that of the heretofore unconnected external and internal parts of the genitalia. In both women and men, one can distinguish two genital centres: the clitoris and the vagina, and the penis and the seminal colliculus or verumontanum. This last is a point in the prostate area of the urethra, one that, surprisingly, is largely unknown but that is a site of intensely pleasurable sensations for many men. The integration of both centres, of inner and outer genitality, is the precondition for genital sexuality. Phallic sexuality, by contrast, is confined largely to the outer genitalia. This is true for both sexes. In the man, it is expressed in a limited sexuality concentrated on the penis, and in the woman, in a reduced form of feminine sexuality that regards only the clitoris as the centre of pleasure. I regard the contrast between clitoral and vaginal orgasm, one established many years ago in a seemingly endless debate, as completely inappropriate. In both sexes, full orgiastic experience presupposes the integration of both parts of the genitals, and their connection in a comprehensive union.

The Oedipus complex is the apex and conclusion of infantile genital organization. Its structuring function, at the synchronic level, is to recognize the limitation of belonging to one sex, and at the diachronic level, to recognize the differences between the generations. At the same time, sexual preference for a given sex crystalizes out of heterosexual and homosexual love for the same- or cross-sex parent. This does not mean a fully determination of sexual orientation, as the Oedipus conflict is worked through at different times in a life history.

With puberty, changes in both body and affect begin, and provide a transition from infantile sexual life into its adult form. As a phase of accelerated and concentrated developmental processes, adolescence is a "second chance" for working through the psychosexual conflicts of early childhood, in particular the Oedipus complex. The perspective of the general seduction theory, which lies at the heart of my conceptualizations, provides an alternative to the Freudian thesis of the "diphasic aspect of human sexual development". Adolescence is not a new beginning, nor a second start of sexual development, but is much more a specific constellation, a nodal point in the development where different reinscriptions are bundled together at different levels. The infantile capacities for pleasure and gratification (the "partial drives") are reinscribed, and no longer tied to primary love-objects. As in the preceding developmental phases, new responses are given here to the "enigmatic messages". The newly acquired genital maturity and reproductive ability plays a prominent role in these responses. This description of developmental goals shows the extent in which the individual during adolescence is subjected to social notions of order. Polymorphously perverse sexuality is socially regulated and placed under the primacy of the genital and of heterosexuality. The Freudian thesis of genital primacy has often been criticized as being a conventionalization of psychoanalytic sexual theory. Correctly so, if the reproductive function becomes central as a result of this primacy and this necessarily implies a valuation of homosexuality and heterosexuality. A different reading is also possible, however. I see the mental representation of the genitals as a kind of "projection surface", a place where the individual, partial drives are integrated into a comprehensive unity. This is clearly not only a restrictive development; such an integrative concept of the primacy of the genitals can also help to explain the other quality of pleasure that arises when sexual maturation occurs. Thus, the adult orgasm differs substantially from the childhood orgasm. In addition, in the case of heterosexuality, in puberty, the pleasure modalities are initially related to the possibility of a pregnancy. For both sexes inner genitality receives new importance with puberty. While this is obvious in the case of female development, the integration of inner and outer genitalia is a central developmental task for the man as well. A phantasmal, playful switching between internalization and externalization in sexual experience becomes possible only if inner genitality is integrated. Finally, the integration of the partial drives is also connected with the integration of the opposite-sex aspects. Thus, the phallic pleasure mode should not be limited to the man and the receptive mode to the woman. Instead both infantile modes should be available, may be in different ways, to both men and women in their love life. The "suspension" of the difference between the sexes also takes place in sexual experience through the "suspension" of the partial drives, which at the same time are integrated "at a higher level" and thereby preserved. In the course of this reinscription, the infantile pleasure and gratification modes are not replaced by that of the genital, but instead, under the influence of the genital, take on a new form and in particular a new quality.

These considerations led me to question a consensus that has existed for decades in the psychoanalytic discourse. From Freud to Melanie Klein to Irene Fast, it was agreed that the male's ability for sexual enjoyment was based on the repression of femininity, of feminine identifications and introjections. Observations made during analysis with male patients led me to doubt this view, however, and thus I try to show that it is the exact reverse: pleasurable sexual experience is the result of the integration of, and not rejection of, elements of the opposite sex. By "integration" I do not mean an intentional, conscious process but rather unconscious psychic work. With the notion of integration, I thus postulate a counter-thesis opposed to the current psychoanalytic concept of a "des-identification", according to which the identifications with the opposite sex acquired in early childhood must be rejected in developing a sexual and gender identity. This seemingly necessary rejection results from heteronormativity and the dichotomy of the sexes. In this, *Geschlecht* is not thought of as a unitary essence that exists in two forms. Instead, this unit is dissolved and two sexes are conceptualized as in a mutually exclusive, polarized, and hierarchical relationship with one another. My critique is not directed at the existence of two sexes but rather at the conceptualization of a polarity instead of a continuum and at normative ascriptions with respect to the male and female sex. Sex identity, following existing theories, develops through demarcation and not through integration of the Other. Psychoanalytically speaking, this requires denial or rejection and projection of the opposite-sex elements. If an identity is constituted in this manner, it necessarily leads to a limitation of behavioural possibilities and experience for the individual, as well as to a devaluation of the Other.

Questioning the sexual dichotomy, and the above thesis that a deepened, pleasurable sexual experience is possible only after the opposite-sex aspects have been integrated, lead to an important insight: The traditional differentiation of sexuality into masculine and feminine types is not psychoanalytically tenable. In Freud's theory of sexuality, the two concepts of genital primacy and infantile sexuality already are difficult to reconcile and exist side by side. While the primacy of the genital established in adolescence does suggest a male or female sexuality that is structured in a sex-specific manner, the polymorphously perverse character of sexuality excludes assigning it to one or the other of the sexes. With my model of human sexuality, I am searching for a new path in psychoanalytic discourse that transcends *Geschlecht* and the polarity between masculinity and femininity. Freud proposed a single-sex, male-oriented model as the basis of his theory, and in subsequent eras efforts were made, and justifiably so, to abandon the notion of the woman as "inferior" in comparison with the man and instead to conceive of her as the "other" sex. In the meantime, there has been a plenitude of studies of femininity, and the continuing, appropriate critique of Freud's notion of femininity has in consequence become part of mainstream psychoanalytic theory formation. In my view, it is now time to cease emphasizing the differences between woman and man and instead to think of commonalties. The significance of difference, however, remains constitutive for psychoanalytic thinking. In speaking of the primacy of the Other, which is of central importance to my own approach, I emphasize its insurmountable difference. However, this difference cannot be generally linked to the relationship between the genders but exists in every relationship between humans. Therefore, my argument does not represent backsliding with respect to feminist insights but quite the opposite: an effort to push the notions of equality further. I am trying to work out the psychic conditions that need to be understood if one wishes to put an end to the continuing hierarchy between woman and man, which is unavoidably associated with the notion of gender differences. In that sense, I have also examined the studies of female sexuality to determine the extent to which they shed light on what is still the "dark continent" of masculinity. This leads to a gender-transcending model of human sexuality that places gender tension not between women and men but rather in every man and every woman.

The unconscious dimension of the sexual is emphasized through the concept of gender tension. This is not a dichotomous, mutually exclusive relationship between the sexes but instead a relationship between masculinity and femininity with aspects that exist both simultaneously and in opposition to one another. When one takes the unconscious into account, it does not make much sense to set a masculine against a feminine sexuality, as sexual experience is more determined by unconscious memories and unconscious fantasies inscribed in the body than it is by anatomy. Rather, it is constituted in every human by gender tension and by the way each individual has experienced that tension in his or her own personal history.

The "suspension" of gender difference in the realm of the sexual additionally puts gender, which has a central significance in modern societies, into question as a structure for ordering society. While ordering functions are without doubt indispensable, by no means do they necessarily need to be tied to *Geschlecht*. The question of what categories could stand in its stead and legitimately lay the basis for power relationships exceeds the bounds of psychoanalysis and needs to be addressed in an interdisciplinary manner by the social sciences.

With this model of a sexuality that transcends *Geschlecht*, I add an additional dissociation to the ones discussed in the introduction: the separation of sexuality from *Geschlecht*. In German, this is disconcerting, since the term *"geschlechtlich"* designates the sexual in addition to referring to gender. Yet in my argument, sexuality is separated from *Geschlecht* understood in a dichotomous manner that, for example, ascribes a phallic pleasure and gratification mode to the man and a receptive mode to the woman. That both modes exist for both men and women not only expands the scope of individual experience but also renders unnecessary a number of questions that have not proved very fruitful in the discourse thus far, such as the question of female desire. Speaking of a genuinely female desire makes as little sense, I think, as assuming that there is a male desire.

What stands out as a major threat, in terms of global climate change, with respect to the relationship between the sexes contributes to a certain easing: the poles are melting.

ACKNOWLEDGEMENTS

I would like to thank my friend and colleague Dr. Helga Kraus, the first reader of this manuscript, for her constructive suggestions, critical commentary, and many encouraging conversations which were of great help to me in clarifying my thoughts and expressing them more precisely.

I would also like to thank Dr. Heinz Beyer of Klett-Cotta Verlag for his pleasant cooperation and Renate Warttman for her careful editing; both helped to transform a manuscript into a book. I am also grateful to Emanuel Kapfinger for his work on the index and bibliography. For the English edition, I want to express my gratitude to Karnac Press, especially to Rod Tweedy for his cordial support and to Catherine Harwood for her highly competent editorial work. My particular thanks go to John Bendix, who, with a high degree of intellectual sensitivity and broad understanding, translated my reflections into English.

Finally, I would like to thank my husband Werner Schneider, and my children Alischa and Nicolas, for the patience they displayed while this book was coming into being.

REFERENCES

Abelin, E. (1980). Triangulation, the role of the father and the origins of core gender identity during the rapprochement subphase. In: R. Lax, S. Bach & A. Burland (Eds.), *Rapprochement* (pp. 151–170). New York: Aronson.

Abraham, K. (1923). Contributions to the theory of the anal character. *International Journal of Psycho-Analysis, 4*: 400–418.

Abraham, K. (1925). The influence of oral erotism on character-formation. *International Journal of Psycho-Analysis, 6*: 247–258.

Adler, A. (1924). *The Practice and Theory of Individual Psychology*. London: K. Paul, Trench, Trubner & Co.

Alizade, A. (2006). *Motherhood in the Twenty-First Century*. London: Karnac.

Alpert, J. (1986). *Psychoanalysis and Women: Contemporary Reappraisals*. Hillsdale, NJ: The Analytic Press.

Ambrosio, G. (2006). The twenty-first century: what changes? In: A. Alizade (Ed.), *Motherhood in the Twenty-First Century* (pp. 11–21). London: Karnac.

Andreas-Salomé, L. (1916). "Anal" und "Sexual". *Imago, 4*: 249–273.

Anzieu, D. (1986). La scène de ménage. In: J.B. Pontalis (Ed.), *L'amour de la haine. Nouvelle Revue de Psychanalyse, 33*: 201–209.

275

Auhagen-Stephanos, U. (2005). Frauen mit unerfülltem Kinderwunsch zwischen Psychoanalyse und Reproduktionstechnik. *Psyche, 54*: 34–54.

Balint, A. (1933). Über eine besondere Form der infantilen Angst. *Zeitschrift für psychoanalytische Pädagogik, 7*: 414–417.

Balint, M. (1935). *Primary Love, and Psycho-analytic Technique*. London: Hogarth.

Bancroft, J. (Ed.) (2003). *Sexual Development in Childhood*. Bloomington: Indiana University Press.

Bassin, D. (1996). Beyond the He and the She: Toward the reconciliation of masculinity and femininity in the postoedipal female mind. *Journal of the American Psychoanalytic Association, 44*: 157–190.

Bayer, L. & Quindeau, I. (2004). *Die unbewusste Botschaft der Verführung. Interdisziplinäre Studien zur Verführungstheorie von Jean Laplanche*. Gießen: Psychosozial.

Becker, S. (2002). Weibliche Perversion. *Zeitschrift für Sexualforschung, 15*: 281–301.

Beier, K. (2007). "Sie sollen Kontrolle lernen". *Die Zeit*, 8 March.

Benedek, T. (1950). Climacterium: A developmental phase. *Psychoanalytic Quarterly, 19*: 1–27.

Benedek, T. (1959). Parenthood as a developmental phase. A contribution to the libido theory. *Journal of the American Psychoanalytic Association, 7*: 389–417.

Benjamin, J. (1986). The alienation of desire: women's masochism and ideal love. In: J. Alpert (Ed.), *Psychoanalysis and Women: Contemporary Reappraisals* (pp. 113–138). Hillsdale, NJ: The Analytic Press.

Benjamin, J. (1988). *The Bonds of Love: Psychoanalysis, feminism, and the problem of domination*. New York: Pantheon.

Benjamin, J. (1993). *Like Subjects, Love Objects: Essays on recognition and sexual difference*. New Haven: Yale University Press.

Berner, W. (2000). Störungen der Sexualität. In: O. Kernberg, B. Dulz & U. Sachsse (Eds.), *Handbuch der Borderline-Störung* (pp. 319–330). Stuttgart: Schattauer.

Berner, W. (2005). Von der Perversion zur Paraphilie. In: I. Quindeau & V. Sigusch (Eds.), *Freud und das Sexuelle. Neue psychoanalytische und sexualwissenschaftliche Perspektiven* (pp. 153–177). Frankfurt: Campus.

Bernstein, D. (1983). The female superego: A different perspective. *International Journal of Psychoanalysis, 64*: 187–201.

Bieber, Irving et al. (1962). *Homosexuality: A psychoanalytic study of male homosexuals*. New York: Basic Books.

Blos, P. (1941). *The Adolescent Personality*. New York: Appleton-Century-Crofts.

Blos, P. (1967). *On Adolescence, a Psychoanalytic Interpretation.* New York: Free Press.

Blum, H. (Ed.) (1977). *Female Psychology.* New York: International Universities Press.

Bödeker, H. (1998). Intersexualität (Hermaphroditismus)—Eine Fingerübung in Compliance? „Dazwischen", „beides" oder „weder noch"? *Beiträge zur feministischen Theorie und Praxis, 49–50:* 99–107.

Boehm, F. (1930). The femininity-complex in men. *International Journal of Psycho-Analysis, 11:* 444–469.

Böllinger, L. (2005). Sadomasochismus 100 Jahre nach den „Drei Abhandlungen" von Freud. In: M. Dannecker & A. Katzenbach (Eds.), *100 Jahre Freuds „Drei Abhandlungen zur Sexualtheorie"—Aktualität und Anspruch* (pp. 43–50). Gießen: Psychosozial-Verlag.

Bohleber, W. (1997). Die Bedeutung der neueren Säuglingsforschung für die psychoanalytische Theorie der Identität. In: H. Keupp & R. Höfer (Eds.), *Identitätsarbeit heute: Klassische und aktuelle Perspektiven der Identitätsforschung* (pp. 93–119). Frankfurt: Suhrkamp.

Boller, N. (2000). Vom Geschlechtswechsel besessen. Ein Beitrag zur Psychoanalyse der Transsexualität. In: M. Dannecker & R. Reiche (Eds.), *Sexualität und Gesellschaft* (pp. 97–110). Frankfurt: Campus.

Bonaparte, M. (1953). *Female Sexuality.* New York: International Universities Press.

Bowlby, J. (1951). *Child Care and the Growth of Love.* Harmondsworth: Penguin.

Bowlby, J. (1969). *Attachment and Loss.* New York: Basic Books.

Braun, C & Otscheret, L. (2004). *Sexualität in der Psychoanalyse: Entwicklungstheorie und psychoterapeutische Praxis.* Frankfurt: Brandes & Apsel.

Brinkmann, L., Schweizer, K. & Richter-Appelt, H. (2007). Geschlechtsidentität und psychische Belastungen von erwachsenen Personen mit Intersexualität. Ergebnisse der Hamburger Intersex Studie. *Zeitschrift für Sexualforschung, 20:* 129–144.

Burzig, G. (1982). Der Psychoanalytiker und der transsexuelle Patient. Ein Beitrag zur notwendigen Auseinandersetzung mit „psycho"-chirurgischen Eingriffen an den Geschlechtsmerkmalen. *Psyche, 36:* 848–856.

Butler, J. (1990). *Gender Trouble: Feminism and the subversion of identity.* New York: Routledge.

Butler, J. (1993a). *Bodies that Matter: On the Discursive limits of 'Sex'.* London: Routledge.

Butler, J. (1993b). Phantasmatic identification and the assumption of sex. In: J. Butler (Ed.), *Bodies that Matter* (pp. 93–119). City: Publisher.

Butler, J. (1997). Melancholy gender/refused identification. *Psychoanalytic Dialogues, 5(2):* 165–180.

Caplan, G. (1959). *Concepts of Mental Health and Consultation*. Washington, DC: US Childrens Bureau.

Chasseguet-Smirgel, J. (1970). *Female sexuality. New psychoanalytic views.* Ann Arbor: University of Michigan Press.

Chasseguet-Smirgel, J. (1974). *Psychoanalyse der weiblichen Sexualität.* Frankfurt: Suhrkamp.

Chasseguet-Smirgel, J. (1981). Loss of reality in perversions—with special reference to fetishism. *Journal of the American Psychoanalytic Association, 29*: 511–534.

Chasseguet-Smirgel, J. (1986). *Creativity and Perversion.* New York: Norton.

Chodorow, N. (1978). *The Reproduction of Mothering: Psychoanalysis and the sociology of gender.* Berkeley: University of California.

Colapinto, J. (2000). *As Nature Made Him: The boy who was raised as a girl.* New York: HarperCollins Publishers.

Daly, C. (1928). Der Menstruationskomplex. *Imago, 14*: 11–75.

Dannecker, M. (1993). Sigmund Freud über Inversion und Homosexualität. In: R. Lautmann (Ed.), *Homosexualität. Handbuch der Theorie- und Forschungsgeschichte* (pp. 159–167). Frankfurt: Campus.

Dannecker, M. (2001). Probleme der männlichen homosexuellen Entwicklung. In: V. Sigusch (Ed.), *Sexuelle Störungen und ihre Behandlung* (pp. 102–123). Stuttgart: Thieme.

Dannecker, M. & Katzenbach, A. (Eds.) (2005). *100 Jahre Freuds „Drei Abhandlungen zur Sexualtheorie"—Aktualität und Anspruch.* Gießen: Psychosozial-Verlag.

Därmann, I. (2004). Von Derrida über Mauss zu Jean Laplanche: Beiträge zu einer Ethnografie und Psychoanalyse der alimentären Gabe und Besessenheit. In: L. Bayer & I. Quindeau (Eds), *Die unbewußte Botschaft der Verführung. Interdisziplinäre Studien zur Allgemeinen Verführungstheorie von Jean Laplanche* (pp. 90–120). Gießen: Psychosozial-Verlag.

Deserno, H. (1999). Männlichkeit und Ödipuskomplex. In: E. Brech, K. Bell & C. Marahrens-Schürg (Eds.), *Weiblicher und männlicher Ödipuskomplex* (pp. 81–110). Göttingen: Vandenhoeck & Ruprecht.

Deserno, H. (2005). Psychische Bedeutungen der inneren Genitalität in der männlichen Adoleszenz. Kasuistischer Beitrag zur unspezifischen Prostatitis. In: V. King & K. Flaake (Eds.), *Männliche Adoleszenz. Sozialisation und Bildungsprozesse zwischen Kindheit und Erwachsensein* (pp. 229–247). Frankfurt: Campus.

Deutsch, H. (1925). *Psychoanalysis of the Sexual Functions of Women.* London: Karnac.

Deutsch, H. (1930). The significance of masochism in the mental life of women. *International Journal of Psycho-Analysis, 11*: 48–60.

Deutsch, H. (1944). *The Psychology of Women: a Psychoanalytic Interpretation* (*Volume I and II*). New York: Grune & Stratton.

Diederichs, P. (1993). Der eigene Körper als Fremder. In: U. Streeck (Ed.), *Das Fremde in der Psychoanalyse* (pp. 324–336). München: Pfeiffer.

Dinnerstein, D. (1976). *The Mermaid and the Minotaur*. New York: Harper & Row.

Dornes, M. (1993). *Der kompetente Säugling*. Frankfurt: Fischer.

Dornes, M. (2005). Infantile Sexualität und Säuglingsforschung. In: I. Quindeau & V. Sigusch (Eds.), *Freud und das Sexuelle. Neue psychoanalytische und sexualwissenschaftliche Perspektiven* (pp. 112–134). Frankfurt: Campus.

Düring, S. (1993). *Wilde und andere Mädchen. Die Pubertät*. Freiburg: Kore.

Düring, S. (1994). Über sequentielle Homo- und Heterosexualität. *Zeitschrift für Sexualforschung, 7*: 193–202.

Düring, S. (1995). Rennen wir offene Türen ein? Die Funktion des Feminismus in der Sexualwissenschaft. In: S. Düring & M. Hauch (Eds.), *Heterosexuelle Verhältnisse* (pp. 145–159). Stuttgart: Enke.

Eich, H. (2005). Es geht kein Weg zurück. Wie der Diskurs über sexuellen Missbrauch zur Verdrängung kindlicher Sexualität beiträgt. In: B. Burian-Langegger (Ed.), *Doktorspiele. Die Sexualität des Kindes* (pp. 167–192). Wien: Picus.

Eisenbud, R. J. (1969). Female Homosexuality: A sweet enfranchisement. In: G. Goldman & D. Milman (Eds.), *The Modern Woman* (pp. 247–271). Springfield: Charles C. Thomas.

Eisenbud, R. J. (1986). Lesbian choice: Transferences to theory. In: J. Alpert (Ed.), *Psychoanalysis and Women: Contemporary Reappraisals* (pp. 215–233). Hillsdale, NJ: The Analytic Press.

Eissler, K. (1939). On certain problems of female sexual development. *Psychoanalytic Quarterly, 8*: 191–210.

Eissler, K. (1958). Notes on problems of technique in the psychoanalytic treatment of adolescents—with some remarks on perversions. *Psychoanalytic Study of the Child, 13*: 223–254.

Ellis, H. (1898). Auto-erotism. A psychological study. *Alienist and Neurologist, 119*: 260–299.

Ellis, H. (1903). *Studies in the Psychology of Sex* (*Volume 3*). Analysis of the Sexual Impulse; Love and Pain. The Sexual Impulse in Women. Philadelphia: F. A. Davis.

Erikson, E. (1959). *Identity and the Life Cycle*. New York: International Universities Press.

Erikson, E. (1964). Reflections on womanhood. *Daedalus, 2*: 582–606.

Fast, Irene. (1984). *Gender Identity: a differentation model*. Hillside NJ: Analytic Press.

Fenichel, O. (1930). Zur Psychologie des Transvestitismus. *Internationale Zeitschrift für Psychoanalyse, 16*: 21–34.

Fenichel, O. (1937). The scopophilic instinct and identification. *International Journal of Psycho-Analysis, 18*: 6–34.

Fenichel, O. (1946). *The Psychoanalytic Theory of Neurosis.* London: Routledge & Kegan Paul.

Ferenczi, S. (1914). The ontogenesis of the interest in money. In: S. Ferenczi, *Sex in Psycho-Analysis. Contributions to Psycho-Analysis* (pp. 319–331). Boston: The Gorham Press, 1916.

Ferenczi, S. (1924). Versuch einer Genitaltheorie. In: S. Ferenczi (Ed.), *Schriften zur Psychoanalyse, (Volume II)* (pp. 317–402). Frankfurt: Fischer.

Ferenczi, S. (1933). Confusion of tongues between adults and the child. In: S. Ferenczi (Ed.), *Final Contributions to the Problems & Methods of Psycho-Analysis* (pp. 156–167). London: Karnac.

Fiedler, P. (2004). *Sexuelle Orientierung und sexuelle Abweichung.* Weinheim: Psychologie Verlags Union.

Fischer, G. & Riedesser, P. (1998). *Lehrbuch der Psychotraumatologie.* München: Reinhardt.

Fliegel, Z. (1973). Feminine psychosexual development in Freudian theory—a historical reconstruction. *Psychoanalytic Quarterly, 42*: 385–408.

Fliegel, Z. (1982). Half a century later: Current status of Freud's controversial views on women. *Psychoanalytic Review, 69*: 7–28.

Fogel, G. & Myers, W. (1991). *Perversions and Near Perversions in Clinical Practice: New psychoanalytic perspectives.* New Haven: Yale University Press.

Fogel, G., Lane, F. & Liebert, R. (1996). *The Psychology of Men: psychoanalytic perspectives.* New Haven: Yale University Press.

Foucault, M. (1977a). *Discipline and Punish: the birth of the prison.* New York: Vintage.

Foucault, M. (1977b). *The History of Sexuality 1. An Introduction.* New York: Pantheon.

Foucault, M. (2005). *Analytik der Macht.* Frankfurt: Suhrkamp.

Freud, A. (1980). Probleme der Pubertät. In: *Die Schriften der Anna Freud (Volume VI).* München: Kindler.

Freud, S. (1896c). The aetiology of hysteria. *S.E., 3*: 187–221.

Freud, S. (1900a). *The Interpretation of Dreams. S.E., 4*: ix–627.

Freud, S. (1905d). *Three Essays on the Theory of Sexuality. S.E., 7*: 123–246.

Freud, S. (1908b). Character and anal erotism. *S.E., 9*: 167–176.

Freud, S. (1908e). Creative writers and day-dreaming. *S.E., 9*: 141–154.

Freud, S. (1909b). *Analysis of a Phobia in a Five-Year-Old Boy. S.E., 10*: 1–150.

Freud, S. (1910c). *Leonardo Da Vinci and a Memory of his Childhood. S.E., 11*: 57–138.

Freud, S. (1910h). A special type of choice of object made by men. *S.E.*, *11*: 163–176.

Freud, S. (1912d). On the universal tendency to debasement in the sphere of love. *S.E.*, *11*: 177–190.

Freud, S. (1914c). On narcissism: an introduction. *S.E.*, *14*: 67–102.

Freud, S. (1915c). *Instincts and their Vicissitudes. S.E.*, *14*: 109–140.

Freud, S. (1915e). The unconscious. *S.E.*, *14*: 159–215.

Freud, S. (1916–17). *Introductory Lectures on Psycho-Analysis. S.E.*, *15*: 1–240; *S.E.*, *16*: 241–463.

Freud, S. (1917c). On transformations of instinct as exemplified in anal erotism. *S.E.*, *17*: 125–134.

Freud, S. (1917e). Mourning and melancholia. *S.E.*, *14*: 237–258.

Freud, S. (1918a). The taboo of virginity. *S.E.*, *11*: 191–208.

Freud, S. (1918b). *From the History of an Infantile Neurosis. S.E.*, *17*: 1–124.

Freud, S. (1919e). "A child is being beaten." *S.E.*, *17*: 175–204.

Freud, S. (1920a). The psychogenesis of a case of homosexuality in a woman. *S.E.*, *18*: 145–172.

Freud, S. (1920g). *Beyond the Pleasure Principle. S.E.*, *18*: 1–64.

Freud, S. (1923b). *The Ego and the Id. S.E.*, *19*: 1–66.

Freud, S. (1923e). The infantile genital organization. *S.E.*, *19*: 139–146.

Freud, S. (1924c). The economic problem of masochism. *S.E.*, *19*: 155–170.

Freud, S. (1924d). The dissolution of the Oedipus complex. *S.E.*, *19*: 171–180.

Freud, S. (1925d). *An Autobiographical Study. S.E.*, *20*: 1–74.

Freud, S. (1925j). Some psychical consequences of the anatomical distinction between the sexes. *S.E.*, *19*: 248–258.

Freud, S. (1927e). Fetishism. *S.E.*, *21*: 147–158.

Freud, S. (1930a). *Civilization and its Discontents. S.E.*, *21*: 57–146.

Freud, S. (1931b). Female sexuality. *S.E.*, *21*: 221–244.

Freud, S. (1933a). *New Introductory Lectures on Psycho-Analysis. S.E.*, *22*: 1–182.

Freud, S. (1937c). Analysis terminable and interminable. *S.E.*, *23*: 209–254.

Freud, S. (1940a). *An Outline of Psycho-Analysis. S.E.*, *23*: 139–208.

Freud, S. (1950a). *Project for a Scientific Psychology. S.E.*, *1*: 281–391.

Friedman, R. M. (1986). The psychoanalytic model of male homosexuality: A historical and theoretical critique. *Psychoanalytic Review*, *73(4)*: 79–115.

Friedman, R. C. (1988). *Male homosexuality: a contemporary psychoanalytic perspective*. New Haven: Yale University Press.

Früh, F. (2005). Warum wird die infantile Sexualität sexuell genannt? In: I. Quindeau & V. Sigusch (Eds.), *Freud und das Sexuelle. Neue psychoanalytische und sexualwissenschaftliche Perspektiven* (pp. 97–111). Frankfurt: Campus.

Gambaroff, M. (1977). Emanzipation macht Angst. In: K-M. Michel & H. Wieser (Eds.), *Kursbuch 47: Frauen* (pp. 1–25). Berlin: Rotbuch.

Gambaroff, M. (1984). Der Einfluss der frühen Mutter-Tochter-Beziehung auf die Entwicklung der weiblichen Sexualität. In: M. Gambaroff (Ed.), *Utopie der Treue* (pp. 75–95). Reinbek: Rowohlt.

Giddens, A. (1993). *The Transformation of Intimacy: Sexuality, love, and eroticism in modern societies*. Stanford: Stanford University Press.

Gissrau, B. (1993). Sigmund Freud über weibliche Homosexualität. In: R. Lautmann (Ed.), *Homosexualität. Handbuch der Theorie- und Forschungsgeschichte* (pp. 168–172). Frankfurt: Campus.

Glover, E. (1933). The relation of perversion-formation to the development of reality-sense. *International Journal of Psycho-Analysis, 14*: 486–504.

Gondek, H-D. (1990). *Angst, Einbildungskraft, Sprache. Ein verbindender Aufriss zwischen Freud—Kant—Lacan*. München: Boer.

Green, A. (1995). Has sexuality anything to do with psychoanalysis? *International Journal of Psycho-Analysis, 76*: 871–883.

Greenacre, P. (1968). Perversions: General considerations regarding their genetic and dynamic background. *Psychoanalytic Study of the Child, 23*: 47–62.

Greenacre, P. (1971). *Emotional Growth. Psychoanalytic Studies of the Gifted and a great Variety of other individuals. (Volumes I and II)*. New York: International Universities Press.

Greenson, R. (1968). Dis-identifying from mother: Its special importance for the boy. *International Journal of Psycho-Analysis, 49*: 370–374.

Hagemann-White, C. (1995). Was tun? Gewalt in der Sexualität verbieten? Gewalt entsexualisieren? In: S. Düring & M. Hauch (Eds.), *Heterosexuelle Verhältnisse* (pp. 160–175). Gießen: Psychosozial 2000.

Hartmann, M. (1943). *Die Sexualität*. Stuttgart: G. Fischer.

Hecker, W. (1985). *Operative Korrekturen des intersexuellen und des fehlgebildeten weiblichen Genitales*. Frankfurt: Springer.

Helfferich, C. (2005). «Das erste Mal»—Männliche sexuelle Initiation in Geschlechterbeziehungen. In: V. King & K. Flaake (Eds.), *Männliche Adoleszenz. Sozialisation und Bildungsprozesse zwischen Kindheit und Erwachsensein* (pp. 183–203). Frankfurt: Campus.

Hettlage-Varjas, A. & Kurz, C. (1995). Von der Schwierigkeit, Frau zu werden und Frau zu bleiben. Zur Problematik weiblicher Identität in den Wechseljahren. *Psyche, 49*: 903–937.

Hiort, Olaf et al. (2003). Puberty in disorders of somatosexual differentiation. *Journal of Pediatric Endocrinology & Metabolism, 16 Suppl* 2: 297–306.

Hirschauer, S. (1993). *Die soziale Konstruktion der Transsexualität: über die Medizin und den Geschlechtswechsel*. Frankfurt: Suhrkamp.

Horney, K. (1924). On the genesis of the castration complex in women. *International Journal of Psycho-Analysis, 5*: 50–65.

Horney, K. (1926). The flight from womanhood: The masculinity-complex in women, as viewed by men and by women. *International Journal of Psycho-Analysis, 7*: 324–339.

Horney, K. (1932). Observations on a specific difference in the dread felt by men and by women respectively for the opposite sex. *International Journal of Psycho-Analysis, 13*: 348–360.

Horney, K. (1933). The denial of the vagina—a contribution to the problem of the genital anxieties specific to women. *International Journal of Psycho-Analysis, 14*: 57–70.

Irigaray, L. (1985). *This Sex which is not one.* Ithaca, NY: Cornell University Press.

Isay, R. (1989). *Being Homosexual: Gay Men and their development.* New York: Farrar, Strauss, Giroux.

Jacobson, E. (1950). Development of the wish for a child in boys. *Psychoanalytic Study of the Child, 5*: 139–152.

Jacobson, E. (1976). Ways of Female Superego Formation and the Female Castration Conflict. *Psychoanalytic Quarterly, 45*: 525–538.

Jarvis, W. (1962). Some effects of pregnancy and childbirth on men. *Journal of the American Psychoanalytic Association, 10*: 689–700.

Jones, E. (1919). Anal erotic character traits. *The Journal of Abnormal Psychology 13(5)*: 261–284.

Jones, E. (1927). The early development of female sexuality. *International Journal of Psycho-Analysis, 8*: 459–472.

Jones, E. (1933). The phallic phase. *International Journal of Psycho-Analysis, 14*: 1–33.

Jones, E. (1935). Early female sexuality. *International Journal of Psycho-Analysis, 16*: 263–273.

Jones, E. (1942). Psychology and Childbirth. In: E. Jones (Ed.), *Papers on Psycho-Analysis* (pp. 384–388). London: Baillière, Tindall & Cox, 1948.

Jones, E. (1953–57). *Sigmund Freud: Life and Work (3 Volumes).* New York: Basic Books.

Kahn-Ladas, A., Whipple, B. & Perry, J. (1982). *The G-Spot and Other Recent Discoveries about Human Sexuality.* New York: Holt, Rinehart, and Winston.

Kamprad, B. & Schiffels, W. (1991). *Im falschen Körper.* Zürich: Kreuz.

Kant, I. (1934). *Religion within the Limits of Reason Alone.* New York: Harper and Brothers.

Kaplan, L. (1984). *Adolescence, the Farewell to Childhood.* New York: Simon and Schuster.

Kernberg, O. (1991). Aggression and love in the relationship of the couple. *Journal of the American Psychoanalytic Association, 38*: 45–70.

Kernberg, O. F. (1995). *Love Relations: Normality and Pathology.* New Haven: Yale University Press.

Kernberg, O. F. (2011). The sexual couple: a psychoanalytic exploration. *Psychoanalytic Review 98 (2)*: 217–45.

Kestenberg, J. (1956). On the development of maternal feelings in early childhood. *Psychoanalytic Study of the Child, 11*: 257–291.

Kestenberg, J. (1968). Outside and inside, male and female. *Journal of the American Psychoanalytic Association, 16*: 457–520.

Kestenberg, J. (1988). Der komplexe Charakter der weiblichen Identität. Betrachtungen zum Entwicklungsverlauf. *Psyche, 42*: 349–364.

King, V. (1992). Geburtswehen der Weiblichkeit—Verkehrte Entbindungen. Zur Konflikthaftigkeit der psychischen Aneignung der Innergenitalität in der Adoleszenz. In: K. Flaake & V. King (Eds.), *Weibliche Adoleszenz. Zur Sozialisation junger Frauen* (pp. 103–125). Frankfurt: Campus.

King, V. (1995). *Die Urszene der Psychoanalyse. Adoleszenz und Geschlechterspannung im Fall Dora.* Stuttgart: Verlag Internationale Psychoanalyse.

King, P. & Steiner, R. (Eds.) (1991). *The Freud-Klein Controversies, 1941–45.* London/New York: Tavistock/Routledge.

Kinsey, A., Pomeroy, W. & Martin, C. (1948). *Sexual Behavior in the Human Male.* Philadelphia: W. B. Saunders.

Kleeman, J. (1966). Genital self-discovery during a boy's second year. A follow-up. *The Psychoanalytic Study of the Child, 21*: 358–392.

Klein, M. (1928). Early stages of the Oedipus conflict. *International Journal of Psycho-Analysis, 9*: 167–180.

Klein, M. (1962). *Das Seelenleben des Kindes und andere Beiträge zur Psychoanalyse.* Stuttgart: Klett-Cotta, 1989.

Klitzing, K. v. (2002). Frühe Entwicklung im Längsschnitt: Von der Beziehungswelt der Eltern zur Vorstellungswelt des Kindes. *Psyche, 56*: 863–887.

Krafft-Ebing, R. v. (1877). Über gewisse Anomalien des Geschlechtstriebs und die klinisch-forensische Verwerthung derselben als eines wahrscheinlich functionellen Degenerationszeichens des centralen Nerven-Systems. *Archiv für Psychiatrie und Nervenkrankheiten, 7*: 291–312.

Krüll, M. (1986). *Freud and his Father.* New York: W.W. Norton.

Kuiper, P. (1962). Probleme der psychoanalytischen Technik in Bezug auf die passiv-feminine Gefühlseinstellung des Mannes, das Verhältnis der beiden Ödipuskomplexe und die Aggression. *Psyche, 16*: 321–344.

Kutter, P. (1989). *Moderne Psychoanalyse: eine Einführung in die Psychologie unbewußter Prozesse.* München: Verlag Internationale Psychoanalyse.

Lackinger, F. (2005). Persönlichkeitsorganisation, Perversion und Sexualdelinquenz. *Psyche, 59*: 1107–1130.

Lang, C. (2006). *Intersexualität. Menschen zwischen den Geschlechtern.* Frankfurt: Campus.

Lange, C. (1994). Das Gleiche ist nicht dasselbe. Subversive Elemente des Paartherapie-Settings im Hinblick auf das Geschlechterverhältnis am Beispiel "Lustlosigkeit". *Zeitschrift für Sexualforschung, 7*: 52–61.

Langer, M. 1992. *Motherhood and Sexuality.* New York: Guilford.

Laplanche, J. (1988). *Die Allgemeine Verführungstheorie und andere Aufsätze.* Tübingen: Edition Diskord.

Laplanche, J. (1989). *New Foundations for Psychoanalysis.* Oxford: Basil Blackwell.

Laplanche, J. (1999a). The unfinished Copernican revolution. In: J. Laplanche (Ed.), *Essays on Otherness* (pp. 53–85). London: Routledge.

Laplanche, J. (1999b). La soi-disant pulsion de mort: une pulsion sexuelle. In: J. Laplanche (Ed.), *Entre séduction et inspiration: L´ homme* (pp. 189–218). Paris: Quadrigue/PUF.

Laplanche, J. & Pontalis, J.-B. (1973). *The Language of Psycho-Analysis.* London: Hogarth.

Laufer, M. & Laufer, M. (1984). *Adolescence and Developmental Breakdown: a Psychoanalytic View.* New Haven: Yale University Press.

Lawrenz, C. & Orzegowski, P. (1988). *Das kann ich keinem erzählen. Gespräche mit Frauen über ihre sexuellen Phantasien.* Frankfurt: Suhrkamp.

Lax, R. (1982). The expectable depressive climacteric reaction. *Bulletin of the Menninger Clinic, 46*: 151–167.

Lax, R. (1997). *Becoming and Being a Woman.* Northvale: Aronson.

Lewes, K. (1988). *The Psychoanalytic Theory of Male Homosexuality.* New York: Simon & Schuster.

Lewin, B. (1930). Kotschmieren, Menses und weibliches Über-Ich. *Internationale Zeitschrift für Psychoanalyse, 16*: 43–56.

Lewin, B. (1939). Some observations on knowledge, belief and the impulse to know. *International Journal of Psychoanalysis, 20*: 426–431.

Lerner, R. & Busch-Rossnagel, N. (1981). *Individuals as Producers of their Development: A life-span perspective.* New York: Academic Press.

Lichtenberg, J. (1989). *Psychoanalysis and Motivation.* Hillsdale, NJ: Analytic Press.

Limentani, A. (1979). The significance of transsexualism in relation to some basic psychoanalytic concepts. *International Review of Psycho-Analysis, 6*: 139–153.

Loch, W. (1967). *Die Krankheitslehre der Psychoanalyse.* Stuttgart: Hirzel.

Lorand, S. (1939). Contribution to the problem of vaginal orgasm. *International Journal of Psychoanalysis, 20*: 432–438.

Lorenzer, A. (1977). *Sprachspiel und Interaktionsformen: Vorträge und Aufsätze zu Psychoanalyse, Sprache und Praxis.* Frankfurt: Suhrkamp.

Lupton, M. (1993). *Menstruation and Psychoanalysis.* Urbana: University of Illinois Press.

Mack-Brunswick, R. (1940). The preoedipal phase of libido development. *Psychoanalytic Quarterly, 9*: 293–319.

Mahler, M., Pine, F. & Bergman, A. (1975). *The Psychological Birth of the Human Infant: Symbiosis and Individuation.* London: Hutchinson.

Masson, J. (1985). *The Complete Letters of Sigmund Freud to Wilhelm Fliess, 1887–1904.* Cambridge: Harvard University Press.

Masters, W. & Johnson, V. (1966). *Human Sexual Response.* Boston: Little, Brown.

May, R. (1986). Männlichkeit in psychoanalytischer Perspektive. In: R. Friedman & I. Lerner (Eds.), *Zur Psychoanalyse des Mannes* (pp. 171–190). Berlin: Springer.

McDougall, J. (1970). Homosexuality in women. In: J. Chasseguet-Smirgel (Ed.), *Female sexuality. New psychoanalytic views* (pp. 171–212). Ann Arbor: University of Michigan Press.

McDougall, J. (1980). *Plea for a Measure of Abnormality.* New York: International Universities Press.

McDougall, J. (1985). *Theaters of the Mind: Illusion and Truth on the Psychoanalytic Stage.* New York: Basic Books.

McDougall, J. (1995). *The Many Faces of Eros: A Psychoanalytic Exploration of Human Sexuality.* New York: W.W. Norton.

Mentzos, S. (1982). *Neurotische Konfliktverarbeitung.* Frankfurt: Fischer.

Mitchell, J. (1974). *Psychoanalysis and Feminism.* New York: Pantheon.

Mitscherlich, A. (1950/51). Wanderversammlung der Südwestdeutschen Psychiater und Neurologen, Badenweiler, 2./3. Juni 1950. I. Erstes Leitthema: Daseinsanalyse. *Psyche, 4*: 226- 234.

Mitscherlich, A. et al. (1950/51a). Rundfrage über ein Referat auf der 66. Wanderversammlung der Südwestdeutschen Psychiater und Neurologen in Badenweiler. *Psyche, 4*: 448–477.

Mitscherlich, A. et al. (1950/51b). Rundfrage über ein Referat auf der 66. Wanderversammlung der Südwestdeutschen Psychiater und Neurologen in Badenweiler. *Psyche, 4*: 626–640.

Mitscherlich-Nielsen, M. (1962). Probleme der psychoanalytischen Technik in Bezug auf die passiv-feminine Gefühlseinstellung des Mannes. *Psyche, 16*: 345–354.

Mitscherlich-Nielsen, M. (1989). Psychoanalyse als Aufklärung.—nur für Männer? In: K. Brede (Ed.), *Was will das Weib in mir?* (pp. 193–244). Freiburg im Breisgau: Kore.

Möslein-Teising, I. (2007). Guter Hoffnung—unter welchen Umständen? Psychoanalytische Bemerkungen zu Schwangerschaft und Geburt. (Lecture given at the Frankfurter Psychoanalytischen Freitagsrunde, 16 November year?).

Moll, A. (1897). *Untersuchungen über die Libido sexualis*. Berlin: Fischer's Medicinische Buchhandlung. H. Kornfeld.

Moll, A. (1912). *The Sexual Life of the Child*. New York: Macmillan.

Money, J. (1988). Homosexuell, bisexuell, heterosexuell. Zum psychoendokrinologischen Forschungsstand. *Zeitschrift für Sexualforschung, 1*: 23–131.

Money, J. & Ehrhardt, A. (1972). *Man & Woman, Boy & Girl: The Differentiation and Dimorphism of Gender Identity from Conception to Maturity*. Baltimore, MD: Johns Hopkins University Press.

Money, J., Hampson, J.G. & Hampson, J.L. (1955). Hermaphroditism: recommendations concerning assignment of sex, change of sex, and psychological management. *Bulletin of the Johns Hopkins Hospital, 97*: 284–300.

Morgenthaler, F. (1974). Die Stellung der Perversionen in Metapsychologie und Technik. *Psyche, 28*: 1087–1098.

Morgenthaler, F. (1980). Homosexualität. In: V. Sigusch (Ed.), *Therapie sexueller Störungen* (pp. 329–367). Stuttgart: Thieme.

Morgenthaler, F. (1988). *Homosexuality, Heterosexuality, Perversion*. Hillsdale, NJ: Analytic Press.

Mulvey, L. (1989). *Visual and Other Pleasures*. Bloomington: Indiana University Press.

Müller-Jung, J. (2005). Das rosarote Gen. Vergebliche Fahndung nach dem homosexuellen Erbgut. *Frankfurter Allgemeine Zeitung*, 8 February year?, p. 34.

Nieden, Sabine zur (2004). *Weibliche Ejakulation*. Gießen: Psychosozial.

Nitzschke, B. (1980). *Männerängste, Männerwünsche*. München: Matthes & Seitz.

Nunner-Winkler, G. (2001). Geschlecht und Gesellschaft. In: H. Joas (Ed.). *Lehrbuch der Soziologie* (pp. 265–288). Frankfurt: Campus.

Nussbaum, M. (1999). The professor of parody. *The New Republic* (March 22).

Oerter, R. & Montada, L. (Eds.) (1982). *Entwicklungspsychologie. Ein Lehrbuch*. München: Schwarzenberg.

Oerter, R. & Montada, L. (Eds.) (1995). *Entwicklungspsychologie. Ein Lehrbuch*. Weinheim: Beltz.

Parin, P. (1986). *Sexualität*. Frankfurt: Athenäum.

Passett, P. (2005). Ein psychoanalytisches Wiederlesen der "Drei Abhandlungen". In: I. Quindeau & V. Sigusch (Eds.), *Freud und das*

Sexuelle. Psychoanalytische und sexualwissenschaftliche Perspektiven (pp. 36–59). Frankfurt: Campus.

Person, E. (1985). The erotic transference in women and in men: Differences and consequences. *Journal of American Academy of Psychoanalysis, 13*: 159–180.

Person, E. & Ovesey, L. (1983). Psychoanalytic theory of gender identity. *Journal of the American Academy of Psychoanalysis, 11*: 203–226.

Person, E. & Ovesey, L. (1993). Psychoanalytische Theorien zur Geschlechtsidentität. *Psyche, 47*: 505–29.

Pfäfflin, F. (1993). *Transsexualität*. Stuttgart: Enke.

Pfäfflin, F. (1994). Zur transsexuellen Abwehr. *Psyche, 48*: 904–931.

Pines, D. (1994). *A Woman's Unconscious use of her body*. New Haven: Yale University Press.

Poluda-Korte, E. (1986). Identität im Fluß. Zur Psychoanalyse weiblicher Adoleszenz im Spiegel des Menstruationserlebens. In: K. Flaake & V. King (Eds.), *Weibliche Adoleszenz. Zur Sozialisation junger Frauen* (pp. 147–165). Frankfurt: Campus.

Poluda-Korte, E. (1993). Der „lesbische Komplex". Das homosexuelle Tabu und die Weiblichkeit: In: E-M. Alves (Ed.), *Stumme Liebe. Der `lesbische Komplex´ in der Psychoanalyse* (pp. 73–132). Freiburg: Kore.

Poluda-Korte, E. (2001). Probleme der weiblichen homosexuellen Orientierung. In: V. Sigusch (Ed.), *Sexuelle Störungen und ihre Behandlung* (pp. 79–101). Stuttgart: Thieme.

Porst, R. (2001). *Manual der Impotenz. Erektions-, Ejakulations- und Hormonstörungen, Peniserkrankungen, weibliche Sexualstörungen*. Bremen: Uni-med.

Quindeau, I. (2004a). *Spur und Umschrift. Die konstitutive Bedeutung von Erinnerung in der Psychoanalyse*. München: Fink.

Quindeau, I. (2004b). Lust auf Anderes. Die Implantation der heterosexuellen Ordnung in der Allgemeinen Verführungsszene. In: L. Bayer & I. Quindeau (Eds.), *Die unbewußte Botschaft der Verführung. Interdisziplinäre Studien zur Allgemeinen Verführungstheorie von Jean Laplanche* (pp. 170–193). Gießen: Psychosozial.

Quindeau, I. (2005). Braucht die Psychoanalyse eine Triebtheorie? In: I. Quindeau & V. Sigusch (Eds.), *Freud und das Sexuelle* (pp. 193–208). Frankfurt: Campus.

Quindeau, I. (2007). Fit for fun? `Sexuelle Funktionsstörungen´ in der Spaßgesellschaft. In: R. Haubl & E. Brähler (Eds.), *Neue moderne Leiden* (pp. 30–48). Gießen: Psychosozial.

Radó, S. (1928). The psychical effects of intoxication: Attempt at a psychoanalytical theory of drug-addiction. *International Journal of Psycho-Analysis, 9*: 301–317.

Radó, S. (1940). A critical examination of the concept of bisexuality. In: S. Radó, *Psychoanalysis of Behavior 1* (pp. 139–150). New York/London: Grune & Stratton.

Radó, S. (1949). An Adaptitional View of Sexual Behavior. In: S. Radó, *Psychoanalysis of Behavior 1* (pp. 186–215). New York/London: Grune & Stratton.

Raguse-Stauffer, B. (1990). Psychoanalytische Überlegungen zu Klimakterium und Menopause. *Zeitschrift für Psychoanalytische Theorie und Praxis, 5*: 322–335.

Rauchfleisch, U. (1994). Die Diskriminierung Homosexueller durch die Psychoanalyse. *Zeitschrift für Sexualforschung, 7*: pp. 217–230.

Rauchfleisch, U. (2002). Hetero-, Homo-, Bisexualität. In: W. Mertens et al. (Eds.), *Handbuch der psychoanalytischen Grundbegriffe* (pp. 280–287). Stuttgart: Kohlhammer.

Rechenberger, I. (1995). Psychosoziale Aspekte bei Intersexualität und Transsexualismus. *Gynäkologe, 28*: 54–58.

Reenkola, E. (2002). *The Veiled Female Core.* New York: Other Press.

Reiche, R. (1970). *Sexuality and Class Struggle.* London: NLB.

Reiche, R. (1984). Sexualität, Identität, Transsexualität. In: M. Dannecker & V. Sigusch (Eds.), *Sexualtheorie und Sexualpolitik* (pp. 51–66). Stuttgart: Enke.

Reiche, R. (1986). Das Geheimnis in der Zündholzschachtel—Gedanken zur latenten Perversion bei der Frau. In: Psychoanalytisches Seminar Zürich (Eds.), *Sexualität* (pp. 89–113). Frankfurt: Syndikat/EVA bei Athenäum.

Reiche, R. (1990). *Geschlechterspannung.* Frankfurt: Fischer.

Reiche, R. (1997). Gender ohne Sex. Geschichte, Funktion und Funktionswandel des Begriffs "Gender". *Psyche, 51*: 926–957.

Reiche, R. (2000). Die Rekonstruktion der zentralen Onaniephantasie in der Analyse eines jungen Homosexuellen. In: M. Dannecker & R. Reiche (Eds.), *Sexualität und Gesellschaft* (pp. 360–382). Frankfurt: Campus.

Reiche, R. (2001a). Der gewöhnliche Weg zur Homosexualität beim Mann. In: W. Bohleber & S. Drews (Eds.), *Die Gegenwart der Psychoanalyse—die Psychoanalyse der Gegenwart* (pp. 288–303). Stuttgart: Klett-Cotta.

Reiche, R. (2001b). Psychoanalytische Therapie sexueller Perversionen. In: V. Sigusch (Ed.), *Sexuelle Störungen und ihre Behandlung* (pp. 439–464). Stuttgart: Thieme.

Reiche, R. (2004a). *Triebschicksal der Gesellschaft. Über den Strukturwandel der Psyche.* Frankfurt: Campus.

Reiche, R. (2004b). Über Judith Butler. *Zeitschrift für Sexualforschung, 17*: 11–25.

Reiche, R. (2005). Das Rätsel der Sexualisierung. In: I. Quindeau & V. Sigusch (Eds.), *Freud und das Sexuelle* (pp. 135–152). Frankfurt: Campus.

Reiche, R. (2006). Das Sexuelle bei Morgenthaler: Verführung, Plombe, Weichenstellung. *Journal für Psychoanalyse, 45/46*: pp. 280–297.

Richter-Appelt, H. (2007). Intersexualität im Wandel. *Zeitschrift für Sexualforschung, 20*: 93–113.

Ricoeur, P. (1970). *Freud and Philosophy: An Essay on Interpretation*. New Haven: Yale University Press.

Rohde-Dachser, C. (1991). *Expedition in den dunklen Kontinent. Weiblichkeit im Diskurs der Psychoanalyse*. Frankfurt: Fischer, 1997.

Rohde-Dachser, C. (1992). Male and female homosexuality. *International Forum of Psychoanalysis, 1*: 67–73.

Roiphe, H. & Galenson, E. (1981). *Infantile Origins of Sexual Identity*. New York: International Universities Press.

Rose, G. (1961). Pregenital aspects of pregnancy fantasies. *International Journal of Psychoanalysis, 42*: 544–549.

Rotter, L. (1934). Zur Psychologie der weiblichen Sexualität. In: A. Benz (Ed.), *Sex-Appeal und männliche Ohnmacht* (pp. 19–32). Freiburg: Kore, 1989.

Rotter, L. (1989). *Sex-Appeal und männlicher Ohnmacht*. Freiburg: Kore.

Schlesier, R. (1981). *Konstruktionen der Weiblichkeit bei Sigmund Freud. Zum Problem von Entmythologisierung und Remythologisierung in der psychoanalytischen Theorie*. Frankfurt: Europäische Verlagsanstalt.

Schlesinger-Kipp, G. (2002). Weibliche Entwicklung in den Wechseljahren. *Psyche, 56*: 1007–1030.

Schmauch, U. (2004). Sexualität und Sozialisation—am Beispiel der wechselseitigen sexuellen Sozialisation zwischen Jugendlichen und ihren Eltern. In: R. Hornung, C. Buddeberg & T. Bucher (Eds.), *Sexualität im Wandel* (pp. 91–113). Zürich: ETH.

Schmidt, G. (2004). *Das neue Der Die Das. Über die Modernisierung des Sexuellen*. Gießen: Psychosozial.

Schmidt, G. (2005). Kindersexualität—Konturen eines dunklen Kontinents. In: B. Burian-Langegger (Ed.), *Doktorspiele. Die Sexualität des Kindes* (pp. 114–128). Wien: Picus.

Schmidt, G., Klusmann, D. & Zeitschel, U. (1992). Veränderungen der Jugendsexualität zwischen 1970 und 1990. *Zeitschrift für Sexualforschung, 5*: 191–217.

Schorsch, E. (1974). Phänomenologie der Transsexualität. Therapie: Geschlechtsumwandlung ohne Alternative. *Sexualmedizin, 3*: 195–198.

Schorsch, E. (1988). Die Medikalisierung der Sexualität. Über Entwicklungen in der Sexualmedizin. *Zeitschrift für Sexualforschung, 1*: 95–112.

Schwarzer, A. (1977). *Der kleine Unterschied und seine großen Folgen*. Frankfurt: Fischer.

Segal, H. (1991). *Wahnvorstellung und künstlerische Kreativität. Ausgewählte Aufsätze*. Stuttgart: Klett-Cotta.

Sherfey, J. (1966). The evolution and nature of female sexuality in relation to psychoanalytic theory. *Journal of the American Psychoanalytical Association, 14*: 28–128.

Sherfey, J. (1972). *The Nature and Evolution of Female Sexuality*. New York: Vintage.

Siegel, E. (1988). *Female Homosexuality: Choice Without Volition—A Psychoanalytic Study*. Hillsdale, NJ: The Analytic Press.

Sies, C. & Nestler, V. (1992). Soll und Haben. Die Wechseljährige zwischen Illusion und Wirklichkeit. *Psyche, 46*: 366–387.

Sigusch, V. (1970). *Exzitation und Orgasmus bei der Frau*. Stuttgart: Enke.

Sigusch, V. (1992). *Geschlechtswechsel*. Hamburg: Klein.

Sigusch, V. (1993). Nachdenken über Feminismus. *Zeitschrift für Sexualforschung, 6*: 36–51.

Sigusch, V. (2001). Kultureller Wandel der Sexualität. In: V. Sigusch (Ed.), *Sexuelle Störungen und ihre Behandlung* (pp. 16–52). Stuttgart: Thieme.

Sigusch, V. (2005a). *Neosexualitäten*. Frankfurt: Campus.

Sigusch, V. (2005b): Freud und die Sexualwissenschaft seiner Zeit. In: I. Quindeau & V. Sigusch (Eds.), *Freud und das Sexuelle* (pp. 15–35). Frankfurt: Campus.

Sigusch, V., Meyenburg, B. & Reiche, R. (1979). Transsexualität. In: V. Sigusch (Ed.), *Sexualität und Medizin* (pp. 249–311). Köln: Kiepenheuer & Witsch.

Simmel, E. (1948). Alcoholism and addiction. *Psychoanalytic Quarterly, 17*: 6–31.

Socarides, C. (1968). *The Overt Homosexual*. New York: Grune & Stratton.

Socarides, C. (1970). A psychoanalytic study of the desire for sexual transformation ("Transsexualism"): The Plaster-of-Paris Man. *International Journal of Psychoanalysis, 51*: 341–349.

Socarides, C. (1978). *Homosexuality*. New York: Aronson.

Spitz, R. (1959). *A Genetic Field Theory of Ego Formation: Its Implications for Pathology*. New York: International Universities Press.

Spitz, R. (1961). Some early prototypes of ego defenses. In: R. Spitz (Ed.), *Vom Dialog* (pp. 238–257). Stuttgart: Klett 1976.

Spitz, R. (1962). Autoerotism re-examined—the role of early sexual behavior patterns in personality Formation. *Psychoanalytic Study of the Child, 17*: 283–315.

Spitz, R. & Wolf, K. (1949). Autoerotism: Some empirical findings and hypotheses on three of its manifestations in the first year of life. *The Psychoanalytic Study of the Child, 3/4*: 85–120.

Springer, A. (1981). *Pathologie der geschlechtlichen Identität. Transsexualismus und Homosexualität. Theorie, Klinik, Therapie*. Wien: Springer.

Stern, D. (1985). *The Interpersonal World of the Infant: A View from Psychoanalysis and Developmental Psychology*. New York: Basic Books.

Stern, D. (2004). *The Present Moment in Psychotherapy and Everyday Life*. New York: W.W. Norton.

Stein, R. (2005). Why perversion? "False love" and the perverse pact. *International Journal of Psychoanalysis*, 86: 775–799.

Stoller, R. (1968). *Sex and Gender. On the Development of Masculinity and Femininity (Volume 1)*. New York: Science House.

Stoller, R. (1975). *Perversion: the Erotic Form of Hatred*. New York: Pantheon.

Sulloway, F. (1979). *Freud, Biologist of the Mind: Beyond the Psychoanalytic Legend*. New York: Basic Books.

Sydow, K. v. (1993). *Lebenslust. Weibliche Sexualität von der frühen Kindheit bis ins hohe Alter*. Bern: Huber.

Sydow, K. v. & Reimer, C. (1995). Psychosomatik der Menopause. Literaturüberblick 1988–1992. *Psychotherapie und medizinische Psychologie, 45*: 225–235.

Thomä, H. (1957). Männlicher Transvestitismus und das Verlangen nach Geschlechtsumwandlung. *Psyche, 11*: 81–124.

Tiefer, L. (1995). *Sex is not a Natural Act*. Boulder: Westview Press.

Torok, M. (1994). The significance of penis envy in women. In: N. Abraham and M. Torok (Eds.), *The Shell and the Kernel (Volume I)* (pp. 41–67). Chicago: University of Chicago Press.

Tyson, P. (1986). Male Gender Identity: Early Developmental Roots. *Psychoanalytic Review, 73*: 1–21.

Ulrich, H. & Karsten, T. (1994). *Messer im Traum. Transsexuelle in Deutschland*. Tübingen: Konkursbuch Verlag.

Waldeck, R. (1988). Der rote Fleck im dunklen Kontinent. Teil I: Das Tabu der Menstruation; Teil II: Die Verletzung der Frau. *Zeitschrift für Sexualforschung, 1*: 189–205 (I) and 337–350 (II).

Waldenfels, B. (2002). *Bruchlinien der Erfahrung. Phänomenologie, Psychoanalyse, Phänomenotechnik*. Frankfurt: Suhrkamp.

Waldenfels, B. (2011). *Phenomenology of the Alien: Basic Concepts*. Evanston: Northwestern University Press.

Welldon, E. (1988). *Mother, Madonna, Whore: The Idealization and Denigration of Motherhood*. London: Free Association Books.

Welldon, E. (2006). Why do you want to have a child? In: A. Alizade (Ed.), *Motherhood in the Twenty-First Century* (pp. 59–71). London: Karnac.

Wisniewski, Amy et al. (2000). Complete Androgen Insensitivity Syndrome: Long-Term Medical, Surgical, and Psychosexual Outcome. *Journal of Clinical Endocrinology & Metabolism, 85(8)*: 2664–2669.

INDEX